Profiles In Hue

To my children
Pete + Sharon

With Love + Best Wishes Always

"Pop" Gene D. Johnson

Feb 18, 2011

Profiles In Hue

George D. Johnson

Other books by George D. Johnson
Except For the Grace-An Autobiography-Trafford Publishing
Light From The Book—Trafford Publishing
More Light From The Book-Xlibris Publishing
What's Wrong With Society and Can it Be Fixed?—Xlibris Publishing
Wisdom—Xlibris Publishing
Wisdom II—Xlibris Publishing
The Lamp Lighter—Xlibris Publishing
The Lamp Lighter Volume II—Xlibris Publishing

To order additional copies of this book, contact:
Xlibris Corporation
1-888-795-4274
www.Xlibris.com
Orders@Xlibris.com
89637

Contents

There are two ways of spreading light;
to be the candle or the mirror that reflects it."
Edith Wharton

"There are two ways of spreading light; to be the candle or the mirror that reflects it."

Edith Wharton

This book is dedicated to the congregation of the First Zion Baptist Church and my sister in Christ, Arlene Prentice who planted the seed for me to undertake the research to make *"Profiles in Hue "possible*. And my further dedication to all of those who expressed their appreciation for my previous publications: Without naming names you who you are.

Please accept my humble thanks, and I pray that God will richly bless you and yours with wisdom, health and peace of mind.

Wisdom for the Journey:

"The only thing new in this world is the history that you don't know"

Harry S Truman

History must be written of, by and for the survivors.

Anonymous

"What is the use of spending one's time in continuous reading, turning the pages of the lives and sayings of holy men, unless we can extract nourishment from them by chewing and digesting this food so that its strength can pass into our inmost heart?"

-Guigo II the Carthusian Monk

Profiles In Hue

Unlike so many books that are read and then put in a book case out of sight this manuscript, like some of my other books, was deliberately designed for coffee table display-with the hope that it will be shared with relatives and friends.

Its construction and pattern was meant to be unconventional—to afford the reader the luxury of finding some thought provoking words of enlightenment and or inspiration on every page.

It is my sincere prayer that others will enjoy reading this work as much as I have enjoyed putting it together.

In His Service,
George D. Johnson

Foreword

To quote George Santayana; "those who cannot remember the past are condemned to repeat it. "And a people without a history are doomed to extinction.

It's upon those quotes that "Profiles in Hue" took root.

"Profiles in Hue" began as a treatise on "Black History." The idea being to acquaint some of our young people with some of the historic's, hardships, defeats and victories of those who came before them. In other words the way it is now is not the way it always was. A lot of dues was paid by a lot of people; in order for many of us to live a better life than they could have ever dreamed possible. Another factor being, so much history about Blacks and other ethnic Americans has been lost, stolen or forgotten. It's essential that we must always try to keep their memories alive along with many other pioneers who helped to make America truly the home of the **free** and the brave.

I never really liked the term "Black History" because of its narrowness. Longevity has taught me to believe there is only one Universal race and that's the human race, comprised of many shades of colors, coming from a single source of **LIGHT**. And upon that belief I could not limit my research to just the history of blacks who have contributed to making the multi—color quilt that covers this great country of ours known as the United States of America. Thus the title of this book: **"Profiles in Hue."**

As I combed the internet in search of the profiles included in this book I was overwhelmed with the wealth of information available: Information that would takes days and months to obtain from public libraries and encyclopedias can be surfaced instantly with a mere click of a mouse.

I could not possibly profile all that I would like to in this book, but I have included just some of those who captured my imagination and inspired me to reach for greater heights. Some I knew personally and a few others I rubbed shoulders with.

What I have tried to do with this book is to whet the appetite for a more in depth look at those who have gone on before us. These few **"Profiles in Hue"**, *are only a few nuggets scratched from the surface of a bottomless mine—rich with education—free for the taking.*

Wisdom for the Journey

Lives of great men all remind us
We can make our lives sublime,
And, departing, leave behind us
Footprints on the sands of time; Henry Wadsworth Longfellow

"I could tell where the lamplighter was by the trail he left behind." Harry Lauder

Part One:

Politics & Religion

In Germany they first came for the Communists and I didn't speak up because I wasn't a Communist. Then they came for the Jews, and I didn't speak up because I wasn't a Jew. Then they came for the trade unionists and I didn't speak up because I wasn't a trade unionist. Then they came for the Catholics, and I didn't speak up because I was a Protestant. Then they came for me—and by that time no one was left to speak up.

Pastor Martin Niemoller

Mankind will never see an end of trouble until . . . lovers of wisdom come to hold political power, or the holders of power . . . become lovers of wisdom.

Plato, The Republic

"By three methods we may learn wisdom: First, by reflection, which is noblest; second, by imitation, which is easiest; and third, by experience, which is the bitterest."

Confucius

Allen, Richard
(1760-1831)

Founder of the African Methodist Episcopal Church, which became one of America's most vigorous black denominations

Born a slave, Allen was converted at the age of seventeen under Methodist preaching. He immediately began to preach the gospel himself, first to his family, then to his master (who was converted), and finally to blacks and whites throughout America. Allen taught himself to read and write, and then after much hard work was able to purchase his freedom.

After working at several trades, all the time preaching as a layman, he arrived in Philadelphia at the age of twenty-six. With several other blacks he worshiped regularly at St. George's Methodist Church. One Sunday in 1787 a distressing incident drove the blacks from that congregation. ***While Allen's friend, Absalom Jones, was praying publicly, white trustees of the church forced him to his seat in an effort to keep him quiet. In response, Jones, Allen, and the other blacks left the church.*** Shortly thereafter, Allen and Jones founded the Free African Society, America's first organization established by blacks for blacks. The nonsectarian society provided mutual aid and spiritual encouragement to Philadelphia's black community. Four years later Jones and Allen left the Society, and Jones eventually became the founder of the Negro Episcopal Church. In 1793 Jones and Allen led other blacks in providing aid to the entire population of Philadelphia during a severe epidemic of yellow fever. Also in 1793 Allen established Bethel Church (Philadelphia) for Negro Methodists. He himself was ordained a Methodist minister in 1799. Because of uneasiness in the predominantly white Methodist church, Allen's congregation and other black Methodist churches organized their own denomination, the African Methodist Episcopal Church, and Richard Allen became its first bishop in 1816. He served this growing body of black Methodists as its widely respected leader until his death in 1831.

Wisdom for the Journey

"It is from numberless diverse acts of courage and belief that human history is shaped. Each time a man stands up for an ideal, or acts to improve the lot of others, or strikes out against injustice, he sends forth a tiny ripple of hope."

~ Robert Francis Kennedy

Frederick Douglass

Frederick Douglass stood at the podium, trembling with nervousness. Before him sat abolitionists who had travelled to the Massachusetts island of Nantucket. Only 23 years old at the time, Douglass overcame his nervousness and gave a stirring, eloquent speech about his life as a slave. Douglass would continue to give speeches for the rest of his life and would become a leading spokesperson for the abolition of slavery and for racial equality.

The son of a slave woman and an unknown white man, "Frederick Augustus Washington Bailey" was born in February of 1818 on Maryland's eastern shore. He spent his early years with his grandparents and with an aunt, seeing his mother only four or five times before her death when he was seven. (**All Douglass knew of his father was that he was white.**) During this time he was exposed to the degradations of slavery, witnessing firsthand brutal whippings and spending much time cold and hungry. When he was eight he was sent to Baltimore to live with a ship carpenter named Hugh Auld. There he learned to read and first heard the words abolition and abolitionists. "Going to live at Baltimore," Douglass would later say, "laid the foundation, and opened the gateway, to all my subsequent prosperity."

Douglass spent seven relatively comfortable years in Baltimore before being sent back to the country, where he was hired out to a farm run by a notoriously brutal "slave breaker" named Edward Covey. **And the treatment he received was indeed brutal. Whipped daily and barely fed, Douglass was "broken in body, soul, and spirit."**

On January 1, 1836, Douglass made a resolution that he would be free by the end of the year. He planned an escape. But early in April he was jailed after his plan was discovered. Two years later, while living in Baltimore and working at a shipyard, Douglass would finally realize his dream: he fled the city on September 3, 1838. Travelling by train, then steamboat, then train, he arrived in New York City the following day. Several weeks later he had settled in New Bedford, Massachusetts, living with his newlywed bride (whom he met in Baltimore and married in New York) under his new name, Frederick Douglass.

Always striving to educate himself, Douglass continued his reading. He joined various organizations in New Bedford, including a black church. He attended Abolitionists' meetings. He subscribed to William Lloyd Garrison's weekly journal, the Liberator. In 1841, he saw Garrison speak at the Bristol Anti-Slavery Society's annual meeting. Douglass was inspired by the speaker, later stating, "No face and form ever impressed me with such sentiments [the hatred of slavery] as did those of William Lloyd Garrison." Garrison, too, was impressed with Douglass, mentioning him in the Liberator. Several days later Douglass gave his speech at the Massachusetts Anti-Slavery Society's annual convention in Nantucket—the speech described at the top of this page. Of the speech, one correspondent reported, "Flinty hearts were pierced, and cold ones melted by his eloquence." Before leaving the island, Douglass was asked to become a lecturer for the Society for three years. It was the launch of a career that would continue throughout Douglass' long life.

Despite apprehensions that the information might endanger his freedom, Douglass published his autobiography, Narrative of the Life of Frederick Douglass, an American Slave, Written by Himself. The year was 1845. Three years later, after a speaking tour of England, Ireland, and Scotland, Douglass published the first issue of the North Star, a four-page weekly, out of Rochester, New York.

Ever since he first met Garrison in 1841, the white abolitionist leader had been Douglass' mentor. But the views of Garrison and Douglass ultimately diverged. Garrison represented the radical end of the abolitionist spectrum. He denounced churches, political parties, even voting. He believed in the dissolution (break up) of the Union. He also believed that the U.S. Constitution was a pro-slavery document. After his tour of Europe and the establishment of his paper, Douglass' views began to change; he was becoming more of an independent thinker, more pragmatic. In 1851 Douglass announced at a meeting in Syracuse, New York, that he did not assume the Constitution was a pro-slavery document, and that it could even "be wielded in behalf of emancipation," especially where the federal government had exclusive jurisdiction. Douglass also did not advocate the dissolution of the Union, since it would isolate slaves in the South. This led to a bitter dispute between Garrison and Douglass that, despite the efforts of others such as Harriet Beecher Stowe to reconcile the two, would last into the Civil War.

Frederick Douglass would continue his active involvement to better the lives of African Americans. He conferred with Abraham Lincoln during the Civil War and recruited northern blacks for the Union Army. After the War he fought for the rights of women and African Americans alike.

Quote: *A little learning, indeed, may be a dangerous thing, but the want of learning is a calamity to any people.*—Frederick Douglass

The Life of Harriet Tubman

Harriet Tubman's life was a monument to courage and determination that continues to stand out in American history. Born into slavery in Maryland, Harriet Tubman freed herself, and played a major role in freeing the remaining millions. After the Civil War, she joined her family in Auburn, NY, where she founded the Harriet Tubman Home.

Harriet Tubman's Life in Slavery

Harriet Ross was born into slavery in 1819 or 1820, in Dorchester County, Maryland. Given the names of her two parents, both held in slavery, she was of purely African ancestry. **She was raised under harsh conditions, and subjected to whippings even as a small child. At the age of 12 she was seriously injured by a blow to the head, inflicted by a white overseer for refusing to assist in tying up a man who had attempted escape.**

At the age of 25, she married John Tubman, a free African American. Five years later, fearing she would be sold South, she made her escape.

Her Escape to Freedom in Canada

Tubman was given a piece of paper by a white neighbor with two names, and told how to find the first house on her path to freedom. At the first house she was put into a wagon, covered with a sack, and driven to her next destination. Following the route to Pennsylvania, she initially settled in Philadelphia, where she met William Still, the **Philadelphia Stationmaster on the Underground Railroad**. With the assistance of Still, and other members of the Philadelphia Anti-Slavery Society, she learned about the workings of the UGRR.

In 1851 she began relocating members of her family to St. Catharine's, (Ontario) Canada West. North Street in St. Catharine's remained her base of operations until 1857. While there she worked at various activities to save to finance her activities as a Conductor on the UGRR, and attended the Salem Chapel BME Church on Geneva Street.

Her Role in the Underground Railroad

After freeing herself from slavery, Harriet Tubman returned to Maryland to rescue other members of her family. In all she is believed to have conducted approximately 300 persons to freedom in the North. The tales of her exploits reveal her highly spiritual nature, as well as a grim determination to protect her charges and those who aided them. **She always expressed confidence that God would aid her efforts, and threatened to shoot any of her charges who thought to turn back.**

When William Still published *The Underground Railroad* in 1871, he included a description of Harriet Tubman and her work. The section of Still's book captioned below begins with a letter from Thomas Garret, the Stationmaster of Wilmington, Delaware. Wilmington and Philadelphia were on the major route followed by Tubman, and by hundreds of others who escaped from slavery in Maryland. For this reason, Still was in a position to speak from his own firsthand knowledge of Tubman's work:

WILMINGTON, 12 mo. 29th, 1854

Esteemed Friend, J. Miller McKim:—We made arrangements last night, and sent away Harriet Tubman, with six men and one woman to Allen Agnew's, to be forwarded across the country to the city. Harriet, and one of the men had worn the shoes off their feet, and I gave them two dollars to help fit them out, and directed a carriage to be hired at my expense, to take them out, but do not yet know the expense . . . .

THOMAS GARRET

Harriet Tubman had been their "Moses," but not in the sense that Andrew Johnson was the "Moses of the colored people." She had faithfully gone down into Egypt, and had delivered these six bondmen by her own heroism. Harriet was a woman of no pretensions, indeed, a more ordinary specimen of humanity could hardly be found among the most unfortunate-looking farm hands of the South. Yet, in point of courage, shrewdness and disinterested exertions to rescue her fellow-men, by making personal visits to Maryland among the slaves, she was without her equal.

Her success was wonderful. Time and again she made successful visits to Maryland on the Underground Rail Road, and would be absent for weeks at a time, running daily risks while making preparations for herself and her passengers. Great fears were entertained for her safety, but she seemed wholly devoid of personal fear. The idea of being captured by slave-hunters or slave-holders seemed never to enter her mind. She was apparently foolproof against all adversaries. While she thus maintained utter personal indifference, she was much more watchful with regard to those she was piloting. Half of her time, she had the appearance of one asleep, and would actually sit down by the road-side and go fast asleep, when on her errands of mercy through the South, yet, she would not suffer one of her party to whimper once, about "giving out and going back," however wearied they might be by the hard travel day and night. She had a very short and pointed rule or law of her own, which implied death to any who talked of giving out and going back. Thus, in an emergency she would give all to understand that "times were very critical and therefore no foolishness would be indulged in on the road." That several who were rather weak-kneed and faint-hearted were greatly invigorated by Harriet's blunt and positive manner and threat of extreme measures, there could be no doubt.

After having once enlisted, "They had to go through ordie." Of course Harriet was supreme, and her followers generally had full faith in her, and would back up any word she might utter. So when she said to them that *"a live runaway could do great harm by going back, but that a dead one could tell no secrets,"* she was sure to have obedience. Therefore, none had to die as traitors on the "middle passage." It is obvious enough, however, that her success in going into Maryland as she did, was attributable to her adventurous spirit and utter disregard of consequences. Her like, it is probable, was never known before or since.

On the road between Syracuse and Rochester, would be found a number of sympathetic Quakers and other abolitionists settled at Auburn. Here also was the home of US Senator and former New York State Governor William H. Seward. Sometime in the mid-1850s, Tubman met Seward and his wife Frances. Mrs. Seward provided a home for Tubman's favorite niece, Margaret, after Tubman helped her to escape from Maryland. In 1857, the Seawards provided a home for Tubman, to which she relocated her parents from St. Catharine's. This home was later sold to her for a small sum, and became her base of operations when she was not on the road aiding fugitives from slavery, and speaking in support of the cause.

Tubman was closely associated with Abolitionist John Brown, and was well acquainted with the other Upstate abolitionists, including Frederick Douglass, Jermain Loguen, and Smith. She worked closely with Brown, and reportedly missed the raid on Harper's Ferry only because of illness.

After the outbreak of the Civil War, Tubman served as a soldier, spy, and a nurse, for a time serving at Fortress Monroe, where Jefferson Davis would later be imprisoned. While guiding a group of black soldiers in South

Carolina, she met Nelson Davis, who was ten years her junior. Denied payment for her wartime service, Tubman was forced, after a bruising fight, to ride in a baggage car on her return to Auburn.

* Note: Harriet Tubman reportedly suffered narcolepsy as a result of the head injury she sustained as a child.

Her Life in Auburn, New York

After the close of the Civil War, Harriet Tubman returned to Auburn, NY. There she married Nelson Davis, and lived in a home they built on South Street, near the original house. This house still stands on the property, and serves as a home for the Resident Manager of the Harriet Tubman Home.

Only twelve miles from Seneca Falls, Tubman helped Auburn to remain a center of activity in support of women's rights. With her home literally down the road, Tubman remained in contact with her friends, William and Frances Seward. In 1908, she built the wooden structure that served as her home for the aged and indigent. Here she worked, and herself was cared for in the period before her death in 1913.

After her death, Harriet Tubman was buried in Fort Hill Cemetery in Auburn [grave], with military honors. She has since received many honors, including the naming of the Liberty Ship Harriet Tubman, christened in 1944 by Eleanor Roosevelt. On June 14, 1914 a large bronze plaque was placed at the Cayuga County Courthouse, and a civic holiday declared in her honor. Freedom Park, a tribute to the memory of Harriet Tubman, opened in the summer of 1994 at 17 North Street in Auburn. In 1995, Harriet Tubman was honored by the federal government with a commemorative postage stamp bearing her name and likeness.

Food for Thought:

The courage of life is often a less dramatic spectacle than the courage of a final moment; but it is no less a magnificent mixture of triumph and tragedy. A man does what he must—in spite of personal consequences, in spite of obstacles and dangers and pressures—and that is the basis of all morality.—John F. Kennedy

What then shall we say to these things? If God is for us, who can be against us? (Romans 8:31)

Hiram Revels

Hiram Rhodes Revels (September 27, 1827-January 16, 1901) was the first African American to serve in the United States Senate. Since he preceded any African American in the House, he was the first African American in the U.S. Congress as well. He represented Mississippi in 1870 and 1871 during Reconstruction. As of 2010, Revels is one of only six African Americans ever to have served in the United States Senate.

Early career

Revels, was born free in Fayetteville, North Carolina, of a free father of mixed white and black ancestry, and a white mother of Scottish heritage. He was tutored by a black woman for his early education. In 1838 he went to live with his brother, Elias B. Revels, in Lincolnton, North Carolina, and was apprenticed as a barber in his brother's shop. Elias Revels died in 1841, and his widow Mary turned over her assets to Hiram before she remarried.

Revels attended the Union County Quaker Seminary in Indiana, and from 1856-57, Knox College in Galesburg, Illinois. He also studied at a black seminary in Ohio. Revels was ordained a minister in 1845. As a minister in the African Methodist Episcopal Church, Revels preached in Indiana, Illinois, Ohio, Tennessee, Missouri, Kansas, and Maryland in the 1850s. *"At times, I met with a great deal of opposition," he later recalled. "I was imprisoned in Missouri in 1854 for preaching the gospel to Negroes, though I was never subjected to violence."* In 1845 he became a minister in Baltimore, Maryland and set up a private school.

As a chaplain Revels helped raise two black Union regiments during the Civil War in Maryland and Missouri, and took part at the battle of Vicksburg in Mississippi.[

Political career

In 1865, Revels returned to his ministry and was assigned briefly to AME churches in Leavenworth, Kansas, and New Orleans, Louisiana. In 1866, he was given a permanent pastorship in Natchez, Mississippi, where he settled with his wife and five daughters, continued his ministerial work, and founded schools for black children.

During Reconstruction, Revels was elected alderman in Natchez in 1868, and he was elected to represent Adams County in the Mississippi State Senate in 1869. As John R. Lynch reports, "so far as known he [Revels] had never voted, had never attended a political meeting, and of course, had never made a political speech. But he was a colored man, and presumed to be a Republican, and believed to be a man of ability and considerably above the average in point of intelligence." In January 1870, Revels presented a remarkable opening prayer in the state legislature. As Lynch says, "That prayer—one of the most impressive and eloquent prayers that had ever been delivered in the [Mississippi] Senate Chamber—made Revels a United States Senator. He made a profound impression upon all who heard him. It impressed those who heard it that Revels was not only a man of great natural ability but that he was also a man of superior attainments."

Election to Senate

At the time, the state legislature elected US senators. Revels was elected by a vote of 81 to 15 in the Mississippi State Senate to finish the term of one of the state's two seats in the US Senate left vacant since the Civil War. The seat had once been held by Albert G. Brown, who withdrew from the US Senate in 1861.

The election of Revels was met with opposition from Southern conservative Democrats who cited the Dred Scott Decision which was considered by many to have been a central cause of the American Civil War. They argued that no black man was a citizen before the 14th Amendment was ratified in 1868. Because election to the Senate required nine years' prior citizenship, opponents of Revels claimed he could not be seated, having been a citizen by law for only two years. Supporters of Revels countered by stating that the Dred Scott decision applied only to those blacks who were of pure African blood. Revels was of mixed black and white ancestry, and therefore exempt, they said, and had been a citizen all his life. This argument prevailed, and on February 25, 1870, Revels, by a vote of 48 to 8, became the first black man to be seated in the United States Senate.

U.S. Senator

Revels spoke for compromise and moderation. A vigorous advocate of racial equality, Revels tried to reassure Senators about the capability of blacks. In his maiden speech to the Senate on March 16, 1870, in a plea to reinstate the black legislators of the Georgia General Assembly who had been illegally ousted by white representatives, he said, "I maintain that the past record of my race is a true index of the feelings which today animate them. They aim not to elevate themselves by sacrificing one single interest of their white fellow citizens."

He served on both the Committee on Education and Labor and the Committee on the District of Columbia. Much of the Senate's attention focused on Reconstruction issues. While Radical Republicans called for continued punishment of ex-Confederates, Revels argued for amnesty and a restoration of full citizenship, provided they swore an oath of loyalty to the United States.

Revel's term lasted one year, February 1870 to March 3, 1871: He quietly, persistently—although for the most part unsuccessfully—worked for equality. He spoke against an amendment proposed by Senator Allen G. Thurman (D-Ohio) to keep the schools of Washington, D.C., segregated. He nominated a young black man to the United States Military Academy, although he was subsequently denied admission: *Revels was successful, however, in championing the cause of black workers who had been barred by their color from working at the Washington Navy Yard.*

Revels was praised in the newspapers for his oratorical abilities. His conduct in the Senate, along with that of the other African Americans who had been seated in the House of Representatives, also prompted a white contemporary, James G. Blaine, to say, "The colored men who took their seats in both Senate and House were as a rule studious, earnest, ambitious men, whose public conduct would be honorable to any race." Some of the bills Hiram Revels was involved with were granting lands and right of way to aid the construction of the New Orleans and Northeastern Railroad (41st Congress 2nd Session S. 712), levees on the Mississippi river (41st Congress 3rd Session S. 1136), and the incorporation of the Grand Tabernacle of Galilean Fishermen (41st Congress 3rd Session S. 1251.)

College president

Revels resigned two months before his term expired and was appointed the first president of Alcorn Agricultural and Mechanical College (now Alcorn State University) located in Claiborne County, Mississippi, where he also taught philosophy. In 1873, Revels took a leave of absence from Alcorn to serve as Mississippi's secretary of state ad interim.

He was dismissed from Alcorn in 1874 when he campaigned against the reelection of Governor of Mississippi Adelbert Ames. He was reappointed in 1876 by the new Democratic administration and served until his retirement in 1882.

On November 6, 1875, Revels, as a Republican, wrote a letter to Republican President Ulysses S. Grant that was widely reprinted. Revels denounced Ames and the Carpetbaggers for manipulating the Black vote for personal benefit, and for keeping alive wartime hatreds:

> *Since reconstruction, the masses of my people have been, as it were, enslaved in mind by unprincipled adventurers, who, caring nothing for country, were willing to stoop to anything no matter how infamous, to secure power to themselves, and perpetuate it . . . . My people have been told by these schemers, when men have been placed on the ticket who were notoriously corrupt and dishonest, that they must vote for them; that the salvation of the party depended upon it; that the man who scratched a ticket was not a Republican. This is only one of the many means these unprincipled demagogues have devised to perpetuate the intellectual bondage of my people . . . . The bitterness and hate created by the late civil strife has, in my opinion, been obliterated in this state, except perhaps in some localities, and would have long since been entirely obliterated, were it not for some unprincipled men who would keep alive the bitterness of the past, and inculcate a hatred between the races, in order that they may aggrandize themselves by office, and its emoluments, to control my people, the effect of which is to degrade them.*

Revels remained active in his ministry. For a time, he served as editor of the *Southwestern Christian Advocate* and taught theology at Shaw College (now Rust College), founded in 1866 in Holly Springs, Mississippi, where Revels and his family made their home. Hiram Revels died on January 16, 1901, while attending a church conference in Aberdeen, Mississippi.

Revel's daughter Susan edited a newspaper in Seattle, Washington. Horace R. Cayton, Jr., co-author of *Black Metropolis*, and labor leader Revels Cayton were his grandsons. ***In 2002, scholar Molefi Kete Asante listed Hiram Rhodes Revels on his list of 100 Greatest African Americans.***

Sojourner Truth

The woman we know as Sojourner Truth was born into slavery in New York as Isabella Baumfree (after her father's owner, Baumfree). She was sold several times, and while owned by the John Dumont family in Ulster County, married Thomas, another of Dumont's slaves. She had five children with Thomas. In 1827, New York law emancipated all slaves, but Isabella had already left her husband and run away with her youngest child. She went to work for the family of Isaac Van Wagenen.

While working for the Van Wagenen's—whose name she used briefly—she discovered that a member of the Dumont family had sold one of her children to slavery in Alabama. Since this son had been emancipated under New York Law, Isabella sued in court and won his return.

Isabella experienced a religious conversion, moved to New York City and to a Methodist perfectionist commune, and there came under the influence of a religious prophet named Mathias. The commune fell apart a few years later, with allegations of sexual improprieties and even murder. Isabella herself was accused of poisoning, and sued successfully for libel. She continued as well during that time to work as a household servant.

In 1843, she took the name Sojourner Truth, believing this to be on the instructions of the Holy Spirit and became a traveling preacher (the meaning of her new name). In the late 1840s she connected with the abolitionist movement, becoming a popular speaker. In 1850, she also began speaking on woman suffrage. Her most famous speech, Ain't I a Woman? was given in 1851 at a women's rights convention in Ohio.

Sojourner Truth met Harriet Beecher Stowe, who wrote about her for the *Atlantic Monthly* and wrote a new introduction to Truth's autobiography, *The Narrative of Sojourner Truth.*

Sojourner Truth moved to Michigan and joined yet another religious commune, this one associated with the Friends. *She was at one point friendly with Millerites, a religious movement that grew out of Methodism and later became the Seventh Day Adventists.*

During the Civil War Sojourner Truth raised food and clothing contributions for black regiments, and met Abraham Lincoln at the White House in 1864. While there, she tried to challenge the discrimination that segregated street cars by race.

After the War ended, Sojourner Truth again spoke widely, advocating for some time a "Negro State" in the west. She spoke mainly to white audiences, and mostly on religion, "Negro" and women's rights, and on temperance, though immediately after the Civil War she tried to organize efforts to provide jobs for black refugees from the war.

Active until 1875, when her grandson and companion fell ill and died, Sojourner Truth returned to Michigan where her health deteriorated and she died in 1883 in a Battle Creek sanatorium of infected ulcers on her legs. She was buried in Battle Creek, Michigan, after a very well-attended funeral.

Wisdom for the Journey

In matters of truth and justice, there is no difference between large and small problems, for issues concerning the treatment of people are all the same.

Albert Einstein

Dred Scott

Dred Scott (1799-September 17, 1858), was an African American slave in the United States who sued unsuccessfully for his freedom in the infamous *Dred Scott v. Sandford* case of 1857. His case was based on the fact that although he and his wife Harriet Scott were slaves, he had lived with his master Dr. John Emerson in states and territories where slavery was illegal according to both state laws and the Northwest Ordinance of 1787, including Illinois and Minnesota (which was then part of the Wisconsin Territory). The United States Supreme Court ruled seven to two against Scott, finding that neither he, nor any person of African ancestry, could claim citizenship in the United States, and therefore Scott could not bring suit in federal court under diversity of citizenship rules. Moreover, Scott's temporary residence outside Missouri did not bring about his emancipation under the Missouri Compromise, since that would improperly deprive Scott's owner of his legal property.

Overview

The case raised the issue of a slave who had lived in a free state. Congress had not asserted whether slaves were free if they set foot upon free soil. The ruling overturned the Missouri Compromise since by the court's logic; any attempt at regulating slavery in the federal Territories deprived a slave owner of his property without due process. This enraged the abolitionist Republicans and further exacerbated sectional sentiments that led to the Civil War.

Scott had traveled with his master Dr. John Emerson, who was in the army and often transferred. Scott's extended stay with his master in Illinois, a free state, gave him the legal standing to make a claim for freedom, as did his extended stay at Fort Snelling in the Wisconsin Territory, where slavery was also prohibited. But Scott never made the claim while living in the free lands—perhaps because he was unaware of his rights at the time, or because he was fearful of possible repercussions. After two years, the army transferred

Emerson to territory where slavery was legal: first to St. Louis, Missouri, then to Louisiana. In just over a year, the recently married Emerson summoned his slave couple. Instead of staying in the free territory of Wisconsin, or going to the free state of Illinois, the two traveled nearly 1250 miles (2000 km), apparently unaccompanied, down the Mississippi River to meet their master. Only after Emerson's death in 1843, when Emerson's widow hired out Scott to an army captain, did Scott seek freedom for himself and his wife. First he offered to buy his freedom from Emerson's widow, Irene Emerson—then living in St. Louis—for US$300, about $7,000 in current value. The offer was refused, leaving Scott to seek freedom through the courts.

Life

Dred Scott was born in Southampton County, Virginia, in the late 1790s as property of the Peter Blow family. It appears that Scott was originally named Sam and had an older brother named Dred. However, when the brother died as a young man, Scott chose to use his brother's name. The Blow family settled near Huntsville, Alabama, where they unsuccessfully tried farming.

In 1830 the Blow family took Scott with them when they relocated to St. Louis, Missouri. They sold Scott to John Emerson, a doctor serving in the United States Army. Scott traveled with Dr. Emerson as he worked throughout Illinois and the Wisconsin Territories, where the Northwest Ordinance prohibited slavery.

In 1836 Dred Scott met a teen-aged slave named Harriet Robinson. Her owner was Major Lawrence Taliaferro, an army officer from Virginia who allowed them to marry and transferred his ownership of Harriet to Dr. Emerson so they could be together. Two years later, Harriet gave birth to their first child, Eliza. In 1840, their daughter Lizzie was born. Scott and his wife would also have two sons, but both died in infancy.

Dr. Emerson would soon meet and marry Irene Sanford, and the Emerson's and Scotts returned to Missouri in 1842. When Dr. Emerson died the following year, his widow took over the estate. Scott petitioned the widow Emerson for his freedom, which she denied.

In 1846, having failed to obtain his freedom, Scott filed suit with the help of a local lawyer. It was tried in 1847 in the state courthouse in St. Louis. The judgment went against Scott, but the presiding judge granted a second trial as hearsay evidence had been introduced. Three years later, a jury decided that Scott and his wife should be freed because of their former residence in Illinois and Wisconsin. The widowed Irene Emerson appealed. The Missouri Supreme Court struck down the lower court ruling in 1852, explaining that: "Times now are not as they were when the previous decisions on this subject were made." The disheartened Scotts were returned to their master's wife.

Irene Emerson remarried Dr. Calvin C. Caffee of anti-slavery and Know-nothing affiliation. Under Missouri law at the time, the powers of estate transferred to her brother, John F. A. Sanford. Because Sanford was a citizen of New York, Scott's lawyers "claimed the case should now be brought before the Federal courts, on the grounds of diverse citizenship."

With the aid of new lawyers (including Montgomery Blair), the Scotts sued in a federal court. They lost the first round and appealed to the United States Supreme Court in *Dred Scott v. Sandford*. (The name is spelled 'Sandford' in the court decision due to a clerical error.) On March 6, 1857, Chief Justice Roger B. Taney delivered the explosive majority opinion. Taney ruled that:

- Any person descended from Africans, whether slave or free, is not a citizen of the United States, according to the Constitution.
- The Ordinance of 1787 could not confer either freedom or citizenship within the Northwest Territory to non-white individuals.
- The provisions of the Act of 1820, known as the Missouri Compromise, were voided as a legislative act, since the act exceeded the powers of Congress, insofar as it attempted to exclude slavery and impart freedom and citizenship to non-white persons in the northern part of the Louisiana Purchase.

In effect, the Court had ruled that African American slaves had no claim to freedom. They were property, not citizens, and could not bring suit in a federal court. Since slaves were private property, the federal government could not revoke a slave owner's rights based on where he lived, thus nullifying the essence of the Missouri Compromise. Taney, speaking for the majority, also ruled that since Scott was considered private property, he was subject to the Fifth Amendment to the United States Constitution, which prohibits taking property from its owner "without due process".

Following the decision, Scott and his family were returned as property to Emerson's widow. In the meantime, her brother John Sanford had been committed to an insane asylum. Ironically, in 1850, Irene Sanford Emerson had remarried. Her new husband, Calvin C. Chaffee, was an abolitionist who shortly after was elected to the United States Congress. An embarrassed Chaffee was apparently unaware that his wife owned the most prominent slave in the United States until one month before the Supreme Court decision. By then it was too late to intervene, and Chaffee was severely criticized for being married to a slave-owner. He persuaded his wife Irene return Scott to his original owners, the Blow family, who had also turned against slavery. As Missouri residents, they could emancipate him.

Dred Scott was formally freed by Henry Taylor Blow on May 26, 1857, less than 3 months after the Supreme Court decision. Scott worked as a porter in St. Louis for about seventeen months before he died from tuberculosis in September 1858. He was survived by his wife Harriet, and his daughters Eliza and Lizzie Scott.

Scott was interred in Calvary Cemetery, St. Louis, Missouri. A local tradition later developed of placing Lincoln pennies on top of Scott's gravestone for good luck.

Harriet Scott was long thought to be buried near her husband, but it was recently proven that she was buried in Greenwood Cemetery in Hillsdale, Missouri. She outlived her husband by 18 years, dying on June 17, 1876.

Legacy

- In 1997, Dred and Harriet Scott were inducted into the St. Louis Walk of Fame.

Their daughter Eliza Scott married and had two sons. Lizzie never married, but following her sister's early death, she helped raise her nephews. One of Eliza's sons died young, but the other married and has descendants. Some descendants of them live in St. Louis to this day.

Turner, Nat
(1800-31)

Nat Turner was a preacher, and the leader of a slave rebellion, born into slavery on October 2 on a plantation in Southampton County, Virginia.

Turner learned to read from one of his master's sons and became a lay preacher, believing himself divinely inspired to lead his people out of bondage.

On the night of August 31, 1831, Turner and several other slaves killed Joseph Travis, Turner's master at the time, and Travis' family. Turner then proceeded to Jerusalem, which was the county seat and where he planned to capture the armory, and in two days and nights with a force of some seventy-five followers, *killed about sixty white people; more than in any other rebellion in the nation's history.*

Turner's rebellion was defeated a few miles from Jerusalem by armed resistance from local whites and the arrival of the state militia, a total force of 3, 000 men.

The Virginia militia captured Turner on October 30, and he was tried on November 5 and *hanged and skinned on November 11.*

In response to fears sparked by the insurrection, as many as 200 innocent blacks were killed by angry whites. The rebellion led to stringent legislation in several Southern states to prohibit the education, movement, and assembly of slaves.

Reflections for the Soul:

Wealth is a tool of freedom, but the pursuit of wealth is the way to slavery.
Frank Herbert

Hatred: slavery's inevitable aftermath. **JOSÉ MARTÍ,**

Father Devine

American religious leader in full **Father Major Jealous Divine**, *original name* **George Baker**—born 1880?, Georgia?, U.S. died Sept. 10, 1965, Philadelphia, Pa.

A prominent African-American religious leader of the 1930s: The Depression-era movement he founded, the Peace Mission, was originally dismissed as a cult, but it still exists and is now generally hailed as an important precursor of the Civil Rights Movement.

Reportedly born on a plantation in Georgia, Baker began his career in 1899 as an assistant to Father Jehovia (Samuel Morris), the founder of an independent religious group. During his early adult years, Baker was influenced by Christian Science and New Thought. In 1912 he left Father Jehovia and emerged several years later as the leader of what would become the Peace Mission movement. He settled first in the New York City borough of Brooklyn and then in Sayville, New York, an all-white community on Long Island, where he lived quietly during the 1920s. His following grew, and in 1931, *when his Sayville neighbors complained about the growing attendance at meetings in his home, Father Divine was arrested and incarcerated for 30 days. When the judge who sentenced him died two days after the sentencing, Father Divine attributed the event to supernatural intervention*. His movement commemorates this event by annually publishing accounts of "divine retribution" visited on wrongdoers.

In 1933 Father Divine and his followers left Sayville for Harlem, where he became one of the most flamboyant leaders of the Depression era. There he opened the first of his Heavens, the residential hotels where his teachings were practiced and where his followers could obtain food, shelter, and job opportunities, as well as spiritual and physical healing.

The movement, whose membership numbered in the tens of thousands at its height during the Great Depression, builds on the principles of Americanism, brotherhood, Christianity, democracy, and Judaism, with the understanding that all "true" religions teach the same basic truths. Members are taught not to discriminate by race, religion, or color, and they live communally as brothers and sisters. Father Divine's teachings were codified in 1936 in the "Righteous Government Platform," which called for an end to segregation, lynching, and capital punishment. Movement members refrain from using tobacco, alcohol, narcotics, and vulgar language, and they are celibate. Moreover, members attempt to embody virtue, honesty, and truth. The movement's teachings also demand "a righteous wage in exchange for a full day's work." Members refuse to accumulate debt, and they possess neither credit nor life insurance.

During the Depression residents of the Heavens paid the minimal fee of 15 cents for meals and a dollar per week for sleeping quarters, a practice that allowed them to maintain their sense of dignity. In the opinion of many, Father Divine affirmed, amid the poverty of the Depression, the abundance of God with the free lavish banquets he held daily.

Heavens were opened across North America as well as in Europe, and, although most of its adherents were African Americans, the movement also attracted many whites (approximately one-fourth of its membership). The Heavens and related businesses brought in millions of dollars in revenue for the Peace Mission. Their success, however, also brought accusations of racketeering against Father Divine that, like the allegations of child abuse that were made against the movement, proved to be unfounded.

In 1942 Father Divine moved to suburban Philadelphia, in part to avoid paying a financial judgment in a suit brought by a former movement member. Four years later he married Edna Rose Ritchings, a Canadian member who, as Mother Divine, succeeded her husband as the movement's leader in 1965. The movement's membership has declined dramatically, however, not least because of the movement's strict dedication to celibacy.

Once dismissed as another cult leader, Father Divine was recognized in the late 20th century as an important social reformer. In the 1930s he was a champion of racial equality and an advocate of the economic self-sufficiency for African Americans that found broad acceptance only with the Civil Rights Movement.

From the Book

"For I was hungry and you gave me food, I was thirsty and you gave me drink, I was a stranger and you welcomed me, I was naked and you clothed me, I was sick and you visited me, I was in prison and you came to me.

Then the righteous will answer him, saying, 'Lord, when did we see you hungry and feed you, or thirsty and give you drink? And when did we see you a stranger and welcome you, or naked and clothe you? And when did we see you sick or in prison and visit you?'

And the King will answer them, 'Truly, I say to you, as you did it to one of the least of these my brothers, you did it to me.'"

(Matthew 25.35-40 ESV)

Bishop C.M. Grace
(Sweet Daddy Grace)

Bishop C.M. Grace, known to his followers as Sweet Daddy Grace, was born in Cape Verde Islands, Portugal in 1884. He came to America in 1903, and settled in New Bedford, Massachusetts. He was the founder, builder and organizer of the United House of Prayer for All People. To his followers he was a spiritual leader, counselor, and father and was affectionately called by them, "Daddy." Later in 1919, he built the first House of Prayer by hand in West Wareham, Massachusetts. He left us with his words stating that another would be chosen from his regular ministers, who would be the spiritual advisory and master of this kingdom.

The flamboyant Bishop C.M. Grace, known as "Sweet Daddy Grace," was an effective evangelist who preached revival in a Pentecostal tradition that included brass "shout bands" and public baptisms.

But his first big success came five years later when he opened a church in Charlotte. The United House of Prayer for All People prided itself on an ecstatic worship style that included speaking in tongues. Grace claimed great powers and developed a line of products including "Daddy Grace" coffee, tea, soaps, and hand creams reputed to have healing properties. By the time of his death in 1960, the church he founded had become a denomination and Grace himself a rich man. Today, the denomination, with about 3.5 million members, has headquarters in Washington, D.C.

A reflection from the BOOK

"Now John answered Him, saying," Teacher, we saw someone who does not follow us casting out demons in Your name, and we forbade him because he does not follow us."

41

But Jesus said, "Do not forbid him, for no one who works a miracle in My name can soon afterward speak evil of Me. For he who is not against us is on our side. For whoever gives you a cup of water to drink in My name, because you belong to Christ, assuredly, I say to you, he will by no means lose his reward." Mark 9:38-41)

Ralph Bunche

Ralph Johnson Bunche was born on August 7, 1904 in Detroit, Michigan. Bunche's family was poor and his father moved from city to city looking for work. Ralph attended Barstow School in Toledo, Ohio and sold newspapers to add to the family income. Bunche would later recall that, "My childhood days were poor days, but happy ones and filled with music." Ralph's mother died when he was thirteen years old, after which his maternal grandmother reared him.

Ralph attended Jefferson High School in Los Angeles. *He experienced racial prejudice when he was not allowed admittance to the Ephebain Society, the citywide honor society.* He was so upset that he wanted to quit school. He did not quit and graduated from high school in 1922 with academic honors. Ralph's grandmother encouraged him to continue his education. After graduation, he entered the University of California at Los Angeles (UCLA). At college Ralph participated in athletic and social activities. He was on the staff of the college newspaper, the "Daily Bruin," and sports editor of the college yearbook.

Although he worked part-time jobs to help pay for his college expenses, he excelled in his subjects. He majored in political science and was elected to Phi Beta Kappa, the most prestigious honor society in the U.S. In 1927, Bunche graduated from UCLA with the highest honors.

Bunche was offered a fellowship from Harvard University. He received a master of arts degree from Harvard in 1928 and took a position at Howard University, the prestigious African American college in Washington, D.C. He served as a political science professor and helped organize the political science department. While at Howard he met Ruth Harris, whom he married in 1930. They had three children, Joan, Jane and Ralph, Jr.

Bunche received a Ph.D. from Harvard University in 1934, becoming the first African-American to receive a doctorate in political science. Bunche traveled to many African countries while studying for his Ph.D. and had an opportunity to meet with many African leaders. In 1936,

Bunche published his first book, "A World View of Race," which was a study of race relations in the U.S. After the publication of his book, Bunche traveled to South Africa to study race relations there.

In 1939, Bunche began working with Gunnar Myrdal, a Swedish sociologist and economist, who was conducting a large scale study on black-white relations in the U.S. In 1944, the results of the research were published in the renowned book, "The American Dilemma: The Negro Problem and Modern Democracy."

During World War II, Bunche served as senior analyst for the National Defense Program Office of Information. He was later promoted to chief of the African section. He also worked at the U.S. State Department and participated in conferences that led to the formation of the United Nations. He was the first African American to serve on the U.S. delegation to the first General Assembly of the united Nations. In 1947, he was appointed director of the Trusteeship Department, and then he became Undersecretary General of the United Nations, becoming the highest U.S. official in the United Nations.

In 1949, Bunche successfully negotiated a truce to the Arab-Israeli conflict. For his work as a mediator for a peaceful resolution, Bunche was awarded the Nobel Peace Prize. In 1950, he became the first African American to receive the Nobel Prize. Bunche gave the Nobel lecture in Oslo, Norway, in which he said, "If today we speak of peace, we also speak of the united Nations, for in this year, peace and the United Nations have become inseparable . . . who could be so unseeing as not to realize that in modern war, victory is illusory; that the harvest of war can be only misery, destruction, and degradation?"

After receiving the Nobel Prize, Bunche continued to work to improve international relations and negotiate for peaceful resolutions throughout the world. In addition to his continued work in the Middle East, he organized and directed United Nations peacekeeping during the Suez and Congo crises. He received over 40 honorary degrees, the National Association for the Advancement of Colored People (NAACP) Spingarn Medal, the Theodore Roosevelt Association Medal of Honor, The Presidential Medal of Honor, and the U.S. Medal of Freedom.

Ralph Bunche died on December 9, 1971. As a tribute, the United Nations General Assembly stood for a moment of silence. In 1980, a steel monolith, entitled "Peace Form On," was erected in a park facing the United Nations. The park is named The Ralph Bunch Park and is dedicated to peace.

From the BOOK

Blessed are the peacemakers, for they shall be called sons of God.
(Mat. 5:9) NKV

Adam Clayton Powell, Jr.

The Reverend and Hon. Mr. **Adam Clayton Powell, Jr.**, (November 29, 1908-April 4, 1972) was an American politician and pastor who represented Harlem, New York City, in the United States House of Representatives (1945-71). *He was the first person of African-American descent elected to Congress from New York.* In 1961, after sixteen years in the House, he became chairman of the Education and Labor Committee. As Chairman, he supported the passage of important social legislation but was removed from his seat by Democratic Representatives-elect of the 90th Congress following allegations of corruption.

Early years

Powell was born in New Haven, Connecticut. His father, Adam Clayton Powell, Sr., was a Baptist minister and pastor of the Abyssinian Baptist Church in the Harlem neighborhood of New York City.

Powell attended Townsend Harris High School. As an undergraduate, he studied at the City College of New York and Colgate University. In 1931, he received a Master of Arts in religious education from Columbia University. He was a member of Alpha Phi Alpha.

During the Great Depression in the 1930s, Powell, a handsome and charismatic figure, became a prominent civil rights leader in Harlem, New York. He developed a formidable public following in the Harlem community through his crusades for jobs and housing. As chairman of the **Coordinating Committee for Employment**, he organized mass meetings, rent strikes, and public campaigns forcing companies and utilities and Harlem Hospital to hire black workers. During the 1939 New York World's Fair, Powell organized a picket line at the Fair's offices in the Empire State Building; as a result, the number of black employees was increased from about 200 to 732. *In 1941, a bus boycott led to the hiring of 200 black workers by the*

Transit Authority, and Powell led a fight to have drugstores in Harlem hire Negro pharmacists.

In 1937, he succeeded his father as Pastor of the Abyssinian Baptist Church. In 1941, with the aid of New York City's use of the Single Transferable Vote, he was elected to the New York City Council as the city's first Black Council representative. He received 65,736 votes, the third best total among the six successful Council candidates.

"Mass action is the most powerful force on earth," Powell once said, adding, "As long as it is within the law, it's not wrong; if the law is wrong, change the law." He was elected to Congress in 1944.

Congressman

In 1944, Powell was elected as a Democrat to represent the Congressional District that included Harlem in the U.S. House of Representatives. He was the first black Congressman from New York State and the first from any Northern state other than Illinois in the Post-Reconstruction Era.

As one of only two black Congressmen, Powell challenged the informal ban on black representatives using Capitol facilities reserved for white members only. He took black constituents to dine with him in the "Whites Only" House restaurant. He clashed with the many segregationists in his own party.

In 1956, Powell broke party ranks and supported President Dwight D. Eisenhower for re-election, saying the civil rights plank in the Democratic Party platform was too weak.

In 1958, he survived a determined effort by the Tammany Hall machine to oust him in the Democratic primary election.

In 1960, Powell forced Bayard Rustin to resign from the Southern Christian Leadership Conference (SCLC) by threatening to discuss Rustin's "immoral" homosexuality in Congress. He was concerned that questions about Rustin adversely affected the reputation and effectiveness of the SCLC.

In 1961, after 15 years in Congress, Powell became chairman of the powerful Education and Labor Committee. In this position, he presided over federal programs for minimum wage increases, Medicaid, expanding the minimum wage to include retail workers, equal pay for women, education and training for the deaf, nursing education, vocational training and standards for wages and work hours, as well as aid for elementary and secondary education. *He orchestrated passage of the backbone of President John Kennedy's "New Frontier" legislation. He also was instrumental in the passage of President Lyndon B. Johnson's "Great Society" social programs and the War on Poverty.*

Powell's committee passed a record number of bills for a single session, a record that still stands (2008). Powell steered some 50 bills through Congress.

He was instrumental in passing legislation that made lynching a federal crime, as well as bills that desegregated public schools. He challenged the Southern practice of charging Blacks a poll tax to vote and stopped racist Congressmen from saying the word "nigger" in sessions of Congress.

However, by the mid-1960s, Powell was increasingly being criticized for mismanaging his committee's budget, taking trips abroad at public expense, and missing sittings of his committee. He was also under attack in his District, where his refusal to pay a slander judgment made him subject to arrest. He spent increasing amounts of time in Florida.

In January 1967, the House Democratic Caucus stripped Powell of his committee chairmanship. The full House refused to seat him until completion of the Judiciary Committee's investigation. Powell urged his supporters to "keep the faith, baby" while the investigation was under way. On March 1, the House voted 307 to 116 to exclude him. Powell said, "On this day, the day of March in my opinion, the end of the United States of America as the land of the free and the home of the brave."

Powell won the Special Election to fill the vacancy caused by his exclusion but did not take his seat. He sued in *Powell v. McCormack* to retain his seat. In November 1968, Powell was again elected. On January 3, 1969, he was seated as a member of the 91st Congress; but he was fined $25,000 and denied seniority. In June 1969, the Supreme Court of the United States ruled that the House had acted unconstitutionally when it excluded Powell, a duly elected member.

Powell's increasing absenteeism was noted. In June 1970, he was defeated in the Democratic primary by Charles B. Rangel. That fall, he failed to get on the November ballot as an Independent; and he resigned as minister at the Abyssinian Baptist Church and moved to his retreat on Bimini. Rangel continues to represent the district (2010).

Death

In April 1972, Powell became gravely ill and was flown to a Miami hospital from his home in Bimini. He died there on April 4, 1972, at the age of 63, from acute prostatitis, according to contemporary newspaper accounts. After his funeral at the Abyssinian Baptist Church in Harlem, New York City, his son Adam III poured his ashes while aloft in a plane and scattered his remains over the waters of his beloved Bimini.

Personal

His first wife was nightclub entertainer Isabel Washington, the sister of actress Fredi Washington. Powell adopted her son Preston, from a previous marriage.

Powell and his second wife, singer Hazel Scott, had a son, Adam Clayton Powell III. Adam Clayton Powell III is Vice Provost for Globalization at the University of Southern California (USC) and one of the world's leading authorities on the use of the Internet for journalists. He named his son Adam Clayton Powell IV.

Powell and his third wife, Puerto Rican Yvette Diago, had a son Adam Clayton Powell Diago, so named in the matrilineal tradition of some Latino cultures. This son changed his name to Adam Clayton Powell IV when he moved to the mainland from Puerto Rico to attend Howard University. This caused confusion because his nephew, only 8 years younger than he, was also named Adam Clayton Powell IV.)

The politician A. C. Powell IV named his son Adam Clayton Powell V. In the 2010 Democratic primary election, A. C. Powell IV lost his challenge to the incumbent Charles B. Rangel for the right to run for Congress in his father's District.

Legacy

Seventh Avenue north of Central Park has been renamed **Adam Clayton Powell Jr. Boulevard**. One of the landmarks along this street is the Adam Clayton Powell Jr. State Office Building. In addition, two schools were named after him, PS 153, at 1750 Amsterdam Ave., and a middle school, IS 172 Adam Clayton Powell, Jr., School of Social Justice, at 509 W. 129th St., which closed in 2009.

Powell was the subject of the 2002 cable television film *Keep the Faith, Baby*, starring Harry Lennix as Powell and Vanessa L. Williams as his second wife, jazz pianist Hazel Scott. The film debuted on February 17, 2002, on premium cable network Showtime and was produced by the Viacom companies Showtime Premium Networks, Paramount Network Television, and Blockbuster on a budget of $6 million. It garnered three NAACP Image Award nominations for Outstanding Television Movie, Outstanding Actor in a Television Movie (Lennix), and Outstanding Actress in a TV Movie (Williams). It won two National Association of Minorities in Cable (NAMIC) Vision Awards for Best Drama and Best Actor in a Television Film (Lennix), the International Press Association's Best Actress in a Television Film Award (Williams), and Reel.com's Best Actor in a Television Film (Lennix). The film's producer was Geoffrey L. Garfield, Powell IV's long-time campaign manager; Monty Ross, a confidant of Spike Lee; and Hollywood veteran Harry J. Ufland. The film was written by Art Washington and directed by Doug McHenry.

A Point to Ponder

*If a man has any greatness in him, it comes to light, not in one **flamboyant** hour, but in the ledger of his daily work.*

Anne Hodki

Martin Luther King, Jr.,

Martin Luther King, Jr., (January 15, 1929-April 4, 1968) was born Michael Luther King, Jr., but later had his name changed to Martin. His grandfather began the family's long tenure as pastors of the Ebenezer Baptist Church in Atlanta, serving from 1914 to 1931; his father has served from then until the present, and from 1960 until his death Martin Luther acted as co-pastor. Martin Luther attended segregated public schools in Georgia, graduating from high school at the age of fifteen; he received the B. A. degree in 1948 from Morehouse College, a distinguished Negro institution of Atlanta from which both his father and grandfather had graduated. After three years of theological study at Crozer Theological Seminary in Pennsylvania where he was elected president of a predominantly white senior class, he was awarded the B.D. in 1951. With a fellowship won at Crozer, he enrolled in graduate studies at Boston University, completing his residence for the doctorate in 1953 and receiving the degree in 1955. In Boston he met and married Coretta Scott, a young woman of uncommon intellectual and artistic attainments. Two sons and two daughters were born into the family.

In 1954, Martin Luther King became pastor of the Dexter Avenue Baptist Church in Montgomery, Alabama. Always a strong worker for civil rights for members of his race, King was, by this time, a member of the executive committee of the National Association for the Advancement of Colored People, the leading organization of its kind in the nation. He was ready, then, early in December, 1955, to accept the leadership of the first great Negro nonviolent demonstration of contemporary times in the United States, the bus boycott described by Gunnar Jahn in his presentation speech in honor of the laureate. The boycott lasted 382 days. On December 21, 1956, after the Supreme Court of the United States had declared unconstitutional the laws requiring segregation on buses, Negroes and whites rode the buses as equals. ***During these days of boycott, King was arrested, his home was*** *bombed, he was subjected to personal abuse, but at the same time he emerged as a Negro leader of the first rank.*

In 1957 he was elected president of the Southern Christian Leadership Conference, an organization formed to provide new leadership for the now burgeoning civil rights movement. The ideals for this organization he took from Christianity; its operational techniques from Gandhi. In the eleven-year period between 1957 and 1968, King traveled over six million miles and spoke over twenty-five hundred times, appearing wherever there was injustice, protest, and action; and meanwhile he wrote five books as well as numerous articles. In these years, he led a massive protest in Birmingham, Alabama, that caught the attention of the entire world, providing what he called a coalition of conscience. and inspiring his "Letter from a Birmingham Jail", a manifesto of the Negro revolution; he planned the drives in Alabama for the registration of Negroes as voters; he directed the peaceful march on Washington, D.C., of 250,000 people to whom he delivered his address, *"I Have a Dream"*, he conferred with President John F. Kennedy and campaigned for President Lyndon B. Johnson*; he was arrested upwards of twenty times and assaulted at least four times;* he was awarded five honorary degrees; was named Man of the Year by *Time* magazine in 1963; and became not only the symbolic leader of American blacks but also a world figure.

At the age of thirty-five, Martin Luther King, Jr., was the youngest man to have received the Nobel Peace Prize. When notified of his selection, he announced that he would turn over the prize money of $54,123 to the furtherance of the civil rights movement.

On the evening of April 4, 1968, while standing on the balcony of his motel room in Memphis, Tennessee, where he was to lead a protest march in sympathy with striking garbage workers of that city, he was assassinated.

Quote:

"I have a dream that one day this nation will rise up and live out the true meaning of its creed: "We hold these truths to be self-evident: that all men are created equal." I have a dream that one day on the red hills of Georgia the sons of former slaves and the sons of former slave owners will be able to sit down together at a table of brotherhood." **MLK**

"I have a dream that my four little children will one day live in a nation where they will not be judged by the color of their skin, but by the content of their character." **MLK**

Part Two:

Arts & Science

Far better is it to dare mighty things, to win glorious triumphs, even though checkered by failure . . . than to rank with those poor spirits who neither enjoy nor suffer much, because they live in a gray twilight that knows not victory nor defeat.

Theodore Roosevelt

Ah, but a man's reach should exceed his grasp. Or what's a heaven for?

Robert Browning

As human beings, our greatness lies not so much in being able to remake the world—that is the myth of the atomic age—as in being able to remake ourselves.

Mohandas Gandhi

Benjamin Banneker

Benjamin Banneker, the son of Robert and Mary Bannaky was born in 1731. His grandfather was a slave from Africa and his grandmother, an indentured servant from England. His grandfather was known as Banna Ka, then later as Bannaky, his grandmother as Molly Walsh. His grandmother was a maid in England who had been sent to Maryland as an indentured servant. When she finished her seven years of bondage, she bought a farm along with two slaves to help her take care of it. Walsh freed both slaves and married one, Bannaky. They had several children, among them a daughter named Mary. When Mary Bannaky grew up, she bought a slave named Robert, married him and had several children, including Benjamin.

Benjamin Banneker grew up on the family farm. Around town it was known as "Bannaky Springs" due to the fresh water springs on the land. Bannaky used ditches and little dams to control the water from the springs for irrigation. His work was so reliable that the Bannaky's crops flourished even in dry spells. The family of free blacks raised good tobacco crops all the time.

Molly, Banneker's grandmother, taught him and his brothers to read, using her Bible as a lesson book. There was no school in the valley for the boys to attend. Then one summer, a Quaker school teacher came to live in the valley. He set up a school for boys. Benjamin Bannaky attended this school. The schoolmaster changed the spelling of his name to Banneker. At school he learned to write and do simple arithmetic.

When Banneker was twenty-one, a remarkable thing happened: he saw a patent watch. The watch belonged to a man named Josef Levi. Banneker was absolutely fascinated with the watch. He had never seen anything like it. Levi gave Banneker his watch. This was to change his life. Banneker took the watch apart to see how it worked. He carved similar watch pieces out of wood and made a clock of his own; the ***first striking clock to be made completely in America.*** Banneker's clock was so precise it struck every hour, on the hour, for forty years. His work on the clock led him to repair watches, clocks and sundials. ***Banneker even helped Joseph Ellicott to build a complex clock. Banneker became close friends with the Ellicott brothers. They lent him books on astronomy and mathematics as well as instruments for observing the stars. Banneker taught himself astronomy and advanced mathematics.***

Banneker's parents died, leaving him the farm since his two sisters had married and moved away. Banneker built a "work cabin" with a skylight to study the stars and make calculations. Working largely alone, with few visitors, he compiled results which he published in his Almanac.

Around this time, Major Andrew Ellicott, George Ellicott's cousin, asked Banneker to help him survey the "Federal Territory". Banneker and Ellicott worked closely with Pierre L'Enfant who was the architect in charge of planning Washington D.C. L'Enfant was suddenly dismissed from the project, due to his temper. When he left, he took the plans with him. Banneker recreated the plans from memory; saving the U.S. government the effort and expense of having someone else design the capital.

Although Banneker studied and recorded his results until he died, he stopped publishing his Almanac due to poor sales. Banneker died on Sunday, October 26, 1806. ***For years he has been referred to as "the first Negro Man of Science".***

Food for Thought

"Only in men's imagination does every truth find an effective and undeniable existence. Imagination, not invention, is the supreme master of art as of life." **Joseph Conrad**

Sacagawea

Sacagawea was the 15 year old Shoshone Indian who assisted the Lewis and Clark expedition around 1804-1806. She, along with her husband, were their guides from the Great Plains to the Pacific Ocean and then back. At around the age of 12 she was kidnapped by the Hidatsa tribe, which was an enemy tribe and was sold into slavery. Later on she was sold to a French-Canadian fur trader named Toussaint Charbonneau who then married Sacagawea and they then had a son whom they named Jean-Baptiste.

Sacagawea was their interpreter and negotiator with the Shoshone tribe and helped Lewis and Clark obtain supplies and horses from the tribe, which was being led by Sacagawea's brother Cameahwait. It is believed that without the help of Sacagawea, the expedition would have been impossible to complete. She went on the expedition with Lewis and Clark with her infant son on her back.

Sacagawea became a very important part of the expedition. Her knowledge of native plants and herbs often helped to feed the people and also knew which plants and roots were good for medicine. When encountering tribes along the way, Sacagawea prevented many battles because the tribes would see that there was an Indian woman with them. That was a clear sign of a non-threatening group. Especially that the woman was carrying a child with her.

In November 1805, when the expedition reached where the Columbia River met the Pacific Ocean, Lewis and Clark held a vote to decide where to settle for the winter. The expedition voted to stay near what is now Astoria, Oregon. They counted Sacagawea's vote as well. She was counted as equally as the men in the group. The corps then built Fort Clatsop and then settled there for the winter.

On the trip back Sacagawea was even more important to their expedition because she knew the areas that they were traveling through and was able to guide the expedition safely back. Sacagawea received no payment for her service but her husband did. He received cash and land for their help on the expedition.

Six years after the expedition, Sacagawea gave birth to a daughter, Lisette. That winter Sacagawea died from what was believed to be an ailment she had her entire adult life, but was aggravated by giving birth to her second child, at the age of 22. Eight months later Clark legally adopted her 2 children. Clark educated Jean-Baptiste. Shortly after his 18th birthday her son was then sent to Europe. There are no records of her daughter and it's unclear if she even survived past infancy.

There is a lot of legends and lore behind the story of Sacagawea. There are no drawings, pictures or descriptions of her, so her appearance is very unclear. Nobody knows what she really looked like. There are other legends associated with her story. *There are monuments and statues dedicated to her and now there is even a one dollar gold coin made in her honor. Her grave is located in Lander, Wyoming.*

Matthew Alexander Henson

Matthew Alexander Henson *(August 8, 1866-March 9, 1955) was an African American explorer and associate of Robert Peary during various expeditions, the most famous being a 1909 expedition which claimed to be the first to reach the Geographic North Pole.*

Life

Henson was born on a farm in Nanjemoy, Maryland on August 8, 1866. He was still a child when his parents Lemuel and Caroline died, and at the age of twelve he went to sea as a cabin boy on a merchant ship. He sailed around the world for the next several years, educating himself and becoming a skilled navigator.

Henson met Commander Robert E. Peary in November 1887 and joined him on an expedition to Nicaragua, with 4 other people that Peary chose. Impressed with Henson's seamanship, Peary recruited him as a colleague. For years they made many trips together, including Arctic voyages in which Henson traded with the Inuit and mastered their language, built sleds, and trained dog teams. In 1909, Peary mounted his eighth attempt to reach the North Pole, selecting Henson to be one of the team of six who would make the final run to the Pole. Before the goal was reached, Peary could no longer continue on foot and rode in a dog sled. Various accounts say he was ill, exhausted, or had frozen toes. In any case, he sent Henson on ahead as a scout. In a newspaper interview Henson said: ***"I was in the lead that had overshot the mark a couple of miles. We went back then and I could see that my footprints were the first at the spot."*** Henson then proceeded to plant the American flag.

Although Admiral Peary received many honors, Henson was largely ignored and spent most of the next thirty years working as a clerk in a federal customs house in New York. But in 1944 Congress awarded him a duplicate of the silver medal given to Peary. Presidents Truman and Eisenhower both honored him before he died in 1955.

In 1912 Matthew Henson wrote the book *A Negro Explorer at the North Pole* about his arctic exploration. Later, in 1947 he collaborated with Bradley Robinson on his biography *Dark Companion*. The 1912 book, along with an abortive lecture tour, enraged Peary who had always considered Henson no more than a servant and saw the attempts at publicity as a breach of faith.

Henson married Lucy Ross in 1906.

During their expeditions, both Henson and Peary fathered children with Inuit women, two of whom were brought to the attention of the American public by S. Allen Counter, who met them on a Greenland expedition.

With an Inuit woman named Akatingwah, Matthew Henson fathered his only child, a son named Anauakaq. After 1909 Henson never saw Akatingwah or his son again, though he did receive updates about them from other explorers for a time. Anauakaq, who died in 1987, arrived in the United States with Kali Peary, Robert Peary's son, on May 29, 1987, to visit his father's family and grave site. Anaukaq and his wife, Aviaq, had five sons who, in turn, had many children of their own who still reside in Greenland.

The "discovery" of Anauakaq and Kali and their meeting with their Henson and Peary relatives were documented in a book and documentary entitled *North Pole Legacy: Black, White and Eskimo*.

Matthew Henson is also a relative of actress Taraji P. Henson ("The Division", *Hustle & Flow*), and the great-great uncle of Annapolis, Maryland native and film Director Stanley V. Henson, Jr. who is the great-great grandson of Matthew Henson's brother and recently worked with Bill Cosby and Dick Gregory on "Sow your dreams" which includes an appearance by Taraji P. Henson. Matthew Henson's father Lemuel Henson is Stanley V. Henson, Jr's great-great-great grandfather.

Honors

The Explorers Club, under its "polar" President Vilhjalmur Stefansson, invited Henson to join its ranks in 1937. Eleven years later the Club reconsidered Henson's membership and instead awarded Henson its highest rank of Honorary Member, an honor reserved for no more than 20 living members at a time.

In 1961 an honorary plaque was installed to mark his Maryland birthplace.

On May 28, 1986, the United States Postal Service issued a 22 cent postage stamp in honor of Henson and Peary; they were previously honored in 1959, but not by name.

On April 6, 1988 Henson was reinterred in Arlington National Cemetery near Peary's monument. Many members from his American family and his Inuit family (Anauakaq's children) were in attendance.

In October 1996, the United States Navy commissioned USNS Henson, a Pathfinder class Oceanographic Survey Ship, in honor of Matthew Henson.

On November 28, 2000, the National Geographic Society awarded the Hubbard Medal to Matthew A. Henson posthumously. Dr. S. Allen Counter petitioned the National Geographic Society for many years to present its most prestigious medal to Henson. He attended the ceremony with Audrey Mebane, Henson's 74-year-old great-niece. The medal was presented at the newly named Matthew A. Henson Earth Conservation Center (MAHECC) in Washington, D.C., and accompanied a scholarship given in Henson's name by NGS.

The Matthew Henson Earth Conservation Center in Washington, D.C. is named for him, as are Matthew Henson State Park in Aspen Hill, Maryland, Matthew Henson Middle School in Pomonkey, Maryland, Matthew Henson Elementary School in Baltimore, Maryland and Matthew Henson Elementary School in Palmer Park, Maryland. Matthew Henson lived for a time in the landmark Dunbar Apartments in Harlem, in New York City.

In 2002, scholar Molefi Kete Asante listed Matthew Henson on his list of 100 Greatest African Americans.

Legacy

Henson's exploits and life were portrayed in the 1998 TV movie *Glory & Honor*. Henson was played by Delroy Lindo, and Henry Czerny played Robert Peary. The film won a Primetime Emmy and a Golden Satellite Award for Lindo's performance as Henson.

Wisdom for the Journey

"A civilized nation can have no enemies, and one cannot draw a line across a map, a line that doesn't even exist in nature and say that the ugly enemy lives on the one side, and good friends live on the other." **Thor Heyerdahl**

Augustus Jackson,
Born April 16, 1808,

African American, Augustus Jackson was a candy confectioner from Philadelphia who created several ice cream recipes and invented an improved method of manufacturing ice cream around 1832.

The origins of ice cream can be traced back to the 4th century B.C. and contrary to popular folklore Augustus Jackson did not invent ice cream itself, however, he was an accomplished businessman and helped to perfect the making of ice cream at that time.

Augustus Jackson—Background

Augustus Jackson left his position as a White House chef to move to Philadelphia in the late 1820s, where he started his own successful catering business. Jackson created several popular ice cream flavors which he distributed packaged in tin cans to the ice cream parlors of Philadelphia. At that time, many African Americans owned ice cream parlors or were ice cream makers in the Philadelphia area. Augustus Jackson was the most successful and his ice cream flavors were well loved.

Augustus Jackson did not apply for any patents.

Wisdom for the Journey

Life is like an ice-cream cone, you have to lick it one day at a time.

Charles M. Schulz

George Washington Carver

It is rare to find a man of the caliber of George Washington Carver. A man who would decline an invitation to work for a salary of more than $100,000 a year (almost a million today) to continue his research on behalf of his countrymen.

Agricultural Chemistry

As an agricultural chemist, Carver discovered three hundred uses for peanuts and hundreds more uses for soybeans, pecans and sweet potatoes. Among the listed items that he suggested to southern farmers to help them economically were his recipes and improvements to/for: adhesives, axle grease, bleach, buttermilk, chili sauce, fuel briquettes, ink, instant coffee, linoleum, mayonnaise, meat tenderizer, metal polish, paper, plastic, pavement, shaving cream, shoe polish, synthetic rubber, talcum powder and wood stain.

However, Carver only applied for three patents.

- #1,522,176, 1/6/1925, Cosmetics & Plant Products
- #1,541,478, 6/9/1925, Paints & Stains
- #1,632,365, 6/14/1927, Paints & Stains

Early Life

George Washington Carver was born in 1864 near Diamond Grove, Missouri on the farm of Moses Carver. He was born into difficult and changing times near the end of the Civil War. *The infant George and his mother were kidnapped by Confederate night-raiders and possibly sent away to Arkansas. Moses Carver found and reclaimed George after the war but his mother had disappeared forever.* The identity of Carver's father remains unknown, although he believed his father was a slave from a neighboring farm. Moses and Susan Carver reared George and his brother as their own children. It was on the Moses' farm where George first fell in love with nature, where he earned the nickname 'The Plant Doctor' and collected in earnest all manner of rocks and plants.

Education

He began his formal education at the age of twelve, which required him to leave the home of his adopted parents. Schools segregated by race at that time with no school available for black students near Carver's home. He moved to Newton County in southwest Missouri, where he worked as a farm hand and studied in a one-room schoolhouse. He went on to attend Minneapolis High School in Kansas. College entrance was a struggle, again because of racial barriers. At the age of thirty, Carver gained acceptance to Simpson College in Indianola, Iowa, where he was the first black student. Carver had to study piano and art and the college did not offer science classes. Intent on a science career, he later transferred to Iowa Agricultural College (now Iowa State University) in 1891, where he gained a Bachelor of Science degree in 1894 and a Master of Science degree in bacterial botany and agriculture in 1897. Carver became a member of the faculty of the Iowa State College of Agriculture and Mechanics (the first black faculty member for Iowa College), teaching classes about soil conservation and chemurgy.

Tuskegee

In 1897, Booker T. Washington, founder of the Tuskegee Normal and Industrial Institute for Negroes, convinced Carver to come south and serve as the school's Director of Agriculture. Carver remained on the faculty until his death in 1943.

At Tuskegee Carver developed his crop rotation method, which revolutionized southern agriculture. He educated the farmers to alternate the soil-depleting cotton crops with soil-enriching crops such as; peanuts, peas, soybeans, sweet potato, and pecans.

Helping the South

America's economy was heavily dependent upon agriculture during this era making Carver's achievements very significant. Decades of growing only cotton and tobacco had depleted the soils of the southern area of the United States of America. The economy of the farming south had been devastated by years of civil war and the fact that the cotton and tobacco plantations could no longer (ab) use slave labor. Carver convinced the southern farmers to follow his suggestions and helped the region to recover.

Carver also worked at developing industrial applications from agricultural crops. During World War I, he found a way to replace the textile dyes formerly imported from Europe. He produced dyes of 500 different shades of dye and he was responsible for the invention in 1927 of a process for producing paints and stains from soybeans. For that he received three separate patents.

God Gave Them to Me

Carver did not patent or profit from most of his products. He freely gave his discoveries to mankind. Most important was the fact that he changed the South from being a one-crop land of cotton, to being multi-crop farmlands, with farmers having hundreds of profitable uses for their new crops. **"God gave them to me" he would say about his ideas, "How can I sell them to someone else?"** In 1940, Carver donated his life savings to the establishment of the Carver Research Foundation at Tuskegee, for continuing research in agriculture.

Honors and Awards

George Washington Carver was bestowed an honorary doctorate from Simpson College in 1928. He was an honorary member of the Royal Society of Arts in London, England. In 1923, he received the Spingarn Medal given every year by the National Association for the Advancement of Colored People. In 1939, he received the Roosevelt medal for restoring southern agriculture. On July 14, 1943, U.S. President Franklin Delano Roosevelt honored Carver with a national monument dedicated to his accomplishments. The area of Carver's childhood near Diamond Grove, Missouri is preserved as a park; this park was the first designated national monument to an African American in the United States.

"He could have added fortune to fame, but caring for neither, he found happiness and honor in being helpful to the world."—Epitaph on the grave of George Washington Carver.

Quote:

I love to think of nature as an unlimited broadcasting station, through which God speaks to us every hour, if we will only tune in. I wanted to know the name of every stone and flower and insect and bird and beast. I wanted to know where it got its color, where it got its life-but there was no one to tell me.

George Washington Carver

From the BOOK

I will lift up my eyes to the hills: From whence comes my help? My help comes from the Lord, Who made heaven and earth. (Psalm 121:1-2)

Edward Goodrich Acheson

Edward Goodrich Acheson patented a method of making an abrasive he named Carborundum—U.S. Patents #492,767 and #615,648.

On February 28, 1893, Edward Goodrich Acheson (1856-1931) patented a method for making an industrial abrasive he called "Carborundum" or silicon carbide. On May 19, 1896, Edward Goodrich Acheson was also issued a patent for an electrical furnace used to produce carborundum. The United States Patent Office named carborundum as one of the 22 patents most responsible for the industrial age (1926). *According to the National Inventors Hall of Fame, "without carborundum, the mass production manufacturing of precision-ground, interchangeable metal parts would be practically impossible."*

Acheson went on to discover that when carborundum was heated to a high temperature it produced an almost pure and perfected form of graphite that could be used as a lubricant. He patented his graphite-making process in 1896.

During his lifetime, Edward Goodrich Acheson was granted 70 patents for industrial abrasives, several graphite products, processes for the reduction of oxides, and refractories.

Earlier in Acheson's career, the inventor had worked for **Thomas A. Edison.** In 1880, Acheson helped in the development of the **incandescent lamp** at Edison's laboratories at Menlo Park, N.J. *By Mary Bellis*

Genius is color blind.

Charles Richard Drew—
June 3, 1904-April 1, 1950

AT A GLANCE:

The American Red Cross blood program of today is a direct result of the work of medical pioneer Dr. Charles Drew, beginning in 1940 and throughout World War II. Dr. Drew was instrumental in developing blood plasma processing, storage and transfusion therapy. His groundbreaking work in the large-scale production of human plasma was eventually used by the U.S. Army and the American Red Cross as the basis for blood banks . . .

The Story:

Dr. Charles Richard Drew was the first person to develop the blood bank. His introduction of a system for the storing of blood plasma revolutionized the medical profession. Drew first utilized his system on the battlefields of Europe and the Pacific during World War II. He organized the world's first blood bank project in 1940—Blood for Britain. He also established the American Red Cross Blood Bank, of which he was the first director.

Drew was born in Washington, D.C. June 3, 1904 to Richard and Nora Drew, and was the oldest of five children. In his youth he seemed headed for a career in athletics and the coaching field rather than for medicine, starring as a four letter man in Dunbar High School, Washington. He went on to study at Amherst College, where he was a star athlete, all-American half-back and captain of his Amherst College football team.

After graduation, Charles Drew was a coach and a biology and chemistry instructor at Morgan State College, Baltimore, Maryland. But a turning point in his life was at hand. It had become his ambition to enter the field of medicine. He resigned his job at Morgan State and went to Montreal, Canada, where he enrolled in McGill University's Medical School. There he was granted two fellowships and was awarded his doctorate of medicine and master of surgery degrees.

For two years following graduation, Dr. Drew was an intern and resident in Montreal hospitals. In 1935, he returned to the United States to accept an appointment as instructor in pathology at the College of Medicine of Howard University in Washington, D.C. During the next two years, he advanced to become assistant professor of surgery.

Dr. Drew showed such promise in his work at Howard University that in 1938, at a time when war clouds were gathering over Europe, he was recommended for one of the Rockefeller fellowships at Columbia aimed at promoting advanced training in all fields of medicine. It was through this fellow ship that he met Dr. John Scudder and began study under him.

Dr. Drew was married in 1939 to Minnie Lenore Robbins, and they had four children, Bebe Roberta, Charlene Rosella, Rhea Sylvia, and Charles Richard, Jr. Shortly after, Dr. Drew earned his Doctor of Medicine degree from Columbia University in 1940, with a 200 page doctoral thesis under the title "Banked Blood: A Study in Blood Preservation".

Drew received an urgent cablegram from a former teacher, who had returned to England. The cable requested 5,000 glass containers of dried plasma for transfusions, plus the same amount three weeks later. A large project was started in August 1940 to collect blood in New York City hospitals for the export of plasma to Britain. Dr. Drew was appointed medical supervisor of the "Plasma for Britain" project. His notable contribution at this time was to transform the test tube methods of many blood researchers, including himself, into the first successful mass production techniques.

By this time it had become apparent that America probably would be drawn into the war. Military authorities in the United States were concerned with the need for a stockpile of blood reserves if hostilities should begin. ***Dr. Drew had emerged as a leading authority on mass transfusion and processing methods.***

After discussions with medical leaders and the American Red Cross, the government asked the Red Cross to establish a pilot program similar to the Plasma for Britain Project but on a smaller scale. Charles Drew was named director of the Red Cross Blood Bank and assistant director of the National

Research Council, in charge of blood collection for the United States Army and Navy. The pilot center was set up through the Red Cross chapter in New York City and began operation in February 1941.

In 1941, Dr. Drew returned to Howard University, where he gained new distinction, particularly in the training of young surgeons. He had spent a total of seven months in the two blood projects, yet in this very brief but productive period of his professional life, he made an outstanding contribution to what was to become a highly successful World War II blood procurement effort.

After Dr. Drew's return to Howard, he was appointed to several scientific committees and received honorary degrees from Virginia State and Amherst Colleges in 1945 and 1947. *He was one of the first of his race to be selected for membership on the American Board of Surgery. He also received the Spingarn Medal of the National Association for the Advancement of Colored People in 1944 for his outstanding contribution to human welfare.*

The experience gained through Dr. Drew's efforts at the Red Cross New York center proved invaluable, and during World War II, 35 blood bank centers were in operation. By war's end, millions of donations had been received by the Red Cross, donations that made possible the saving of thousands of lives of wounded U.S. servicemen lives that would have been lost in earlier wars when blood therapy was unknown.

Mankind suffered a great loss in 1950 when, at the age of 45, Dr. Drew was killed in an automobile accident while driving to a scientific conference. His pioneering medical work has endured. How many lives have been saved because of his genius at turning basic biological research into practical production methods is impossible to determine. But it is a certainty that mankind owes a debt of gratitude to Charles Richard Drew.

Quote:

"In nothing do men more nearly approach the gods than in giving health to men." ~Cicero

Vivien Theodore Thomas

Vivien Theodore Thomas (August 29, 1910-November 26, 1985) was an African-American surgical technician who developed the procedures used to treat blue baby syndrome in the 1940s. He was an assistant to surgeon Alfred Blalock in Blalock's experimental animal laboratory at Vanderbilt University in Nashville, Tennessee and later at the Johns Hopkins University in Baltimore, Maryland. *Without any education past high school, Thomas rose above poverty and racism to become a cardiac surgery pioneer and a teacher of operative techniques to many of the country's most prominent surgeons. Vivien Thomas was the first African American without a doctorate degree to perform open heart surgery on a white patient in the United States.*

Early life

Thomas was born in New Iberia, Louisiana. The grandson of a slave, he attended Pearl High School (named for a Union sympathizer Joshua Fenton Pearl and now known as Pearl Cohn Comprehensive High School) in Nashville in the 1920s. Even though it was racially segregated, the school provided him with a decent education. Thomas had hoped to go to college and become a doctor, but the Great Depression derailed his plans. He worked at Fisk University in the summer of 1929 doing carpentry but was laid off in the fall. In the wake of the stock market crash in October, Thomas put his educational plans on hold, and, through a friend, in February 1930 he secured a job as laboratory assistant to Dr. Alfred Blalock at Vanderbilt University. Although Blalock had hired Thomas to clean the cages and feed the laboratory dogs used for surgical experiments, he discovered Thomas' extraordinary eye-hand coordination developed during his carpenter work. When Blalock found that Thomas had an equally sharp intellect, Thomas began doing more laboratory work and less maintenance. ***Thomas was*** *classified and paid as a janitor, despite that by the mid 1930s he was doing the work of a postdoctoral researcher in the lab.*

Before meeting Blalock, Thomas married Clara and had two daughters. When Nashville's banks failed nine months after starting his job with Blalock and Thomas' savings were wiped out, he abandoned his plans for college and medical school, relieved to have even a low-paying job as the Great Depression deepened.

Working with Blalock

Thomas and Blalock did groundbreaking research into the causes of hemorrhagic and traumatic shock. This work later evolved into research on Crush syndrome and saved the lives of thousands of soldiers on the battlefields of World War II. In hundreds of flawlessly executed experiments, the two disproved traditional theories which held that shock was caused by toxins in the blood. Blalock, a highly original scientific thinker and something of an iconoclast, had theorized that shock resulted from fluid loss outside the vascular bed and that the condition could be effectively treated by fluid replacement. Assisted by Thomas, he was able to provide incontrovertible proof of this theory, and in so doing, he gained wide recognition in the medical community by the mid 1930s. At this same time, Blalock and Thomas began experimental work in vascular and cardiac surgery, defying medical taboos against operating upon the heart. It was this work that laid the foundation for the revolutionary lifesaving surgery they were to perform at Johns Hopkins a decade later.

Working at Johns Hopkins

By 1940, the work Blalock had done with Thomas placed him at the forefront of American surgery, and when he was offered the position of Chief of Surgery at his alma mater Johns Hopkins in 1941, he requested that Thomas accompany him. Thomas arrived in Baltimore with his family in June of that year, confronting a severe housing shortage and a level of racism worse than they had endured in Nashville. *Hopkins, like the rest of Baltimore, was rigidly segregated, and the only black employees at the institution were janitors. When Thomas walked the halls in his white lab coat, heads turned.*

Blue baby syndrome

In 1943, while pursuing his shock research, Blalock was approached by renowned pediatric cardiologist Dr. Helen Taussig, who was seeking a surgical solution to a complex and fatal four-part heart anomaly called Tetralogy of Fallot (also known as blue baby syndrome, although other cardiac anomalies produce blueness, or cyanosis). In infants born with this defect, blood is shunted past the lungs, thus creating oxygen deprivation and a blue pallor. Having treated many such patients in her work in Hopkins' Harriet Lane Home, Taussig was desperate to find a surgical cure. According to the accounts in Thomas' 1985 autobiography and in a 1967 interview with medical historian Peter Olch, Taussig suggested only that it might be possible to "reconnect the pipes" in some way to increase the level of blood flow to the lungs but did not suggest how this could be accomplished. Blalock and Thomas realized immediately that the answer lay in a procedure they had perfected for a different purpose in their Vanderbilt work, involving the anastomosis, or joining, of the subclavian to the pulmonary artery, which had the effect of increasing blood flow to the lungs.

Thomas was charged with the task of first creating a blue baby-like condition in a dog, and then correcting the condition by means of the pulmonary-to-subclavian anastomosis. *Among the dogs on whom Thomas operated was one named Anna, who became the first long-term survivor of the operation and the only animal to have her portrait hung on the walls of Johns Hopkins.* In nearly two years of laboratory work, involving some 200 dogs, Thomas was ultimately able to replicate only two of the four cardiac anomalies involved in Tetralogy of Fallot. He did demonstrate that the corrective procedure was not lethal, thus persuading Blalock that the operation could be safely attempted on a human patient. Even though Thomas knew he was not allowed to operate on patients at that time, he still followed Blalock's rules and assisted him during surgery.

Decisive surgery

On November 29, 1944, the procedure was first tried on an eighteen-month-old infant named Eileen Saxon. The blue baby syndrome had made her lips and fingers turn blue, with the rest of her skin having a very faint blue tinge. She could only take a few steps before beginning to breathe heavily. *Because no instruments for cardiac surgery then existed, Thomas adapted the needles and clamps for the procedure from those in use in the animal lab. During the surgery itself, at Blalock's request, Thomas stood on a step stool at Blalock's shoulder and coached him step by step through the procedure, Thomas having performed the operation hundreds of times on a dog, Blalock only once, as Thomas' assistant.* The surgery was not completely successful, though it did prolong the infant's life for several more months. Blalock and his team operated again on an 11-year-old girl, this time with complete success, and the patient was able to leave the hospital three weeks after the surgery. Next, they operated upon a six-year-old boy, who dramatically regained his color at the end of the surgery. ***The three cases formed the basis for the article that was published in the May 1945 issue of the Journal of the American Medical Association, giving credit to Blalock and Taussig for the procedure. Thomas received no mention.***

News of this groundbreaking story circulated around the world via the Associated Press. Newsreels touted the event, greatly enhancing the status of Johns Hopkins and solidifying the reputation of Blalock, who had been regarded as a maverick up until that point by some in the Hopkins old guard. ***Thomas' contribution remained unacknowledged, both by Blalock and by Hopkins.*** Within a year, the operation known as the Blalock-Taussig shunt had been performed on more than 200 patients at Hopkins, with parents bringing their suffering children from thousands of miles away.

Thomas' surgical techniques included one he developed in 1946 for improving circulation in patients whose great vessels (the aorta and the pulmonary artery) were transposed. A complex operation called an atrial septectomy, the procedure was executed so flawlessly by Thomas that Blalock, upon examining the nearly undetectable suture line, was prompted to remark, ***"Vivien, this looks like something the Lord made."***

To the host of young surgeons Thomas trained during the 1940s, he became a figure of legend, the model of a dexterous and efficient cutting surgeon. "Even if you'd never seen surgery before, you could do it because Vivien made it look so simple," the renowned surgeon Denton Cooley told *Washingtonian* magazine in 1989. "There wasn't a false move, not a wasted motion, when he operated." Surgeons like Cooley, along with Alex Haller, Frank Spencer, Rowena Spencer, and others credited Thomas with teaching them the surgical technique that placed them at the forefront of medicine in the United States. ***Despite the deep respect Thomas was accorded by these surgeons and by the many black lab technicians he trained at Hopkins, he was not well paid. He sometimes resorted to working as a bartender, often at Blalock's parties. This led to the peculiar circumstance of his serving drinks to people he had been teaching earlier in the day.*** Eventually, after negotiations on his behalf by Blalock, he became the highest paid technician at Johns Hopkins by 1946, and by far the highest paid African-American on the institution's rolls. Although Thomas never wrote or spoke publicly about his ongoing desire to return to college and obtain a medical degree, his widow, the late Clara Flanders Thomas, revealed in a 1987 interview with *Washingtonian* writer Katie McCabe that her husband had clung to the possibility of further education throughout the Blue Baby period and had only abandoned the idea with great reluctance.

Mrs. Thomas stated that in 1947, Thomas had investigated the possibility of enrolling in college and pursuing his dream of becoming a doctor, but had been deterred by the inflexibility of Morgan State University, which refused to grant him credit for life experience and insisted that he fulfill the standard freshman requirements. Realizing that he would be 50 years old by the time he completed college and medical school, Thomas decided to give up the idea of further education.

Relations with Blalock

Blalock's approach to the issue of Thomas' race was complicated and contradictory throughout their 34-year partnership. On the one hand, he defended his choice of Thomas to his superiors at Vanderbilt and to Hopkins colleagues, and he insisted that Thomas accompany him in the operating room during the first series of tetralogy operations. On the other hand, there were limits to his tolerance, especially when it came to issues of pay, academic acknowledgment, and his social interaction outside of work.

After Blalock's death from cancer in 1964 at the age of 65, Thomas stayed at Hopkins for 15 more years. In his role as director of Surgical Research Laboratories, he mentored a number of African-American lab technicians as well as Hopkins' first black cardiac resident, Dr. Levi Watkins, Jr., whom Thomas assisted with his groundbreaking work in the use of the Automatic Implantable Defibrillator.

Thomas' nephew, Koco Eaton, graduated from the Johns Hopkins Medical School; trained by many of the same physicians his uncle had trained. Eaton trained in orthopedics and is now the team doctor for the Tampa Bay Rays.

Institutional acknowledgment

In 1968, the surgeons Thomas trained—who had then become chiefs of surgical departments throughout America—commissioned the painting of his portrait (by Bob Gee, oil on canvas, 1969, The Johns Hopkins Alan Mason Chesney Medical Archives) and arranged to have it hung next to Blalock's in the lobby of the Alfred Blalock Clinical Sciences Building.

In 1976, Johns Hopkins University presented Thomas with an honorary doctorate. However, because of certain restrictions, he received an Honorary Doctor of Laws, rather than a medical doctorate, but it did allow the staff and students of Johns Hopkins Hospital and Johns Hopkins Medical School to call him doctor. Thomas was also appointed to the faculty of Johns Hopkins Medical School as Instructor of Surgery.

Legacy

Following his retirement in 1979, Thomas began work on an autobiography, *Partners of the Heart: Vivien Thomas and his Work with Alfred Blalock*, ISBN 0-8122-1634-2. He died on November 26, 1985 of pancreatic cancer, at age 75, and the book was published just days later. Having learned about Thomas on the day of his death, *Washingtonian* writer Katie McCabe brought his story to public attention for the first time in a 1989 article entitled **"Like Something the Lord Made"**, which won the 1990 National Magazine Award for Feature Writing and inspired filmmaker Andrea Kalin to make the PBS documentary *Partners of the Heart"*, which was broadcast in 2003 on PBS' American Experience and won the Organization of American Historians' Erik Barnouw Award for Best History Documentary in 2004. McCabe's article, brought to Hollywood by Washington, D.C. dentist Irving Sorkin, formed the basis for the Emmy and Peabody Award-winning 2004 HBO film *Something the Lord Made*.

Thomas' legacy as an educator and scientist continued with the institution of the Vivien Thomas Young Investigator Awards, given by the Council on Cardiovascular Surgery and Anesthesiology beginning in 1996. In 1993, the Congressional Black Caucus Foundation instituted the Vivien Thomas Scholarship for Medical Science and Research sponsored by GlaxoSmithKline. In the fall of 2004, the Baltimore City Public School System opened the Vivien T. Thomas Medical Arts Academy, and on January 29, 2008, MedStar Health unveiled the first "Rx for Success" program at the Academy, joining the conventional curriculum with specialized coursework geared to the health care professions. In the halls of the school hangs a replica of Thomas' portrait commissioned by his surgeon-trainees in 1968. The Journal of Surgical Case Reports (JSCR) announced in January 2010 that their annual prizes for the best case report written by a doctor and best case report written by a medical student would be named after Thomas.

Wisdom for the Journey:

The genius of the United States is not best or most in its executives or legislatures, nor in its ambassadors or authors or colleges, or churches, or parlors, nor even in its newspapers or inventors, but always most in the common people. **Walt Whitman**

God and Nature first made us what we are, and then out of our own created genius we make ourselves what we want to be. Follow always that great law. Let the sky and God be our limit and Eternity our measurement. **Marcus Garvey**

Jealousy is the tribute mediocrity pays to genius. **Fulton J. Sheen**

Part Three:

Labor & Industry

Everyone has the right to a standard of living adequate for the health and well-being of himself and his family, including food, clothing, housing, medical care and necessary social services, and the right to security in the event of unemployment, sickness, disability, widowhood, old age or other lack of livelihood.
   —Universal Declaration of Human Rights, Article 25, passed unanimously by the United Nations General Assembly in December, 1948

Labor is prior to, and independent of, capital. Capital is only the fruit of labor, and could never have existed if labor had not first existed. Labor is the superior of capital, and deserves much the higher consideration.—**Abraham Lincoln**

Historically: Jesus was a Carpenter. (Mark 6:3)NKJV

Denmark Vesey

Denmark Vesey (1767-1822), an African American who fought to liberate his people from slavery, planned an abortive slave insurrection.

Denmark Vesey, whose original name was Telemanque, was born in West Africa. As a youth, he was captured, sold as a slave, and brought to America. In 1781 he came to the attention of a slaver, Capt. Vesey, who was "struck with the beauty, alertness, and intelligence" of the boy. Vesey, a resident of Charleston, S.C., acquired the boy. The captain had "no occasion to repent" his purchase of Denmark, who "proved for 20 years a most faithful slave."

In 1800 Vesey won a $1,500 lottery prize, with which he purchased his freedom and opened a carpentry shop. Soon this highly skilled artisan became "distinguished for [his] great strength and activity. Among his color he was always looked up to with awe and respect" by both black and white Americans. He acquired property and became prosperous.

Nevertheless, Vesey was not content with his relatively successful life. He hated slavery and slaveholders. This brilliant man versed himself in all the available antislavery arguments and spoke out against the abuse and exploitation of his own people.

Believing in equality for everyone and vowing never to rest until his people were free, he became the political provocateur, agitating and moving his brethren to resist their enslavement. Selecting a cadre of exceptional lieutenants, Vesey began organizing the black community in and around Charleston to revolt. He developed a very sophisticated scheme to carry out his plan. The conspiracy included over 9,000 slaves and "free" blacks in Charleston and on the neighboring plantations.

The revolt, which was scheduled to occur on July 14, 1822, was betrayed before it could be put into effect. As rumors of the plot spread, Charleston was thrown into a panic. Leaders of the plot were rounded up. Vesey and 46 other were condemned, and even four whites were implicated in the revolt. On June 23 Vesey was hanged on the gallows for plotting to overthrow slavery.

After careful examination of the historical record, the judgment of Sterling Stuckey remains valid: *"Vesey's example must be regarded as one of the most courageous ever to threaten the racist foundations of America . . . . He stands today, as he stood yesterday . . . as an awesome projection of the possibilities for militant action on the part of a people who have for centuries been made to bow down in fear."*

Quote:

"The only way a man can ride your back is when it's bent." MLK

Isaac Myers

Isaac Myers's (1835—1891) life after 1865 represented an example of the anticipation with which most of black Baltimore viewed the end of slavery and legal inequality in the U.S. Myers stood near the center of a leadership cadre charged with shaping the conversion not only from slavery to freedom, but more importantly perhaps, from free people to equal citizen. Social work, political activism, entrepreneurship, inter-racial cooperation, intra-community networking, represented the vehicles for meeting this charge.

A caulker by trade, this native Baltimorean was born free like so many other blacks in the city (the overwhelming majority after the 1820s). The caulking trade specifically, and ship-building/maritime industries in general of Baltimore were historical inter-racial, using freeman and slaves simultaneously. By the close of the U.S. Civil War (1861—1865) with the consequent end of slavery, blacks were systematically pushed out of this type of employment to make room for growing numbers of whites in the city. This reality led to the organization by Myers and others of the Chesapeake Marine Railway and Dry Dock Company.

The historical significance of Isaac Myers rises above the establishment of this company, however. He was a key Republican organizer during the high point of black involvement with the party in Baltimore. He also did complete the groundwork for organization of black workers into labor unions during the late-nineteenth century. In fact, until his death, he represented the broad possibilies and reluctant opportunities open to blacks in the unique situation of nineteenth century Baltimore.

Wisdom for the Journey

We are a continuum. Just as we reach back to our ancestors for our fundamental values, so we, as guardians of that legacy, must reach ahead to our children and their children. And we do so with a sense of sacredness in that reaching. **Paul Tsongas**

Madame C.J. Walker
(1867-1919)

Sarah Breedlove McWilliams Walker, better known as Madame CJ Walker or Madame Walker, together with Marjorie Joyner revolutionized the hair care and cosmetics industry for African American women early in the 20th century.

Early Years

Madame CJ Walker was born in 1867 in poverty-stricken rural Louisiana. The daughter of former slaves, she was orphaned at the age of seven. Walker and her older sister survived by working in the cotton fields of Delta and Vicksburg, Mississippi. She married at age fourteen and her only daughter was born in 1885. After her husband's death two years later, she traveled to St. Louis to join her four brothers who had established themselves as barbers. Working as a laundrywoman, she managed to save enough money to educate her daughter, and became involved in activities with the National Association of Colored Women.

Inspired by Need

During the 1890s, Sarah began to suffer from a scalp ailment that caused her to lose some of her hair. Embarrassed by her appearance, she experimented with a variety of home-made remedies and products made by another black woman entrepreneur, Annie Malone. In 1905, Sarah became a sales agent for Malone and moved to Denver, where she married Charles Joseph Walker.

Madam Walker's Wonderful Hair Grower

Changing her name to Madame CJ Walker, Sarah founded her own business and began selling her own product called Madam Walker's Wonderful

Hair Grower, a scalp conditioning and healing formula. To promote her products, she embarked on an exhausting sales drive throughout the South and Southeast selling her products door to door, giving demonstrations, and working on sales and marketing strategies. In 1908, she opened a college in Pittsburgh to train her "hair culturists."

The Walker System

Eventually, her products formed the basis of a thriving national corporation employing at one point over 3,000 people. Her Walker System, which included a broad offering of cosmetics, licensed Walker Agents, and Walker Schools offered meaningful employment and personal growth to thousands of Black women. Madame Walker's aggressive marketing strategy combined with relentless ambition led her to be labeled as the ***first known African-American woman to become a self-made millionaire.***

Having amassed a fortune in fifteen years, this pioneering businesswoman died at the age of 52. Her prescription for success was perseverance, hard work, faith in herself and in God, "honest business dealings" and of course, quality products. ***"There is no royal flower-strewn path to success,"*** she once observed. "And if there is, I have not found it—for if I have accomplished anything in life it is because I have been willing to work hard."

Improved Permanent Wave Machine

An employee of Madame CJ Walker's empire, Marjorie Joyner invented an improved permanent wave machine. This device patented in 1928, curled or "permed" women's hair for a relatively lengthy period of time. ***The wave machine was popular among women white and black allowing for longer-lasting wavy hair styles.*** Joyner went on to become a prominent figure in Madame CJ Walker's industry, though she never profited directly from her invention, the assigned intellectual property of the Walker Company.

Madame Walker on Herself

I got my start by giving myself a start.

"I am a woman who came from the cotton fields of the South. From there I was promoted to the washtub. From there I was promoted to the cook kitchen. And from there I promoted myself into the business of manufacturing hair goods and preparations. I have built my own factory on my own ground"

- I had to make my own living and my own opportunity. But I made it! Don't sit down and wait for the opportunities to come. Get up and make them.
- One night I had a dream, and in that dream a big black man appeared to me and told me what to mix up for my hair. I made up my mind I would begin to sell it.
- I am not satisfied in making money for myself. I endeavor to provide employment for hundreds of the women of my race.
- There is no royal flower-strewn path to success. And if there is, I have not found it for if I have accomplished anything in life it is because I have been willing to work hard.
- Perseverance is my motto.—Madame Walk

Wisdom for the Journey

Difficult things take a long time, impossible things a little longer.
                                                        ~*André A. Jackson*

Look at a stone cutter hammering away at his rock, perhaps a hundred times without as much as a crack showing in it. Yet at the hundred-and-first blow it will split in two, and I know it was not the last blow that did it, but all that had gone before. **Jacob A. Riis**

A. Philip Randolph

Asa Philip Randolph (April 15, 1889—May 16, 1979) was a prominent twentieth century African American civil rights leader and founder of the Brotherhood of Sleeping Car Porters, which was a huge victory for labor and especially for African American labor organizing.

Early Years

Randolph was born in Crescent City, Florida. He never grew up being "racially internalized", meaning that he never saw himself any less than the white kids around him. His father was a minister of the A.M.E. Church who moved the family to Jacksonville, Florida in 1891. In 1911, Randolph moved to New York City's Harlem in hope of becoming an actor.

Randolph's parents objected to his dramatic aspirations, so while at the City College of New York, he switched his studies to politics and economics. While at City College, he met his future wife, Lucille Green. Green was a former teacher who had opened a lucrative beauty salon when her first husband died. During their marriage, Randolph's political activities would sometimes cause Lucille to lose customers.

Also at City College, Randolph met Chandler Owen, a sociology and political science student at Columbia University. Together, they were influenced by Hubert Harrison and then formed the radical Harlem magazine, The Messenger, in 1917 which espoused socialist views. He ran, unsuccessfully, as the Socialist candidate for New York's Secretary of State in the 1921 election.

Union organizer

Randolph had some experience in labor organization, having organized a union of elevator operators in New York City in 1917. In 1925, Randolph organized the Brotherhood of Sleeping Car Porters. This was the first serious effort to form a labor union for the employees of the Pullman Company, which was a major employer of African-Americans. With amendments to the Railway Labor Act in 1934, porters were granted rights under federal law, and membership in the Brotherhood jumped to more than 7,000. After years of bitter struggle, the Pullman Company finally began to negotiate with the Brotherhood in 1935, and agreed to a contract with them in 1937, winning $2,000,000 in pay increases for employees, a shorter workweek, and overtime pay. The Brotherhood was associated with the American Federation of Labor.

Civil rights leader

Randolph emerged as one of the most visible spokespersons for African-American civil rights. In 1941, he, Bayard Rustin, and A. J. Muste proposed a March on Washington to protest racial discrimination in war industries. The March was cancelled after President of the United States Franklin D. Roosevelt issued the Fair Employment Act. Some militants felt betrayed by the cancellation because Roosevelt's pronouncement only pertained to defense industries and not the armed forces themselves. In 1947, Randolph formed the Committee against Jim Crow in Military Service, later renamed the League for Non-Violent Civil Disobedience. President Harry S. Truman abolished racial segregation in the armed forces through Executive Order 9981 on July 26, 1948.

Randolph was also notable in his support for restrictions on immigration.

In 1950, along with Roy Wilkins, Executive Secretary of the NAACP, and Arnold Aronson, a leader of the National Jewish Community Relations Advisory Council, Randolph founded the Leadership Conference on Civil Rights (LCCR). LCCR has since become the nation's premier civil rights coalition, and has coordinated the national legislative campaign on behalf of every major civil rights law since 1957.

Randolph also helped Rustin and Martin Luther King Jr. to organize the March on Washington for Jobs and Freedom on August 28, 1963. As the U.S. civil rights movement gained momentum in the early 1960s and came to the forefront of the nation's consciousness, his rich baritone voice was often heard on television news programs addressing the nation on behalf of African-Americans engaged in the struggle for voting rights and an end to discrimination in public accommodations.

Honors and Awards

On September 14, 1964, Lyndon B. Johnson presented Randolph with the Presidential Medal of Freedom.

Wisdom for the Journey

All of the great leaders have had one characteristic in common: it was the willingness to confront unequivocally the major anxiety of their people in their time. This, and not much else, is the essence of leadership. ~John Kenneth Galbraith

Part Four:

Law, Education & Literature

One who breaks an unjust law that conscience tells him is unjust, and who willingly accepts the penalty of imprisonment in order to arouse the conscience of the community over its injustice, is in reality expressing the highest respect for law. **Martin Luther King, Jr.**

"Education makes people easy to lead, but difficult to drive; easy to govern, but impossible to enslave." **Henry Peter Broughan**

*A mind once stretched by a new idea never regains its original dimensions.—***Anonymous**

"Books are the carriers of civilization. Without books, history is silent, literature dumb, science crippled, thought and speculation at a standstill." **Barbara Tuchman**

In a real sense, people who have read good literature have lived more than people who cannot or will not read. It is not true that we have only one life to live; if we can read, we can live as many more lives and as many kinds of lives as we wish. **S. I. Hayakawa**

Prince Hall

Prince Hall (c.1735-December 4, 1807), was a tireless abolitionist and a leader of the free black community in Boston. Hall tried to gain New England's enslaved and free blacks a place in some of the most crucial spheres of society, Freemasonry, education and the military. He is considered the founder of **"Black Freemasonry"** in the United States, known today as Prince Hall Freemasonry. Hall formed the African Grand Lodge of North America. Prince Hall was unanimously elected its Grand Master and served until his death in 1807. He also lobbied tirelessly for education rights for black children and a back-to-Africa movement. *Many historians regard Prince Hall as one of the more prominent African American leaders throughout the early national-period of the United States.*

Early Life and Manumission

Prince Hall's life history has been a subject of debate. William Grimshaw's 1903 "Official History of Freemasonry Among the Colored People of North America" began the story that Prince Hall was born in Barbados to a white father and mulatto mother who fled to the British colony of Massachusetts where Hall became a Methodist minister. Black Freemasonry scholars have for the most part, rejected Grimshaw's account due to inconsistencies.

Charles Wesley, a historian (not the founder of Methodism), put together an alternative history for Prince Hall through compilations of archival sources. He claimed that Prince Hall was enslaved to the tanner William Hall at age eleven in Boston. Prince Hall may have become literate on his own, or through the direct help of white people. Some New Englanders made a point of teaching slaves and Free Blacks to read and write. Documents in Massachusetts showing that slave-owner William Hall freed a man named Prince Hall on April 9, 1765 cannot be conclusively linked to any one individual as there exists record of no fewer than 21 males named Prince

Hall, and several other men named Prince Hall were living in Boston at that time.

It is extremely hard to conclusively say which man in either case is actually Prince Hall. At the time Hall was supposedly freed, there were no less than 21 black males named Prince hall in Boston. But it is certain that by 1770 Prince Hall was a free, literate, black man living in Boston.

Leadership

The details surrounding Prince Hall's life involving abolitionism and masonry are more certain than his early life. He attempted various approaches to advance black rights. He was politically active, petitioning for the abolition of slavery in Massachusetts and fought for laws to protect free blacks in Massachusetts from kidnapping by slave traders. He proposed a *back-to-Africa* movement and pressed for equal education and funding for black and white school children, even operating a school in his own home. He showed his prowess in debate early on, citing Christian teachings in a petition that spoke out against slavery to fellow Christians in a predominantly church-attending Massachusetts legislature.

His role as a business entrepreneur, Free Mason, and politician significantly improved the lives of many African Americans living in New England. Tax records in 1775 Boston, Massachusetts, show that Hall was involved in several business ventures throughout the city. The records show Hall's connections with a leather, tanner, caterer, and merchant business. Hall's businesses were easily recognizable on Water Street by his mark of the Golden Fleece. Hall used these business forums as an educational medium for African American youth as well as a theatrical stage for public activities involving the Black Free Mason community.

After the American Revolution ended, many African Americans who served in the ranks or as aids during the war expected equality from the whites whom they had stood next to against the British. Prince Hall soon emerged in the high profile realm of politics and was instrumental in proposing several pieces of legislation that would improve the lives of African Americans throughout New England. However, the situation soon became apparent that the African American place in society had budged little throughout the duration of the war. In addition to proposing legislation, Hall also hosted a variety of different events for African Americans including theater events as well as educational forums. Prince Hall's role of an educator of the African American youth as well as a politician may very well have been just as instrumental as his foundation of the African American Free Masonry Lodge.

Involvement in American Revolutionary War

Hall urged the enlistment of both enslaved and freed blacks for the attempt to free the American colonies from British control. Hall was concerned with the development of the colonies if they gained independence. He was certain that involvement of blacks in the construction of the new nation would be the first step toward the complete freedom for all blacks. The Massachusetts Committee of Safety declined Hall's proposal to allow blacks the opportunity to fight for the colonies. Prince Hall and supporters of his cause petitioned the Committee by comparing Britain's ruling of the colonies with the enslavement of blacks. A proclamation from England guaranteed blacks that if they enlisted in the British army instead of the Continental they would be freed at the end of the war. *Only after the British Army began to use blacks in their troops did the Colonial Army change its decision to block admission of blacks into the military.*

It is very likely that because of his strong support for the revolutionary cause Prince Hall had served in the Massachusetts militia during the American Revolutionary War. It is again unclear definitively whether he served or not since at least six men from Massachusetts who were named "Prince Hall" served in the military during the war.

A Freemason

The Masonic fraternity was extremely attractive to free blacks of the eighteenth century. Prince Hall and his followers saw Freemasonry as a platform where racial differences did not exist. The Masonic ideals greatly appealed to Hall, especially the beliefs in liberty, equality and peace. Prior to the American Revolutionary War, Prince Hall and fourteen other free black men petitioned for the admittance to the white Boston St. John's Lodge. They were turned away. Some whites were irate of the audacity for blacks applying to be Masons. Due to the resistance of colonial Masonries, Hall looked elsewhere and on March 6, 1775, Hall and fifteen other free blacks were initiated into the Masonry by members of the Irish Military Lodge No. 441. The Lodge was attached to the British forces stationed in Boston. Hall and the other freedmen founded African Lodge No. 1 with Prince Hall named as Grand Master.

A problem quickly arose for black men wishing to become Masons in the newly formed United States: the members of a Lodge must agree unanimously in an anonymous vote to accept a petitioner to receive the degrees. As a consequence of the unanimity requirement, if just one member of a lodge did not want black men in his Lodge, his vote was enough to cause the petitioner's rejection. This sentiment can be seen in the letter of General Albert Pike to his brother in 1875 where he says, "I am not inclined to mettle in the matter. I took my obligations to white men, not to Negroes. When I have to accept Negroes as brothers or leave Masonry, I shall leave it." **Thus, although exceptions did exist, Masonic Lodges and Grand Lodges in the United States generally excluded African Americans.** And since the vote is conducted anonymously, this created a second problem: since no one knew who had voted against the applicant, it was impossible to identify a member as pursuing a policy of racism. This allowed even a tiny number of prejudiced members to effectively deny membership to black petitioners, and in some cases even exclude black men who had legitimately been made Masons in integrated jurisdictions. **Thus there arose a system of racial segregation in American Masonry, which remained in place until the 1960s and which persists in some jurisdictions even to this day.**

When the British Army left Boston in 1776, the black Masons had limited power. They could meet as a lodge, take part in the Masonic procession on St. John's Day, and bury their dead with Masonic rites but could not confer Masonic degrees or perform any other essential functions of a fully operating Lodge. It took nine years of petitioning white American Lodges before they appealed to the less prejudiced lodges in England. They applied to the Grand Lodge of England for a warrant March 2, 1784. While waiting to hear from England, Prince Hall applied to mainstream Masonic authorities for a temporary full warrant in the meantime. They were unsuccessful. However, they were granted a second permit to continue with their original, though limited, operations that covered the period until Hall heard back from the Grand Lodge. The first meeting place was a lodge room they prepared in "Golden Fleece" which was located near Boston Harbor. They later met at Kirby Street Temple in Boston.

Eventually, the grand master of the Mother Grand Lodge of England, H. R. H. The Duke of Cumberland issued a charter for the African Lodge No. 1 later renamed African Lodge no. 459 September 29, 1784. But the charter was not received until April, 29, 1787 due to complications. The Lodge was organized under the warrant May 6, 1781. Shortly after, black masons elsewhere in the United States began contacting Prince Hall with requests to establish Lodges in their own cities. Consistent with European Masonic practices at the time, African Lodge granted their requests and served as Mother Lodge to new black Lodges in Newport, Rhode Island in 1799, Philadelphia, Providence and New York.

By 1779 there were at least thirty-four members in the Boston black lodge, a sizeable number that was overlooked by mainstream Boston Masons. Unfortunately, integration with the American white Masons was not impending.

The dream that black Masonry and white Masonry would become simply Freemasonry had to be either abandoned or, at least, indefinitely postponed. Instead, the blacks concentrated on recognition from the whites. Recognition required that white Masons state that black Masonry, descending from Prince Hall of Massachusetts, was legitimate and not "clandestine." That it had received its charter from the English Grand Lodge and was thus entitled to all Masonic rights such as inter-visitation between black and white lodges without prejudice. Many Grand Masters hoped that ultimately recognition would lead to integration but they knew it would be a long time before that happened.

In 1791, black Freemasons met in Boston and formed the African Grand Lodge of North America. Prince Hall was unanimously elected its Grand Master and served until his death in 1807. (The claim that he was appointed Provincial Grand Master for North America in 1791 appears to have been fabricated.) The African Grand Lodge was later renamed the Prince Hall Grand Lodge in his honor. In 1827 the African Grand Lodge declared its independence from the United Grand Lodge of England, as the Grand Lodge of Massachusetts had done 45 years earlier. It also stated its independence from all of the white Grand Lodges in the United States.

Today, predominantly black Prince Hall Grand Lodges exist in the United States, Canada, the Caribbean and Liberia, governing Prince Hall Lodges throughout the world. Hall's legacy as a freemason and a leader has survived with the lodges. As a Georgia Mason noted, the original local lodge rules written by Prince Hall and his followers in the late 18th century were the first set of regulations drafted by colored men for self government in the United States and Masonry ever since has striven to teach its members 'the fundamentals of central government' which is the basis of American life." After nearly two centuries of controversy, the Grand Lodge of England was asked to decide the matter of Prince Hall Masonic legitimacy. Carefully studying the records, the Grand Lodge of England concluded that the Prince Hall Grand Lodge of Massachusetts was indeed entitled to Masonic recognition and this against the tradition that, *per* state, only one recognized Masonic body should exist.

Attempted Reforms and Legislation

Prince Hall is recognized as a black leader due to an unrelenting effort to engage the Massachusetts' legislature in the cause for blacks. He repeatedly joined groups requesting the legislative body to end slavery in the state. He also petitioned for state support for black schools, and even opened one in his own home. As with many of his previous appeals, this one went unattended, and yet, his emancipatory efforts helped create an enduring tradition of Black activism.

Hall put much of his energy into education. Literate himself, he believed that education was an extremely important skill to teach black children to get them on even footing with whites. He is known for speeches and petitions he gave on furthering his cause. Prince Hall' "1792 Charge", "1797 Charge" and his 1787 Petition are his most recognizable writings. Hall had a way with words that could lead many to follow in his strong beliefs. In a speech given to the Boston African Masonic Lodge, *Hall stated, "My brethren, let us not be cast down under these and many other abuses we at present labor under: for the darkest is before the break of day . . . . Let us remember what a dark day it was with our African brethren, six years ago, in the French West Indies. Nothing but the snap of the whip was heard, from morning to evening". Halls' 1792 Charge, focused on the abolition of slavery in his home state of Massachusetts. He addressed how United States' Black Leaders were important to the shaping of the country and unity.* In his 1797 Charge, Hall spoke more about the treatment and hostility that blacks faced while living in the United States. He also gave recognition to the black revolutionaries in the Haitian Revolution.

A strong advocate for black equality, Prince Hall was also involved in the back-to-Africa movement. In the 1780s Hall approached the legislature once again requesting funds for voluntary emigration to Africa. In January of 1773, Prince Hall and seventy three other African American delegates presented an emigration plea to the Massachusetts Senate. This plea explained that the African Americans would be better suited to the warm climate of Africa and that they would be able to endure the lifestyle. However this failed. Hall felt that it was the most appropriate solution in order for blacks to gain some semblance of equality. Hall fought even harder for the movement when a group of freed black men were captured and detained while making their way to Africa. With all the information that Prince Hall had received he believed that blacks would be well suited back in Africa as leaders by using lessons they learned in America. However, due to a lack of support and enthusiasm for the movement, Hall decided to turn his efforts towards equality in education.

Education played a significant role in Prince Hall's life. As a slave, Hall was taught to read and write by his master. Some northern slave-owners believed it was a good idea to teach their slaves to become literate. By experiencing how crucial education was, Hall used his leadership to ask the Massachusetts congress for a school program for black children. Hall cited the same platform for fighting the American Revolution of "Taxation without Representation." Although Hall's arguments were logical, his two attempts at passing legislation through the Massachusetts Senate both resulted in failure. Denied equal funding, Hall was not to be deterred and eventually started a school program for free black children out of his own home. Prince Hall emphasized classical education and Liberal Arts.

Quote:

Education is not preparation for life; education is life itself.

~John Dewey

Harriet Beecher Stowe—
Uncle Tom's Cabin

American writer and philanthropist, ***best-known for the anti-slavery novel Uncle Tom's Cabin (1851-52).*** Stowe wrote the work in reaction to the Fugitive Slave Act of 1850, which made it illegal to assist an escaped slave. ***In the story 'Uncle Tom' of the title is bought and sold three times and finally beaten to death by his last owner.*** The book was quickly translated into 37 languages and it sold in five years over half a million copies in the United States. *Uncle Tom's Cabin* was also among the most popular plays of the 19th century.

*"**Eliza made her desperate retreat across the river just in the dusk of twilight. The gray mist of evening, rising slowly from the river, enveloped her as she disappeared up the bank, and the swollen current and floundering masses of ice presented a hopeless barrier between her and her pursuer.**" (From Uncle Tom's Cabin)*

Harriet Beecher Stowe was born in Litchfield, Connecticut, into a large family. She had two sisters (Catharine and Mary), one half-sister (Isabella), five brothers (William, Edward, George, Henry Ward, and Charles), and two half-brothers (Thomas and James). Harriet herself was the seventh child of her parents, Lyman and Roxana Beecher. "Wisht it had been a boy!" said her father after her birth. Lyman was a controversial Calvinist preacher, who saw himself as a soldier of Christ. Roxana, a granddaughter of General Andrew Ward, died of tuberculosis at 41-Harriet was four at that time. Two years later a stepmother took over the household.

Stowe was named after her aunt, Harriet Foote, who influenced deeply her thinking, especially with her strong belief in culture. Samuel Foote, her uncle, encouraged her to read works of Lord Byron and Sir Walter Scott. When Stowe was eleven, she entered the seminary at Hartford, Connecticut, kept by her elder sister Catharine. The school had advanced curriculum and she learned languages, natural and mechanical science, composition, ethics, logic, mathematics—subjects that were generally taught to male students. Four years later she was employed as an assistant teacher. Her father married again—he became the president of lane Theological Seminary.

Catharine and Harriet founded a new seminary, the Western Female Institute. With her sister Stowe wrote a children's geography book. In 1834 Stowe began her literary career when she won a prize contest of the *Western Monthly Magazine*, and soon Stowe was a regular contributor of stories and essays. Her first book, *The Mayflower*, appeared in 1843.

In 1836 Stowe married Calvin Ellis Stowe, a professor at her father's theological seminary. He was a widower; his late wife had been Stowe's friend. The early years of their marriage were marked by poverty. Over the next 14 years Stowe had 7 children. In 1850 Calvin Stowe was offered a professorship at Bowdoin, and they moved to Brunswick, Maine. *In Cincinnati Stowe had come in contact with fugitive slaves. She learned about life in the South from her own visits there and saw how cruel slavery was.* In addition the Fugitive Slave Law, passed by Congress in 1850, arose much protest—giving shelter or assistance to an escaped slave became a crime. And finally a personal tragedy, the death of her infant Samuel from cholera, led Stowe to compose her famous novel. It was first published in the anti-slavery newspaper *The National Era*, from June 1851 to April 1852, and later in book form. **The story was to some extent based on true events and the life of Josiah Henson. "I could not control the story, the Lord himself wrote it," Stowe once said. "I was but an instrument in His hands and to Him should be given all the praise." When Abraham Lincoln met the author he joked, "So you're the little woman who wrote the book that started this Great War."** Uncle Tom's Cabin was smuggled into Russia in Yiddish to evade the czarist censor. Leo Tolstoy praised the work and it remained enormously popular also after the Revolution.

"I s'pect I growed. Don't think nobody never made me." (from *Uncle Tom's Cabin*)

Stowe's fame opened her doors to the national literary magazines. She started to publish her writings in *The Atlantic Monthly* and later in *Independent* and in *Christian Union*. For some time she was the most celebrated woman writer in *The Atlantic Monthly* and in the New England literary clubs. In 1853, 1856, and 1859 Stowe made journeys to Europe, where she became friends with George Eliot, Elisabeth Barrett Browning, and Lady Byron. However, the British public opinion turned against her when she charged Lord Byron with incestuous relations with his half-sister. In *Lady Byrin Vindicated* (1870) she accused him in the writing. Both the magazine *Atlantic*, where the text first appeared, and Stowe, suffered.

Attacks on the veracity of her portrayal of the South led Stowe to publish *The Key to Uncle Tom's Cabin* (1853), in which she presented her source material. A second anti-slavery novel, *Dred: A Tale of the Great Dismal Swamp* (1856), told the story of a dramatic attempt at slave rebellion.

> *In Uncle Tom's Cabin the pious old Uncle Tom is sold by his well-intentioned Kentucky owner, Mr. Shelby, who has fallen into debts. The trader also singles out little Harry, Eliza's child, but Eliza takes Harry and heads for the river. Uncle Tom submits to his fate. He is bought first by the idealistic Augustine St Clare after saving her daughter, Little Eva, who falls from the deck of a riverboat. In his New Orleans house, Uncle Tom makes friends with Eva's black friend, the impish Topsy. "Never was born!' persisted Topsy . . . 'never had no father, nor mother, nor nothin'. I was raised by a speculator, with lots of others." Eva dies from a weakened constitution, and St. Clare is killed in an accident—he is stabbed while trying to separate two brawling men. Tom is sold to the villainous Simon Legree, a Yankee and a brutal cotton plantation owner. "I don't go for savin' niggers. Use up, and buy more,'s my way," he says. Two of Uncle Tom's female slaves, Cassy and Emmeline, pretend to escape and go into hiding. Tom will not reveal their whereabouts and Legree has his lackeys Quimbo and Sambo beat the unprotesting Tom to the point of death. Tom forgives them and dies, just as Mr. Shelby's son arrives to buy him back. Shelby decides to fight for the Abolitionist cause. A parallel plot centers on Eliza, her little child, and her husband George who escape to freedom in Canada using the 'underground railroad.' Other important characters are Miss Ophelia St. Clare, a New England spinster, and Marks, the slave catcher. Cassy meets on the boat north Madame de Throux, sister of George Harris, Eliza's husband. The Harris family leaves for Africa and George Shelby frees his slaves.*

After the Civil War the sales of the novel declined. The sentimentality and religiosity of the story was considered a drawback. ***The first film adaptation was made in 1903. 'Uncle Tom' was used negatively, meaning white paternalism and black passivity, undue subservience to white people on the part of black people.*** In the 1970s *Uncle Tom's Cabin*, with its strong female characters, started to attract the attention of feminist critics, but Stowe's vision found new defenders. ***However, Tom's passivity was compared to Gandhi's strategy of peaceful resistance.***

Stowe's later works did not gain the same popularity as *Uncle Tom's Cabin*. She published novels, studies of social life, essays, and a small volume of religious poems. The Stowes lived in Hartford in summer and spent their winters in Florida, where they had a luxurious home. *The Pearl of Orr's Island*

(1862), *Old-Town Folks* (1869), and *Poganuc People* (1878) were partly based on her husband's childhood reminiscences and are among the first examples of local color writing in New England. *Poganuc People* was Stowe's last novel. Her mental faculties failed in 1888, two years after the death of her husband. She died on July 1, 1896 in Hartford, Connecticut.

Quote:

As long as the mind is enslaved, the body can never be free. Psychological freedom, a firm sense of self-esteem, is the most powerful weapon against the long night of physical slavery. MARTIN LUTHER KING, *speech, Aug. 16, 1967*

Booker Taliaferro Washington
Born: (1856-1915)

Occupation: Lecturer, Civil Rights/Human Rights Activist, Educational Administrator, Professor, Organization Executive/Founder, Author/Poet

Booker T. Washington was born a slave in Hale's Ford, Virginia, reportedly on April 5, 1856. After emancipation, his family was so poverty stricken that he worked in salt furnaces and coal mines beginning at age nine. Always an intelligent and curious child, he yearned for an education and was frustrated when he could not receive good schooling locally. When he was 16 his parents allowed him to quit work to go to school. They had no money to help him, so *he walked 200 miles to attend the Hampton Institute in Virginia and paid his tuition and board there by working as the janitor.*

Dedicating himself to the idea that education would raise his people to equality in this country, Washington became a teacher. He first taught in his home town, then at the Hampton Institute, and then in 1881, he founded the Tuskegee Normal and Industrial Institute in Tuskegee, Alabama. As head of the Institute, he traveled the country unceasingly to raise funds from blacks and whites both; soon he became a well-known speaker.

In 1895, Washington was asked to speak at the opening of the Cotton States Exposition, an unprecedented honor for an African American. His Atlanta Compromise speech explained his major thesis, that blacks could secure their constitutional rights through their own economic and moral advancement rather than through legal and political changes. Although his conciliatory stand angered some blacks who feared it would encourage the foes of equal rights, whites approved of his views. Thus his major achievement was to win over diverse elements among Southern whites, without whose support the programs he envisioned and brought into being would have been impossible.

In addition to Tuskegee Institute, which still educates many today, Washington instituted a variety of programs for rural extension work, and helped to establish the National Negro Business League. Shortly after the election of President William McKinley in 1896, a movement was set in motion that Washington be named to a cabinet post, but he withdrew his name from consideration, preferring to work outside the political arena. He died on November 14, 1915.

Quote:

There is a class of colored people who make a business of keeping the troubles, the wrongs, and the hardships of the Negro race before the public. Having learned that they are able to make a living out of their troubles, they have grown into the settled habit of advertising their wrongs-partly because they want sympathy and partly because it pays. Some of these people do not want the Negro to lose his grievances, because they do not want to lose their jobs.—Booker T. Washington

W.E.B. DuBois

Introduction

William Edward Burghardt DuBois, to his admirers, was by spirited devotion and scholarly dedication, an attacker of injustice and a defender of freedom.

A harbinger of Black Nationalism and Pan-Africanism, he died in self-imposed exile in his home away from home with his ancestors of a glorious past—Africa.

Labeled as a "radical," he was ignored by those who hoped that his massive contributions would be buried along side of him. But, as Dr. Martin Luther King, Jr. wrote, "history cannot ignore W.E.B. DuBois because history has to reflect truth and Dr. DuBois was a tireless explorer and a gifted discoverer of social truths. His singular greatness lay in his quest for truth about his own people. There were very few scholars who concerned themselves with honest study of the black man and he sought to fill this immense void. The degree to which he succeeded disclosed the great dimensions of the man."

His Formative Years

W.E.B. DuBois was born on February 23, 1868 in Great Barrington, Massachusetts. At that time Great Barrington had perhaps 25, but not more than 50, Black people out of a population of about 5,000. Consequently, there were little signs of overt racism there. Nevertheless, its venom was distributed through a constant barrage of suggestive innuendoes and vindictive attitudes of its residents. This mutated the personality of young William from good natured and outgoing to sullen and withdrawn. This was later reinforced and strengthened by inner withdrawals in the face of real discriminations. His demeanor of introspection haunted him throughout his life.

104

While in high school DuBois showed a keen concern for the development of his race. At age fifteen he became the local correspondent for the *New York Globe*. And in this position he conceived it his duty to push his race forward by lectures and editorials reflecting upon the need of Black people to politicize themselves.

DuBois was naturally gifted intellectually and took pleasurable pride in surpassing his fellow students in academic and other pursuits. Upon graduation from high school, he, like many other New England students of his caliber, desired to attend Harvard. However, he lacked the financial resources to go to that institution. But with the aid of friends and family, and a scholarship he received to Fisk College (now University), he eagerly headed to Nashville, Tennessee to further his education.

This was DuBois' first trip south. And in those three years at Fisk (1885-1888) his knowledge of the race problem became more definite. *He saw discrimination in ways he never dreamed of, and developed a determination to expedite the emancipation of his people. Consequently, he became a writer, editor, and an impassioned orator: And in the process acquired a belligerent attitude toward the color bar.*

Also, while at Fisk, DuBois spent two summers teaching at a county school in order to learn more about the South and his people. There he learned first hand of poverty, poor land, ignorance, and prejudice. But most importantly, he learned that his people had a deep desire for knowledge.

After graduation from Fisk, DuBois entered Harvard (via scholarships) classified as a junior. As a student his education focused on philosophy, centered in history. It then gradually began to turn toward economics and social problems. As determined as he was to attend and graduate from Harvard, he never felt himself a part of it. Later in life he remarked "I was in Harvard but not of it." He received his bachelor's degree in 1890 and immediately began working toward his master's and doctor's degree.

DuBois completed his master's degree in the spring of 1891. However, shortly before that, ex-president Rutherford B. Hayes, the current head of a fund to educate Negroes, was quoted in the *Boston Herald* as claiming that they could not find one worthy enough for advanced study abroad. DuBois' anger inspired him to apply directly to Hayes. His credentials and references were impeccable. He not only received a grant, but a letter from Hayes saying that he was misquoted. DuBois chose to study at the University of Berlin in Germany. It was considered to be one of the world's finest institutions of higher learning. And DuBois felt that a doctor's degree from there would infer unquestionable preparation for ones life's work.

During the two years DuBois spent in Berlin, he began to see the race problems in the Americas, Africa, and Asia, and the political development of Europe as one. This was the period of his life that united his studies of history, economics, and politics into a scientific approach of social research.

DuBois had completed a draft of his dissertation and needed another semester or so to finish his degree. But the men over his funding sources decided that the education he was receiving there was unsuitable for the type of work needed to help Negroes. They refused to extend him any more funds and encouraged him to obtain his degree from Harvard. Which of course he was obliged to do. His doctoral thesis, *The Suppression of the African Slave Trade in America*, remains the authoritative work on that subject, and is the first volume in Harvard's Historical Series.

Easing On Down the Road

At the age of twenty-six, with twenty years of schooling behind him, DuBois felt that he was ready to begin his life's work. He accepted a teaching job at Wilberforce in Ohio at the going rate of $800.00 per year. (He also had offers from Lincoln in Missouri and Tuskegee in Alabama.)

The year 1896 was the dawn of a new era for DuBois. With his doctorate degree and two undistinguished years at Wilberforce behind him, he readily accepted a special fellowship at the University of Pennsylvania to conduct a research project in Philadelphia's seventh ward slums. This responsibility afforded him the opportunity to study Blacks as a social system.

DuBois plunged eagerly into his research. *He was certain that the race problem was one of ignorance.* And he was determined to unearth as much knowledge as he could, thereby providing the "cure" for color prejudice. His relentless studies led into historical investigation, statistical and anthropological measurement, and sociological interpretation. The outcome of this exhaustive endeavor was published as *The Philadelphia Negro. "It revealed the Negro group as a symptom, not a cause; as a striving, palpitating group, and not an inert, sick body of crime; as a long historic development and not a transient occurrence." This was the first time such a scientific approach to studying social phenomena was undertaken, and as a consequence DuBois is acknowledged as the father of Social Science.*

After the completion of the study, DuBois accepted a position at Atlanta University to further his teachings in sociology. For thirteen years there he wrote and studied Negro morality, urbanization, Negroes in business, college-bred Negroes, the Negro church, and Negro crime. He also repudiated the widely held view of Africa as a vast cultural cipher by presenting a historical version of complex, cultural development throughout Africa. His studies left no stone unturned in his efforts to encourage and help social reform . . . It is said that because of his outpouring of information "there was no study made of the race problem in America which did not depend in some degree upon the investigations made at Atlanta University."

During this period an ideological controversy grew between DuBois and Booker T. Washington, which later grew into a bitter personal battle. Washington from 1895, when he made his famous "Atlanta Compromise" speech, to 1910 was the most powerful black man in the America. Whatever grant, job placement or any endeavor concerning Blacks that influential whites received was sent to Washington for endorsement or rejection. Hence, the "Tuskegee Machine" became the focal point for Black input/output. DuBois was not opposed to Washington's power, but rather, he was against his ideology/methodology of handling the power. On one hand Washington decried *political* activities among Negroes, and on the other hand dictated Negro political objectives from Tuskegee.

Washington argued the Black people should temporarily forego "political power, insistence on civil rights, and higher education of Negro youth. They should concentrate all their energies on industrial education*." **DuBois believed in the higher education of a "Talented Tenth" who through their knowledge of modern culture could guide the American Negro into a higher civilization. (See Chapter 4, "Science and Empire" in DuBois' Dusk of Dawn.)**

The culmination of the conflict came in 1903 when DuBois published his now famous book, *The Souls of Black Folks*. The chapter entitled "Of Booker T. Washington and Others" contains an analytical discourse on the general philosophy of Washington. DuBois edited the chapter himself to keep the most controversial and bitter remarks out of it. Nevertheless, it still was more than enough to incur Washington's continued contempt for him.

In the early summer of 1905 Washington went to Boston to address a rally. While speaking he was verbally assaulted by William Monroe Trotter (a Harvard college friend of DuBois). The subsequent jailing of Trotter on trumped-up charges, apparently by Washingtonites, raised the wrath of DuBois. This incident caused DuBois to solicit help from others "for organized determination and aggressive action on the part of men who believe in *Negro freedom and growth*. (Emphasis mine)

Twenty-nine men from fourteen states answered the call in Buffalo, New York. Five months later in January of 1906 the "Niagara Movement" was formed. So called after the cite of the meeting place-the Canadian side of Niagara Falls. (They were prevented from meeting on the U.S. side.) Its objectives were to advocate civil justice and abolish caste discrimination. The downfall of the group was attributed to public accusations of fraud and deceit instigated and engineered presumably by Washington advocates, and DuBois' inexperience with organizations and the internal strain from the dynamic personality of Trotter. In 1909 all members of the Niagara Movement save one *(Trotter, who despised and distrusted whites and their objectives) merged with some white liberals and thus the National Association for the Advancement of Colored People (NAACP) was born.* DuBois was not altogether pleased with the group but agreed to stay on as Director of Publications and Research.

The main artery for distributing NAACP policy and news concerning Blacks was the *Crisis* magazine, which DuBois autocratically governed as its editor-in-chief for some twenty-five years. He was of no mind to follow pedantically the Associations views, and therefore wrote *only* that which he felt could lift the coffin lid off his people.

His hot, raking editorials oftentimes lead to battles within the ranks of the Association. Besides this, the NAACP was, at that time, under the leadership of whites, to which DuBois objected. He always felt that Blacks should lead and that if whites were to be included at all, it should be in a supportive role. The meteoric and sustained rise in the circulation of the *Crisis*, making it self-supporting, tranquilized the moderates within the Association. This afforded DuBois the ability to continue his assault on the injustices heaped upon the Blacks.

World War I had dramatic affects on the lives of Black folks. Firstly, the Armed Forces refused Black inductees, but finally relinquished and put the "colored folks" in subservient roles. Secondly, while the war was raging, Blacks in the southern states were moving north where industry was desperately looking for workers. Ignorant, frightened whites, led by capitalist instigators, were fearful that Blacks would totally consume the job market. Thus, lynching ran rampant. Finally, after the war, Black veterans returned home to the same racist country they had fought so heroically to defend.

Dr. DuBois, using the *Crisis* as his vehicle, hurled thunderbolts of searing script, scorching the "dusty veil," and revealing the innards of a country whose quivering heart beat bigotry. So vitriolic and eloquent was his pen, that subsequent reaction from his followers caused congressional action to:

1. *Inaugurate the opening of Black officer training schools.*
2. *Bring forth legal action against lynchers.*
3. *Set up a federal work plan for returning veterans.*

His articles never quit. The countryside was inundated with DuBoisian unmitigated protest. This period marked the height of DuBois' popularity. The *Crisis* magazine subscription rate had grown from 1000 in 1909 to over 10,000 in May of 1919. His "Returning Soldier" editorial climaxed the period.

"By the God of Heaven, we are cowards and jackasses if now that the war is over, we do not marshal every ounce of our brain and brawn to fight the forces of hell in our own land.

We return.
We return from fighting.
We return fighting!
Make way for Democracy! We saved it in France, and by the great Jehovah, we will save it in the United Stated of America, or know the reason why."

Shortly after the Armistice was signed, DuBois sailed for France in 1919 to represent the NAACP as an observer at the Peace Conference. While there he decided it was an opportune time to organize a Pan-African conference to bring attention to the problems of Africans around the world. While this was not the first Pan-African Congress (the first one was held in 1900), he had long been interested in the movement.

While the concept was lauded by a few revolutionaries, it failed because of lack of interest by the more influential Black organizations.

DuBois realized that for Africans could be free anywhere, they must be free everywhere. He therefore decided to hold another Pan-African meeting in 1921. While this one was better organized, he was dealt double trouble. First, following the war, "a political and social revolution, economic upheaval and depression, national and racial hatred made a setting in which any such movement was entirely out of the Question." More importantly, however, was the encounter with the astonishing Marcus Garvey.

"Unlike DuBois, Garvey was able to gain mass support and had tremendous appeal." He established the Universal Negro Improvement Association (UNIA) for the purpose of uniting Africa and her descendants. He instituted the visionary concept of buying ships for overseas trade and travel; he issued forth uncompromising orations on race relations and inspiration ("Up you mighty people. You can accomplish what you will!"); and held pageants and parades through **"Harlem" with red, black, and green liberation flags flying (The colors symbolizes the skin, the blood, and the hopes and growth potential of Black people. The green is also symbolic of the earth.). His methodology was refreshing and inspiring.** And it was in direct contrast to the intellectual style of DuBois.

DuBois' first efforts were to explain away the Garvey movement and ignore it. But it was a mass movement and could not be ignored.

Later, when Garvey began to collect money for his steamship line, DuBois characterized him as "a hard-working idealist, but his methods are bombastic, wasteful, illogical and almost illegal." Marcus Garvey, choosing to ignore the critiques of DuBois, continued with his undertakings until charges of fraud was brought forth against him. He was imprisoned and upon his release, he was exiled from the United States. He died in 1941.

The conflict between the two men was amplified by the white press. It also served to debilitate the progress of the future planned Pan-African Congress. Nevertheless, DuBois held his conference in 1923, and as expected the turnout was small.

When the conference was concluded, he set sail for Africa for the first time. During the trip through "the eternal world of Black folk" he made a characteristic observation—"The world brightens as it darkens." His racial romanticism was given free reign as he wrote—"The spell of Africa is upon me . . ."

Ideology Change

Returning home from his African experience, DuBois had a chance to reflect upon his past. DuBois noted how America tactically side-stepped the issues of color, and how his approach of **"*educate and agitate*"** appeared to fall on deaf ears. He felt that his ideological approach to the "problem of the twentieth century" had to be revised.

The Russian Revolution of 1917 illuminated and made clear the change in his basic thought. The revolution concerned itself with the problem of poverty. "Russia was trying to put into the hands of those people who do the world's work the power to guide and rule the state for the best welfare of the masses." DuBois' trip to Russia in 1927, his learning about Marx and Engels, his seeing the beginning of a new nation form with regard to class, prompted him to say—"My day in Russia was the day of communist beginnings."

"He could no longer support integration as present tactics and relegated it to a long range goal. Unable to trust white politicians, white capitalists of white workers he invested everything in the segregated socialized economy." (Shades of Washingtonianism?) His ideology carried over to his editorials in the *Crisis* magazine.

By 1930 he had become thoroughly convinced that the basic policies and ideals of the NAACP must be modified and/or discarded. There were two alternatives:

1. Change the board of directors of the NAACP (who were mostly white) so as to substitute a group which agreed with his program.
2. LEAVE THE ORGANIZATION.

By 1933 DuBois decided his financial, organizational and ideological battles with the NAACP were unendurable, and he recommended that the *Crisis* suspend its operation. (The *Crisis* magazine, however, is still in existence today.)

He resumed his duties at Atlanta University and there upon completed two major works. His book *Black Reconstruction* dealt with the socio-economic development of the nation after the Civil War. This masterpiece portrayed the contributions of the Black people to this period, whereas before, the Blacks were always portrayed as disorganized and chaotic. His second book of this period, *Dusk of Dawn*, was completed in 1940 and expounded his concepts and views on both the African's and African American's quest for freedom.

As in years past, DuBois never relented in attacks upon imperialism, especially in Africa. (His book entitled *The World and Africa* was written as a contradiction to the pseudo-*historians who consistently omitted Africa from world history.*) In 1945 he served as an associate consultant to the American delegation at the founding conference of the United Nations in San Francisco. He charged the world organization with planning to be dominated by imperialist nations and not intending to intervene on the behalf of colonized countries. He announced that the fifth Pan-African Congress would convene to determine what pressure could be applied to the world powers.

This conference was dotted with an all-star cast:

1. Kwame Nkruma-dedicated revolutionary, father of Ghanaian independence, and first president of Ghana.
2. George Padmore-an international revolutionary, often called the "Father of African Emancipation," who later became Kwame Nkrumah's advisor on African Affairs.
3. Jomo Kenyatta-called the "burning Spear," reputed leader of the Mau Mau uprising, and first president of independent Kenya.

The congress elected DuBois International President and cast him a "Father of Pan-Africanism."

Thus, "W.E.B. DuBois entered into his last phase as a protest propagandist, committed beyond a single social group to a world conception of proletarian liberation."

Alienation

Always antagonizing and making guilty groups feel extremely uncomfortable, he wrote in 1949: *"We want to rule Russia and cannot rule Alabama."* As s member of the left-wing American Labor Party he wrote: "Drunk with power, we (the U.S.) are leading the world to hell in a new colonialism with the same old human slavery, which once ruined us, to a third world war, which will ruin the world."

As the chairman of the Peace Information Center, he demanded the outlawing of atomic weapons. The Secretary of State denounced it as Soviet propaganda. Jumping at the chance to quiet "that old man," the U.S. Department of Justice ordered DuBois and others to register as agents of a "foreign principal." DuBois refused and was immediately indicted under the Foreign Agents Registration Act. Sufficient evidence was lacking, therefore DuBois was acquitted. The subversive activity initiated by the U.S. government acted as a catalyst in the alienation DuBois already felt for the present system. His feelings were heard around the world in 1959. ***While in Peking he told a large audience—"In my own country for nearly a century I have been nothing but a NIGGER."*** By the time the U.S. press published the account, he was residing in Ghana; an expatriate from the United States. President Nkruma welcomed DuBois and asked him to direct the government-sponsored *Encyclopedia Africana*. The offer was accepted graciously and a year later, in the final months of his life, DuBois became a Ghanaian citizen and an official member of the Communist party.

Free At Last

On August 27, 1963, on the eve of the March on Washington, DuBois died in Accra, Ghana.

His role as a pioneering Pan-Africanist was memorialized by the few who understood the genius of the man and neglected by the many who were afraid that his loquacious espousals would unite the oppressed throughout the world into revolution.

Quote:

"Human beings are so made that the ones who do the crushing feel nothing; it is the person crushed who feels what is happening. Unless one has placed oneself on the side of the oppressed, to feel with them, one cannot understand." Simone Weil

James Weldon Johnson
(1871-1938)

Johnson was born in Jacksonville, Florida, the son of Helen Louise Dillet and James Johnson. His brother was the composer J. Rosamond Johnson. Johnson was first educated by his mother (a musician and a public school teacher—the first female, black teacher in Florida at a grammar school) and then at Edwin M. Stanton School. His mother imparted to him her considerable love and knowledge of English literature and the European tradition in music. At the age of 16 he enrolled at Atlanta University, from which he graduated in 1894. In addition to his bachelor's degree, he also completed some graduate coursework there. The achievement of his father, headwaiter at the St. James Hotel, a luxury establishment built when Jacksonville was one of Florida's first winter havens, gave young Jimmie the wherewithal and the self-confidence to pursue a professional career. Molded by the classical education for which Atlanta University was best known, Johnson regarded his academic training as a trust given him in the expectation that he would dedicate his resources to black people. Johnson was also a prominent member of Phi Beta Sigma Fraternity, Inc.

He served in several public capacities over the next 35 years, working in education, the diplomatic corps, civil rights activism, literature, poetry, and music. In 1904 Johnson went on Theodore Roosevelt's presidential Campaign. Theodore Roosevelt appointed Johnson as U.S. consul at Puerto Cabello, Venezuela from 1906-1908 and then Nicaragua from 1909-1913.

In 1910, Johnson married Grace Nail while he was a United States Consul in Nicaragua. They had met several years earlier in New York when Johnson was working as a songwriter. A cultured and well-educated New Yorker, Grace Nail Johnson became an accomplished artist in pastels and collaborated with her husband on a screenwriting project.

Education and law

In the summer of 1891 the Atlanta University freshman had gone to a rural district in Georgia to instruct the children of former slaves. "In all of my experience there has been no period so brief that has meant so much in my education for life as the three months I spent in the backwoods of Georgia," Johnson wrote. "I was thrown for the first time on my own resources and abilities." James Weldon Johnson graduated from Atlanta University in 1894. He would later receive an honorary Master's degree in 1904. After graduation he returned to Stanton, a school for African American students in Jacksonville, until 1906, where, at the young age of 23, he became principal. As principal Johnson found himself the head of the largest public school in Jacksonville regardless of race. *For his work Johnson received a paycheck less than half of what was offered to a white colleague possessing a comparable position. Johnson improved education by adding the ninth and tenth grades*. Algebra, English composition, physical geography and bookkeeping were a part of the added ninth grade course. The tenth grade course consisted of geometry, English literature, elementary physics, history and Spanish. Johnson later resigned from his position as principal.

In 1897, Johnson was the first African American admitted to the Florida bar Exam since Reconstruction. He was also the first Negro in Duval County to seek admission to the state bar. In order to receive entry Johnson underwent a two-hour examination before three attorneys and a judge. He later recalled that *one of the examiners, not wanting to see a black man admitted, left the room.*

In December 1930, Johnson resigned from the leadership of the NAACP to accept the Spence Chair of Creative Literature at Fisk University in Nashville, where he lectured not only on literature but also on a wide range of issues to do with the life and civil rights of black Americans. The position had been especially created for him, largely out of recognition of his achievements as a poet, editor, and critic during the heyday of the Harlem Renaissance in the 1920s. He held this position until his death in an automobile accident in 1938. Enjoying unusual success as a songwriter for Broadway shows, Johnson moved easily in the upper echelons of African American society in Brooklyn, New York where he met his future wife, Grace Nail.

Diplomacy

In 1906 Johnson was consul of Puerto Cabello, Venezuela. In 1909, he transferred to Corinto, Nicaragua. During his stay at Corinto a rebellion occurred against President Adolfo Diaz. Johnson proved himself an effective diplomat under times of strain. During his work in the Foreign Service, Johnson became a published poet, with work printed in *The Century Magazine* and in *The Independent*.

Literature and anthology

During his six-year stay in Hispanic America he completed his most famous book *The Autobiography of an Ex-Colored Man* which was published anonymously in 1912. It was only during 1927 that Johnson admitted his authorship—stressing that it was not a work of autobiography but mostly fictional. Other works include *The Book of American Negro Spirituals* (1925), *Black Manhattan* (1930), his exploration of the contribution of African-Americans to the culture of New York, and *Negro Americans, What Now?* (1934), a book advocating civil rights for African Americans. Johnson was also an anthologist. His anthologies concerned African-American themes and were part of the Harlem Renaissance of the 1920s and 1930s. He also wrote the melody for the song *Dem Bones*.

Poetry

In 1922, he edited *The Book of American Negro Poetry*, which the Academy of American Poets calls "a major contribution to the history of African-American literature." One of the works for which he is best remembered today, *God's Trombones: Seven Negro Sermons in Verse*, was published in 1927 and celebrates the tradition of the folk preacher. In 1917, Johnson published *50 Years and Other Poems*.

Activism

While attending Atlanta University Johnson became known as an influential campus speaker. He won the Quiz Club Contest in English Composition and Oratory in 1892. The contest topic was "The Best Methods of Removing the Disabilities of Caste from the Negro". In addition, Johnson founded the newspaper the *Daily American* and in 1895 and became its editor. The newspaper concerned both political and racial topics. It was terminated a year later due to financial difficulty. These early endeavors were the start of what would prove to be a long period of activism.

Johnson became further involved with political activism during 1904 when he accepted a position as the treasurer of the Colored Republican Club started by Charles W. Anderson. A year later he became the president of the club. His duties as president included organizing political rallies. During 1914 Johnson became editor of the editorial page of the *New York Age*, an influential African American weekly newspaper that had supported Booker

T. Washington in his propaganda struggle with fellow African American W. E. B. Du Bois during the early twentieth century. Johnson's writing for the *Age* displayed the political gift that soon made him famous.

In the fall of 1916, because Johnson excelled as a reconciler of differences among those whose ideological agendas seemed to preclude unified, cooperative action, he was asked to become the national organizer for the National Association for the Advancement of Colored People (NAACP). Opposing race riots in northern cities and the lynching's that pervaded the South during and immediately after the end of World War I, Johnson engaged the NAACP in mass tactics, such as a silent protest parade down New York's Fifth Avenue in which ten thousand African Americans took part on July 28, 1917. In 1920 Johnson was elected to manage the NAACP, the first African American to hold this position. While serving the NAACP from 1914 through 1930 Johnson started as an organizer and eventually became the first black male secretary in the organization's history. In 1920, he was sent by the NAACP to investigate conditions in Haiti, which had been occupied by U.S. Marines since 1915. Johnson published a series of articles in *The Nation*, in which he described the American occupation as being brutal and offered suggestions for the economic and social development of Haiti. These articles were reprinted under the title *Self-Determining Haiti*. Throughout the 1920s he was one of the major inspirations and promoters of the Harlem Renaissance trying to refute condescending white criticism and helping young black authors to get published. While serving in the NAACP Johnson was involved in sparking the drive behind the Dyer Anti-Lynching Bill of 1921.

Shortly before his death, Johnson supported efforts by Ignatz Waghalter, a Polish-Jewish composer who had escaped the Nazis, to establish a classical orchestra of African-American musicians. According to musical historian James Nathan Jones, the formation of the "American Negro Orchestra" represented for Johnson "the fulfillment of a dream he had for thirty years."

James Weldon Johnson died during 1938 while vacationing in Wiscasset, Maine, when the car he was driving was hit by a train. His funeral in Harlem was attended by more than 2000 people.

Legacy

"Lift Every Voice and Sing"—often called "The Negro National Hymn," "The Negro National Anthem," "The Black National Anthem," or "The African-American National Anthem"—is a song written as a poem by

James Weldon Johnson (1871-1938) and set to music by his brother John Rosamond Johnson (1873-1954) in 1900.

Food for thought:

Education is expensive;
Ignorance is free.

Carter G. Woodson
(1875—1950)

Historian

Carter G. Woodson, *known as the Father of Negro History*, set for himself the goal of providing a scientific and historical account of people of African ancestry. Born to former slaves, he educated himself as a youth and went on to earn a Ph.D. from Harvard University in 1912. Among his highly influential writings are *The Education of the Negro Prior to 1861* and *The Negro in Our History.* Although his six volume Encyclopedia Africana remained unfinished at the time of his death, his works are the foundation for countless other writers on African American history. ***One of Dr. Woodson's achievements was the organization in 1926 of the first Negro History Week, which has evolved over the years to become what is currently known as African American History Month.***

Wisdom for the Journey

We should emphasize not Negro History, but the Negro in history. What we need is not a history of selected races or nations, but the history of the world void of national bias, race hate, and religious prejudice.

~Carter Woodson, 1926

Laundry is the only thing that should be separated by color.

~Author Unknown

Marcus Garvey

Marcus Mosiah Garvey, Jr., National Hero of Jamaica (17 August 1887-10 June 1940 was a publisher, journalist, entrepreneur, Black Nationalist, Pan-Africanist, and orator. Marcus Garvey was founder of the Universal Negro Improvement Association and African Communities League (UNIA-ACL).Prior to the twentieth century, leaders such as Prince Hall, Martin Delany, Edward Wilmot Blyden, and Henry Highland Garnet advocated the involvement of the African Diaspora in African affairs. Garvey was unique in advancing a Pan-African philosophy to inspire a global mass movement focusing on Africa known as Garveyism. Promoted by the UNIA as a movement of *African Redemption*, Garveyism would eventually inspire others, ranging from the Nation of Islam, to the Rastafarian movement (which proclaims Garvey as a prophet). The intention of the movement was for those of African ancestry to "redeem" Africa and for the European colonial powers to leave it. His essential ideas about Africa were stated in an editorial in the *Negro World* titled "African Fundamentalism" where he wrote:

> *"Our union must know no clime, boundary, or nationality . . .*
> *let us hold together under all climes and in every country . . ."*

Early years

Garvey was born in St. Ann's Bay, Jamaica to Marcus Mosiah Garvey, Sr., JB a mason, and Sarah Jane Richards, a domestic worker and farmer. Of eleven siblings, only Marcus and his sister Indiana reached maturity. Garvey's father was known to have a large library, and it was from his father that Marcus gained his love for reading. Sometime in the year 1900, Garvey entered into an Apprenticeship with his uncle, Alfred Burrowes. Like Garvey Sr., Burrowes had an extensive library, of which young Garvey made good use. Garvey attended elementary and middle school in Jamaica until he was about fourteen, he left St. Ann's Bay for Kingston, where he found employment as a compositor in the printing house of P. A. Benjamin, Limited. He was a master printer and foreman at Benjamin when, in November 1907, he was elected vice-president of the Kingston Union. However, he was fired when he joined a strike by printers in late 1908. Having been blacklisted for his stance in the strike, he later found work at the Government Printing Office. In 1909, his newspaper *The Watchman* began publication, but it only lasted for three issues.

In 1910 Garvey left Jamaica and began traveling throughout the Central American region. He lived in Costa Rica for several months, where he worked as a time-keeper on a banana plantation. He began work as editor for a daily newspaper titled *La Nacionale* in 1911. Later that year, he moved to Colón, Panama, where he edited a biweekly newspaper before returning to Jamaica in 1912.

After years of working on the Caribbean, Garvey left Jamaica to live in London from 1912 to 1914, where he attended Birkbeck College, worked for the *African Times and Orient Review*, published by Dusé Mohamed Ali, and sometimes spoke at Hyde Park's Speakers' Corner.

Founding and Projects of the UNIA-ACL

During his travels, Garvey became convinced that uniting Blacks was the only way to improve their condition. Towards that end, he departed England on 14 June 1914 aboard the S.S. Trent, reaching Jamaica on 15 July 1914. He founded the Universal Negro Improvement Association (UNIA) in August 1914 as a means of uniting all of Africa and its Diaspora into "one grand racial hierarchy." Amy Ashwood, who would later be Garvey's first wife, was among the founders. As the group's first President-General, *Garvey's goal was "to unite all people of African ancestry of the world to one great body to establish a country and absolute government of their own."*

Following much reflection the following day and night about what he learned, he named the organization the Universal Negro Improvement Association and African Communities (Imperial) League."

After corresponding with Booker T. Washington, Garvey arrived in the U.S. on 23 March 1916 aboard the S.S. *Tallac* to give a lecture tour and to raise funds to establish a school in Jamaica modeled after Washington's Tuskegee Institute. Garvey visited Tuskegee, and afterward, visited with a number of Black leaders. After moving to New York, he found work as a printer by day. He was influenced by Hubert Harrison. At night he would speak on street corners, much like he did in London's Hyde Park. It was then that Garvey perceived a leadership vacuum among people of African ancestry. On 9 May 1916, he held his first public lecture in New York City at St Mark's Church in-the-Bowery and undertook a 38-state speaking tour.

In May 1917, Garvey and thirteen others formed the first UNIA division outside Jamaica and began advancing ideas to promote social, political, and economic freedom for Blacks. On 2 July, the East St. Louis riots broke out. On July 8, Garvey delivered an address, titled "The Conspiracy of the East St. Louis Riots," at Lafayette Hall in Harlem. During the speech, he declared the riot was "one of the bloodiest outrages against mankind." By October, rancor within the UNIA had begun to set in. A split occurred in the Harlem division, with Garvey enlisted to become its leader; although he technically held the same position in Jamaica.

Garvey next set about the business of developing a program to improve the conditions of those of African ancestry "at home and abroad" under UNIA auspices. On 17 August 1918, publication of the widely distributed *Negro World* newspaper began. Garvey worked as an editor without pay until November 1920. By June 1919 the membership of the organization had grown to over two million.

On 27 June 1919, the Black Star Line of Delaware was incorporated by the members of the UNIA, with Garvey as President. By September, it obtained its first ship. Much fanfare surrounded the inspection of the S.S. *Yarmouth* and its rechristening as the S.S. *Frederick Douglass* on 14 September 1919. Such a rapid accomplishment garnered attention from many.

One person who noticed was Edwin P. Kilroe, Assistant District Attorney in the District Attorney's office of the County of New York. Kilroe began an investigation into the activities of the UNIA, without finding any evidence of wrongdoing or mismanagement. After being called to Kilroe's office numerous times, Garvey wrote an editorial on Kilroe's activities for the *Negro World*. Garvey was arrested and indicted for criminal libel in relation to the article, but charges were dismissed after Garvey published a retraction.

While in his Harlem office at 56 West 156th Street on 14 October 1919, Garvey received a visit from George Tyler, who told him that Kilroe "had sent him" to get Garvey. Tyler then pulled a .38-caliber revolver and fired four shots, wounding Garvey in the right leg and scalp. Garvey was taken to the hospital and Tyler arrested. The next day, it was let out that Tyler had committed suicide by leaping from the third tier of the Harlem jail as he was being taken to his arraignment.

By August 1920, the UNIA claimed four million members. That month, the International Convention of the UNIA was held. With delegates from all over the world in attendance, over 25,000 people filled Madison Square Garden on 1 August to hear Garvey speak.

Another of Garvey's ventures was the Negro Factories Corporation. His plan called for creating the infrastructure to manufacture every marketable commodity in every big U.S. industrial center, as well as in Central America, the West Indies, and Africa. Related endeavors included a grocery chain, restaurant, publishing house, and other businesses.

Convinced that Blacks should have a permanent homeland in Africa, Garvey sought to develop Liberia.

The Liberia program, launched in 1920, was intended to build colleges, universities, industrial plants, and railroads as part of an industrial base from which to operate. However, it was abandoned in the mid-1920s after much opposition from European powers with interests in Liberia. In response to suggestions that he wanted to take all Americans of African ancestry back to Africa, he wrote, "We do not want all the Negroes in Africa. Some are no good here, and naturally will be no good there."

Garvey has been credited with creating the biggest movement of people of African descent. This movement that took place in the 1920s is said to have had more participation from people of African descent than the Civil Rights Movement. In essence the UNIA was the largest Pan-African movement.

Charge of mail fraud

In a memorandum dated 11 October 1919, J. Edgar Hoover, special assistant to the Attorney General and head of the General Intelligence Division (or "anti-radical division") of The Bureau of Investigation or BOI (after 1935, the Federal Bureau of Investigation), wrote a memorandum to Special Agent Ridgely regarding Marcus Garvey. In the memo, Hoover wrote that:

> *"Unfortunately, however, he [Garvey] has not as yet violated any federal law whereby he could be proceeded against on the grounds of being an undesirable alien, from the point of view of deportation."*

Sometime around November 1919 an investigation by the BOI was begun into the activities of Garvey and the UNIA. Toward this end, the BOI hired James Edward Amos, Arthur Lowell Brent, Thomas Leon Jefferson, James Wormley Jones, and Earl E. Titus as its first five African-American agents. Although initial efforts by the BOI were to find grounds upon which to deport Garvey as "an undesirable alien", a charge of mail fraud was brought against Garvey in connection with stock sales of the Black Star Line after the U.S. Post Office and the Attorney General joined the investigation.

The accusation centered on the fact that the corporation had not yet purchased a ship with the name "Phyllis Wheatley". Although one was pictured with that name emblazoned on its bow on one of the company's stock brochures, it had not actually been purchased by the BSL and still had the name "Orion". The prosecution produced as evidence a single empty envelope which it claimed contained the brochure. During the trial, a man by the name of Benny Dancy testified that he didn't remember what was in the envelope, although he regularly received brochures from the Black Star Line. Another witness for the prosecution, Schuyler Cargill, perjured himself after admitting to having been told to mention certain dates in his testimony by Chief Prosecutor Maxwell S. Mattuck. Furthermore, he admitted that he could not remember the names of any coworkers in the office, including the timekeeper who punched employees' time cards. Ultimately, he acknowledged being told to lie by Postal Inspector F.E. Shea. He said Shea told him to state that he mailed letters containing the purportedly fraudulent brochures. The Black Star Line did own and operate several ships over the course of its history and was in the process of negotiating for the disputed ship at the time the charges were brought. Assistant District Attorney, Leo H. Healy, who was, before he became a District Attorney, attorney for Harris McGill and Co., the sellers of the first ship, the S. S. Yarmouth, to the Black Star Line Inc., was also a key witness for the government during the trial.

Of the four Black Star Line officers charged in connection with the enterprise, only Garvey was found guilty of using the mail service to defraud. His supporters called the trial fraudulent. While there were serious accounting irregularities within the Black Star Line and the claims he used to sell Black Star Line stock could be considered misleading, Garvey's supporters still contest that the prosecution was a politically motivated miscarriage of justice, given the above-mentioned false statement testimony and Hoover's explicit regret that Garvey had committed no crimes.

When the trial ended on 23 June 1923, Garvey had been sentenced to five years in prison. Garvey blamed Jewish and Roman Catholic jurors and federal judge Julian Mack, a former president of the Zionist Organization of America, for his conviction. He felt they had been biased because of their political objections to his meeting with the acting imperial wizard of the Ku Klux Klan the year before. In 1928, Garvey told a journalist: "When they wanted to get me they had a Jewish judge try me, and a Jewish prosecutor. I would have been freed but two Jews on the jury held out against me ten hours and succeeded in convicting me, whereupon the Jewish judge gave me the maximum penalty."

He initially spent three months in the Tombs Jail awaiting approval of bail. While on bail, he continued to maintain his innocence, travel, speak and organize the UNIA. After numerous attempts at appeal were unsuccessful, he was taken into custody and began serving his sentence at the Atlanta Federal Penitentiary on 8 February 1925. Two days later; he penned his well known

"First Message to the Negroes of the World from Atlanta Prison" wherein he makes his famous proclamation:

> *"Look for me in the whirlwind or the storm, look for me all around you, for, with God's grace, I shall come and bring with me countless millions of black slaves who have died in America and the West Indies and the millions in Africa to aid you in the fight for Liberty, Freedom and Life."*

Professor Judith Stein has stated, "his politics were on trial."

Garvey's sentence was eventually commuted by President Calvin Coolidge. Upon his release in November 1927, Garvey was deported via New Orleans to Jamaica, where a large crowd met him at Orrett's Wharf in Kingston. A huge procession and band converged on UNIA headquarters.

Criticism

On October 4, 1916, the *Daily Gleaner* newspaper in Kingston published a letter written by the Very Rev. Fr. Raphael Morgan, a Jamaican-American priest of the Ecumenical Patriarchate, together with over a dozen other like-minded Jamaican-Americans, who wrote in to protest Garvey's lectures. Garvey's views on Jamaica, they felt, were damaging to both the reputation of their homeland and its people, enumerating several objections to Garvey's stated preference for the prejudice of the American whites over that of English whites. Garvey's response was published a month later, in which he called the letter a conspiratorial fabrication meant to undermine the success and favor he had gained while in Jamaica and in the United States.

While W. E. B. Du Bois felt that the Black Star Line was "original and promising," he added that "Marcus Garvey is, without doubt, the most dangerous enemy of the Negro race in America and in the world. He is either a lunatic or a traitor." Du Bois feared that Garvey's activities would undermine his efforts toward black rights.

Garvey suspected Du Bois was prejudiced against him because he was a Caribbean native with darker skin. Du Bois once described Marcus Garvey as "a little, fat black man; ugly, but with intelligent eyes and a big head." Garvey called Du Bois "purely and simply a white man's nigger" and "a little Dutch, a little French, a little Negro . . . a mulatto . . . a monstrosity." This led to an acrimonious relationship between Garvey and the NAACP. Garvey accused Du Bois of paying conspirators to sabotage the Black Star Line to destroy his reputation.

At the National Conference of the Universal Negro Improvement Association in 1921 a Los Angeles delegate Noah Thompson spoke on the floor complaining on the lack of transparency in the group's financial accounts. When accounts were prepared Thompson highlighted several sections with what he felt were irregularities.

Garvey recognized the influence of the Ku Klux Klan, and in early 1922, he went to Atlanta, Georgia, for a conference with KKK imperial giant Edward Young Clarke.

According to Garvey, "I regard the Klan, the Anglo-Saxon clubs and White American societies, as far as the Negro is concerned, as better friends of the race than all other groups of hypocritical whites put together. I like honesty and fair play. You may call me a Klansman if you will, but, potentially, every white man is a Klansman, as far as the Negro in competition with whites socially, economically and politically is concerned, and there is no use lying." Leo H. Healy publicly accused Garvey of being a member of the Ku Klux Klan in his testimony during the mail fraud trial.

After Garvey's entente with the Ku Klux Klan, a number of African American leaders appealed to U.S. Attorney General Harry M. Daugherty to have Garvey incarcerated.

Later years

In 1928, Garvey travelled to Geneva to present the Petition of the Negro Race. This petition outlined the worldwide abuse of Africans to the League of Nations. In September 1929, he founded the People's Political Party (PPP), Jamaica's first modern political party, which focused on workers' rights, education, and aid to the poor.

Also in 1929, Garvey was elected councilor for the Allman Town Division of the Kingston and St. Andrew Corporation (KSAC). However, he lost his seat because of having to serve a prison sentence for contempt of court. But, in 1930, Garvey was re-elected, unopposed, along with two other PPP candidates.

In April 1931, Garvey launched the Edelweiss Amusement Company. He set the company up to help artists earn their livelihood from their craft. Several Jamaican entertainers—Kidd Harold, Ernest Cupidon, Bim & Bam, and Ranny Williams—went on to become popular after receiving initial exposure that the company gave them.

In 1935, Garvey left Jamaica for London. He lived and worked in London until his death in 1940. During these last five years, Garvey remained active and in touch with events in war-torn Ethiopia (then known as Abyssinia) and in the West Indies. In 1937, he wrote the poem *Ras Nasibu Of Ogaden* in honor of Ethiopian Army Commander (*Ras*) Nasibu Emmanual. In 1938, he gave evidence before the West Indian Royal Commission on conditions there. Also in 1938 he set up the School of African Philosophy in Toronto to train UNIA leaders. He continued to work on the magazine *The Black Man*.

In 1937, a group of Garvey's American supporters called the Peace Movement of Ethiopia openly collaborated with Mississippi Senator Theodore Bilbo in the promotion of a repatriation scheme introduced in the US Congress as the Greater Liberia Act. In the Senate, Bilbo was a supporter of Franklin Roosevelt's New Deal. ***Bilbo was an outspoken supporter of segregation and white supremacy and, attracted by the ideas of Black separatists like Garvey, Bilbo proposed an amendment to the federal work-relief bill on 6 June 1938, proposing to deport 12 million black Americans to Liberia at federal expense to relieve unemployment.*** He took the time to write a book titled *Take Your Choice, Separation or Mongrelization,* advocating the idea. Garvey praised him in return, saying that Bilbo had "done wonderfully well for the Negro".

During this period, Evangeline Rondon Paterson the grandmother of the current (55th) Governor of New York, David Paterson served as his secretary.

Death

On 10 June 1940, Garvey died after two strokes, putatively after reading a mistaken, and negative, obituary of himself in the *Chicago Defender* which stated, in part, that Garvey died "broke, alone and unpopular". Because of travel conditions during World War II, he was interred at Kensal Green Cemetery in London. Rumors claimed that Garvey was in fact poisoned on a boat on which he was travelling and that was where and how he actually died.

In 1964, his remains were exhumed and taken to Jamaica. On 15 November 1964, the government of Jamaica, having proclaimed him Jamaica's first national hero, re-interred him at a shrine in National Heroes Park.

Personal life

Marcus Garvey was married twice: to the Jamaican Pan-African activist Amy Ashwood (married 1919 divorced 1922), who worked with him in the early years of UNIA; then to the journalist and publisher Amy Jacques (married 1922). The latter was mother to his two sons, Marcus III (born 17 September 1930) and Julius.

Influence

Garvey's memory has been kept alive. Schools, colleges, highways, and buildings in Africa, Europe, the Caribbean, and the United States have been named in his honor. The UNIA red, black, and green flag has been adopted as the Black Liberation Flag. Since 1980, Garvey's bust has been housed in the Organization of American States' Hall of Heroes in Washington, D.C.

Malcolm X's parents, Earl and Louise Little, met at a UNIA convention in Montreal. Earl was the president of the UNIA division in Omaha, Nebraska and sold the *Negro World* newspaper, for which Louise covered UNIA activities.

Kwame Nkrumah named the national shipping line of Ghana the Black Star Line in honor of Garvey and the UNIA. Nkrumah also named the national soccer team the Black Stars as well. The black star at the center of Ghana's flag is also inspired by the Black Star Line.

During a trip to Jamaica, Martin Luther King and his wife Coretta Scott King visited the shrine of Marcus Garvey on 20 June 1965 and laid a wreath. In a speech he told the audience that Garvey *"was the first man of color to lead and develop a mass movement. He was the first man on a mass scale and level to give millions of Negroes a sense of dignity and destiny. And make the Negro feel he was somebody."*

King was also the posthumous recipient of the first Marcus Garvey Prize for Human Rights on 10 December 1968 issued by the Jamaican Government and presented to King's widow.

The United States of Africa first saw light in a 1924 poem by Garvey and is still discussed.

There have been pop culture references to Marcus Garvey since he first came on the international scene. Garvey is cited repeatedly in a diverse variety of books, songs and films. He is mentioned particularly frequently in blues, reggae, jazz and hip hop music.

In 2002, scholar Molefi Kete Asante listed Marcus Garvey on his list of 100 Greatest African Americans.

Rastafari and Garvey

Rastafarians consider Garvey a religious prophet, and sometimes even the reincarnation of Saint John the Baptist. This is partly because of his frequent statements uttered in speeches throughout the 1920s, usually along the lines of "Look to Africa, when a black king shall be crowned for the day of deliverance is at hand!"

His beliefs deeply influenced the Rastafari, who took his statements as a prophecy of the crowning of Haile Selassie I of Ethiopia. Early Rastas were associated with his Back-to-Africa movement in Jamaica. This early Rastafari movement was also influenced by a separate, proto-Rasta movement known as the Afro-Athlican Church that was outlined in a religious text known as the Holy Piby—where Garvey was proclaimed to be a prophet as well. Thus, the Rastafari movement can be seen as an offshoot of Garveyite philosophy.

As his beliefs have greatly influenced Rastafari, he is often mentioned in reggae music.

Garvey himself never identified with the Rastafari movement, and was, in fact, raised as a Methodist who went on to become a Catholic.

Wisdom for the Journey

"God and Nature first made us what we are, and then out of our own created genius we make ourselves what we want to be. Follow always that great law. Let the sky and God be our limit and Eternity our measurement."

Marcus Garvey

"Intelligence rules the world, ignorance carries the burden . . ."

—*Marcus Garvey*

Benjamin Mays
(ca. 1894-1984)

A distinguished African American minister, educator, scholar, and social activist, Benjamin Mays is perhaps best known as the longtime president of Morehouse College in Atlanta.

He was also a significant mentor to civil rights leader Martin Luther King Jr. and was among the most articulate and outspoken critics of segregation before the rise of the modern civil rights movement in the United States. Mays also filled a leadership role in several significant national and international organizations, among them the National Association for the Advancement of Colored People (NAACP), the International Young Men's Christian Association (YMCA), the World Council of Churches, the United Negro College Fund, the National Baptist Convention, the Urban League, the Southern Conference for Human Welfare, the Southern Conference Educational Fund, and the Peace Corps Advisory Committee.

Education

Benjamin Elijah Mays was born on August 1, 1894 or 1895 in a rural area outside Ninety-Six, South Carolina. He was the youngest of eight children born to Louvenia Carter and Hezekiah Mays, tenant farmers and former slaves. A consistent theme in Mays's boyhood and early adulthood was his quest for education against overwhelming odds. He refused to be circumscribed by the widespread poverty and racism of his place of birth. After some struggle he gained acceptance to Bates College in Maine. After completing his B.A. there in 1920, Mays entered the University of Chicago as a graduate student, earning an M.A. in 1925 and a Ph.D. in the School of Religion in 1935.

Career and Accomplishments

Mays's education at Chicago was interrupted several times, first by stints as a teacher at Morehouse and at South Carolina State College. During his tenure at the latter, he met his future wife, Sadie Gray. They were married for forty-three years, from 1926 until her death in 1969. Mays's work for the Urban League and the YMCA similarly postponed his doctoral efforts. In 1933, with coauthor Joseph Nicholson, Mays published a groundbreaking study entitled *The Negro's Church*, which described the unique origins and character of this central African American institution, offering a critique of some of its problematic clerical practices.

Less than a year before completing his dissertation at Chicago in the spring of 1935, Mays accepted a position as dean of the School of Religion at Howard University in Washington, D.C. Mays distinguished himself as an effective administrator, elevating the Howard program to legitimacy and distinction among schools of religion. During his tenure there, Mays also traveled a great deal, which would become a consistent aspect of his career. Perhaps the most significant of these travels was a trip in 1936 to India, where he spoke at some length with Mahatma Gandhi, anticipating an exchange of ideas that would come to fruition during the civil rights movement some years later. Mays also continued his scholarly efforts. In 1938 he published *The Negro's God, as Reflected in His Literature*, a study of the image and concept of God in African American Christianity.

In 1940 Mays became the president of Morehouse College. There he enjoyed his greatest influence on events in the history of the United States, rising to national prominence. **His most famous student at Morehouse was Martin Luther King Jr.** During King's years as an undergraduate at Morehouse in the mid-1940s, the two developed a close relationship that continued until King's death in 1968. Mays's unwavering emphasis on two ideas in particular—the dignity of all human beings and the incompatibility of American democratic ideals with American social practices—became vital strains in the language of King and the civil rights movement. Although Mays's essays and sermons throughout his years at Morehouse related these ideas, their clearest explication came in his book *Seeking to Be a Christian in Race Relations*, published in 1957.

As an administrator at Morehouse, Mays expanded and streamlined the structure of the institution and enhanced its academic reputation. He was a highly successful fundraiser, securing the needed financial support for Morehouse to pursue its educational goals. Beyond such practical concerns, Mays left a legacy of prominent Morehouse graduates and lent the college his own inimitable style, characterized by rigor and enthusiasm for the Morehouse mission.

After his retirement in 1967 from Morehouse, Mays remained active in several social and political organizations of prominence and was in demand as a speaker and lecturer. He published two autobiographies in these years, *Born to Rebel* (1971), and *Lord, the People Have Driven Me On* (1981). He died in 1984.

Thoughts worth remembering

An education isn't how much you have committed to memory, or even how much you know. It's being able to differentiate between what you know and what you don't. **Amatole France**

"I once knew a man who could speak seven languages fluently; but I never heard him make an intelligent statement in one of them."

Mary Jane McLeod
1877-1955

Mary Jane McLeod was born in South Carolina, the fifteenth of seventeen children. Scholarships enabled her to attend Scotia Seminary and Moody Bible Institute. Turned down when she applied to go to Africa as a missionary, she returned to the South. She met and married Albertus Bethune, and began to teach school.

In Daytona, Florida, in 1904 she scraped together $1.50 to begin a school with just five pupils. She called it the Daytona Literary and Industrial School for Training Negro Girls. A gifted teacher and leader, Mrs. Bethune ran her school with a combination of unshakable faith and remarkable organizational skills. She was a brilliant speaker and an astute fund raiser. She expanded the school to a high school, then a junior college, and finally it became Bethune-Cookman College.

Continuing to direct the school, she turned her attention to the national scene, where she became a forceful and inspiring representative of her people. First through the National Council of Negro Women, then within Franklin Roosevelt's New Deal in the National Youth Administration, she worked to attack discrimination and increase opportunities for Blacks. Behind the scenes as a member of the "Black cabinet," and in hundreds of public appearances, she strove to improve the status of her people.

On May 18, 1955, Bethune died of a heart attack. Her death was followed by editorial tributes in newspapers all over America. The Oklahoma City Black Dispatch stated she was, "Exhibit No. 1 for all who have faith in American and the democratic process." *The Atlanta Daily World said her life was, "One of the most dramatic careers ever enacted at any time upon the stage of human activity." And in the Pittsburgh Courier, it was stated, "In any race or nation she would have been an outstanding personality and made a noteworthy contribution because her chief attribute was her indomitable soul."* The mainstream press praised her as well. Christian Century suggested, "The story of her life should be taught every school child for generations to come." The New York Times noted she was, "one of the most potent factors in the growth of interracial goodwill in America." The Washington Post read, "So great were her dynamism and force that it was almost impossible to resist her . . . Not only her own people, but all America has been enriched and ennobled by her courageous, ebullient spirit." Her hometown newspaper, the Daytona Beach Evening News printed, "To some she seemed unreal, something that could not be . . . What right had she to greatness? . . . *The lesson of Mrs. Bethune's life is that genius knows no racial barriers."*

Food for Thought

Any intelligent fool can make things bigger, more complex, and more violent. It takes a touch of genius—and a lot of courage—to move in the opposite direction.

~**E.F. Schumacher**

Genius may have its limitations, but stupidity is not thus handicapped.

Elbert Hubbard

Roy Wilkins

Roy Wilkins (August 30, 1901-September 8, 1981) was a prominent civil rights activist in the United States from the 1930s to the 1970s. *Wilkins' most notable role was in his leadership of the National Association for the Advancement of Colored People (NAACP).*

Early career

Born in St. Louis, Missouri, Wilkins graduated from the University of Minnesota with a degree in sociology in 1923. He worked as a journalist at The Minnesota Daily and became editor of St. Paul Appeal, an African-American newspaper. After he graduated he became the editor of the Kansas City Call. In 1929, he married social worker Aminda "Minnie" Badeau; the couple had no children.

Between 1931 and 1934, Wilkins was assistant NAACP secretary under Walter Francis White. When W. E. B. Du Bois left the organization in 1934, he replaced him as editor of The Crisis, the official magazine of the NAACP. From 1949-50 Wilkins chaired the National Emergency Civil Rights Mobilization, which comprised more than 100 local and national groups.

In 1950, Wilkins—along with A. Philip Randolph, founder of the Brotherhood of Sleeping Car Porters, and Arnold Aronson, a leader of the National Jewish Community Relations Advisory Council—founded the Leadership Conference on Civil Rights (LCCR). LCCR has become the premier civil rights coalition, and has coordinated the national legislative campaign on behalf of every major civil rights law since 1957.

Leading the NAACP

In 1955, Roy Wilkins was chosen to be the executive secretary of the NAACP and in 1964 he became its executive director. He had an excellent reputation as an articulate spokesperson for the civil rights movement.

One of his first actions was to provide support to civil rights activists in Mississippi who were being subject to a "credit squeeze" by members of the White Citizens Councils.

Wilkins backed a proposal suggested by Dr. T.R.M. Howard of Mound Bayou, Mississippi, who headed the Regional Council of Negro Leadership, a leading civil rights organization in the state. Under the plan, black businesses and voluntary associations shifted their accounts to the black-owned Tri-State Bank of Memphis, Tennessee. By the end of 1955, about $280,000 had been deposited in Tri-State for this purpose. The money enabled Tri-State to extend loans to credit-worthy blacks who were denied loans by white banks. Wilkins participated in the March on Washington (August 1963) which he helped organize, the Selma to Montgomery marches (1965), and the March Against Fear (1966).

He believed in achieving reform by legislative means, testified before many Congressional hearings and conferred with Presidents Kennedy, Johnson, Nixon, Ford, and Carter. Wilkins strongly opposed militancy in the movement for civil rights as represented by the **"black power"** movement. He was a strong critic of racism in any form regardless of its creed, color or political motivation, and also espoused the principles of nonviolence.

Wilkins was also a member of Omega Psi Phi, a fraternity with a civil rights focus, and one of the intercollegiate Greek-letter fraternities established for African Americans.

In 1968, Wilkins also served as chair of the U.S. delegation to the International Conference on Human Rights.

In 1977, at the age of 76, Wilkins retired from the NAACP and was succeeded by Benjamin Hooks. He was honored with the title *Director Emeritus of the NAACP* in the same year. Roy Wilkins died on September 8, 1981 in New York City of heart problems related to a pacemaker implanted on him in 1979 due to his irregular heartbeat. In 1982, his autobiography *Standing Fast: The Autobiography of Roy Wilkins* was published posthumously.

"The players in this drama of frustration and indignity are not commas or semicolons in a legislative thesis; they are people, human beings, citizens of the United States of America."

Legacy

Gil Scott-Heron mentioned Wilkins in his most famous spoken word song "The Revolution Will Not Be Televised" with this lyric: "There will be no slow motion or still life of Roy Wilkins strolling through Watts in a red, black and green liberation jumpsuit that he has been saving for just the proper occasion."

During his later life Wilkins was frequently referred to as the 'Senior Statesman' of the U.S. Civil Rights Movement.

The Roy Wilkins Centre for Human Relations and Human Justice was established in the University of Minnesota's Humphrey Institute of Public Affairs in 1992.

In 2002, Molefi Kete Asante listed Roy Wilkins on his list of the 100 Greatest African Americans.

Criticisms

Wilkins was a staunch liberal and proponent of American values during the Cold War, and denounced suspected and actual communists within the civil rights movement. He has been criticized by some, on the left of the civil rights movement, such as Daisy Bates, Robert F. Williams, and Fred Shuttlesworth, for his cautious approach, his suspicion of grassroots organizations, and his conciliatory attitude towards white anti-communism, which was considered detrimental to the post-war civil rights movement.

James Mercer Langston Hughes

James Mercer Langston Hughes, (February 1, 1902-May 22, 1967) was an American poet, novelist, playwright, short story writer, and columnist. He was one of the earliest innovators of the new literary art form jazz poetry. *Hughes is best-known for his work during the Harlem Renaissance. He famously wrote about the Harlem Renaissance, saying that "Harlem was in vogue".*

Ancestry and childhood:

Langston Hughes was born in Joplin, Missouri, the second child of school teacher Carrie (Caroline) Mercer Langston and her husband James Nathaniel Hughes (1871-1934). Both parents were mixed-race, and Langston Hughes was of African American, European American and Native American descent. He grew up in a series of Midwestern small towns. *Both his paternal and maternal great-grandmothers were African American, and both his paternal and maternal great-grandfathers were white: one of Scottish and one of Jewish descent.* Hughes was named after both his father and his grand-uncle, John Mercer Langston who, in 1888, became the first African American to be elected to the United States Congress from Virginia. Hughes' maternal grandmother Mary Patterson was of African American, French, English and Native American descent. One of the first women to attend Oberlin College, she first married Lewis Sheridan Leary, also of mixed race. He joined the men in John Brown's Raid on Harper's Ferry in 1859 and died from his wounds.

In 1869 Mary Patterson Leary married again, into the elite, politically active Langston family. Her second husband was Charles Henry Langston, of African American, Native American, and Euro-American ancestry. He and his younger brother John Mercer Langston worked for the abolitionist cause and helped lead the Ohio Anti-Slavery Society in 1858.

Charles Langston later moved to Kansas where he was active as an educator and activist for voting and rights for African Americans. Charles and Mary's daughter Caroline Mercer Langston was the mother of Langston Hughes. Hughes' father left his family and later divorced Carrie. He went to Cuba, and then Mexico, seeking to escape the enduring racism in the United States. After the separation of his parents, while his mother travelled seeking employment, young Langston was raised mainly by his maternal grandmother Mary Patterson Langston in Lawrence, Kansas. Through the black American oral tradition and drawing from the activist experiences of her generation, Mary Langston instilled in the young Langston Hughes a lasting sense of racial pride. He spent most of childhood in Lawrence, Kansas. After the death of his grandmother, he went to live with family friends, James and Mary Reed, for two years. Because of the unstable early life, his childhood was not an entirely happy one, but it was one that heavily influenced the poet he would become. Later, Hughes lived again with his mother Carrie in Lincoln, Illinois, who had remarried when he was still an adolescent, and eventually in Cleveland, Ohio, where he attended high school. The Hughes' home in Cleveland was sold in foreclosure in 1918; the 2.5-story, wood-frame house on the city's east side was sold at a sheriff's auction in February for $16,667.

While in grammar school in Lincoln, Illinois, Hughes was elected class poet. Hughes stated in retrospect he thought it was because of the stereotype that African Americans have rhythm. "I was a victim of a stereotype. There were only two of us Negro kids in the whole class and our English teacher was always stressing the importance of rhythm in poetry. *Well, everyone knows, except us, that all Negroes have rhythm, so they elected me as class poet.*" During high school in Cleveland, Ohio, he wrote for the school newspaper, edited the yearbook, and began to write his first short stories, poetry, and dramatic plays. His first piece of jazz poetry, "'When Sue Wears Red", was written while he was still in high school. It was during this time that he discovered his love of books. From this early period in his life, Hughes would cite as influences on his poetry the American poets Paul Laurence Dunbar and Carl Sandburg.

Relationship with father and Columbia

Hughes had a very poor relationship with his father. He lived with his father in Mexico for a brief period in 1919. Upon graduating from high school in June 1920, Hughes returned to live with his father, hoping to convince him to provide money to attend Columbia University. Hughes later said that, prior to arriving in Mexico again: "I had been thinking about my father and his strange dislike of his own people. I didn't understand it, because I was a Negro, and I liked Negroes very much. Initially, his father had hoped for Hughes to attend a university abroad, and to study for a career in engineering. On these grounds, he was willing to provide financial assistance to his son. James Hughes did not support his son's desire to be a writer. Eventually, Hughes and his father came to a compromise and Hughes would study engineering, so long as he could attend Columbia. His tuition provided, Hughes left his father after more than a year of living with him. While at Columbia in 1921, Hughes managed to maintain a B+ grade average. He left in 1922 because of racial prejudice within the institution, and his interests revolved more around the neighborhood of Harlem than his studies, though he continued writing poetry.

Adulthood

Hughes worked various odd jobs, before serving a brief tenure as a crewman aboard the S.S. *Malone* in 1923, spending six months traveling to West Africa and Europe. In Europe, Hughes left the S.S. *Malone* for a temporary stay in Paris.

During his time in England in the early 1920s, Hughes became part of the black expatriate community. In November 1924, Hughes returned to the U. S. to live with his mother in Washington, D.C. Hughes again found work doing various odd jobs before gaining white-collar employment in 1925 as a personal assistant to the historian Carter G. Woodson at the Association for the Study of African American Life and History. Not satisfied with the demands of the work and its time constraints that limited his writing, Hughes quit to work as a busboy in a hotel. It was while working as a busboy that Hughes would encounter the poet Vachel Lindsay. Impressed with the poems Hughes showed him, Lindsay publicized his discovery of a new black poet. By this time, Hughes' earlier work had already been published in magazines and was about to be collected into his first book of poetry. The following year, Hughes enrolled in Lincoln University, a historically black university in Chester County, Pennsylvania. There he became a member of the Omega Psi Phi Fraternity, a black fraternal organization founded at Howard University in Washington, D.C. Thurgood Marshall, who later became an Associate Justice of the Supreme Court of the United States, was an alumnus and classmate of Langston Hughes during his undergraduate studies at Lincoln University.

Hughes earned a B.A. degree from Lincoln University in 1929. He then moved to New York. Except for travels to the Soviet Union and parts of the Caribbean, Hughes lived in Harlem as his primary home for the remainder of his life. *Some academics and biographers today believe that Hughes was homosexual and included homosexual codes in many of his poems, similar in manner to Walt Whitman, whose work Hughes cited as another influence on his poetry. Hughes' story "Blessed Assurance" deals with a father's anger over his son's effeminacy and queerness. To retain the respect and support of black churches and organizations and avoid exacerbating his precarious financial situation, Hughes remained closeted.*

Arnold Rampersad, the primary biographer of Hughes, determined that Hughes exhibited a preference for other African-American men in his work and life. However, Rampersad denies Hughes' homosexuality in his biography as well. Rampersad comes to the conclusion that Hughes was probably asexual and passive in his sexual relationships. He did, however show a respect and love for his fellow white man (and woman). Still, others argue for Hughes' homosexuality: his love of black men is evidenced in a number of reported unpublished poems to an alleged black male lover.

Death

On May 22, 1967, Langston Hughes died from complications after abdominal surgery, related to prostate cancer, at the age of 65. His ashes are interred beneath a floor medallion in the middle of the foyer leading to the auditorium named for him within the Arthur Schomburg Center for Research in Black Culture in Harlem. The design on the floor covering his cremated remains is an African cosmogram titled *Rivers*. The title is taken from the poem *The Negro Speaks of Rivers* by Hughes. Within the center of the cosmogram and precisely above the ashes of Hughes are the words *My soul has grown deep like the rivers.*

Career

First published in *The Crisis* in 1921, the verse that would become Hughes' signature poem, "The Negro Speaks of Rivers", appeared in his first book of poetry *The Weary Blues* in 1926:Hughes' life and work were enormously influential during the Harlem Renaissance of the 1920s alongside those of his contemporaries, Zora Neale Hurston, Wallace Thurman, Claude McKay, Countee Cullen, Richard Bruce Nugent, and Aaron Douglas, who, collectively (with the exception of McKay), created the short-lived magazine *Fire!! Devoted to Younger Negro Artists.*

Hughes and his contemporaries were often in conflict with the goals and aspirations of the black middle class, and of those considered to be the midwives of the Harlem Renaissance, W. E. B. Du Bois, Jessie Redmon Fauset, and Alain LeRoy Locke, whom they accused of being overly excessive in accommodating and assimilating eurocentric values and culture for social equality. A primary expression of this conflict was the former's depiction of the "low-life", that is, the real lives of blacks in the lower social-economic strata and the superficial divisions and prejudices based on skin color within the black community. Hughes wrote what would be considered the manifesto for him and his contemporaries published in *The Nation* in 1926,

> *"The Negro Artist and the Racial Mountain"*
> *The younger Negro artists who create now intend to express our individual dark-skinned selves without fear or shame.*
> *If white people are pleased we are glad. If they are not, it doesn't matter. We know we are beautiful. And ugly, too.*
> *The tom-tom cries, and the tom-tom laughs. If colored people are pleased we are glad. If they are not, their displeasure doesn't matter either. We build our temples for tomorrow, strong as we know how, and we stand on top of the mountain free within ourselves.*

Hughes was unashamedly black at a time when blackness was démodé, and he didn't go much beyond the themes of black is beautiful as he explored the black human condition in a variety of depths. His main concern was the uplift of his people, of whom he judged himself the adequate appreciator, and whose strengths, resiliency, courage, and humor he wanted to record as part of the general American experience. Thus, his poetry and fiction centered generally on insightful views of the working class lives of blacks in America, lives he portrayed as full of struggle, joy, laughter, and music. Permeating his work is pride in the African American identity and its diverse culture. **"My seeking has been to explain and illuminate the Negro condition in America and obliquely that of all human kind,"** Hughes is quoted as saying. Therefore, in his work he confronted racial stereotypes, protested social conditions, and expanded African America's image of itself; a "people's poet" who sought to reeducate both audience and artist by lifting the theory of the black artistic into reality. An expression of this is the poem "My People"

> *The night is beautiful,*
> *So the faces of my people.*
>
> *The stars are beautiful,*
> *So the eyes of my people*
>
> *Beautiful, also, is the sun.*
> *Beautiful, also, are the souls of my people.*

Moreover, Hughes stressed the importance of a racial consciousness and cultural nationalism devoid of self-hate that united people of African descent and Africa across the globe and encouraged pride in their own diverse black folk culture and black aesthetic. ***Langston Hughes was one of the few black writers of any consequence to champion racial consciousness as a source of inspiration for black artists.*** His African-American race consciousness and cultural nationalism would influence many foreign black writers, such as Jacques Roumain, Nicolás Guillén, Léopold Sédar Senghor, and Aimé Césaire. With Senghor and Césaire and other French-speaking writers of Africa and of African descent from the Caribbean like René Maran from Martinique and Léon Damas from French Guiana in South America, the works of Hughes helped to inspire the concept that became the Négritude movement in France where a radical black self-examination was emphasized in the face of European colonialism. ***Langston Hughes was not only a role model for his calls for black racial pride instead of assimilation, but the most important technical influence in his emphasis on folk and jazz rhythms as the basis of his poetry of racial pride.***

In 1930, his first novel, *Not Without Laughter*, won the Harmon Gold Medal for literature. The central character of the story is a boy named Sandy whose family must deal with a variety of struggles imposed upon them due to their race and class in society in addition to relating to one another. Hughes's first collection of short stories came in 1934 with *The Ways of White Folks*. These stories provided a series of vignettes revealing the humorous and tragic interactions between whites and blacks. Overall, these stories are marked by a general pessimism about race relations, as well as a scornful realism. He received a Guggenheim Fellowship in 1935.

The same year Hughes established his theater troupe in Los Angeles, his ambition to write for the movies materialized when he co-wrote the screenplay for *Way Down South*. Further hopes by Hughes to write for the lucrative movie trade were thwarted because of racial discrimination within the industry. Through the black publication Chicago Defender, Hughes in 1943 gave creative birth to *Jesse B. Semple*, often referred to and spelled *Simple*, the everyday black man in Harlem who offered musings on topical issues of the day. He received offers to teach at a number of colleges, but seldom did. In 1947, Hughes taught at Atlanta University. Hughes, in 1949, spent three months at University of Chicago Laboratory Schools as a visiting lecturer. He wrote novels, short stories, plays, poetry, operas, essays, and works for children, and, with the encouragement of his best friend and writer, Arna Bontemps, and patron and friend, Carl Van Vechten, two autobiographies, *The Big Sea* and *I Wonder as I Wander*, as well as translating several works of literature into English.

During the mid–1950s and –1960s, Hughes' popularity among the younger generation of black writers varied as his reputation increased worldwide. With the gradual advancement toward racial integration, many black writers considered his writings of black pride and its corresponding subject matter out of date. They considered him a racial chauvinist. He in turn found a number of writers like James Baldwin lacking in this same pride, over intellectualizing in their work, and occasionally vulgar.

Hughes wanted young black writers to be objective about their race, but not to scorn it or flee it. He understood the main points of the Black Power movement of the 1960s, but believed that some of the younger black writers who supported it were too angry in their work. Hughes's work *Panther and the Lash* was posthumously published in 1967 and was intended to show solidarity and understanding with these writers, but with more skill and devoid of the most virile anger and terse racial prejudice some showed toward whites. Hughes still continued to have admirers among the larger younger generation of black writers, whom he often helped by offering advice and introducing them to other influential persons in the literature and publishing communities. This latter group, including Alice Walker, whom Hughes discovered, looked upon Hughes as a hero and an example to be emulated in degrees and tones within their own work. ***One of these young black writers observed of Hughes, "Langston set a tone, a standard of brotherhood and friendship and cooperation, for all of us to follow. You never got from him, 'I am the Negro writer,' but only 'I am a Negro writer.' He never stopped thinking about the rest of us."***

Political views

Hughes, like many black writers and artists of his time, was drawn to the promise of Communism as an alternative to a segregated America. Many of his lesser-known political writings have been collected in two volumes published by the University of Missouri Press and reflect his attraction to Communism. An example is the poem "A New Song".

In 1932, Hughes became part of a group of blacks who went to the Soviet Union to make a film depicting the plight of African Americans in the United States. The film was never made, but Hughes was given the opportunity to travel extensively through the Soviet Union and to the Soviet-controlled regions in Central Asia, the latter parts usually closed to Westerners. While there, he met African-American Robert Robinson, living in Moscow and unable to leave. In Turkmenistan, Hughes met and befriended the Hungarian polymath Arthur Koestler. Hughes also managed to travel to China and Japan before returning to the States.

Hughes' poetry was frequently published in the CPUSA newspaper and he was involved in initiatives supported by Communist organizations, such as the drive to free the Scottsboro Boys. Partly as a show of support for the Republican faction during the Spanish Civil War, in 1937 Hughes traveled to Spain as a correspondent for the *Baltimore Afro-American* and other various African-American newspapers. Hughes was also involved in other Communist-led organizations like the John Reed Clubs and the League of Struggle for Negro Rights. He was more of a sympathizer than an active participant. He signed a statement in 1938 supporting Joseph Stalin's purges and joined the American Peace Mobilization in 1940 working to keep the U.S. from participating in World War II.

Hughes initially did not favor black American involvement in the war because of the persistence of discriminatory U.S. Jim Crow laws existing while blacks were encouraged to fight against Fascism and the Axis powers. He came to support the war effort and black American involvement in it after deciding that blacks would also be contributing to their struggle for civil rights at home.

Hughes was accused of being a Communist by many on the political right, but he always denied it. When asked why he never joined the Communist Party, he wrote "it was based on strict discipline and the acceptance of directives that I, as a writer, did not wish to accept." In 1953, he was called before the Senate Permanent Subcommittee on Investigations led by Senator Joseph McCarthy. Following his appearance, he distanced himself from Communism and was subsequently rebuked by some who had previously supported him on the Radical Left. Over time, Hughes would distance himself from his most radical poems. In 1959 his collection of *Selected Poems* was published. He excluded his most controversial work from this group of poems.

Stage and film depictions

Hughes' life has been depicted in many stage and film productions. *Hannibal of the Alps* by Michael Dinwiddie and *Paper Armor* by Eisa Davis are plays by African-American playwrights which deal with Hughes' sexuality. In the 1989 film, *Looking for Langston*, **British filmmaker Isaac Julien claimed Hughes as a black gay icon** —Julien thought that Hughes' sexuality had historically been ignored or downplayed. In the film *Get on the Bus*, directed by Spike Lee, a black gay character, played by Isaiah Washington, invokes the name of Hughes and punches a homophobic character while commenting, "This is for James Baldwin and Langston Hughes." Film portrayals of Hughes include Gary LeRoi Gray's role as a teenage Hughes in the 2003 short subject film *Salvation* (based on a portion of his autobiography *The Big Sea*) and Daniel Sunjata as Hughes in the 2004 film *Brother to Brother. Hughes' Dream Harlem*, a documentary by Jamal Joseph, examines Hughes' works and environment.

Literary archives

The Beinecke Rare Book and Manuscript Library at Yale University holds the Langston Hughes papers (1862-1980) and the Langston Hughes collection (1924-1969) containing letters, manuscripts, personal items, photographs, clippings, artworks, and objects that document the life of Hughes. The Langston Hughes Memorial Library on the campus of Lincoln University, as well as at the James Weldon Johnson Collection within the Yale University also hold archives of Hughes' work.

Honors and awards

- 1943, Lincoln University awarded Hughes an honorary Litt.D.
- 1960, the NAACP awarded Hughes the Spingarn Medal for distinguished achievements by an African American.
- 1961 National Institute of Arts and Letters.
- 1963 Howard University awarded Hughes an honorary doctorate.
- 1973, the first Langston Hughes Medal was awarded by the City College of New York.
- 1979, Langston Hughes Middle School was created in Reston, Virginia.
- 1981, New York City Landmark status was given to the Harlem home of 2002 The United States Postal Service added the image of Langston Hughes to its Black Heritage series of postage stamps.
- **2002, scholar Molefi Kete Asante listed Langston Hughes on his list of 100 Greatest African Americans.**

Points to Ponder

The skill of writing is to create a context in which other people can think.
Edwin Schlossberg

How vain it is to sit down to write when you have not stood up to live.
Henry David Thoreau, Journal, 19 August 1851

If you don't have the time to read, you don't have the time or the tools to write.
Stephen King

Thurgood Marshall,
Supreme Court Justice

Born in Baltimore, Maryland on July 2, 1908, Thurgood Marshall was the grandson of a slave. His father, William Marshall, instilled in him from youth an appreciation for the United States Constitution and the rule of law. After completing high school in 1925, Thurgood followed his brother, William Aubrey Marshall, at the historically black Lincoln University in Chester County, Pennsylvania. His classmates at Lincoln included a distinguished group of future Black leaders such as the poet and author Langston Hughes, the future President of Ghana, Kwame Nkrumah, and musician Cab Calloway. Just before graduation, he married his first wife, Vivian "Buster" Burey. Their twenty-five year marriage ended with her death from cancer in 1955.

In 1930, he applied to the University of Maryland Law School, but was denied admission because he was Black. This was an event that was to haunt him and direct his future professional life. Thurgood sought admission and was accepted at the Howard University Law School that same year and came under the immediate influence of the dynamic new dean, Charles Hamilton Houston, who instilled in all of his students the desire to apply the tenets of the Constitution to all Americans. Paramount in Houston's outlook was the need to overturn the 1898 Supreme Court ruling, Plessy v. Ferguson which established the legal doctrine called, "separate but equal." Marshall's first major court case came in 1933 when he successfully sued the University of Maryland to admit a young African American Amherst University graduate named Donald Gaines Murray. Applauding Marshall's victory, author H.L. Mencken wrote that the decision of denial by the University of Maryland Law School was "brutal and absurd," and they should not object to the "presence among them of a self-respecting and ambitious young Afro-American well prepared for his studies by four years of hard work in a class A college."

Thurgood Marshall followed his Howard University mentor, Charles Hamilton Houston to New York and later became Chief Counsel for the National Association for the Advancement of Colored People (NAACP). During this period, Mr. Marshall was asked by the United Nations and the United Kingdom to help draft the constitutions of the emerging African nations of Ghana and what is now Tanzania. It was felt that the person who so successfully fought for the rights of America's oppressed minority would be the perfect person to ensure the rights of the White citizens in these two former European colonies. After amassing an impressive record of Supreme Court challenges to state-sponsored discrimination, including the landmark Brown v. Board decision in 1954, President John F. Kennedy appointed Thurgood Marshall to the U.S. Court of Appeals for the Second Circuit. In this capacity, he wrote over 150 decisions including support for the rights of immigrants, limiting government intrusion in cases involving illegal search and seizure, double jeopardy, and right to privacy issues. Biographers Michael Davis and Hunter Clark note that, *"none of his (Marshall's) 98 majority decisions was ever reversed by the Supreme Court."* In 1965 President Lyndon Johnson appointed Judge Marshall to the office of U.S. Solicitor General. Before his subsequent nomination to the United States Supreme Court in 1967, Thurgood Marshall won 14 of the 19 cases he argued before the Supreme Court on behalf of the government. *Indeed, Thurgood Marshall represented and won more cases before the United States Supreme Court than any other American.*

Until his retirement from the highest court in the land, Justice Marshall established a record for supporting the voiceless American. Having honed his skills since the case against the University of Maryland, he developed a profound sensitivity to injustice by way of the crucible of racial discrimination in this country. *As an Associate Supreme Court Justice, Thurgood Marshall leaves a legacy that expands that early sensitivity to include all of America's voiceless. Justice Marshall died on January 24, 1993.*

Wisdom for the Journey

There may be times when we are powerless to prevent injustice, but there must never be a time when we fail to protest. Elie Wiesel

Rosa Parks Biography

Pioneer of Civil Rights

Rosa Parks Date of birth: February 4, 1913
Date of death: October 24, 2005

Most historians date the beginning of the modern civil rights movement in the United States to December 1, 1955. That was the day when an unknown seamstress in Montgomery, Alabama refused to give up her bus seat to a white passenger. ***This brave woman, Rosa Parks, was arrested and fined for violating a city ordinance, but her lonely act of defiance began a movement that ended legal segregation in America, and made her an inspiration to freedom-loving people everywhere.***

Rosa Parks was born Rosa Louise McCauley in Tuskegee, Alabama to James McCauley, a carpenter, and Leona McCauley, a teacher. At the age of two she moved to her grandparents' farm in Pine Level, Alabama with her mother and younger brother, Sylvester. At the age of 11 she enrolled in the Montgomery Industrial School for Girls, a private school founded by liberal-minded women from the northern United States. The school's philosophy of self-worth was consistent with Leona McCauley's advice to "take advantage of the opportunities, no matter how few they were."

Opportunities were few indeed. "Back then," Mrs. Parks recalled in an interview, "we didn't have any civil rights. It was just a matter of survival, of existing from one day to the next. ***I remember going to sleep as a girl hearing the Klan ride at night and hearing a lynching and being afraid the house would burn down.***" In the same interview, she cited her lifelong acquaintance with fear as the reason for her relative fearlessness in deciding to appeal her conviction during the bus boycott. "I didn't have any special fear," she said. "It was more of a relief to know that I wasn't alone."

After attending Alabama State Teachers College, the young Rosa settled in Montgomery, with her husband, Raymond Parks. The couple joined the local chapter of the NAACP and worked quietly for many years to improve the lot of African-Americans in the segregated south.

"I worked on numerous cases with the NAACP," Mrs. Parks recalled, "but we did not get the publicity. There were cases of flogging, peonage, murder, and rape. We didn't seem to have too many successes. It was more a matter of trying to challenge the powers that be, and to let it be known that we did not wish to continue being second-class citizens."

The bus incident led to the formation of the Montgomery Improvement Association, led by the young pastor of the Dexter Avenue Baptist Church, Dr. Martin Luther King, Jr. The association called for a boycott of the city-owned bus company. The boycott lasted 382 days and brought Mrs. Parks, Dr. King, and their cause to the attention of the world. A Supreme Court Decision struck down the Montgomery ordinance under which Mrs. Parks had been fined, and outlawed racial segregation on public transportation.

In 1957, Mrs. Parks and her husband moved to Detroit, Michigan where Mrs. Parks served on the staff of U.S. Representative John Conyers. The Southern Christian Leadership Council established an annual Rosa Parks Freedom Award in her honor.

After the death of her husband in 1977, Mrs. Parks founded the Rosa and Raymond Parks Institute for Self-Development. The Institute sponsors an annual summer program for teenagers called Pathways to Freedom. The young people tour the country in buses, under adult supervision, learning the history of their country and of the civil rights movement. President Clinton presented Rosa Parks with the Presidential Medal of Freedom in 1996. She received a Congressional Gold Medal in 1999.

When asked if she was happy living in retirement, Rosa Parks replied, "I do the very best I can to look upon life with optimism and hope and looking forward to a better day, but I don't think there is any such thing as complete happiness. It pains me that there is still a lot of Klan activity and racism. I think when you say you're happy, you have everything that you need and everything that you want, and nothing more to wish for. I haven't reached that stage yet."

Mrs. Parks spent her last years living quietly in Detroit, where she died in 2005 at the age of 92. *After her death, her casket was placed in the rotunda of the United States Capitol for two days, so the nation could pay its respects to the woman whose courage had changed the lives of so many. She is the only woman and second African American in American history to lie in state at the Capitol, an honor usually reserved for Presidents of the United States.*

Quote:

Courage is contagious. When a brave man takes a stand, the spines of others are often stiffened. **Billy Graham**

Daisy Bates
(civil rights activist)

Daisy Lee may "Gatson" Bates (November 11, 1914 in Huttig, Arkansas-November 4, 1999 in Little Rock, Arkansas) *was an American civil rights activist, publisher and writer who played a leading role in the Little Rock integration crisis of 1957.*

Bates' mother was murdered while resisting three local white men who were attempting to rape her. Her father left the family shortly after her mother's death and she was raised by friends of the family, Orle and Susie Smith.

At the age of 15, Daisy became the object of an older man's attention. L.C. Bates, an insurance salesman who had also worked on newspapers in the South and West. L.C. dated her for several years, and they married in 1942, living in Little Rock. The Bates decided to act on a dream of theirs, to run their own newspaper, leasing a printing plant that belonged to a church publication and inaugurating the Arkansas State Press. The first issue appeared on May 9, 1941. The paper became an avid voice for civil rights even before a nationally recognized movement had emerged.

In 1952, Daisy Bates was elected president of the Arkansas State Conference of NAACP branches.

Little Rock integration crisis

Bates and her husband were important figures in the Little Rock Integration Crisis in 1957. The Bates published a local black newspaper, the *Arkansas State Press*, which publicized violations of the Supreme Court's desegregation rulings. Bates guided and advised the nine students, known as the Little Rock Nine, when they attempted to enroll at Little Rock Central High School, a previously all white school, in 1957. The students' attempts to enroll provoked a confrontation with Arkansas Governor Orval Faubus,

150

who called out the National Guard to prevent the students from entering the school. White mobs met at the school, threatening to kill the black students; these mobs harassed not only activists but also northern journalists who came to cover the story. Bates was a pivotal figure in that seminal moment of the civil rights movement. As a publisher and journalist, she was also a witness and advocate on a larger scale. In 1998, a spokeswoman for Ms. Bates stated that she had always felt guilty for her role in the Little Rock Central High School event since it had been her responsibility to notify one of the young ladies that they were delaying the entrance into Central High School. The family of the child had no phone and the father did not return from work until 3 in the morning. Ms. Bates fell asleep before she was able to deliver the message to the family and the girl attempted to attend her first day at the segregated school alone.

The city council instructed the Little Rock police chief to arrest Bates and other NAACP officials; she and the local branch president surrendered voluntarily. They were charged with failing to provide information about members for the public record, in violation of a city ordinance. Though Bates was charged a fine by the judge, NAACP lawyers appealed and eventually won a reversal in the United States Supreme Court.

President Dwight D. Eisenhower intervened by federalizing the Arkansas National Guard and dispatching the 101st Airborne Division to Little Rock to ensure that the court orders were enforced.

Their involvement in the Little Rock Crisis resulted in the loss of much advertising revenue to their newspaper and it was forced to close in 1959. In 1960, Daisy Bates moved to New York City and wrote her memoir, *The Long Shadow of Little Rock*, which won a 1988 National Book Award.

Later life

Then Bates moved to Washington, D.C. and worked for the Democratic National Committee. She also served in the administration of President Lyndon Baines Johnson working on anti-poverty programs. In 1965, she suffered a stroke and returned to Little Rock.

In 1968 she moved to the rural black community of Mitchellville, Desha County, Arkansas. She concentrated on improving the lives of her neighbors by establishing a self-help program which was responsible for new sewer systems, paved streets, a water system, and community center.

Bates revived the Arkansas State Press in the 1980s after L.C. Bates, her husband, died in 1980.

In 1986 the University of Arkansas Press republished *The Long Shadow of Little Rock*, which became the first reprinted edition ever to earn an American Book Award. The following year she sold the newspaper, but continued to act as a consultant. Little Rock paid perhaps the ultimate tribute, not only to Bates but to the new era she helped initiate, by opening the Daisy Bates Elementary School and by making the third Monday in February "George Washington's Birthday and Daisy Gatson Bates Day" an official state holiday.

Bates died in Little Rock, Arkansas on November 4, 1999.

Food for Thought

There can be no higher law in journalism than to tell the truth and to shame the devil. **Walter Lippmann**

Medgar Evers

Known today more for his struggles for civil rights in Mississippi and his untimely death at the hands of an assassin than for his writings, Medgar Evers nevertheless left behind an impressive record of achievement.

Medgar Wiley Evers was born July 2, 1925, near Decatur, Mississippi, and attended school there until he was inducted into the army in 1943. After serving in Normandy, he attended Alcorn College (now Alcorn State University), majoring in business administration. While at Alcorn, he was a member of the debate team, the college choir, and the football and track teams, and he also held several student offices and was editor of the campus newspaper for two years and the annual for one year. In recognition of his accomplishments at Alcorn, he was listed in Who's Who in American Colleges.

Evers and his wife moved to Jackson, where they worked together to set up the NAACP office, and he began investigating violent crimes committed against blacks and sought ways to prevent them. His boycott of Jackson merchants in the early 1960s attracted national attention, and his efforts to have James Meredith admitted to the University of Mississippi in 1962 brought much-needed federal help for which he had been soliciting. Meredith was admitted to Ole Miss, a major step in securing civil rights in the state, but an ensuing riot on campus left two people dead, and Evers' involvement in this and other activities increased the hatred many people felt toward Evers.

On June 12, 1963, as he was returning home, Medgar Evers was killed by an assassin's bullet. Black and white leaders from around the nation came to Jackson for his funeral and then gathered at Arlington National Cemetery for his interment. Following his death, his brother, Charles, took over Medgar's position as state field secretary for the NAACP. **The accused killer, a white supremacist named Byron De La Beckwith, stood trial twice in the 1960s, but in both cases the all-white juries could not reach a verdict. Finally, in a third trial in 1994 (and thirty-one years**

after Evers' murder), Beckwith was convicted and sentenced to life in prison.

The legacy of Medgar Evers is everywhere present in the Mississippi of today. This peaceful man, who had constantly urged that "violence is not the way" but who paid for his beliefs with his life was a prominent voice in the struggle for civil rights in Mississippi. Many tributes have been paid to Medgar Evers over the years, including a book by his widow, *"For Us, the Living"*, but perhaps the greatest tribute can be found in changes noted in Mississippi Black History Makers: "Ten years after Medgar's death the national office of the NAACP reported that Mississippi had 145 black elected officials and that blacks were enrolled in each of the state's public and private institutions of higher learning . . . . In 1970, according to statistics compiled by the Department of Health, Education, and Welfare, more than one-fourth or 26.4 percent of black pupils in Mississippi public schools attended integrated schools with at least a 50 percent white enrollment. **When Medgar died in 1963, only 28,000 blacks were registered voters. By 1971, there were 250,000 and by 1982 over 500,000.**" *Attributed to John B. Padgett*

"The legacy of heroes is the memory of a great name and the inheritance of a great example." *Benjamin Disraeli*

Aloysius Leon Higginbotham, Jr.

A. Leon Higginbotham "was born on February 25, 1928, in Trenton, N.J. Higginbotham attended Purdue University from 1944-46 and then transferred to Antioch College where he earned a B.A. 1949. Three years later in 1952 he graduated with high honors from Yale University Law School. After an active legal career including many years as a federal judge, he died on December 14, 1998. He was married twice and had four children.

He held a variety of positions early in his career including stints as a Philadelphia County assistant district attorney (1953-54); a partner in the law firm of Norris, Green, Harris & Higginbotham, in Philadelphia (1954-62); a special hearing officer for conscientious objectors for the U.S. Justice Department (1960-62); a commissioner of the Federal Trade Commission (1962-64); and a commissioner of the Pennsylvania Human Relations Commission (1961-62). Then, from 1964 until his retirement in 1993, he was a federal judge serving first a federal district court judge for the U.S. District Court for the East District (1964-77) then on the U.S. Court of Appeals Third Circuit (1977-93). He then he was counsel to Paul, Weiss, Rifkind, Wharton (1993-98) and a professor at Harvard University's John F. Kennedy School of Government (1993-98) and he served as an international mediator of first South African election in which blacks were allowed to vote in 1994.

"Among his many awards are the nation's highest civilian award—the Presidential Medal of Freedom (1995), the Raoul Wallenberg Humanitarian Award (1994), the Spingarn Medal (1996) and numerous honorary degrees.

"Judge Higginbotham was a life-long champion of individual rights liberties as an advocate, judge, and author."

Food for Thought

Crimes were committed to punish crimes, and crimes were committed to prevent crimes. The world has been filled with prisons and dungeons, with chains and whips, with crosses and gibbets, with thumbscrews and racks, with hangmen and heads-men—and yet these frightful means and instrumentalities have committed far more crimes than they have prevented . . . . Ignorance, filth, and poverty are the missionaries of crime. As long as dishonorable success outranks honest effort—as long as society bows and cringes before the great thieves, there will be little ones enough to fill the jails.

~Robert Ingersoll, Crimes against Criminals

Somebody recently figured out that we have 35 million laws to enforce the Ten Commandments.

~Attributed to both Bert Masterson and Earl Wilson

Part Five:

Armed Forces

"Every gun that is made, every warship launched, every rocket signifies, in the final sense, a theft from those who hunger and are not fed, from those who are cold and are not clothed. The world in arms is not spending money alone. It is spending the sweat of its laborers, the genius of its scientists, and the hopes of its children."—**Dwight D. Eisenhower**

FROM THE BOOK

"He shall judge between many peoples, and rebuke strong nations afar off; They shall beat their swords into plowshares, And their spears into pruning hooks; Nation shall not lift up sword against nation, neither shall they learn war anymore."(Micah 4:3)

Buffalo Soldiers

Buffalo Soldiers was a name given to two cavalry regiments and two infantry regiments. These United States Army units were made up entirely of African American soldiers.

In 1866 two U.S. Army African American regiments were formed, the 9th and 10th cavalries: Members of these two cavalry units and two all-black infantry regiments, the 24th and 25th, came to be called Buffalo Soldiers. By 1867, the first Buffalo Soldier units were sent to the West to fight Indians and protect settlers, cattle herds, and railroad crews. Indians gave the troops the name of Buffalo Soldiers, probably because their short, dark, curly hair resembled the mane of the buffalo. In the 1950s, Buffalo Soldier regiments were disbanded when all military services were integrated.

Buffalo Soldiers originally were members of the U.S. 10th Cavalry Regiment of the United States Army, formed on September 21, 1866 at Fort Leavenworth, Kansas.

The nickname was given to the "Negro Cavalry" by the Native American tribes they fought; the term eventually became synonymous with all of the African-American regiments formed in 1866:

Although several African-American regiments were raised during the Civil War to fight alongside the Union Army (including the 54th Massachusetts Volunteer Infantry and the many United States Colored Troops Regiments), the *"Buffalo Soldiers" were established by Congress as the first peacetime all-black regiments in the regular U.S. Army.*

On September 6, 2005, Mark Matthews, who was the oldest living Buffalo Soldier, died at the age of 111. He was buried at Arlington National Cemetery.

Etymology

Sources disagree on how the nickname "Buffalo Soldiers" began. According to the Buffalo Soldiers National Museum, the name originated with the Cheyenne warriors in the winter of 1867, the actual Cheyenne translation being "Wild Buffalo." However, writer Walter Hill documented the account of Colonel Benjamin Grierson, who founded the 10th Cavalry regiment, recalling an 1871 campaign against the Comanche tribe. Hill attributed the origin of the name to the Comanche due to Grierson's assertions. Some sources assert that the nickname was given out of respect for the fierce fighting ability of the 10th cavalry. Other sources assert that Native Americans called the black cavalry troops "buffalo soldiers" because of their dark curly hair, which resembled a buffalo's coat. Still other sources point to a combination of both legends. The term *Buffalo Soldiers* became a generic term for all African-American soldiers. It is now used for U.S. Army units that trace their direct lineage back to the 9th and 10th Cavalry, units whose service earned them an honored place in U.S. history.

Service

During the American Civil War, the U.S. government formed regiments known as the United States Colored Troops, composed of black soldiers. After the war, Congress reorganized the Army and authorized the formation of two regiments of black cavalry with the designations 9th and 10th U.S. Cavalry, and four regiments of black infantry, designated the 38th, 39th, 40th and 41st Infantry Regiments (Colored). The 38th and 41st were reorganized as the 25th Infantry Regiment, with headquarters in Jackson Barracks in New Orleans, Louisiana, in November 1869. The 39th and 40th were reorganized as the 24th Infantry Regiment, with headquarters at Fort Clark, Texas, in April 1869. All of these units were composed of black enlisted men commanded by both white and black officers. These included the first commander of the 10th Cavalry Benjamin Grierson, the first commander of the 9th Cavalry Edward Hatch, Medal of Honor recipient Louis H. Carpenter, the unforgettable Nicholas M. Nolan and the first black graduate of West Point Henry O. Flipper.

Indian Wars

From 1866 to the early 1890s, these regiments served at a variety of posts in the Southwestern United States (Apache Wars) and Great Plains regions. They participated in most of the military campaigns in these areas and earned a distinguished record. Thirteen enlisted men and six officers from these four regiments earned the Medal of Honor during the Indian Wars. In addition to the military campaigns, the "Buffalo Soldiers" served a variety of roles along the frontier from building roads to escorting the U.S. mail. On 17 April 1875, regimental headquarters for the 9th and 10th Cavalries were transferred to Fort Concho, Texas. Companies actually arrived at Fort Concho in May 1873. At various times from 1873 through 1885, Fort Concho housed 9th Cavalry companies A-F, K, and M, 10th Cavalry companies A, D-G, I, L, and M, 24th Infantry companies D-G, and K, and 25th Infantry companies G and K.

A lesser known action was the 9th Cavalry's participation in the fabled Johnson County War, an 1892 land war in Johnson County, Wyoming between small farmers and large, wealthy ranchers. It culminated in a lengthy shootout between local farmers, a band of hired killers, and a sheriff's posse. The 6th Cavalry was ordered in by President Benjamin Harrison to quell the violence and capture the band of hired killers. Soon afterward, however, the 9th Cavalry was specifically called on to replace the 6th. The 6th Cavalry was swaying under the local political and social pressures and was unable to keep the peace in the tense environment.

The Buffalo Soldiers responded within about two weeks from Nebraska, and moved the men to the rail town of Suggs, Wyoming, creating "Camp Bettens" despite a racist and hostile local population. One soldier was killed and two wounded in gun battles with locals. Nevertheless, the 9th Cavalry remained in Wyoming for nearly a year to quell tensions in the area.
1898-1918

After the Indian Wars ended in the 1890s, the regiments continued to serve and participated in the 1898 Spanish-American War (including the Battle of San Juan Hill) in Cuba, where five more Medals of Honor were earned.

The regiments took part in the Philippine-American War from 1899 to 1903 and the 1916 Mexican Expedition.

In 1918 the 10th Cavalry fought at the Battle of Ambos Nogales, where they assisted in forcing the surrender of the federal Mexican and German forces.

Buffalo soldiers fought in the last engagement of the Indian Wars: the small Battle of Bear Valley in southern Arizona which occurred in 1918 between U.S. cavalry and Yaqui natives.

Park Rangers

Another little-known contribution of the Buffalo Soldiers involved eight troops of the 9th Cavalry Regiment and one company of the 24th Infantry Regiment who served in California's Sierra Nevada as some of the first national park rangers. In 1899, Buffalo Soldiers from Company H, 24th Infantry Regiment briefly served in Yosemite National Park, Sequoia National Park and General Grant (Kings Canyon) National Parks.

U.S. Army regiments had been serving in these national parks since 1891, but until 1899 the soldiers serving were white. Beginning in 1899, and continuing in 1903 and 1904, African-American regiments served during the summer months in the second and third oldest national parks in the United States (Sequoia and Yosemite). Because these soldiers served before the National Park Service was created (1916), they were "park rangers" before the term was coined.

A lasting legacy of the soldiers as park rangers is the Ranger Hat (popularly known as the Smokey Bear Hat.) Although not officially adopted by the Army until 1911, the distinctive hat crease, called a Montana Peak, (or pinch,) can be seen worn by several of the "Buffalo Soldiers" in park photographs dating back to 1899. Soldiers serving in the Spanish American war began to recrease the Stetson hat with a Montana "pinch" to better shed water from the torrential tropical rains. Many retained that distinctive "pinch" upon their return to the U.S. The park photographs in all likelihood show Buffalo Soldiers who were veterans from that 1898 war.

One particular Buffalo Soldier stands out in history: Captain Charles Young who served with Troop "I", 9th Cavalry Regiment in Sequoia National Park during the summer of 1903. Charles Young was the third African American to graduate from the United States Military Academy. At the time of his death, he was the highest ranking African American in the U.S. military. He made history in Sequoia National Park in 1903 by becoming Acting Military Superintendent of Sequoia and General Grant National Parks. Charles Young was also the first African American superintendent of a national park. During Young's tenure in the park, he named a Giant Sequoia for Booker T. Washington. Recently, another Giant Sequoia in Giant Forest was named in Captain Young's honor. Some of Young's descendants were in attendance at the ceremony.

In 1903, 9th Cavalrymen in Sequoia built the first trail to the top of Mount Whitney, the highest mountain in the contiguous United States. They also built the first wagon road into Sequoia's Giant Forest, the most famous grove of Giant Sequoia trees in Sequoia National Park.

In 1904, 9th Cavalrymen in Yosemite built an arboretum on the South Fork of the Merced River in the southern section of Yosemite National Park. This arboretum had pathways and benches, and some plants were identified in both English and Latin. Yosemite's arboretum is considered to be the first museum in the National Park System. The NPS cites a 1904 report, where Yosemite superintendent (Lt. Col.) John Bigelow, Jr. declared the arboretum "To provide a great museum of nature for the general public free of cost . . ."

Unfortunately, the forces of developers, miners and greed cut the boundaries of Yosemite in 1905 and the arboretum was nearly destroyed.

In the Sierra Nevada, the Buffalo Soldiers regularly endured long days in the saddle, slim rations, racism, and separation from family and friends. As military stewards, the African American cavalry and infantry regiments protected the national parks from illegal grazing, poaching, timber thieves, and forest fires. Yosemite Park Ranger Shelton Johnson researched and interpreted the history in an attempt to recover and celebrate the contributions of the Buffalo Soldiers of the Sierra Nevada.

In total, 23 "Buffalo Soldiers" received the Medal of Honor during the Indian Wars.

West Point

On March 23, 1907, the United States Military Academy Detachment of Cavalry was changed to a "colored" unit. This had been a long time coming. It had been proposed in 1897 at the "Cavalry and Light Artillery School" at Fort Riley, Kansas that West Point Cadets learn their riding skills from the black non-commissioned officers who were considered the best. The one hundred man detachment from the 9th Cavalry served to teach future officers at West Point riding instruction, mounted drill and tactics until 1947.

Systemic prejudice

The "Buffalo Soldiers" were often confronted with racial prejudice from other members of the U.S. Army. Civilians in the areas where the soldiers were stationed occasionally reacted to them with violence. Buffalo Soldiers were attacked during racial disturbances in: General of the Armies John J. Pershing is a controversial figure regarding the Buffalo Soldiers. He served with the 10th Cavalry from October 1895 to May 1897. He served again with them for less than six months in Cuba. *Because he saw the "Buffalo Soldiers" as good soldiers, he was looked down upon and called "Nigger Jack" by white cadets and officers at West Point.* It was only later during the Spanish-American War that the press changed that insulting term to "Black Jack." During World War I Pershing bowed to political and progressive racial policies of President of the United States Woodrow Wilson, Secretary of War Newton D. Baker and the southern Democratic Party with its "separate but equal" philosophy. For the first time in American history, Pershing allowed American soldiers (African-Americans) to be under the command of a foreign power.

World War I

The Buffalo Soldiers did not participate with the American Expeditionary Force (AEF) during World War I, but experienced non-commissioned officers were provided to other segregated black units for combat service—such as the 317th Engineer Battalion. The Soldiers of the 92nd Infantry Division (United States) and the 93rd Infantry Division (United States) were the first Black Americans to fight in France. The four regiments of 93rd fought under French command for the duration of the war.

In August 1918, the 10th Cavalry supported the 35th Infantry Regiment in a border skirmish, the Battle of Ambos Nogales, in which German military advisors fought along with Mexican soldiers. This was the only battle during World War I where Germans engaged and died in combat against United States soldiers in North America.

Battle of Ambos Nogales

The 35th Infantry Regiment was stationed at Nogales, Arizona on August 27, 1918; when at about 4:10 PM, a gun battle erupted unintentionally when a Mexican civilian attempted to pass through the border, back to Mexico, without being interrogated at the U.S. Customs house. After the initial shooting, reinforcements from both sides rushed to the border. For the Americans, the reinforcements were the 10th Cavalry, off duty 35th Regimental soldiers and militia. Hostilities quickly escalated and several soldiers were killed and others wounded on both sides. A cease fire was arranged later after the US forces took the heights south of Nogales.

World War II

Early in the 20th century, the Buffalo Soldiers found themselves being used more as laborers and service troops rather than as active combat units. During World War II the 9th and 10th Cavalry Regiments were disbanded, and the soldiers were moved into service-oriented units, along with the entire 2nd Cavalry Division. One of the infantry regiments, the 24th Infantry Regiment, served in combat in the Pacific theater. Another was the 92nd Infantry Division, AKA the "Buffalo Division", which served in combat during the Italian Campaign in the Mediterranean theater. Another was the 93rd Infantry Division—including the 25th Infantry Regiment—which served in the Pacific theater.

Despite some official resistance and administrative barriers, black airmen were trained and played a part in the air war in Europe, gaining a reputation for skill and bravery (see Tuskegee Airmen). In early 1945, after the Battle of the Bulge, American forces in Europe experienced a shortage of combat troops. The embargo on using black soldiers in combat units was relaxed. The American Military History says:

Faced with a shortage of infantry replacements during the enemy's counteroffensive, General Eisenhower offered Negro soldiers in service units an opportunity to volunteer for duty with the infantry. More than 4,500 responded, many taking reductions in grade in order to meet specified requirements. The 6th Army Group formed these men into provisional companies, while the 12th Army Group employed them as an additional platoon in existing rifle companies. The excellent record established by these volunteers, particularly those serving as platoons, presaged major postwar changes in the traditional approach to employing Negro troops.

Korean War and integration

The 24th Infantry Regiment saw combat during the Korean War and was the last segregated regiment to engage in combat. The 24th was deactivated in 1951, and its soldiers were integrated into other units in Korea. On December 12, 1951, the last Buffalo Soldier units, the 27th Cavalry and the 28th (Horse) Cavalry, were disbanded. The 28th Cavalry was inactivated at Assi-Okba, Algeria in April 1944 in North Africa, and marked the end of the regiment.

There are monuments to the Buffalo Soldiers in Kansas at Fort Leavenworth and Junction City. Then-Chairman of the Joint Chiefs of Staff Colin Powell, who initiated the project to get a statue to honor the Buffalo Soldiers when he was posted as a brigadier general to Fort Leavenworth, was guest speaker for the unveiling of the Fort Leavenworth monument in July 1992.

Controversy

In the last decade, the employment of the Buffalo Soldiers by the United States Army in the Indian Wars has led many historians to call for the "critical reappraisal" of the "Negro regiments." In this viewpoint, shared by most historians, the Buffalo Soldiers were used as mere shock troops or accessories to the forcefully-expansionist goals of the U.S. government at the expense of the Native Americans and other minorities.

A Thought worth Remembering:

"A man who is good enough to shed his **blood** *for his country is good enough to be given a square deal afterwards. More than that no man is entitled to, and less than that no man shall have."* **Theodore Roosevelt**

Benjamin Oliver Davis, Sr.

Brigadier General **Benjamin Oliver Davis, Sr.** (July 1, 1877-November 26, 1970) was an American general and the father of Benjamin O. Davis Jr. He was the first African-American general in the United States Army.

Benjamin O. Davis, Sr., was born in Washington, D.C., on July 1, 1877. His biographer Marvin Fletcher (author of *America's First Black General, Benjamin O. Davis, Sr., 1880-1970*) has presented evidence of his birth records indicating that he was born in May 1880 and later lied about his age so that he could enlist in the Army without the permission of his parents. It is the earlier date that appears on his grave at Arlington National Cemetery, however. He was a student at Howard University when—as a result of the start of the War with Spain—he entered the military service on July 13, 1898 as a temporary first lieutenant of the 8th United States Volunteer Infantry. He was mustered out on March 6, 1899, and on June 18, 1899, he enlisted as a private in Troop I, U.S. 9th Cavalry Regiment *(one of the original Buffalo Soldier regiments)*, of the Regular Army. He then served as corporal and squadron sergeant major, and on February 2, 1901, he was commissioned a second lieutenant of Cavalry in the Regular Army.

Military service

Benjamin Oliver Davis, Sr. was born in Washington, D.C. on July 1, 1877 to Louis P. H. and Henrietta Davis. He attended M Street High School in Washington where he participated in the school's cadet program. During the Spanish-American War, Davis briefly served in Company D, 1st Separate Battalion of the Washington D.C. National Guard. On 10 July 1898, Davis joined the 8th U.S. Volunteer Infantry Regiment as a first lieutenant of Company G. The 8th United States Volunteer Infantry was stationed at Chickamauga Park, Georgia, from October 1898 until the unit was disbanded in March 1899.

166

On 14 June 1899, Davis enlisted in the Regular Army. He was assigned to Troop I, 3rd Squadron, 9th Cavalry at Ft. Duchesne, Utah, first as the troop's clerk and then as squadron sergeant major. In the spring of 1901, Troop I was assigned to the Philippines. In August 1901, he was assigned to Troop F, 10th Cavalry, where Davis assumed the duties of a second lieutenant after passing an officers' qualification test. Troop F returned to the United States in August 1902. Davis was then stationed at Fort Washakie, Wyoming, where he also served for several months with Troop M. In September 1905, he was assigned to Wilberforce University in Ohio as Professor of Military Science and Tactics, a post that he filled for four years.

In November 1909, shortly after being ordered to Regimental Headquarters, 9th Cavalry, Davis was reassigned for duty to Liberia. He left the United States for Liberia in April 1910, and served as a military attaché reporting on Liberia's military forces until October 1911. He returned to the United States in November 1911. In January 1912, Davis was assigned to Troop I, 9th Cavalry, stationed at Fort D. A. Russell, Wyoming. In 1913, the 9th Cavalry was assigned to patrol the Mexican-United States border.

In February 1915, Davis was again assigned to Wilberforce University as Professor of Military Science and Tactics. From 1917 to 1920, Davis was assigned to the 9th Cavalry at Camp Stotsenburg, Philippine Islands, as supply officer, commander of 3rd Squadron, and then of 1st Squadron. He reached the temporary rank of lieutenant colonel, but returned to the United States in March 1920 with the rank of captain.

Davis was assigned to the Tuskegee University, Alabama, as the Professor of Military Science and Tactics from 1920 to 1924. He then served for five years as an instructor with 2nd Battalion, 372nd Regiment, Ohio National Guard, in Cleveland, Ohio. In September 1929, Davis returned to Wilberforce University as Professor of Military Science and Tactics. He was assigned to the Tuskegee Institute in the early part of 1931, and remained there for six years as Professor of Military Science and Tactics. During the summer months of 1930 to 1933, Davis escorted pilgrimages of World War I Gold Star Mothers and Widows to the burial places of their loved ones in Europe.

In August 1937, Davis returned to Wilberforce University as Professor of Military Science and Tactics. Davis was assigned to the 369th Regiment, New York National Guard, during the summer of 1938, and took command of the regiment a short time later. Davis was promoted to Brigadier General on 25 October 1940, becoming the first African-American general in the United States Army.

Davis became Commanding General of 4th Brigade, 2nd Cavalry Division at Fort Riley, Kansas, in January 1941. About six months later, he was assigned to Washington, D.C. as an assistant in the Office of the Inspector General. While serving in the Office of the Inspector General, Davis also served on the Advisory Committee on Negro Troop Problems. From 1941 to 1944, Davis conducted inspection tours of African-American soldiers in the United States Army. From September to November 1942 and again from July to November 1944, Davis made inspection tours of African-American soldiers stationed in Europe.

On 10 November 1944, Davis was reassigned to work under Lieutenant General John C. H. Lee as Special Assistant to the Commanding General, Communications Zone, and European Theater of Operations. He served with the General Inspectorate Section, European Theater of Operation (later the Office of the Inspector General on Europe) from January through May 1945. While serving in the European Theater of Operations, Davis was influential in the proposed policy of integration using replacement units.

After serving in the European Theater of Operations for more than a year, Davis returned to Washington, D.C. as Assistant to the Inspector General. In 1947 he was assigned as a Special Assistant to the Secretary of the Army. In this capacity, he was sent to Liberia in July 1947 as a representative of the United States for the African country's centennial celebration. On 20 July 1948, after fifty years of military service, Davis retired in a public ceremony with President Harry S. Truman presiding.

From July 1953 through June 1961, he served as a member of the American Battle Monuments Commission. Davis died on 26 November 1970 at Great Lakes Naval Hospital in Chicago, Illinois, and was buried at Arlington National Cemetery.

Promotions

He was promoted to first lieutenant on March 30, 1905; to captain on December 24, 1915; to major (temporary) on August 5, 1917; and to lieutenant colonel (temporary) on May 1, 1918. He reverted to his permanent rank of captain on October 14, 1919, and was promoted to lieutenant colonel on July 1, 1920; to colonel on February 18, 1930; to brigadier general (temporary) on October 25, 1940. He was retired on July 31, 1941, and recalled to active duty with the rank of brigadier general the following day.

Decorations and honors

General Davis' U.S. military decorations included the Distinguished Service Medal (DSM) and Bronze Star. His DSM medal, awarded by General Order 10, dated February 22, 1945, stated that Benjamin O. Davis was awarded the DSM "for exceptionally meritorious service to the Government in a duty of great responsibility from June 1941 to November 1944." The War

Department release issued about General Davis' DSM on February 11, 1945, included the following citation:

> *For exceptionally meritorious service to the Government in a duty of great responsibility from June, 1941, to November, 1944, as an Inspector of troop units in the field, and as special War Department consultant on matters pertaining to Negro troops. The initiative, intelligence and sympathetic understanding displayed by him in conducting countless investigations concerning individual soldiers, troop units, and components of the War Department brought about a fair and equitable solution to many important problems which have since become the basis of far-reaching War Department policy. His wise advice and counsel have made a direct contribution to the maintenance of soldier morale and troop discipline and has been of material assistance to the War Department and to responsible commanders in the field of understanding personnel matters as they pertain to the individual soldier.*

Additionally, Davis was awarded an Honorary Degree of LL.D. from Atlanta University, Atlanta, Georgia. His foreign awards and honors include of the Croix de Guerre with Palm from France and the Grade of Commander of the Order of the Star of Africa from Liberia.

A Point to Ponder

*"I believe that a man is the strongest **soldier** for daring to die unarmed."*
Mahatma Gandhi

Doris (Dorie) Miller,
American Hero

Famous for firing a 50 caliber Browning anti-aircraft machine gun for 15 minutes during the attack until he ran out of ammo. (Ordinarily this is not unusual—except that Dorie was the Ships Cook!) He was awarded the Navy Cross for his actions beyond the call of duty.

Highlights of his career

Dorie was the ship's heavyweight boxing champ on board the USS *West Virginia* (BB-48).

Dorie was awarded the Navy Cross by Admiral Chester W. Nimitz, on board USS *Enterprise* (CV-6) at Pearl Harbor, 27 May 1942, for heroism on board USS *West Virginia* (BB-48) during the Pearl Harbor Attack, 7 December 1941.

He was killed on 24 November 1943 in the line of duty while serving in action on board the USS *Liscome Bay* (CVE-56) during Operation Galvanic, (the seizure of Makin and Tarawa Atolls in the Gilbert Islands). While cruising near Butaritari Island, a single torpedo from Japanese submarine *I-175* struck the escort carrier near the stern. The aircraft bomb magazine detonated a few moments later, sinking the warship within minutes.

In 1973, the USS *Miller* (FF-1091), a *Knox*-class frigate, was named in honor of Doris Miller.

The Full Story

Doris Miller, known as "Dorie" to shipmates and friends, was born in Waco, Texas, on 12 October 1919, to Henrietta and Conery Miller. He had three brothers, one of which served in the Army during World War II. While attending Moore High School in Waco, he was a fullback on the football team and he worked on his father's farm.

On 16 September 1939, he enlisted in the U.S Navy as Mess Attendant, Third Class, at Dallas, Texas, so he could travel, and earn money for his family. He later was commended by the Secretary of the Navy, was advanced to Mess Attendant, Second Class and First Class, and subsequently was promoted to Ship's Cook, Third Class.

Following training at the Naval Training Station, Norfolk, Virginia, Miller was assigned to the ammunition ship USS *Pyro* (AE-1) where he served as a Mess Attendant.

On 2 January 1940 was transferred to USS *West Virginia* (BB-48), where he became the ship's heavyweight boxing champion.

In July 1940 he had temporary duty aboard USS *Nevada* (BB-36) at Secondary Battery Gunnery School.

On August 3 1940, he returned to *West Virginia*, and was serving in that battleship when the Japanese attacked Pearl Harbor on 7 December 1941.

On 7 December 1941, Miller had arisen at 6 a.m., and was collecting laundry when the alarm for general quarters sounded. He headed for his battle station, the antiaircraft battery magazine amidship, only to discover that torpedo damage had wrecked it, so he went on deck. Because of his physical prowess, he was assigned to carry wounded fellow Sailors to places of greater safety. Then an officer ordered him to the bridge to aid the mortally wounded Captain of the ship.

He subsequently manned a 50 caliber Browning anti-aircraft machine gun until he ran out of ammunition and was ordered to abandon ship.

Miller described firing the machine gun during the battle, a weapon which he had not been trained to operate: ***"It wasn't hard. I just pulled the trigger and she worked fine. I had watched the others with these guns. I guess I fired her for about fifteen minutes. I think I got one of those Jap planes. They were diving pretty close to us."***

During the attack, Japanese aircraft dropped two armored piercing bombs through the deck of the battleship and launched five 18-inch aircraft torpedoes into her port side. Heavily damaged by the ensuing explosions, and suffering from severe flooding below decks, the crew abandoned ship while *West Virginia* slowly settled to the harbor bottom. Of the 1,541 men on *West Virginia* during the attack, 130 were killed and 52 wounded. Subsequently refloated, repaired, and modernized, the battleship served in the Pacific theater through to the end of the war in August 1945.

Miller was commended by the Secretary of the Navy Frank Knox on 1 April 1942, and on 27 May 1942 he received the Navy Cross, which Fleet Admiral (then Admiral) Chester W. Nimitz, the Commander in Chief, Pacific Fleet personally presented to Miller on board aircraft carrier USS *Enterprise* (CV-6) for his extraordinary courage in battle. Speaking of Miller, Nimitz remarked:

This marks the first time in this conflict that such high tribute has been made in the Pacific Fleet to a member of his race and I'm sure that the future will see others similarly honored for brave acts.

On 13 December 1941, Miller reported to USS *Indianapolis* (CA-35), and subsequently returned to the west coast of the United States in November 1942. Assigned to the newly constructed USS *Liscome Bay* (CVE-56) in the spring of 1943, Miller was on board that escort carrier during Operation Galvanic, the seizure of Makin and Tarawa Atolls in the Gilbert Islands. *Liscome Bay*'s aircraft supported operations ashore between 20-23 November 1943. At 5:10 a.m. on 24 November, while cruising near Butaritari Island, a single torpedo from Japanese submarine *I-175* struck the escort carrier near the stern. The aircraft bomb magazine detonated a few moments later, sinking the warship within minutes. Listed as missing following the loss of that escort carrier, Miller was officially presumed dead 25 November 1944, a year and a day after the loss of *Liscome Bay*. Only 272 Sailors survived the sinking of *Liscome Bay*, while 646 died.

In addition to the Navy Cross, Miller was entitled to the Purple Heart Medal; the American Defense Service Medal, Fleet Clasp; the Asiatic-Pacific Campaign Medal; and the World War II Victory Medal.

Commissioned on 30 June 1973, USS *Miller* (FF-1091), a *Knox*-class frigate, was named in honor of Doris Miller.

On 11 October 1991, Alpha Kappa Alpha Sorority dedicated a bronze commemorative plaque of Miller at the Miller Family Park located on the U.S. Naval Base, Pearl Harbor. *From history.navy.mil*

Quote:

"A hero is an ordinary individual who finds the strength to persevere and endure in spite of overwhelming obstacles." **Christopher Reeve**

Navajo-Code talkers

A code talker was a term used to describe people who talk using a coded language. It is frequently used to describe Native Americans who served in the United States Marine Corps whose primary job was the transmission of secret tactical messages. Code talkers transmitted these messages over military telephone or radio communications nets using formal or informally developed codes built upon their native languages. Their service was very valuable because it enhanced the communications security of vital front line operations during World War II.

The name *code talker is* strongly associated with bilingual Navajo speakers specially recruited during World War II by the Marines to serve in their standard communications units in the Pacific Theater. Code talking, however, was pioneered by Choctaw Indians serving in the U.S. Army during World War I. These soldiers are referred to as Choctaw Code Talkers.

Other Native American code talkers were used by the United States Army during World War II, using Cherokee, Choctaw, Lakota, Meskwaki, and Comanche soldiers. Soldiers of Basque ancestry were used for code talking by the US Marines during World War II in areas where other Basque speakers were not expected to be operating.

Use of Cherokee

The first known use of Native Americans in the American military to transmit messages under fire was a group of Cherokee troops utilized by the American 30th Infantry Division serving alongside the British during the Second Battle of the Somme. According to the Division Signal Officer, this took place in September 1918. Their outfit was under British command at the time.

Use of Choctaw

In the days of World War I, company commander Captain Lawrence of the U. S. Army overheard Solomon Louis and Mitchell Bobb conversing in the Choctaw language. He found eight Choctaw men in the battalion. Eventually, fourteen Choctaw men in the Army's 36th Infantry Division trained to use their language in code. They helped the American Expeditionary Force win several key battles in the Meuse-Argonne Campaign in France, during the final big German push of the war. *Within 24 hours after the Choctaw language was pressed into service, the tide of the battle had turned. In less than 72 hours the Germans were retreating and the Allies were in full attack.*
These solders are now known as the Choctaw Code Talkers.

Use of Comanche

Adolf Hitler knew about the successful use of code talkers during World War I. He sent a team of some thirty anthropologists to learn Native American languages before the outbreak of World War II. However, it proved too difficult for them to learn the many languages and dialects that existed. Because of Nazi German anthropologists' attempts to learn the languages, the U.S. Army did not implement a large-scale code talker program in the European Theater. Fourteen Comanche code talkers took part in the Invasion of Normandy, and continued to serve in the 4th Infantry Division during further European operations. *Comanches of the 4th Signal Company compiled a vocabulary of over 100 code terms using words or phrases in their own language. Using a substitution method similar to the Navajo, the Comanche code word for tank was "turtle", bomber was "pregnant airplane", machine gun was "sewing machine" and Adolf Hitler became "crazy white man."*
Two Comanche code-talkers were assigned to each regiment, the rest to 4th Infantry Division headquarters. Shortly after landing on Utah Beach on June 6, 1944, the Comanches began transmitting messages. Some were wounded but none killed.
In 1989, the French government awarded the Comanche code-talkers the Chevalier of the National Order of Merit. On 30 November 1999, the United States Department of Defense presented Charles Chibitty with the Knowlton Award.

Use of Navajo

Philip Johnston proposed the use of Navajo to the United States Marine Corps at the beginning of World War II. Johnston, a World War I veteran, was raised on the Navajo reservation as the son of a missionary to the Navajos, and was one of the few non-Navajos who spoke their language fluently. Because Navajo has a complex grammar, is not nearly mutually intelligible enough with even its closest relatives within the Na-Dene family to provide meaningful information, and was an unwritten language, Johnston saw Navajo as answering the military requirement for an undecipherable code. Navajo was spoken only on the Navajo lands of the American Southwest, and its syntax and tonal qualities, not to mention dialects, make it unintelligible to anyone without extensive exposure and training. One estimate indicates that at the outbreak of World War II fewer than 30 non-Navajos, none of them Japanese, could understand the language.

Early in 1942, Johnston met with Major General Clayton B. Vogel, the commanding general of Amphibious Corps, Pacific Fleet, and his staff. Johnston staged tests under simulated combat conditions which demonstrated that Navajos could encode, transmit, and decode a three-line English message in 20 seconds, versus the 30 minutes required by machines at that time. The idea was accepted, with Vogel recommending that the Marines recruit 200 Navajos. The first 29 Navajo recruits attended boot camp in May 1942. This first group then created the Navajo code at Camp Pendleton, Oceanside, California. The Navajo code was formally developed and modeled on the Joint Army/Navy Phonetic Alphabet that uses agreed-upon English words to represent letters. As it was determined that phonetically spelling out all military terms letter by letter into words—while in combat—would be too time consuming, some terms, concepts, tactics and instruments of modern warfare were given uniquely formal descriptive nomenclatures in Navajo (the word for "potato" being used to refer to a hand grenade, or "tortoise" to a tank, for example). Several of these portmanteaus (such as gofasters referring to running shoes, ink stick for pens) entered Marine Corps vocabulary and are commonly used today to refer to the appropriate objects.

A codebook was developed to teach the many relevant words and concepts to new initiates. The text was for classroom purposes only, and was never to be taken into the field. The code talkers memorized all these variations and practiced their rapid use under stressful conditions during training. Uninitiated Navajo speakers would have no idea what the code talkers' messages meant; they would hear only truncated and disjointed strings of individual, unrelated nouns and verbs.

The Navajo code talkers were commended for their skill, speed and accuracy accrued throughout the war. At Iwo Jima, Major Howard Connor, 5th Marine Division signal officer, had six Navajo code talkers working around the clock during the first two days of the battle. These six sent and received over 800 messages, all without error. Connor later stated, ***"Were it not for the Navajos, the Marines would never have taken Iwo Jima."***

176 George D. Johnson

As the war progressed, additional code words were added on and incorporated program-wide. In other instances, informal short-cut code words were devised for a particular campaign and not disseminated beyond the area of operation. To ensure a consistent use of code terminologies throughout the Pacific Theater, representative code talkers of each of the U.S. Marine divisions met in Hawaii to discuss shortcomings in the code, incorporate new terms into the system, and update their codebooks. These representatives in turn trained other code talkers who could not attend the meeting.

The deployment of the Navajo code talkers continued through the Korean War and after, until it was ended early in the Vietnam War.

Cryptographic properties

Non-speakers would find it extremely difficult to accurately distinguish unfamiliar sounds used in these languages. Additionally, a speaker who has acquired a language during their childhood sounds distinctly different from a person who acquired the same language in later life, thus reducing the chance of successful impostors sending false messages. Finally, the additional layer of an alphabet cipher was added to prevent interception by native speakers not trained as code talkers, in the event of their capture by the Japanese. A similar system employing Welsh was used by British forces, but not to any great extent during World War II. Welsh was used more recently in the Balkan peace-keeping efforts for non-vital messages.

Navajo was an attractive choice for code use because few people outside the Navajo themselves had ever learned to speak the language. Virtually no books in Navajo had ever been published. Outside of the language itself, the Navajo spoken code was not very complex by cryptographic standards and would likely have been broken if a native speaker and trained cryptographers worked together effectively. The Japanese had an opportunity to attempt this when they captured Joe Kieyoomia in the Philippines in 1942 during the Bataan Death March. Kieyoomia, a Navajo Sergeant in the U.S. Army, but not a code talker, was ordered to interpret the radio messages later in the war. However, since Kieyoomia had not participated in the code training, the messages made no sense to him. When he reported that he could not understand the messages, his captors tortured him. Given the simplicity of the alphabet code involved, it is probable that the code could have been broken easily if Kieyoomia's knowledge of the language had been exploited more effectively by Japanese cryptographers. *The Japanese Imperial Army and Navy never cracked the spoken code.*

Post-war recognition

The code talkers received no recognition until the declassification of the operation in 1968. In 1982, the code talkers were given a Certificate of Recognition by U.S. President Ronald Reagan, who also named August 14, 1982 "Navajo Code Talkers Day".

On December 21, 2000 the U.S. Congress passed, and President Bill Clinton signed, Public Law 106-554, 114 Statute 2763, which awarded the Congressional Gold Medal to twenty-nine World War II Navajo code talkers. In July 2001, U.S. President George W. Bush personally presented the Medal to four surviving code talkers (the fifth living code talker was not able to attend) at a ceremony held in the Capitol Rotunda in Washington, DC. Gold medals were presented to the families of the 24 code talkers no longer living.

On September 17, 2007, 18 Choctaw code talkers were posthumously awarded the Texas Medal of Valor from the Adjutant General of the State of Texas for their World War I service. On December 13, 2007, H.R. 4544, the Code Talker Recognition Act, was introduced to the House of Representatives. The Code Talker Recognition Act recognizes every code talker who served in the United States military with a Congressional Gold Medal for his tribe and a silver medal duplicate to each code talker, including eight Meskwakis.

Popular culture

The 2002 movie *Windtalkers* was a fictional story based on Navajo code talkers who were enlisted in the U.S. Marine Corps in World War II. The movie was criticized for featuring the Navajo characters only in supporting roles, not as the primary focus of the film. The film's plot was fabricated about white bodyguards being ordered to kill them should they fall into enemy hands. It was further criticized for its use of stereotypes of both Native Americans and East Asians.

The 1959 movie *Never So Few* features Charles Bronson as Sgt. John Danforth, a Navajo code talker.

Quote:

"Never was so much owed by so many to so few"

Red Ball Express

The Red Ball Express was an enormous convoy system created by Allied forces to supply their forward-area combat units moving through Europe following the breakout from the D-Day beaches in Normandy. The term "Red Ball" was a railroad phrase referring to express shipping. The system lasted only three months, from August 25 to November 16, 1944, when the port facilities at Antwerp, Belgium were opened. Almost 75% of all Red Ball drivers were African Americans, able-bodied soldiers who were denied front-line service because of racial discrimination, but who had been attached to various units for other duties. The term Red Ball is often used incorrectly to refer to all WWII European supply convoys by historians and the veterans themselves.

African Americans Gain Fame as World War II Red Ball Express Drivers

WASHINGTON, Feb. 15, 2002-"When Gen. Patton said for you to be there, you were there if you had to drive all day and all night. Those trucks just kept running. They'd break down, we'd fix them and they'd run again," said James D. Rookard, a truck driver with the famous World War II Red Ball Express.

Army Gen. George S. Patton's bold armored advance across France in 1944 is credited historically as a significant contribution to the Allied victory in Europe in World War II. The Allied breakout from Normandy and the French hedgerow country in the summer started a race to Paris and points north and east. Patton stretched his supply line to near-collapse.

Since an army without gas, bullets and food would quickly be defeated, the Army Transportation Corps created a huge trucking operation called the "Red Ball Express" on Aug. 21, 1944. Supply trucks started rolling Aug. 25 and continued for 82 days. Men like Rookard, then 19, played a major role in the Nazis' defeat by ensuring U.S. and Allied war fighters had what they needed to sweep across France into Germany.

Nearly 75 percent of all Red Ball Express drivers, like Rookard, were African American. That's because well before and during the war, U.S. commanders in general believed African Americans had no mettle or guts for combat. Consequently, the Army relegated blacks primarily to "safe" service and supply outfits and the Navy assigned them as mess stewards. All Marines are combat troops—the Corps refused to take blacks at all until 1942.

"Red Ball Express" was the Army code name for a truck convoy system that stretched from St. Lo in Normandy to Paris and eventually to the front along France's northeastern borderland. The route was marked with red balls. On an average day, 900 fully loaded vehicles were on the Red Ball route round-the-clock with drivers officially ordered to observe 60-yard intervals and a top speed of 25 miles per hour.

At the Red Ball's peak, 140 truck companies were strung out with a round trip taking 54 hours as the route stretched nearly 400 miles to First Army and 350 to Patton's Third. Rookard recalled convoys rolling all day every day regardless of the weather. Night driving was hard because of blackout rules.

"We had to drive slowly at night because we had to use 'cat eyes,' and you could hardly see," he said. "If you turned on your headlights, the Germans could bomb the whole convoy. So we had to feel our way down the road." "Cat—eyes" were slitted headlight covers that reduced light to a dim beam on the highway.

Nobody wanted to invite air or ground ambushes—only some trucks had .50-caliber machine guns for defense, he said. The drivers carried only carbines.

The strain on personnel and equipment began to show. Drivers wanted to live up to their growing reputation among combat units and reporters, who sent home news stories about their exploits. They regularly began to ignore speed and weight limits and their own fatigue. The number of one—vehicle accidents climbed. The solution was easy—the Army assigned relief drivers to ride shotgun.

"We hauled anything Gen. Patton needed," said Rookard, who was drafted into the Army in March 1943 and was discharged in December 1946. "We took supplies all the way to the front line, back and forth, back and forth. Some of the fellows ran into ambushes, but my company, Company C, 514th Quartermaster Regiment, wasn't. We were lucky, because there was shooting all around us. The Germans had 'buzz bombs' (V-1 missiles). They were set to fly a certain amount of miles and (then) drop just like a bomb. We had to watch out for those.

"My worst memories of being in the Red Ball Express were seeing trucks get blown up and being afraid that I might get killed," said Rookard of Maple Heights, Ohio. "There were dead bodies and dead horses on the highways after bombs dropped. I was scared, but I did my job, hoping for the best. Being young and about 4,000 miles away from home, anybody would be scared."

Rookard, who became a Cleveland city truck driver after the war and retired in 1986, said the only fond memory he has is that of the French people, who treated African Americans nice.

"Some of the white soldiers told the French people that black soldiers had tails and stuff like that," he said. "But other than that, our company didn't have too much trouble with segregation and discrimination."

When the program ended in mid-November 1944, Red Ball Express truckers had delivered 412,193 tons of gas, oil, lubricants, ammunition, food and other essentials. By then, 210,209 African Americans were serving in Europe and 93,292 of them were in the Quartermaster Corps.

By Rudi Williams American Forces Press Service

Daniel James, Jr.

Daniel "Chappie" James Jr. (February 11, 1920-February 25, 1978) was a fighter pilot in the U.S. Air Force, who in 1975 became the first African American to reach the rank of four-star general.

Military career
World War II

James graduated from the Tuskegee Institute in 1942 where he received a Bachelor of Science degree in physical education. He continued civilian pilot training under the government-sponsored Civilian Pilot Training Program. He remained at Tuskegee as a civilian instructor pilot in the Army Air Corps Aviation Cadet Program until January 1943, when he entered the program as a cadet and received his commission as a second lieutenant later that July. Throughout the remainder of the war James trained pilots for the all-black 99th Pursuit Squadron. He did not see combat until the Korean War.

Korean War

In September 1949, James went to the Philippines as flight leader for the 12th Fighter-Bomber Squadron, 18th Fighter Wing at Clark Field. In July 1950 he left for Korea, where he flew 101 combat missions in P-51 Mustang and F-80 aircraft.

James returned to the United States, and in July 1951 went to Otis Air Force Base, Massachusetts as an all-weather jet fighter pilot with the 58th Fighter-Interceptor Squadron, later becoming operations officer. In April 1953 he became commander of the 437th Fighter-Interceptor Squadron, and assumed command of the 60th Fighter-Interceptor Squadron in August 1955. While stationed at Otis, he received the Massachusetts Junior Chamber of Commerce 1954 award of "Young Man of the Year" for his outstanding community relations efforts. On August 15, 1954 he appeared as a contestant on the game show What's My Line? He graduated from the Air Command and Staff College in June 1957.

James next was assigned to Headquarters U.S. Air Force as a staff officer in the Air Defense Division of the Office of the Deputy Chief of Staff for Operations. In July 1960 he was transferred to the Royal Air Force Bentwaters in England, where he served successively as assistant director of operations and then director of operations, 81st Tactical Fighter Wing; commander, 92nd Tactical Fighter Squadron; and deputy commander for operations for the 81st Wing. In September 1964 James was transferred to Davis-Monthan Air Force Base, Arizona, where he was director of operations training and later deputy commander for operations for the 4453rd Combat Crew Training Wing.

Vietnam War

James went to Ubon Royal Thai Air Force Base, Thailand in December 1966, as deputy commander for operations, 8th TFW. In June 1967, under Colonel Robin Olds, he was named wing vice commander when Col. Vermont Garrison completed his tour. Both in their mid-40s, they formed a legendary team nicknamed *"Blackman and Robin." James flew 78 combat missions into North Vietnam, many in the Hanoi/Haiphong area, and led a flight in the "Operation Bolo" MiG sweep in which seven Communist MiG-21s were destroyed, the highest total kill of any mission during the Vietnam War.*

He was named vice commander of the 33rd TFW at Eglin Air Force Base, Florida, in December 1967. While stationed at Eglin, the Florida State Jaycees named James as Florida's "Outstanding American of the Year" for 1969, and he received the Jaycee Distinguished Service Award. He was transferred to Wheelus Air Base in the Libyan Arab Republic in August 1969 as Commander of the 7272nd Fighter Training Wing.

James became Deputy Assistant Secretary of Defense (Public Affairs) in March 1970 and was designated principal Deputy Assistant Secretary of Defense (Public Affairs) in April 1973. On September 1, 1974, he assumed duty as vice commander of the Military Airlift Command (MAC), headquartered at Scott Air Force Base, Illinois.

James was promoted to four-star grade and assigned as commander in chief of NORAD/ADCOM at Peterson Air Force Base, Colorado, on September 1, 1975. In these dual capacities he had operational command of all United States and Canadian strategic aerospace defense forces. On December 6, 1977, he assumed duty as special assistant to the Chief of Staff, U.S. Air Force.

General James was widely known for his speeches on Americanism and patriotism, for which he was editorialized in numerous national and international publications. Excerpts from some of the speeches have been read into the Congressional Record. He was awarded the George Washington Freedom Foundation Medal in both 1967 and 1968. He received the Arnold Air Society Eugene M. Zuckert Award in 1970 for outstanding contributions to Air Force professionalism. His citation read " . . . fighter pilot with a magnificent record, public speaker, and eloquent spokesman for the American Dream we so rarely achieve."

Later achievements

Other civilian awards that General James received included the following: Builders of a Greater Arizona Award (1969); Phoenix Urban League Man of the Year Award, Distinguished Service Achievement Award from Kappa Alpha Psi Fraternity (1970); American Legion National Commander's Public Relations Award, Veteran of Foreign Wars Commander in Chief's Gold Medal Award and Citation (1971); Capital Press Club, Washington, D.C., Salute to Black Pioneers Award (1975); and, all in 1976, the Air Force Association Jimmy Doolittle Chapter Man of the Year Award, Florida Association of Broadcasters' Gold Medal Award, American Veterans of World War II Silver Helmet Award, United Service Organization Liberty Bell Award, Blackbook Minority Business and Reference Guidance Par Excellence Award, American Academy of Achievement Golden Plate Award, United Negro College Fund's Distinguished Service Award, Horatio Alger Award, VFW Americanism Medal, Bishop Wright Air Industry Award, and the Kitty Hawk Award (Military). He was awarded honorary doctor of laws degrees from the University of West Florida in 1971; the University of Akron in 1973; Virginia State College in 1974; Delaware State College in 1975; and St. Louis University in 1976. He was named honorary national commander of the Arnold Air Society in 1971.

General James died of a heart attack on February 25, 1978, just two weeks after his 58th birthday and three weeks following his retirement from the Air Force.

General James's son, Lieutenant General Daniel James III, also served in the United States Air Force and in the Texas Air National Guard. He served from 1995 to 2002 as the Adjutant General of the Texas National **Guard (the first African American to hold the post)**, and as Director of the Air National Guard from 2002 to 2006. In the summer of 2006, he retired from the Air Force at the rank of Lieutenant General after 38 years of total commissioned service, on active duty and as an Air Guardsman.

"No bird soars too high if he soars with his own wings"

William Blake

Samuel Gravely Jr.
Navy's First Black Admiral

Samuel Lee Gravely Jr. made history by becoming the first African American to command a naval fleet

Gravely, the first black admiral achieved a number of other accomplishments in a storied, 38-year naval career that began as a fireman apprentice in the Naval Reserve in 1942.

In the 1960s, he became the first African American to command a Navy warship, when he was executive officer and acting commanding officer of the destroyer Theodore E. Chandler. In the Vietnam War, he was placed in command of the destroyer Taussig and later the guided missile frigate Jouett, *making him the first African American to command a major naval warship.*

He went on to command a cruiser destroyer group, the 11th Naval District and the 3rd Fleet.

"His leadership inspired a generation of Americans to make the most of every opportunity," said Adm. Vern Clark, chief of naval operations.

A quiet, unassuming man, who was known more as a listener than a talker, Gravely was promoted to rear admiral in 1971 during a ceremony aboard the Jouett in San Diego.

"His view was that he liked the Navy," said his wife, Alma Gravely of Haymarket. "He was happy just doing his job and doing it well. And as he was doing it, he strived to climb the ranks."

In 1976, Gravely was placed in command of the 3rd Fleet in the Pacific after a reorganization of Navy forces. After two years, he was named director of the Defense Communications Agency in Washington, a post he held until his retirement from active military duty in 1980.

In retirement, he worked as a consultant and tended to a lifelong hobby of raising pigeons.

A Richmond native Gravely joined the Naval Reserve after his second year at Virginia Union University. He entered the Navy's college V-12 program in 1943. After attending Midship School at UCLA and Columbia University, he received an officer's commission the next year.

His first assignment as an ensign took him to a naval training station in Illinois, where he was assistant battalion commander for new recruits. Near the end of the war, he was assigned to a submarine-chasing patrol craft that had a predominantly African American crew.

He left active duty after the war and remained in the Naval Reserve. He completed a bachelor's degree at Virginia Union University before being recalled to duty during the Korean War.

His awards included the Legion of Merit, the Bronze Star and the Meritorious Service Medal.

While the military services were under a presidential order to desegregate, Gravely was assigned as a Navy recruiter in Washington.

In addition to his wife of 58 years, survivors include two children and two brothers.

A Point to Ponder:

What you leave behind is not what is engraved in stone monuments, but what is woven into the lives of others. **Pericles**

Part Six:

Sports & Entertainment

Life is like a play—we merely go through the stages of our life acting it out.

All the world's a stage, And all the men and women merely players: They have their exits and their entrances; And one man in his time plays many parts.

From Shakespeare's As You Like It, *1600:*

So be your part great or small, we should play it well or not at all.

Nate Love

The most famous black cowboy of all:

Nate Love, also know as Deadwood Dick, was ***born a slave*** in Tennessee. He had a love of the free and wild life on the range. Soon he was known as a good all around cowboy.

Nate found a Texas outfit that had delivered its herd and was preparing to go back down to Texas. There were several good black cowboys in the outfit. After sharing breakfast with the crew, Nate asked the trail boss for a job. The boss agreed if Nate could break a horse named ***Good Eye, the wildest horse in the outfit***. Bronco Jim, another black cowboy gave Nate some pointers and Nate rode that horse. He said later that it was the toughest ride he had ever had.

The work was very hard. Nate rode through hailstorms so violent that only strong men could withstand them. The first time he met hostile Indians, he admitted he was too scared to run. After going through a number of such trials he adjusted to the ways of the cattle country and could handle any problem,

Nate had a forty-five and he took every chance he could to practice with it and he got very good with it. There came a time when he could shoot better than any of his friends.

Nate left the Texas Panhandle, and rode into Arizona where he got a job working for an outfit on the Gila River. He had ridden many of the trails of the southwest and he believed that he was a capable cowboy: While in Arizona working with Mexican vaqueros, he learned to speak Spanish like a native and he became very good at reading brands.

In the spring of 1876, Nate Love's outfit received orders to deliver three thousand steer to Deadwood City in the Dakota Territory. They arrived July 3rd. The town was getting ready for the 4th of July. The mining men and gamblers had gotten together and organized a contest with $200 prize money. Nate said that six of the dozen men in the contest were Black. Each black cowboy was to rope, throw, tie bridles, and saddle a mustang in the shortest possible time. The wildest horses were chosen for this event. Nate roped, threw, tied bridles, saddled, and mounted his mustang in exactly nine minutes. The next competitor took twelve minutes and thirty seconds. In the rifle and Colt events, shooting at 100 and 250 yards with 14 shots, Nate placed all of his shots in the bulls' eye and 10 of the 12 pistol shots in the bulls' eye.

Nate Love was the obvious winner and along with the prize money, the town gave Nate the title of **"Deadwood Dick"**.

Cowboy Wisdom

It's better to be a has-been than a never was.
Generally, you ain't learnin' nothing when your mouth's a-jawin'.

William (Will, Bill) Pickett

William (Will, Bill) Pickett was a legendary cowboy from Taylor, Texas of black and Indian descent. He was born December 5, 1870, at the Jenks-Branch community on the Travis County line. He died April 2, 1932, near Ponca City, Oklahoma.

From 1905 to 1931, the Miller brothers' 101 Ranch Wild West Show was one of the great shows in the tradition begun by William F. *"Buffalo Bill"* Cody in 1883. The 101 Ranch Show introduced bulldogging (steer wrestling), an exciting rodeo event invented by Bill Pickett, one of the show's stars.

Riding his horse, Spradley, Pickett came alongside a Longhorn steer, dropped to the steer's head, twisted its head toward the sky, and bit its upper lip to get full control. *Cow dogs of the Bulldog breed were known to bite the lips of cattle to subdue them. That's how Pickett's technique got the name "bulldogging."* As the event became more popular among rodeo cowboys, the lip biting became increasingly less popular until it disappeared from steer wrestling altogether. Bill Pickett, however, became an immortal rodeo cowboy, and his fame has grown since his death.

He died in 1932 as a result of injuries received from working horses at the 101 Ranch. His grave is on what is left of the 101 Ranch properties, near Ponca City, Oklahoma. Pickett was inducted into the National Rodeo Hall of Fame in 1972 for his contribution to the sport.

Bill Pickett was the second of thirteen children born to Thomas Jefferson and Mary Virginia Elizabeth (Gilbert) Pickett, both of whom were former slaves. He began his career as a cowboy after completing the fifth grade. Bill soon began giving exhibitions of his roping, riding and bulldogging skills, passing a hat for donations.

By 1888, his family had moved to Taylor, Texas, and Bill performed in the town's first fair that year. He and his brothers started a horse-breaking business in Taylor, and Bill was a member of the National Guard and a deacon of the Baptist church. In December 1890, Bill married Maggie Turner.

Known by the nicknames "The Dusky Demon" and "The Bull-Dogger," Pickett gave exhibitions in Texas and throughout the West. His performance in 1904 at the Cheyenne Frontier Days (America's best-known rodeo) was considered extraordinary and spectacular. He signed on with the 101 Ranch show in 1905, becoming a full-time ranch employee in 1907. The next year, he moved his wife and children to Oklahoma.

He later performed in the U.S., Canada, Mexico, South America, and England, and became the first black cowboy movie star. *Had he not been banned from competing with white rodeo contestants, Pickett might have become one of the greatest record-setters in his sport.* He was often identified as an Indian, or some other ethnic background other than black, to be allowed to compete.

Bill Pickett died April 2, 1932, after being kicked in the head by a horse. Famed humorist Will Rogers announced the funeral of his friend on his radio show. In 1989, years after being honored by the National Rodeo Hall of Fame, Pickett was inducted into the Prorodeo Hall of Fame and Museum of the American Cowboy at Colorado Springs, Colorado. A 1994 U.S. postage stamp meant to honor Pickett accidentally showed one of his brothers.

Cowboy Proverbs

"Never kick a cow chip on a hot day"
"Don't interfere with something that ain't bothering you none"

Black Cowboys

Black Cowboys, legendary African American figures who drove great cattle herds across the early West. Idealized in motion pictures, television, and books, the cowboy serves as the great American icon, representing courage, hardiness, and independence.

Yet images of black cowboys have been scarce in popular culture, giving the false impression that African Americans were not among the men and women who settled the West. In fact, by the time the huge cattle drives of cowboy legend ended, at least 5,000 black men had worked as cowboys. The word cowboy refers to the men who drove herds of cattle from ranchland in Texas over hundreds of miles of rough and dangerous terrain to the stockyards in the North, a trip taking two to three months. A typical crew consisted of one trail chief, eight cowboys, a wrangler to take care of the horses, and a cook. One historian estimates that an average crew would have included two or three black cowboys.

African Americans came to cattle country most often as slaves, brought by white landowners who hoped to take advantage of the fertile Texas soil to grow cotton (see Slavery in the United States). Once there, many whites began ranching, often selling or trading their slaves for livestock. By the start of the American Civil War in 1861, Texas had over 180,000 black inhabitants and close to four million head of cattle. When the war ended four years later, ranching, with its dependence on cowboys, became the dominant industry.

Although black cowboys seldom became trail chiefs or owned their own stock—although some did, usually those who had been free men before the war—they encountered less discrimination along the cattle trail than in most other occupations at the time. While riding herd, black and white cowboys depended upon each other. They lived, ate, and slept together.

The demands of the trail, which included dangerous snakes and wolves, treacherous rivers and mountains, and the threat of attack from Native Americans, made most cowboys transcend their prejudices. One black cowboy, Nat Love (also known as Deadwood Dick), summed up the cowboy code, "There a man's work was to be done, and a man's life to be lived, and when death was to be met, he met it like a man."

If life on the trail was arduous, life in the cattle market towns, like Dodge City, Kansas, and Cheyenne, Wyoming, was wide open and lawless. Despite the efforts of marshals such as Wyatt Earp and Bat Masterson, thieves, rustlers, and gunslingers were abundant. *Although the majority of black cowboys, like the majority of whites, were tough but law-abiding, there were a few famous black outlaws. One, known as Cherokee Bill, was as bloodthirsty as Billy the Kid and was hanged before his 20th birthday.*

By around 1890 the cowboy's world had changed. Railroad lines had rendered long drives unnecessary, and barbed-wire fences now blocked the legendary Chisholm and Western trails. Some old cowboys, like Love, found work as Pullman porters. Others continued to work on ranches as broncobusters who tamed wild mustangs. Still others, like Bill Pickett, put their riding, roping, or shooting skills to use on the rodeo and vaudeville circuits.

More Cowboy Wisdom:

Some men talk 'cause they got somethin' to say. Others talk 'cause they got to say somethin.

Never wrestle with a pig, You both get all dirty, and the pig likes it.

There are three kinds of men, The one that learns by reading, The few who learn by observation, and the rest of them have to pee on the electric fence for themselves.

W.C. Handy

William Christopher Handy was born on November 16, 1873, in Florence, Alabama. He grew up in a log cabin that his grandfather had built on what is now called College Street. As a young child, he displayed a keen interest in music and his intuitive ear could catalog the musical notes of songbirds, the whistles from nearby river boats, and even the rhythms of the Tennessee River. However, musical talent, especially the playing of musical instruments, was frowned upon by his family and church.

Despite Handy's lack of encouragement, he longed to own a guitar that he had seen in a local shop window and he secretly saved the money he made by picking berries and nuts and making lye soap. When he had finally saved enough money to buy the guitar, he proudly brought it home to his shocked and dismayed family. Handy's father made him take the guitar back and exchange it for a dictionary.

Handy joined a local blues band as a teenager, but he kept this fact a secret from his parents. He purchased a cornet from a fellow band member and spent every free minute practicing it. An exceptional student in school, he placed near the top of his class. In September of 1892, Handy traveled to Birmingham to take a teaching exam, which he passed easily. He obtained a teaching job in Birmingham but soon learned that the teaching profession paid poorly. He quit the position and found work at a pipe works plant in nearby Bessemer.

During his free time, he organized a small string orchestra and taught musicians how to read notes. He formed a quartet called the "Lauzetta Quartet". When the group read about the upcoming World's Fair in Chicago, they decided to attend. The trip to Chicago was long and arduous. To pay their way, group members performed at odd jobs along the way. They finally arrived in Chicago only to learn that the World's Fair had been postponed for a year. The group then headed to St. Louis but working conditions there proved to be very bad. The Laurzetta Quartet disbanded and Handy subsequently left St. Louis for Evansville, Indiana.

In Evansville, Handy's luck changed dramatically. He joined a successful band which performed throughout the neighboring cities and states. While performing at a barbecue in Henderson, Kentucky, he met Elizabeth Price, and they married shortly afterwards (on July 19, 1896).

Handy received a letter from a musician friend in August of 1896, inviting him to join a minstrel group called "Mahara's Minstrels." He saw this as a great opportunity even though minstrel groups (traveling bands that roamed from city to city) were not highly regarded. Handy and his new wife Elizabeth traveled to Chicago where Handy took the job with Mahara's Minstrels at a salary of $6 per week. The three-year minstrel tour took them throughout the southwestern states of Texas and Oklahoma, across the Southeast through Tennessee and Georgia, and south to Florida and eventually to Cuba. Life on the road was not an easy way to make a living and Elizabeth especially grew weary of it. Following their return from Cuba, the group headed north again, stopping along the way for a performance in Huntsville, Alabama. Handy decided to stay in Florence with his family for a much needed rest.

While in Florence, Elizabeth gave birth to the first of six children (a daughter named Lucille) on June 29, 1900 in Florence. During this time, Handy was approached by W.H. Councill, President of Agricultural and Mechanical College in Normal, Alabama, about a teaching position. The university was one of two black colleges in the state of Alabama at the time (the other being Tuskegee University). Handy accepted the offer and became a faculty member in September of that year.

He was soon disheartened to discover that American music was often cast aside by the college and instead emphasized inferior foreign music considered to be "classical". It also became apparent that Handy was being underpaid and he could make much more money touring with the minstrel group. After a dispute with President Councill, Handy resigned his position and rejoined the Mahara Minstrels to tour states in the Midwest and Pacific Northwest. In 1903, he received an offer to direct a black band called the Knights of Pythias in Clarksdale, Mississippi. This job proved to be very rewarding and Handy remained there for six years.

In 1909, Handy and his band moved to Memphis, Tennessee where they established their headquarters on the famous Beale Street. ***Handy's years of observing the reactions of white people to native black music as well as his own study of the music, habits and attitudes of his race, began to affect his music sparking the beginnings of what would later be called "the blues."*** The first composition of this type was a campaign song that Handy composed for E. H. Crump, a Memphis candidate for mayor who was running on a reform platform. The song, "Mr. Crump," was later titled "Memphis Blues" and became very popular.

"Memphis Blues" was such a huge success that Handy published it in 1912. Although he sold the rights to the song for a mere $100, his musical style had been asserted and in 1914, at the age of 40, he published his most famous composition, *"St. Louis Blues."* Handy began to write and publish prolifically and his popularity soared. He opened his own publishing business and worked steadily throughout the 1920s and 1930s despite problems with his vision. His eyes had been sensitive since childhood and the heavy demands of his career took their toll on his vision. In 1943, he lost his balance and fell from a subway station which caused him to go totally blind.

In addition to composing, Handy worked laboriously at compiling blues tunes which he published in a book called *Blues: An Anthology* in 1926. He later published *Negro Authors And Composers of the United States* (1935), and *Unsung Americans Sung* (1944). His biography, *Father of the Blues* was published in 1941.

Handy's wife, Elizabeth, died in 1937. Handy later married Irma Louise Logan in 1954 at the age of 80. He suffered a stroke one year later and was confined to a wheelchair. Still a very popular figure, Handy's 84th birthday party was held at the Waldorf-Astoria with more than 800 people attending.

He died on March 28, 1958 of acute bronchial pneumonia at the age of 84. He was buried in Woodlawn Cemetery, Bronx, New York with many notables attending the funeral service and an estimated 150,000 people along the funeral route.

W.C. Handy has been called "the Father of the Blues" having single-handedly introduced a new style of music to the world. He acknowledged that he did not invent the blues but merely transcribed them and presented them to a worldwide audience. There have been many honors bestowed upon Handy since his death. In Memphis, a city park is named after him and in his hometown of Florence, Alabama; the log cabin where he was born has been restored and turned into a museum which houses mementos from his life. The city of Florence also holds an annual music festival in his honor. *Attributed to—Phillip Oliver*

Wisdom for the Journey

Blues is a natural fact, is something that a fellow lives. If you don't live it you don't have it. Young people have forgotten to cry the blues. Now they talk and get lawyers and things. **Big Bill Broonzy**

The history of a people is found in its songs.—George Jellinek

Jack Johnson (boxer)

John Arthur ("Jack") Johnson (March 31, 1878-June 10, 1946), *nicknamed the "Galveston Giant", was an American boxer, the second African American Boxing Champion, and the first African American world heavyweight boxing champion (1908-1915).*

Early life

Johnson was born in Galveston, Texas, the third child and first son of Henry and Tina "Tiny" Johnson, former slaves who worked at blue-collar jobs to raise six children and taught them how to read and write. He dropped out of school after just five or six years of education to get a job as a dock worker in Galveston.

Professional boxing career

Johnson's boxing style was very distinctive. He developed a more patient approach than was customary in that day: playing defensively, waiting for a mistake, and then capitalizing on it. Johnson always began a bout cautiously, slowly building up over the rounds into a more aggressive fighter. He often fought to punish his opponents rather than knock them out, endlessly avoiding their blows and striking with swift counters. He always gave the impression of having much more to offer and, if pushed, he could punch powerfully.

Johnson's style was very effective, but it was criticized in the press as being cowardly and devious. By contrast, World Heavyweight Champion "Gentleman" Jim Corbett had used many of the same techniques a decade earlier, and was praised by the press as "the cleverest man in boxing". Corbett was white.

By 1902, Johnson had won at least 50 fights against both white and black opponents. Johnson won his first title on February 3, 1903, beating "Denver" Ed Martin over 20 rounds for the World Colored Heavyweight Championship.

His efforts to win the full title were thwarted, as world heavyweight champion James J. Jeffries refused to face him then. ***Black and white boxers could meet in other competitions, but the world heavyweight championship was off limits to them.*** However, Johnson did fight former champion Bob Fitzsimmons in July 1907, and knocked him out in two rounds.

Johnson finally won the world heavyweight title on December 26, 1908; a full six years after Lightweight Champion Joe Gans became the first African American boxing champion. Johnson's victory over the reigning world champion, Canadian Tommy Burns, in Sydney, came after stalking Burns around the world for two years and taunting him in the press for a match. The fight lasted fourteen rounds before being stopped by the police in front of over 20,000 spectators. The title was awarded to Johnson on a referee's decision as a T.K.O, but he had clearly beaten the champion.

After Johnson's victory over Burns, racial animosity among whites ran so deep that Jack London called out for a "Great White Hope" to take the title away from Johnson. As title holder, Johnson thus had to face a series of fighters billed by boxing promoters as "great white hopes", often in exhibition matches. In 1909, he beat Frank Moran, Tony Ross, Al Kaufman, and the middleweight champion Stanley Ketchel. The match with Ketchel was keenly fought by both men until the 12th and last round, when Ketchel threw a right to Johnson's head, knocking him down. Slowly regaining his feet, Johnson threw a straight to Ketchel's jaw, knocking him out, along with some of his teeth, several of which "supposedly" were embedded in Johnson's glove. His fight with Philadelphia Jack O'Brien was a disappointing one for Johnson: though weighing 205 pounds (93 kg) to O'Brien's 161 pounds (73 kg), he could only achieve a six-round draw with the great middleweight.

The "Fight of the Century"

In 1910, former undefeated heavyweight champion James J. Jeffries came out of retirement and said, "I feel obligated to the sporting public at least to make an effort to reclaim the heavyweight championship for the white race . . . . I should step into the ring again and demonstrate that a white man is king of them all." Jeffries had not fought in six years and had to lose weight to get back to his championship fighting weight.

The fight took place on July 4, 1910 in front of 20,000 people, at a ring built just for the occasion in downtown Reno, Nevada. Johnson proved stronger and more nimble than Jeffries. In the 15th round, after Jeffries had been knocked down twice for the first time in his career, his people called it quits to prevent Johnson from knocking him out.

The "Fight of the Century" earned Johnson $65,000 and silenced the critics, who had belittled Johnson's previous victory over Tommy Burns as "empty," claiming that Burns was a false champion since Jeffries had retired undefeated.

Riots and aftermath

The outcome of the fight triggered race riots that evening—the Fourth of July—all across the United States, from Texas and Colorado to New York and Washington, D.C. Johnson's victory over Jeffries had dashed white dreams of finding a "great white hope" to defeat him. Many whites felt humiliated by the defeat of Jeffries.

Blacks, on the other hand, were jubilant, and celebrated Johnson's great victory as a victory for racial advancement. Black poet William Waring Cuney later highlighted the black reaction to the fight in his poem *"My Lord, What a Morning"*. Around the country, blacks held spontaneous parades and gathered in prayer meetings.

Some "riots" were simply blacks celebrating in the streets. In certain cities, like Chicago, the police did not disturb the celebrations. But in other cities, the police and angry white citizens tried to subdue the revelers. Police interrupted several attempted lynchings. In all, "riots" occurred in more than 25 states and 50 cities. ***About 23 blacks and two whites died in the riots, and hundreds more were injured.***

Film of the bout

A number of leading American film companies joined forces to shoot footage of the Jeffries-Johnson fight and turn it into a feature-length documentary film, at the cost of $250,000. The film was distributed widely in the U.S. and was exhibited internationally as well. As a result, Congress banned prizefight films from being distributed across state lines in 1912; the ban was lifted in 1940. ***In 2005, the film of the Jeffries-Johnson "Fight of the Century" was entered into the United States National Film Registry as being worthy of preservation.***

In the United States, many states and cities banned the exhibition of the Johnson-Jeffries film. The movement to censor Johnson's black supremacy took over the country within three days after the fight. It was a spontaneous movement, mobilized by the Christian lobby and police forces, and endorsed by former President Theodore Roosevelt.

Loss of the title

On April 5, 1915, Johnson lost his title to Jess Willard, a working cowboy from Kansas who started boxing when he was twenty-seven years old. With a crowd of 25,000 at Oriental Park Racetrack in Havana, Cuba, Johnson was K.O.'d in the 26th round of the scheduled 45-round fight, which was co-promoted by Roderick James "Jess" McMahon and a partner. Johnson found that he could not knock out the giant Willard, who fought as a counterpuncher, making Johnson do all the leading. Johnson aged 37, although having won almost every round, began to tire after the 20th round, and was visibly hurt by heavy body punches from Willard in rounds preceding the 26th round knockout. Johnson is said by many to have spread rumors that he took a dive, but Willard is widely regarded as having won the fight outright. Willard said, "If he was going to throw the fight, I wish he'd done it sooner. It was hotter than hell out there".

In a famous photo showing Johnson lying on the mat after being knocked down and during the ten count, he can be seen shielding his eyes from the glare of the tropical sun with his glove.

Personal life

Johnson was an early example of the celebrity athlete in the modern era, appearing regularly in the press and later on radio and in motion pictures. He earned considerable sums endorsing various products, including patent medicines, and indulged several expensive hobbies such as automobile racing and tailored clothing, as well as purchasing jewelry and furs for his wives. He even challenged champion racer Barney Oldfield to a match auto race at the Sheepshead Bay, New York one mile (1.6 km) dirt track. Oldfield, far more experienced, easily out-distanced Johnson, ending any thoughts the boxer might have had about becoming a professional driver. Once, when he was pulled over for a $50 speeding ticket (a large sum at the time), he gave the officer a $100 bill; the officer protested that he couldn't make change for that much, Johnson told him to keep the change, as he was going to make his return trip at the same speed. Johnson was also interested in opera (his favorite being *Il Trovatore*) and in history—he was an admirer of Napoleon Bonaparte, believing him to have risen from a similar origin to his own. *In 1920, Johnson opened a night club in Harlem; he sold it three years later to a gangster, Owney Madden, who renamed it the Cotton Club.*

Johnson constantly flouted conventions regarding the social and economic "place" of Blacks in American society. *As a Black man, he broke a powerful taboo in consorting with White women, and would constantly and arrogantly verbally taunt men (both white and black) inside and outside the ring. Johnson was pompous about his affection for white women, and imperious about his physical prowess, both in and out of the ring.* Asked the secret of his staying power by a reporter who

202 | George D. Johnson

had watched a succession of women parade into, and out of, the champion's hotel room, Johnson supposedly said "Eat jellied eels and think distant thoughts".

Johnson was married three times. All of his wives were white, a fact that caused considerable controversy at the time. In January 1911, Johnson married Etta Terry Duryea. A Brooklyn socialite and former wife of businessman Charles Duryea, she met Johnson at a car race in 1909. Their romantic involvement was very turbulent. Beaten many times by Johnson and suffering from severe depression, she committed suicide in September 1912, shooting herself with a revolver.

Less than three months later, on 4 December 1912, Johnson married Lucille Cameron. *After Johnson married Cameron, two ministers in the South recommended that Johnson be lynched. Cameron divorced him in 1924 because of infidelity.*

The next year, Johnson married Irene Pineau. When asked by a reporter at Johnson's funeral what she had loved about him, she replied, "I loved him because of his courage. He faced the world unafraid. There wasn't anybody or anything he feared." Johnson had no children.

Prison sentence

On October 18, 1912, Johnson was arrested on the grounds that his relationship with Lucille Cameron violated the Mann Act against "transporting women across state lines for immoral purposes" due to her being a prostitute. Cameron, soon to become his second wife, refused to cooperate and the case fell apart. Less than a month later, Johnson was arrested again on similar charges. This time the woman, another prostitute named Belle Schreiber with whom he had been involved in 1909 and 1910, testified against him, and he was convicted by a jury in June 1913. The conviction was despite the fact that the incidents used to convict him took place prior to passage of the Mann Act. He was sentenced to a year and a day in prison.

Johnson skipped bail, and left the country, joining Lucille in Montreal on June 25, before fleeing to France. For the next seven years, they lived in exile in Europe, South America and Mexico. Johnson returned to the U.S. on 20 July 1920. He surrendered to Federal agents at the Mexican border and was sent to the United States Penitentiary, Leavenworth to serve his sentence. He was released on July 9, 1921.

There have been recurring proposals to grant Johnson a posthumous presidential pardon. A bill requesting President George W. Bush to pardon Johnson in 2008, passed the House, but failed to pass in the Senate. In April 2009, Senator John McCain, along with Representative Peter King, filmmaker Ken Burns and Johnson's great niece, Linda Haywood, requested a presidential pardon for Johnson from President Barack Obama. On July 29, 2009, Congress passed a resolution calling on President Obama to issue a pardon.

While incarcerated, Johnson found need for a tool that would help tighten loosened fastening devices, and modified a wrench for the task. He patented his improvements on April 18, 1922, as US Patent 1,413,121.

Later life

Johnson continued fighting, but age was catching up with him. He fought professionally until 1938, losing 7 of his last 9 bouts, losing his final fight to Walter Price, by a 7th-round TKO.

On June 10, 1946, Johnson died in a car crash on U.S. Highway 1 near Franklinton, North Carolina, a small town near Raleigh, North Carolina, after racing angrily from a diner that refused to serve him. He was taken to the closest black hospital, Saint Agnes Hospital in Raleigh. He was 68 years old at the time of his death. He was buried next to Etta Duryea Johnson at Graceland Cemetery in Chicago. His grave was initially unmarked, but a stone that bears only the name "Johnson" now stands above the plots of Jack, Etta, and Irene Pineau.

Legacy

Johnson was inducted into the Boxing Hall of Fame in 1954, and is on the roster of both the International Boxing Hall of Fame and the World Boxing Hall of Fame. In 2005, the United States National Film Preservation Board deemed the film of the 1910 Johnson-Jeffries fight "historically significant" and put it in the National Film Registry.

Johnson's skill as a fighter and the money that it brought made it impossible for him to be ignored by the establishment. In the short term, the boxing world reacted against Johnson's legacy. But Johnson foreshadowed, in many ways, perhaps one of the most famous boxers of all time, Muhammad Ali. In fact, Ali often spoke of how he was influenced by Jack Johnson. Ali identified with Johnson because he felt America ostracized him in the same manner because of his opposition to the Vietnam War and affiliation with the Nation of Islam. In his autobiography, Ali relates how he and Joe Frazier agreed that Johnson and Joe Louis were the greatest boxers of all.

In 2002, scholar Molefi Kete Asante listed Jack Johnson on his list of 100 Greatest African Americans.

Popular culture

Johnson's story is the basis of the play and subsequent 1970 movie *The Great White Hope*, starring James Earl Jones as Johnson (known as Jack Jefferson in the movie), and Jane Alexander as his love interest. In 2005, filmmaker Ken Burns produced a 2-part documentary about Johnson's life, *Unforgivable Blackness: The Rise and Fall of Jack Johnson*, based on the 2004 nonfiction book of the same name by Geoffrey C. Ward.

Folksinger and blues musician Leadbelly references Johnson in a song about the *Titanic*: "*Jack Johnson wanna get on board, Captain said I ain't hauling no coal. Fare thee, Titanic, fare thee well. When Jack Johnson heard that mighty shock, mighta seen the man do the Eagle rock. Fare thee, Titanic, fare thee well*" (The Eagle Rock was a popular dance at the time). In 1969, American folk singer Jamie Brockett reworked the Leadbelly song into a satirical talking blues called "The Legend of the U.S.S. Titanic". It should be noted there is no convincing evidence that Johnson was in fact refused passage on the *Titanic* because of his race, as these songs allege.

Miles Davis's 1970 (see 1970 in music) album *A Tribute to Jack Johnson* was inspired by Johnson. The end of the record features the actor Brock Peters (as Johnson) saying:

> "*I'm Jack Johnson. Heavyweight champion of the world. I'm black. They never let me forget it. I'm black all right! I'll never let them forget it!*"

Food for Thought:

Boxing is the only sport you can get your brain shook, your money took and your name in the undertaker book. **Joe Frazier**

The bell that tolls for all in boxing belongs to a cash register. **Bob Verdi**

Noble Sissle

Personal Information

Born on July 10, 1889, in Indianapolis, IN; died on December 17, 1975, in Tampa, FL.
Education: Butler University, attended; DePauw University, attended.

Career

Songwriter, bandleader, vocalist, and instrumental performer. Organized hotel band in Indianapolis, 1915; moved to Baltimore and met Eubie Blake, 1915; joined dance orchestra of James Reese Europe, 1917; toured Europe with 369th Infantry Regimental Band, 1917-19; toured U.S. with Blake as Dixie Duo, 1919-20; with Blake, wrote hit all-black musical *Shuffle Along*, 1921; with Blake, wrote musical *Chocolate Dandies*, 1924; toured Europe with Blake, 1925-26; formed orchestra that toured Europe, 1928-31; led Noble Sissle Orchestra and performed at leading U.S. clubs and hotels, 1930s and 1940s; toured with USO Camp Show, 1945-46; worked as disc jockey in New York City, mid-1950s;

Life's Work

Noble Sissle was one of African-American music's unsung tradition-builders. As half of the duo that composed *Shuffle Along*, he helped to bring African-American creativity to a new level on the Broadway stage. As a bandleader, Sissle nurtured the careers of vocalist Lena Horne and other important musicians, and he participated fundamentally in the popularization of African-American jazz and pop in Europe.

Sissle was born in Indianapolis, Indiana, on July 10, 1889. His father was a minister and church organist, and his first musical appearances

206 George D. Johnson

came as a boy soprano in a Methodist church choir. Sissle studied music in the public schools of Indianapolis and Cleveland, Ohio, where his family moved for a time. While still in his teens, Sissle was touring the Midwest as part of vaudeville and gospel quartets. He enrolled at Indiana's Butler University in 1913 and later transferred to DePauw, but music held a stronger grip on his attentions. With interest in dancing being spurred by the rise of black-influenced popular music such as ragtime, Sissle was tapped to organize a dance orchestra at the Severin Hotel in Indianapolis.

Met Eubie Blake

Moving to Baltimore in 1915, Sissle landed a job singing with a vocal group called Joe Porter's Serenaders. Performing in a Baltimore park one evening, he met James Hubert "Eubie" Blake, a ragtime pianist who was a star of the city's music scene and was known up and down the East Coast. The two men hit it off creatively; Sissle had written lyrics for a song called "It's All Your Fault," and soon Blake had set it to music. The pair found immediate success when Sophie Tucker, one of the leading white female vocal stars of the day, introduced the song at a Baltimore performance.

Sissle briefly led a band in Coconut Grove, Florida; with this experience under his belt he was hired into the dance orchestra of New York bandleader James Reese Europe, whom he had known since his Indianapolis days. The so-called "society bands" of which Europe's was the best known were not jazz bands but were important predecessors of jazz, furnishing syncopated dance music for the fox trots and other new dances of African-American origin that had seized the fancy of American young people. Sissle became a vocalist and guitarist with Europe's group

The entrance of the U.S. into World War I in 1917 saw both Europe and Sissle joining the Army and successfully combining military service with their musical activities. Europe formed the 369th Infantry Regimental Band, a group of musical, black servicemen who entertained European audiences with the latest American dance styles; Sissle performed on drums with the group. *The 369th Infantry Regimental Band was a smash success, and Sissle thus became one of the first African-American musicians to find and enjoy the appreciation of audiences across the Atlantic.* He joined the group on tour in France after the war ended, but the tour ended with Europe's murder by one of his band members in 1919.

Refused to Wear Blackface

Back in the U.S., Sissle reunited with Blake and the pair formed a vaudeville act called the Dixie Duo. This act differed from other African-American stage presentations of the day in two important respects. First, Sissle and Blake worked, not in theaters that catered primarily to blacks, but, rather, in the circuit under the control of the Keith firm, one of the country's leading theatrical promoters. ***Sissle and Blake were able to partly break down the segregated seating arrangements that prevailed in many theaters.*** Most important, though they did not entirely eliminate the stereotypes of blacks that pervaded even African-American productions of the day, they did not wear the burnt-cork blackface makeup that was conventional for both white and black minstrel performers. ***Sissle and Blake are thus credited with a major step in the creation of a more dignified image for African-American entertainers.***

In 1921 Sissle and Blake joined with several other veteran black performers to mount a full-scale musical of their own, *Shuffle Along*. Again, Sissle was the lyricist, Blake the composer. **Shuffle Along was one of the first all-black productions to appear on Broadway, and it, too, broke down barriers. Sissle's book for the show included romantic love scenes between black characters, and at the opening performance the company feared ridicule and anger from its white audience.** But *Shuffle Along* became a smash, running for more than 500 performances and grossing the impressive total of eight million dollars.

The show's plot involved a satirical treatment of the political leaders of a fictional all-black town. It included an upbeat song called ***"I'm Just Wild About Harry"*** that became not only a pop standard but also an insurance policy for Sissle's old age when it was revived as part of the 1948 campaign of President Harry Truman and entered upon a fresh round of royalty-producing performances. *Shuffle Along* inaugurated the careers of future stars Josephine Baker and Paul Robeson, who were part of the company. Sissle and Blake, riding high, joined forces again on *The Chocolate Dandies* (1924) and other shows, and went on tour in Europe as *"the American Ambassadors of Syncopation."*

Remained in Europe

Although they continued to work together occasionally for the rest of their lives, Sissle and Blake parted ways in 1926; one of the issues was that Blake wanted to return to the U.S., while Sissle hoped to pursue opportunities in France's expanding jazz scene. Encouraged by songwriter Cole Porter, Sissle put together a band of top jazz expatriates that included clarinetist Sidney Bechet. Touring with this group and also as a singer, Sissle remained in Europe for several years, sometimes returning to the U.S. for brief engagements. Sissle's band gained renown in Europe; he is underappreciated as a contributor to the Americanization of European musical tastes. At one

British date, the future King Edward VIII was said to have played drums with Sissle's group.

Sissle re-formed his orchestra in America when he returned home in late 1930, and enjoyed a successful career in the 1930s and 1940s even though he was no longer in the forefront of jazz developments. Sissle and Blake reunited for the Broadway show *Shuffle Along of 1933*; it was less successful than its predecessor but spawned another significant career—that of **Nat "King" Cole**, who performed on keyboards. Yet another performer whose career Sissle helped along was that of Lena Horne, who became the featured female vocalist with his orchestra in the mid-1930s. Sissle returned to Europe to entertain U.S. troops during World War II and led his orchestra well into the 1950s. In later years he lived comfortably, working as a disc jockey and overseeing his copyrights; unlike many other black musicians, Sissle had succeeded in maintaining ownership of many of his works. He died in Tampa, Florida, on December 17, 1975.

Points to Ponder

The discovery of song and the creation of musical instruments both owed their origin to a human impulse which lies much deeper than conscious intention: the need for rhythm in life . . . the need is a deep one, transcending thought, and disregarded at our peril. ~**Richard Baker**

Music is the universal language of mankind. **Henry Wadsworth Longfellow**

The Apollo Theater

The Apollo Theater in New York City is one of the most famous music halls in the United States, and the most famous club associated almost exclusively with African-American performers. It is listed on the National Register of Historic Places, and was the home of Showtime at the Apollo, a nationally syndicated television variety show consisting of new talent.

The theater is located at 253 W. 125th Street in the New York City borough of Manhattan, specifically in Harlem, one of the United States' most historically significant traditionally black neighborhoods.

Creation and rise

An Apollo Hall was founded in the mid-1800s by former Civil War General Edward Ferrero as a dance hall and ballroom. Upon the expiration of his lease in 1872, the building was converted to a theater, which closed shortly before the turn of the century.

However, the name "Apollo Theater" lived on. In 1913 or 1914, a new building, designed by the architect George Keister, and who also patterned the First Baptist Church in the City of New York, opened at 253 West 125th Street as **Hurtig and Seamon's New (Burlesque) Theater**, operated by noted burlesque producers Jules Hurtig and Harry Seamon, who obtained a 30-year lease. It remained in operation until 1928, when Bill Minsky took over. The song "I May Be Wrong (But I Think You're Wonderful)" by Harry Sullivan and Harry Ruskin, written in 1929, became the theme song of the theater. Sidney S. Cohen, president of the Motion Picture Theater Owners of America, purchased the Apollo in 1932 upon Minsky's death. Sources vary as to the next transfer. According to the Apollo Theater Foundation, Cohen sold it in 1934 to Frank Schiffman and Leo Brecher, who renamed the hall the **125 Street Apollo** and reopened it on January 26, 1934, with an advertisement in the *New York Age* that referred to the Apollo as "the finest theater in Harlem" After Cohen's death, business partner Morris Sussman teamed with Schiffman, who ran the Harlem Opera House, and a merger between the two theaters was formed.

The Harlem Renaissance was occurring at the time, following the World War I-era Great Migration of blacks from the southern U.S. states, and Schiffman and Brecher opened with "a colored review" entitled "Jazz a la Carte", featuring Ralph Cooper, Benny Carter and his orchestra, and "16 Gorgeous Hot Steppers", with all proceeds donated to the Harlem Children's Fresh Air Fund. Schiffman's motivation for featuring black talent and entertainment was not only because the neighborhood had become black over a long period of gradual migration, but because black entertainers were cheaper to hire, and Schiffman could offer quality shows for reasonable rates. ***For many years, Apollo was the only theater in New York City to hire black talent.***

Ella Fitzgerald made her singing debut at 17 at the Apollo, on November 21, 1934. Fitzgerald's performances pulled in a weekly audience at the Apollo and she won the opportunity to compete in one of the earliest of its "Amateur Nights". She had originally intended to go on stage and dance, but intimidated by the Edwards Sisters, a local dance duo, she opted to sing instead, in the style of Connie Boswell. She sang Hoagy Carmichael's "Judy" and "The Object of My Affection"; a song recorded by the Boswell Sisters, and won the first prize of US$25.00.

The Apollo grew to prominence during the Harlem Renaissance of the pre-World War II years. In 1934, it introduced its regular Amateur Night shows hosted by Ralph Cooper. Billing itself as a place "where stars are born and legends are made, ***"the Apollo became famous for launching the careers of artists such as Ella Fitzgerald, Billie Holiday, James Brown, Diana Ross & The Supremes, Gladys Knight & the Pips, The Jackson 5, Patti LaBelle, Marvin Gaye, Luther Vandross, Stevie Wonder, Aretha Franklin, Ben E. King, Mariah Carey, The Isley Brothers, Lauryn Hill, and Sarah Vaughan. The Apollo also featured the performances of old-time vaudeville favorites like Tim Moore, Stepin Fetchit, Dewey "Pigmeat" Markham, Clinton "Dusty" Fletcher, John "Spider Bruce" Mason, and Johnny Lee, as well as younger comics like Godfrey Cambridge. One unique feature of the Apollo was "the executioner" a man with a broom who would sweep performers off the stage if the highly vocal and opinionated audiences began to call for their removal.***

Later years and decline

On August 16, 1957, Buddy Holly was allegedly the first white rock and roll performer to play at the Apollo. That claim is challenged by Jo-Ann

Campbell who performed November 30, 1956, and also the week of May 3, 1957, Jimmy Cavallo and the House Rockers who say they performed there in December 1956, and Dale Hawkins, who says he performed there in July 1957, about a month before Holly. Jimi Hendrix won the first place prize in an amateur musician contest at the Apollo in 1964.

The club fell into decline in the 1960s and 1970s, and was converted into a movie theater in 1975.

Transformation and renovation

The Apollo was revived in 1983, when Inner City Broadcasting, a firm owned by former Manhattan borough president Percy E. Sutton purchased the building. It obtained federal, state, and city landmark status, and fully reopened in 1985 The Little Rascals, produced by former actor Jimmy Hawkins, performed at a fiftieth anniversary show at the Apollo that year. The musical duo Hall & Oates played the grand reopening in 1987, which was released on an album that year.

In 1991, the Apollo was purchased by the State of New York.

On December 15, 2005, the Apollo Theater launched the first phase of its refurbishment, costing an estimated $65 million. The first phase included the facade and the new light-emitting diode (LED) marquee. *Attendees and speakers at the launch event included President Bill Clinton, New York Mayor Michael Bloomberg and Time Warner CEO Richard Parsons.*

On December 28, 2006, the body of James Brown, who had died a few days before, was displayed at an Apollo Theater memorial covered heavily by the news media.

As of 2009 it is run by the nonprofit Apollo Theater Foundation Inc., and draws an estimated 1.3 million visitors annually.

The Jazz Foundation of America has celebrated its annual benefit concert known as **"A Great Night in Harlem"** at the famous Apollo Theater for the every year since 2001. The concert will features over 50 musicians performing Big Band, Gospel, Jazz and Blues music. The event has been hosted by the likes of Bill Cosby, Danny Glover, Danny Aiello, Michael Imperioli, Mario Van Peebles and Chevy Chase. The performers include Elvis Costello, Lou Reed, Norah Jones, Dr. John, Sweet Georgia Brown, Dave Brubeck, Frank Fosters' Loud Minority Big Band, Gary Brown, Phil Woods, Frank Wess, Davell Crawford, Jimmy Heath, Randy Weston, Dr. Michael White's Original Liberty Brass Band, Cecil Bridgewater, Nnenna Freelon, Ron Carter, Odetta, Johnnie Mae Dunson, Beverly Watkins, and many others. The Jazz Foundation of America provides emergency assistance and long-term support to jazz and blues musicians. The foundation was a leading force in providing relief to Gulf Coast musicians after Hurricane Katrina.

Food for Thought:

"Young people must learn that none of the exciting and entertaining fun things are worth it if they take you off the path that will lead you back home to your Heavenly Father." **William R. Bradford**

Bert Williams III

Born: 1874
Died: March 4, 1922

Pioneer of the Stage:

W. C. Fields, star of the silent screen, called Bert Williams "the funniest man I ever saw and the saddest." As a central figure on America's vaudeville circuit, Williams sang, danced, and pantomimed in clubs, cabarets, and theaters across the country. Williams was one of, if not the most famous, African-American performers in the 1900s.

In an age when the "white vaudeville stage did not welcome black performers," Williams pioneered an important role for black performers who had so profoundly shaped the genre. With unfortunate regularity, he was often the only African American on stage. In the 1900s Williams was the toast of the cities he toured, and in 1904 he played a command performance in England for King Edward VII.

Facing Racism:

Racial prejudice shaped Williams' career. Unlike many other blackface performers, Williams did not play for laughs at the expense of other African Americans or black culture. Instead, he based his humor on universal situations in which any members of his audience might find themselves. In the style of vaudeville, Williams performed in blackface makeup like his white counterparts. Blackface worked like a double mask for him. It emphasized the difference between Williams, his fellow vaudevillians, and his white audiences.

Many white vaudevillians refused to appear on the same bill with Williams, and others complained that his material, which he wrote

213

himself, was better than theirs. Williams, like many black performers, faced discrimination from the hotels and restaurants in which he often performed. Hotels routinely refused to let Williams ride in the same elevators used by their white patrons. He once told a friend how much such seemingly petty discrimination hurt. "It wouldn't be so bad. . . . if I didn't hear the applause [from his performance] still ringing in my ears."

Early Life:

Williams was born in New Providence, Nassau, in the British West Indies, in 1874. He became a showman in 1893, when he joined Martin and Seig's Mastodon Minstrels. While performing with the Minstrels he met African American song-and-dance man George Walker, and the two men teamed up. The twosome debuted in New York's Casino Theatre in 1898 in a short-lived show, "The Gold Bug." Their act consisted of songs, dance, and quick-paced patter that centered on Walker trying to convince the slower Williams to join him in get-rich-quick schemes. Williams and Walker's popular act continued until Walker's death in 1911.

Ziegfeld Follies:

Williams struck out on his own when, in 1909, Walker became too ill to perform. In 1910 Florenz Ziegfeld hired Williams to be one of the stars of "The Ziegfeld Follies." He performed in the "Follies" almost continually, and his national popularity and fame grew. ***In 1918 Williams broke another color line when he topped the bill at New York City's Palace.*** Williams became famous for his pantomimed poker game. In this skit a single spotlight illuminated Williams' head and shoulders as he mimicked all the gestures of the player, from drawing cards to losing the game. The popularity of this skit led to a brief film career in the summer of 1916 when Williams appeared in the film A NATURAL BORN GAMBLER. In addition to the poker-game skit, Williams introduced many popular songs to audiences across the country, such as "You Ain't So Warm," "Nobody," "That's Harmony," and "You Got the Right Church but the Wrong Pew."

Later Life:

In 1920 Williams left the "Follies" and signed with another New York company, the Shubert's. On 21 February 1922 Williams collapsed onstage while touring with the production of "Under the Bamboo Tree." Williams returned to New York City, where he died a month later.

Quote:

"If vaudeville had died, television was the box they put it in."

Larry Gelbart

Thomas Andrew Dorsey

(July 1, 1899, Villa Rica, Georgia—January 23, 1993, Chicago).

He is known as "the father of black gospel music" and was at one time so closely associated with the field that songs written in the new style were sometimes known as "dorseys." Earlier in his life he was a leading blues pianist known as Georgia Tom.

As formulated by Dorsey, gospel music combines Christian praise with the rhythms of jazz and the blues. His conception also deviates from what had been, to that time, standard hymnal practice by referring explicitly to the self, and the self's relation to faith and God, rather than the individual included into the group via belief.

Dorsey was the music director at Pilgrim Baptist Church in Chicago from 1932 until the late 1970s. His best known composition, **"Take My Hand, Precious Lord"**, was performed by Mahalia Jackson and was a favorite of the Rev. Martin Luther King Jr., and "Peace in the Valley", which was a hit for Red Foley in 1951 and has been performed by dozens of other artists, including Queen of Gospel Albertina Walker, Elvis Presley and Johnny Cash.

In 2002, the Library of Congress honored his album *Precious Lord: New Recordings of the Great Songs of Thomas A. Dorsey* (1973), by adding it to the United States National Recording Registry.

Life and career

Dorsey's father was a minister and his mother a piano teacher. He learned to play blues piano as a young man. After studying music formally in Chicago, he became an agent for Paramount Records. He put together a band for Ma Rainey called the "Wild Cats Jazz Band" in 1924.

He started out playing at rent parties with the names **Barrelhouse Tom** and **Texas Tommy**, but he was most famous as **Georgia Tom**. As Georgia

Tom, he teamed up with Tampa Red (Hudson Whittaker) with whom he recorded the raunchy 1928 hit record "Tight Like That", a sensation, selling seven million copies. In all, he is credited with more than 400 blues and jazz songs.

Dorsey began recording gospel music alongside blues in the mid 1920s. This led to his performing at the National Baptist Convention in 1930, and becoming the bandleader of two churches in the early 1930s.

His first wife, Nettie, who had been Rainey's wardrobe mistress, died in childbirth in 1932 along with his first son. In his grief, he wrote his most famous song, one of the most famous of all gospel songs, "Precious Lord, Take My Hand"

Unhappy with the treatment received at the hands of established publishers, Dorsey opened the first black gospel music publishing company, Dorsey House of Music. He also founded his own gospel choir and was a founder and first president of the National Convention of Gospel Choirs and Choruses.

His influence was not limited to African American music, as white musicians also followed his lead. "Precious Lord" has been recorded by Albertina Walker, Elvis Presley, Mahalia Jackson, Aretha Franklin, Clara Ward, Dorothy Norwood, Jim Reeves, Roy Rogers, and Tennessee Ernie Ford, among hundreds of others. It was a favorite gospel song of the Rev. Martin Luther King, Jr.; and was sung at the rally the night before his assassination, and, per his request, at his funeral by Mahalia Jackson. *It was also a favorite of President Lyndon B. Johnson, who requested it to be sung at his funeral.* Dorsey was also a great influence on other Chicago-based gospel artists such as Albertina Walker and The Caravans and Little Joey McClork.

Dorsey wrote "Peace in the Valley" for Mahalia Jackson in 1937, which also became a gospel standard. He was the first African American elected to the Nashville Songwriters Hall of Fame and also the first in the Gospel Music Association's Living Hall of Fame. In 2007, he was inducted as a charter member of the Gennett Records Walk of Fame in Richmond, Indiana. His papers are preserved at Fisk University, along with those of W.C. Handy, George Gershwin, and the Fisk Jubilee Singers.

Dorsey's works have proliferated beyond performance, into the hymnals of virtually all American churches and of English-speaking churches worldwide.

Thomas was a member of the Omega Psi Phi Fraternity, Incorporated.

He died in Chicago, Illinois and was interred there in the Oak Woods Cemetery.

A Point to Ponder:

"Music has a very powerful and wonderful influence in establishing feelings and moods that can lift and elevate your thoughts and your actions. But because it is so powerful, it is cleverly used by the adversary to stimulate your thoughts, feelings, and moods, to pollute and poison your mind and cause you to do things you would not otherwise consider doing." (Ardeth G. Kapp)

Eubie Blake

Born: February 7, 1883
Died: February 12, 1983

Eubie Blake grew up to the sounds of ragtime music, and before the turn of the century was playing piano in sporting houses and other similar establishments. He was a composer too, and in 1915 joined forces with Noble Sissle; they played in vaudeville as a double act and wrote together extensively. In 1921 Sissle and Blake wrote the score for a Broadway show—a remarkable accomplishment for blacks at that time. "Shuffle Along," which starred Flournoy Miller, Aubrey Lyles, Gertrude Saunders, and Sissle himself (with Blake on the piano), included several admirable songs, including "Bandana Days," "Gypsy Blues," "Love Will Find a Way," "Everything Reminds Me of You," "Shuffle Along," and "If You've Never Been Vamped by a Brown Skin (You've Never Been Vamped at All)."

There was also one enormous hit, "I'm Just Wild About Harry," which became popular at the time for artists such as Marion Harris, Ray Miller, and Paul Whiteman, among others, and gave a boost to Harry S. Truman's election campaign in 1948. Blake contributed to other Broadway musicals and revues such as "Elsie," Andre Charlot's "Revue of 1924," and Lew Leslie's "Blackbirds of 1930." For the latter, he and Andy Razaf wrote "Baby Mine," *"That Lindy Hop,"* "My Handy Man Ain't Handy No More," and another substantial hit, the lovely reflective ballad "Memories of You." After one more Broadway musical, "Swing It" (1937), Blake reunited with Sissle for a time, and then spent much of World War II entertaining troops with the USO.

In the '50s Blake demonstrated and lectured on ragtime, but his day seemed to be past. Then, in 1969, at the age of 86, Blake's fortunes were revived when John Hammond recorded the old man playing piano and talking about his life. The concurrent vogue for ragtime helped his comeback and the next years were filled with honors, recordings, concerts, festivals, and television appearances; in 1978, his life and music were celebrated in a Broadway show, "Eubie," which was also televised in the USA and later staged in London. In 1983 Blake contributed to the lists of favorite quotations when, on the occasion of his 100th birthday, he said: *"If I'd known I was going to live this long, I would've taken better care of myself."* He died five days later.

Wisdom for the Journey

"Never trust anyone who wants what you've got. Friend or no, envy is an overwhelming emotion." **Eubie Blake**

Bessie Smith

(April 15, 1894-September 26, 1937) was an American blues singer.

Sometimes referred to as *"The Empress of the Blues,"* Smith was the most popular female blues singer of the 1920s and 1930s. She is often regarded as one of the greatest singers of her era and, along with Louis Armstrong, a major influence on subsequent jazz vocalists.

Life

The 1900 census indicates that Bessie Smith was born in Chattanooga, Tennessee in July 1892. However, the 1910 census recorded her birthday as April 15, 1894, a date that appears on all subsequent documents and was observed by the entire Smith family. Census data also contributes to controversy about the size of her family. The 1870 and 1880 censuses report three older half-siblings, while later interviews with Smith's family and contemporaries did not include these individuals among her siblings.

Bessie Smith was the daughter of Laura (née Owens) and William Smith. William Smith was a laborer and part-time Baptist preacher (he was listed in the 1870 census as a "minister of the gospel", in Moulton, Lawrence, Alabama.) He died before his daughter could remember him. By the time she was nine, she had lost her mother as well. Her older sister Viola took charge of caring for her siblings.[

To earn money for their impoverished household, Bessie Smith and her brother Andrew began acting on the streets of Chattanooga as a duo: she singing and dancing, he accompanying her on guitar. Their favorite location was in front of the White Elephant Saloon at Thirteenth and Elm streets in the heart of the city's African-American community.

In 1904, her oldest brother, Clarence, covertly left home by joining a small traveling troupe owned by Moses Stokes. "If Bessie had been old enough, she would have gone with him," said Clarence's widow, Maud. "That's why he left without telling her, but Clarence told me she was ready, even then. Of course, she was only a child."

In 1912, Clarence returned to Chattanooga with the Stokes troupe. He arranged for its managers, Lonnie and Cora Fisher, to give Smith an audition. She was hired as a dancer rather than a singer, because the company also included the notable singer Ma Rainey.

By the early 1920s, Smith had starred with Sidney Bechet in *How Come?*, a musical that made its way to Broadway. She spent several years working out of Atlanta, Georgia's 81 Theater, and performing in black theaters along the East Coast. Following a run-in with the producer of *How Come?*, Smith was replaced by Alberta Hunter and returned to Philadelphia, where she had taken up residence.

There, she met and fell in love with Jack Gee, a security guard whom she married on June 7, 1923, just as her first recordings were being released by Columbia Records. ***The marriage was a stormy one, with infidelity on both sides.*** During the marriage, Smith became the biggest headliner on the black Theater Owners Booking Association (T.O.B.A.) circuit. Her show sometimes featured as many as 40 troupers and made her the highest-paid black entertainer of her day. Gee was impressed by the money, but never adjusted to show business life, or to Smith's bisexuality. In 1929, when Smith learned of Gee's affair with Gertrude Saunders, another performer, she ended the marriage, though she never sought a divorce.

Smith eventually found a common-law husband in an old friend, Richard Morgan, who was Lionel Hampton's uncle and the antithesis of her husband. She stayed with him until her death.

Career

All contemporary accounts indicate that while Rainey did not teach Smith to sing, she probably helped her develop a stage presence. Smith began forming her own act around 1913, at Atlanta's "81" Theater. By 1920, Smith had established a reputation in the South and along the Eastern Seaboard.

In 1920, sales figures for "Crazy Blues," an Okeh Records recording by singer Mamie Smith (no relation) pointed to a new market. The recording industry had not directed its product to blacks, but the success of the record led to a search for female blues singers. Bessie Smith was signed by Columbia Records in 1923 and her first session for Columbia was February 15, 1923. For most of 1923, her records were issued on Columbia's regular A—series; when the label decided to establish a "race records" series, Smith's "Cemetery Blues" (September 26, 1923) was the first issued.

She scored a big hit with her first release, a coupling of "Gulf Coast Blues" and "Downhearted Blues", which its composer Alberta Hunter had already turned into a hit on the Paramount label. Smith became a headliner on the black T.O.B.A. circuit and rose to become its top attraction in the 1920s. *Working a heavy theater schedule during the winter months and doing tent tours the rest of the year (eventually traveling in her own railroad car), Smith became the highest-paid black entertainer of her day. Columbia nicknamed her "Queen of the Blues," but a PR-minded press soon upgraded her title to "Empress".*

She made some 160 recordings for Columbia, often accompanied by the finest musicians of the day, most notably Louis Armstrong, James P. Johnson, Joe Smith, Charlie Green and Fletcher Henderson.

Broadway

Smith's career was cut short by a combination of the Great Depression (which all but put the recording industry out of business) and the advent of "talkies", which spelled the end for vaudeville. She never stopped performing, however. While the days of elaborate vaudeville shows were over, Smith continued touring and occasionally singing in clubs. In 1929, she appeared in a Broadway flop called *Pansy*, a musical in which top critics said she was the only asset.

Film

In 1929, Smith made her only film appearance, starring in a two-reeler titled *St. Louis Blues*, based on W. C. Handy's song of the same name. In the film, directed by Dudley Murphy and shot in Astoria, she sings the title song accompanied by members of Fletcher Henderson's orchestra, the Hall Johnson Choir, pianist James P. Johnson and a string section—a musical environment radically different from any found on her recordings.

Swing era

In 1933, John Hammond, who also mentored Billie Holiday, asked Smith to record four sides for Okeh (which had been acquired by Columbia Records in 1925). He claimed to have found her in semi-obscurity, working as a hostess in a speakeasy on Philadelphia's Ridge Avenue. Bessie Smith worked at Art's Cafe on Ridge Avenue, but not as a hostess and not until the summer of 1936. In 1933, when she made the Okeh sides, Bessie was still touring. Hammond was known for his selective memory and gratuitous embellishments.

Bessie Smith was paid a non-royalty fee of $37.50 for each selection and these Okeh sides, which were her last recordings. Made November 24, 1933, they serve as a hint of the transformation she made in her performances as she shifted her blues artistry into something that fit the "swing era". The relatively modern accompaniment is notable. The band included such swing era musicians as trombonist Jack Teagarden, trumpeter Frankie Newton, tenor saxophonist Chu Berry, pianist Buck Washington, guitarist Bobby Johnson, and bassist Billy Taylor. Benny Goodman, who happened to be recording with Ethel Waters in the adjoining studio, dropped by and is barely audible on one selection. Hammond was not entirely pleased with the results, preferring to have Smith revisit her old blues groove. Her "Take Me for a Buggy Ride" and "Gimme a Pigfoot" continues to be ranked among her most popular recordings.

Death

On September 26, 1937, Smith was critically injured in a car accident while traveling along U.S. Route 61 between Memphis, Tennessee, and Clarksdale, Mississippi. Her lover, Richard Morgan, was driving and, probably mesmerized by the long stretch of straight road, misjudged the speed of a slow-moving truck ahead of him. Tire marks at the scene suggested that Morgan tried to avoid the truck by driving around its left side, but he hit the rear of the truck side-on at high speed. The tailgate of the truck sheared off the wooden roof of Smith's old Packard. Smith, who was in the passenger seat, probably with her right arm or elbow out the window, took the full brunt of the impact. Morgan escaped without injuries.

The first people on the scene were a Memphis surgeon, Dr. Hugh Smith (no relation), and his fishing partner Henry Broughton. In the early 1970s, Dr. Smith gave a detailed account of his experience to Bessie's biographer Chris Albertson. This is the most reliable eyewitness testimony about the events surrounding Bessie Smith's death.

After stopping at the accident scene, Dr. Smith examined Bessie Smith, who was lying in the middle of the road with obviously severe injuries. He estimated she had lost about a half-pint of blood, and immediately noted a major traumatic injury to her right arm; it had been almost completely severed at the elbow. But Dr. Smith was emphatic that this arm injury alone did not cause her death. Although the light was poor, he observed only minor head injuries. He attributed her death to extensive and severe crush injuries to the entire right side of her body, consistent with a "sideswipe" collision.

Broughton and Dr. Smith moved the singer to the shoulder of the road. Dr. Smith dressed her arm injury with a clean handkerchief and asked Broughton to go to a house about 500 feet off the road to call an ambulance.

By the time Broughton returned, about 25 minutes had elapsed since the accident and Bessie Smith was in shock. Time passed with no sign of the ambulance, so Dr. Smith suggested that they take her into Clarksdale in his car. He and Broughton had almost finished clearing the back seat when they heard the sound of a car approaching at high speed. Dr. Smith flashed his lights in warning, but the oncoming car failed to stop and plowed into the doctor's car at full speed. It sent his car careening into Bessie Smith's overturned Packard, completely wrecking it. The oncoming car ricocheted off Dr. Smith's car into the ditch on the right, barely missing Broughton and Bessie Smith.

The young couple in the new car did not have life-threatening injuries. Two ambulances arrived on the scene from Clarksdale; one from the black hospital, summoned by Mr. Broughton, the other from the white hospital, acting on a report from the truck driver, who had not seen the accident victims.

Bessie Smith was taken to Clarksdale's Afro-American Hospital where her right arm was amputated. She died that morning without regaining consciousness. After Smith's death, an often repeated but now discredited story emerged about the circumstances; namely, that she had died as a result of having been refused admission to a "whites only" hospital in Clarksdale. Jazz writer/producer John Hammond gave this account in an article in the November 1937 issue of *Down Beat* magazine. The circumstances of Smith's death and the rumor promoted by Hammond formed the basis for Edward Albee's 1959 one-act play *The Death of Bessie Smith*.

"The Bessie Smith ambulance would not have gone to a white hospital, you can forget that." Dr. Smith told Albertson. "Down in the Deep South cotton country, no ambulance driver, or white driver, would even have thought of putting a colored person off in a hospital for white folks."

Smith's funeral was held in Philadelphia on Monday, October 4, 1937. Her body was originally laid out at Upshur's funeral home. As word of her death spread through Philadelphia's black community, the body had to be moved to the O.V. Catto Elks Lodge to accommodate the estimated 10,000 mourners who filed past her coffin on Sunday, October 3. Contemporary newspapers reported that her funeral was attended by about seven thousand people. Far fewer mourners attended the burial at Mount Lawn Cemetery, in nearby Sharon Hill. Gee thwarted all efforts to purchase a stone for his estranged wife, once or twice pocketing money raised for that purpose.

The grave remained unmarked until August 7, 1970, when a tombstone—paid for by singer Janis Joplin and Juanita Green, who as a child had done housework for Smith—was erected.

The Afro-American Hospital, now the Riverside Hotel in Clarksdale, was the site of the dedication of the fourth historic marker on the Mississippi Blues Trail.

Quotes:

"White folks hear the blues come out, but they don't know how it got there."
Ma Rainey

"It is from the blues that all that may be called American music derives its most distinctive characteristics."—**James Weldon Johnson**

Marian Anderson

Marian Anderson (February 27, 1897-April 8, 1993) was an American contralto and *one of the most celebrated singers of the twentieth century*. Music critic Alan Blyth said "Her voice was a rich, vibrant contralto of intrinsic beauty." Most of her singing career was spent performing in concert and recital in major music venues and with major orchestras throughout the United States and Europe between 1925 and 1965. Although she was offered contracts to perform roles with many important European opera companies, Anderson declined all of these, preferring to perform in concert and recital only. She did, however, perform opera arias within her concerts and recitals. She made many recordings that reflected her broad performance repertoire of everything from concert literature to lieder to opera to traditional American songs and spirituals.

An African-American, Anderson became an important figure in the struggle for black artists to overcome racial prejudice in the United States during the mid twentieth century. In 1939, the Daughters of the American Revolution (DAR) refused permission for Anderson to sing to an integrated audience in Constitution Hall. Their race-driven refusal placed Anderson into the spotlight of the international community on a level usually only found by high profile celebrities and politicians. With the aid of President Franklin D. Roosevelt and First Lady Eleanor Roosevelt, Anderson performed a critically acclaimed open-air concert on Easter Sunday, in 1939 on the steps of the Lincoln Memorial in Washington, D.C. to a crowd of more than 75,000 people and a radio audience in the millions. She continued to break barriers for black artists in the United States, notably becoming the first black person, American or otherwise, to perform at the Metropolitan Opera in New York City on January 7, 1955. Her performance as Ulrica in Giuseppe Verdi's Un ballo in maschera at the Met was the only time she sang an opera role on stage. Anderson later became an important symbol of grace and beauty during the civil rights movement in the 1960s, notably singing at the March on Washington for Jobs and Freedom in 1963. She also worked for several years as a delegate to the United Nations Human Rights Committee and as a "goodwill ambassadress" for the United States Department of State. The recipient of numerous awards and honors, Anderson was notably awarded the Presidential Medal of Freedom in 1963, the Kennedy Center Honors in 1978, the National Medal of Arts in 1986, and a Grammy Lifetime Achievement Award in 1991.

Early life and career

Anderson was born on February 27, 1897 in Philadelphia, Pennsylvania, the daughter of John Berkley Anderson and the former Annie Delilah Rucker. Her father sold ice and coal in downtown Philadelphia at the Reading Terminal and eventually opened a small liquor business as well, ironic for a man who did not drink alcohol himself. Prior to her marriage, Anderson's mother had briefly attended the Virginia Seminary and College in Lynchburg and had worked as a schoolteacher in Virginia. However, having not completed a degree, she was unable to teach in Philadelphia, *a law that was only applied to black teachers and not white ones.* She therefore earned an income looking after small children. Marian was the eldest of the three Anderson children. Her two sisters, Alice (later spelled Alyse) (1899-1965) and Ethel (1902-1990), also became singers. Ethel (married name DePreist) became mother to noted conductor James DePreist.

Anderson's parents were both devout Christians and the whole family was highly active in the Union Baptist Church in South Philadelphia. Marian's Aunt Mary (John Berkley's sister) was particularly active in the church's musical life and, noticing her niece's talent, convinced her to join the junior church choir at the age of six. As a part of the choir she got to perform solos and duets, often with Aunt Mary who also had a fine voice. Marian was also taken by her aunt to concerts at local churches, the YMCA, and other community music events throughout the city. Anderson credited her aunt's influence as the reason she pursued a singing career. Beginning as young as six, her aunt arranged for Marian to sing for local functions where she was often paid 25 or 50 cents for singing a few songs. As she got into her early teens, Marian began to make as much as four or five dollars for singing; a considerable amount of money for the early 20th century. At the age of 10, Marian joined the People's Chorus under the direction of singer Emma Azalia Hackley, where she was often given solos.

When Marian was 12, her father was accidentally struck on the head while at work at the Reading Terminal, just a few weeks before Christmas of 1909. He died of heart failure a month later at age 34. Marian and her family moved into the home of her father's parents, Grandpa Benjamin and Grandma Isabella Anderson. **Her grandfather had been born a slave and had experienced emancipation in the 1860s.** He was the first of the Anderson family to settle in South Philadelphia, and when Marian moved into his home the two became very close. Sadly he died only about a year after the family moved in.

Throughout her teenage years, Marian remained active in her church's musical activities, now heavily involved in the adult choir. She attended Stanton Grammar School, graduating from there in the summer of 1912. Her family, however, could not afford to send her to high school, nor could they pay for any music lessons. Undaunted, Marian continued to perform wherever she could and learn from anyone who was willing to teach her. She joined the Baptists' Young People's Union and the Camp Fire Girls which provided her with some limited musical opportunities. Eventually the directors of the People's Chorus and the pastor of her church, Reverend Wesley Parks, along with other leaders of the black community, banded together to help out Marian. They raised the money she needed to get singing lessons with Mary S. Patterson and to attend South Philadelphia High School, from which she graduated in 1921.

After high school, Marian applied to an all-white music school, the Philadelphia Music Academy (now University of the Arts), but was turned away because she was black. The woman working the admissions counters replied, "We don't take colored" when she tried to apply. Undaunted, Anderson pursued studies privately with Giuseppe Boghetti and Agnes Reifsnyder in her native city through the continued support of the Philadelphia black community. She met Boghetti through the principal of her high school. Marian auditioned for him singing 'Deep River' and he was immediately brought to tears.

In 1925 Anderson got her first big break when she won first prize in a singing competition sponsored by the New York Philharmonic. As the winner she got to perform in concert with the orchestra on August 27, 1925; a performance that scored immediate success with both audience and music critics. Anderson remained in New York to pursue further studies with Frank La Forge. During the time Arthur Judson, whom she had met through the NYP, became her manager. **Over the next several years, she made a number of concert appearances in the United States, but racial prejudice prevented her career from gaining much momentum.** In 1928, she sang for the first time at Carnegie Hall. Eventually she decided to go to Europe where she spent a number of months studying with Mme Charles Cahier before launching a highly successful European singing tour.

European fame and the 1939 Lincoln Memorial concert

In 1930 Anderson made her European debut in a concert at Wigmore Hall in London where she was received enthusiastically. She spent the early 1930s touring throughout Europe where she did not encounter the racial prejudices she had experienced in America. In the summer of 1930 she went to Scandinavia where she met the Finnish pianist Kosti Vehanen who became her regular accompanist and her vocal coach for many years. She also met Jean Sibelius through Vehanen after he had heard her in a concert in Helsinki. Moved by her performance, Sibelius invited them to his home and asked his wife to bring champagne in place of the traditional coffee. Sibelius commented to Anderson of her performance that he felt that she had been able to penetrate the Nordic soul. The two struck up an immediate friendship which further blossomed into a professional partnership, and for many years Sibelius altered and composed songs for Anderson to perform. He notably made a new arrangement of the song *Solitude* and dedicated it to Anderson in 1939. Originally *The Jewish Girl's Song* from his 1906 incidental music to *Belshazzar's Feast*, it later became the "Solitude" section of the orchestral suite derived from the incidental music.

In 1934 impresario Sol Hurok offered Anderson a better contract than she previously had with Arthur Judson. He became her manager for the rest of her performing career and it is only through his persuasion that she came back to perform in America. In 1935, Anderson made her first recital appearance in New York at Town Hall which received highly favorable reviews by music critics. She spent the next four years touring throughout the United States and Europe. She was offered opera roles by several European houses but, due to her lack of acting experience, Anderson declined all of these offers. She did, however, record a number of opera arias in the studio which became bestsellers.

Anderson, accompanied by Vehanen, continued to tour throughout Europe during the mid 1930s. She visited Eastern European capitals and Russia and returned again to Scandinavia, where "Marian fever" had spread to small towns and villages where she had thousands of fans. She quickly became a favorite of many conductors and composers of major European orchestras, and drew a large fan base among European audiences. **During a 1935 tour in Salzburg, the famed conductor Arturo Toscanini told her she had a voice "heard once in a hundred years."** Once he heard her sing, he knew instantly that with a rich voice like hers, there was no way that she could fail

In the late 1930s, Anderson gave about 70 recitals a year in the United States. Although by now quite famous, her stature did not completely end the prejudice she confronted as a young black singer touring the United States. She was still denied rooms in certain

American hotels and was not allowed to eat in certain American restaurants.

In 1939, the Daughters of the American Revolution (DAR) refused permission for Anderson to sing to an integrated audience in Constitution Hall. At the time, Washington D.C. was a segregated city and black patrons were upset that they had to sit at the back of Constitution Hall. The District of Columbia Board of Education also declined a request to use the auditorium of a white public high school. As a result of the ensuing furor, thousands of DAR members, including First Lady Eleanor Roosevelt, resigned.

The Roosevelt's, with Walter White, then-executive secretary of the National Association for the Advancement of Colored People, and Anderson's manager, impresario Sol Hurok, then persuaded Secretary of the Interior Harold L. Ickes to arrange an open air Marian Anderson concert on the steps of the Lincoln Memorial. The concert was performed on Easter Sunday, April 9, and Anderson was accompanied, per usual, by Vehanen. They began the performance with a dignified and stirring rendition of "My Country, 'Tis of Thee". The event attracted a crowd of more than 75,000 of all colors and was a sensation with a national radio audience of millions.

Mid life and career

During World War II and the Korean War, Marian Anderson participated by entertaining the troops in hospitals and bases. In 1943, Anderson finally sang at Constitution Hall at the invitation of the DAR to an integrated audience as part of a benefit for the American Red Cross. She said of the event, "When I finally walked onto the stage of Constitution Hall, I felt no different than I had in other halls. There was no sense of triumph. I felt that it was a beautiful concert hall and I was very happy to sing there." *By contrast, the District of Columbia Board of Education continued to bar her from using the high school auditorium in the District of Columbia.*

On July 17, 1943, in Bethel, Connecticut, Anderson became the second wife of a man who had asked her to marry him when they were teenagers, architect Orpheus H. Fisher (1900—1986), known as *King*. By this marriage she had a stepson, James Fisher, from her husband's previous marriage to Ida Gould. The couple had purchased a 100-acre (0.40 km²) farm in Danbury, Connecticut, three years earlier in 1940 after an exhaustive search throughout New York, New Jersey and Connecticut. *Many purchases were attempted but thwarted by property sellers due to racial discrimination.* The Danbury property transaction was initially disputed by the seller as well, after he discovered the couple was African Americans. Through the years Fisher built many outbuildings on the property that became known as Marianna Farm, including an acoustic rehearsal studio he designed for his wife. The property remained Anderson's home for more than 50 years.

On January 7, 1955, Anderson became the first African-American to perform with the Metropolitan Opera in New York. On that occasion, she sang the part of Ulrica in Giuseppe Verdi's *Un ballo in maschera* (opposite Zinka Milanov, then Herva Nelli, as Amelia) at the invitation of director Sir Rudolf Bing. Anderson said later about the evening, "The curtain rose on the second scene and I was there on stage, mixing the witch's brew. I trembled, and when the audience applauded and applauded before I could sing a note, I felt myself tightening into a knot." Although she never appeared with the company again after this production, Anderson was named a permanent member of the Metropolitan Opera company. The following year she published her autobiography, *My Lord, What a Morning*, which became a bestseller.

In 1957, she sang for President Dwight D. Eisenhower's inauguration and toured India and the Far East as a goodwill ambassadress through the U.S. State Department and the American National Theater and Academy. She traveled 35,000 miles (56,000 km) in 12 weeks, giving 24 concerts. After that, President Eisenhower appointed her as a delegate to the United Nations Human Rights Committee. In 1958 she was officially designated delegate to the United Nations, a formalization of her role as "goodwill ambassadress" of the U.S. which she had played earlier.

On January 20, 1961 she sang for President John F. Kennedy's inauguration, and in 1962 she performed for President Kennedy and other dignitaries in the East Room of the White House, and also toured Australia. She was active in supporting the civil rights movement during the 1960s, giving benefit concerts for the Congress of Racial Equality, the National Association for the Advancement of Colored People and the America-Israel Cultural Foundation. In 1963, she sang at the March on Washington for Jobs and Freedom. That same year she was one of the original 31 recipients of the newly reinstituted Presidential Medal of Freedom (which is awarded for "especially meritorious contributions to the security or national interest of the United States, World Peace or cultural or other significant public or private endeavors"), and she also released her album, *Snoopycat: The Adventures of Marian Anderson's Cat Snoopy*, which included short stories and songs about her beloved black cat. **In 1965, she christened the nuclear-powered ballistic-missile submarine, USS *George Washington Carver*.** That same year Anderson concluded her farewell tour, after which she retired from public performance. The international tour began at Constitution Hall on Sunday October 24, 1964 and ended at Carnegie Hall on April 18, 1965.

Later life

Although Anderson retired from singing in 1965, she continued to appear publicly. On several occasions she narrated Aaron Copland's *Lincoln Portrait*, including a performance with the Philadelphia Orchestra at Saratoga in 1976, conducted by the composer. Her achievements were recognized and honored with many prizes, including the UN Peace Prize in 1972, the University of Pennsylvania Glee Club Award of Merit in 1973, the Congressional Gold Medal in 1977, the Kennedy Center Honors in 1978, the George Peabody Medal in 1981, the National Medal of Arts in 1986, and a Grammy Award for Lifetime Achievement in 1991. In 1980, the United States Treasury Department coined a half-ounce gold commemorative medal with her likeness, and in 1984 she was the first recipient of the Eleanor Roosevelt Human Rights Award of the City of New York. She has been awarded honorary doctoral degrees from Howard University, Temple University and Smith College. She also received the Silver Buffalo Award in 1990, the highest award given to adults by the Boy Scouts of America.

In 1986, Anderson's husband, Orpheus Fisher, died after 43 years of marriage. Anderson remained in residence at Marianna Farm until 1992, one year before her death. Although the bucolic property was sold to developers, various preservationists as well as the City of Danbury fought to protect Anderson's studio. Their efforts proved successful and the Danbury Museum and Historical Society received a grant from the State of Connecticut, relocated the structure, restored it, and opened it to the public in 2004. In addition to seeing the studio, visitors can see photographs and memorabilia from milestones in Anderson's career.

Marian Anderson died of congestive heart failure on April 8, 1993, at age 96. She had suffered a stroke a month earlier. She died in Portland, Oregon at the home of her nephew, conductor James DePreist. She is interred at Eden Cemetery, in Collingdale, Pennsylvania, a suburb of Philadelphia.

Legacy

The life and art of Marian Anderson has inspired several writers and artists. In 1999 a one act musical play entitled *My Lord, What a Morning: The Marian Anderson Story* was produced by the Kennedy Center. In 2001, the 1939 documentary film, *Marian Anderson: the Lincoln Memorial Concert* was selected for preservation in the United States National Film Registry by the Library of Congress as being "culturally, historically, or aesthetically significant". Anderson's 1939 concert at the Lincoln Memorial also forms a centre point of Richard Powers' novel *The Time of Our Singing* (2003).

In 2002, scholar Molefi Kete Asante listed Marian Anderson on his list of 100 Greatest African Americans.

On January 27, 2005, a commemorative U.S. postage stamp honored Marian Anderson as part of the Black Heritage series. Anderson is also pictured on the US$5,000 Series I United States Savings Bond.

Marian Anderson Award

The Marian Anderson Award was originally established in 1943 by Anderson after she was awarded the $10,000 Bok Prize that year by the city of Philadelphia. Anderson used the award money to establish a singing competition to help support young singers; recipients of which include Camilla Williams (1943, 1944), Nathaniel Dickerson (1944), Louise Parker (1944), Rawn Spearman (1949), Georgia Laster (1951), Betty Allen (1952), Shirlee Emmons (1953), Judith Raskin (1952, 1953), Miriam Holman (1954), Shirley Verrett (1957), and Joyce Mathis (1967). Eventually the prize fund ran out of money and it was disbanded. Florence Quivar was the last recipient of this earlier award in 1976.

In 1990 the award was re-established and has dispensed $25,000 annually. In 1998 the prize was restructured with the "Marian Anderson Award" going to an established artist, not necessarily a singer, who exhibits leadership in a humanitarian area. A separate prize, the "Marian Anderson Prize for Emerging Classical Artists" is given to promising young classical singers.

Wisdom for the Journey

As human beings, our greatness lies not so much in being able to remake the world—that is the myth of the atomic age—as in being able to remake ourselves. **Mohandas Gandhi**

"I Can Do All Things through Christ Who Strengthens Me"

Philippians 4:13

Jim Thorpe

Jacobus Franciscus "Jim" Thorpe (Sac and Fox (Sauk): **Wa-Tho-Huk**) (May 28, 1888-March 28, 1953) *was an American athlete of mixed ancestry (mixed Caucasian and American Indian). Considered one of the most versatile athletes of modern sports, he won Olympic gold medals for the 1912 pentathlon and decathlon, played American football (collegiate and professional), and also played professional baseball and basketball. He lost his Olympic titles after it was found he was paid for playing two seasons of semi-professional baseball before competing in the Olympics, thus violating the amateurism rules.*

Of Native American and European American ancestry, Thorpe grew up in the Sac and Fox nation in Oklahoma. He played as part of several All-American Indian teams throughout his career, and "barnstormed" (played mainly in small towns) as a professional basketball player with a team composed entirely of American Indians.

His professional sports career ended during the Great Depression; and Thorpe struggled to earn a living after that. He worked several odd jobs, struggled with alcoholism, and lived his last years in failing health and poverty. In 1983, 30 years after his death, the International Olympic Committee (IOC) restored his former Olympic medals to him.

Early life

Information about Thorpe's birth, name, and ethnic background varies widely. He was born in Indian Territory, but no birth certificate has been found. Thorpe was generally considered born on May 28, 1888, near the town of Prague, Oklahoma. He was christened "Jacobus Franciscus Thorpe" in the Catholic Church.

Thorpe's parents were of mixed-race ancestry and both were Catholic. His father, Hiram Thorpe, had an Irish father and a Sac and Fox Indian mother. His mother, Charlotte Vieux, had a French father and a Potawatomi mother, a descendant of Chief Louis Vieux. Thorpe was raised as a Sac and Fox, and his native name was *Wa-Tho-Huk*, translated as "path lighted by great flash of lightning" or, more simply, "Bright Path". As was the custom for Sac and Fox, Thorpe was named for something occurring around the time of his birth, in this case the light brightening the path to the cabin where he was born. Thorpe's mother was Roman Catholic and raised her children in that faith, which Thorpe observed throughout his adult life.

Together with his twin brother, Charlie, Thorpe attended school in Stroud, Oklahoma at the Sac and Fox Indian Agency School. Charlie died of pneumonia when he was nine years old. Charlie had helped Jim through school. Thereafter Thorpe absconded from school on several occasions. Hiram Thorpe then sent him to the present-day Haskell Indian Nations University, in Lawrence, Kansas, so that he would not abscond again. When his mother died of childbirth complications two years later, Thorpe became depressed. After several arguments with his father, he left home to work on a horse ranch.

In 1904, Thorpe returned to his father and decided to attend Carlisle Indian Industrial School in Carlisle, Pennsylvania. There his athletic ability was recognized and he was coached by Glenn Scobey "Pop" Warner, one of the most influential coaches of early American football history. Later that year, Hiram Thorpe died from gangrene poisoning after being wounded in a hunting accident. Thorpe again dropped out of school. He resumed farm work for a few years and then returned to Carlisle Indian Industrial School, where his athletic career commenced.

College career

Thorpe reportedly began his athletic career at Carlisle in 1907 when he walked past the track and beat the school's high jumpers with an impromptu 5-ft 9-in jump while still wearing street clothes. His earliest recorded track and field results are from 1907. In addition, he also competed in football, baseball, lacrosse and even ballroom dancing, winning the 1912 inter-collegiate ballroom dancing championship. Reportedly, Pop Warner was hesitant to allow Thorpe, his best track and field athlete, to compete in a physical game such as football. Thorpe, however, convinced Warner to let him participate in some plays against the school team's defense; Warner assumed he would be tackled easily and give up the idea of playing football. Thorpe "ran around past and through them not once, but twice." He then walked over to Warner and said, "Nobody is going to tackle Jim," while flipping him the ball.

Thorpe gained nationwide attention for the first time in 1911. As a running back, defensive back, placekicker, and punter for his school's football team, Thorpe scored all of his team's points—four field goals and a touchdown—in an 18-15 upset of Harvard. His team finished the season 11-1. The next year, Carlisle won the national collegiate championship largely as a result of his efforts—he scored 25 touchdowns and 198 points. Carlisle's 1912 record included a 27-6 victory over Army. In that game, Thorpe's 92-yard touchdown was nullified by a teammate's penalty; the next play, Thorpe scored a 97-yard touchdown. Future President Dwight Eisenhower injured his knee in that game trying to tackle Thorpe. Eisenhower recalled of Thorpe in a 1961 speech, "Here and there, there are some people who are supremely endowed. My memory goes back to Jim Thorpe. He never practiced in his life, and he could do anything better than any other football player I ever saw." Thorpe was awarded All-American honors in both 1911 and 1912.

In the spring of 1912 he started training for the Olympics. He had confined his efforts to the jumps, the hurdles and the shot-put but now he undertook the pole vault, the javelin, discus, the hammer and the fifty-six-pound weight. In the Olympic trials held at Celtic Park in New York, his all-round ability stood out in all these events and so he riveted a claim to a place on the team that went to Sweden.

Olympic career

For the 1912 Summer Olympics in Stockholm, Sweden, two new multi-event disciplines were included, the pentathlon and the decathlon. A pentathlon based on the ancient Greek event had been organized at the 1906 Summer Olympics. The 1912 version consisted of the long jump, the javelin throw, 200-meter dash, the discus throw and the 1500-meter run.

The decathlon was a relatively new event of modern athletics, although it had been part of American track meets since the 1880s and a version had been featured on the program of the 1904 St. Louis Olympics. The events of the new decathlon differed slightly from the American version. Both events seemed appropriate for Thorpe, who was so versatile that he alone had constituted Carlisle's team in several track meets. He could run the 100-yard dash in 10 seconds flat, the 220 in 21.8 seconds, the 440 in 51.8 seconds, the 880 in 1:57, the mile in 4:35, the 120-yard high hurdles in 15 seconds, and the 220-yard low hurdles in 24 seconds. He could long jump 23 ft 6 in and high-jump 6 ft 5 in. He could pole vault 11 feet, put the shot 47 ft 9 in, throw the javelin 163 feet, and throw the discus 136 feet.

Thorpe entered the U.S. Olympic trials for both the pentathlon and the decathlon. He won the awards easily, winning three events, and was named to the pentathlon team, which also included future International Olympic Committee (IOC) president Avery Brundage. There were only a few candidates for the decathlon team, and the trials were cancelled.

His schedule in the Olympics was busy. Along with the decathlon and pentathlon, he competed in the long-jump and high-jump. The first competition was the pentathlon; Thorpe won four of the five events and placed third in the javelin, an event in which he had not competed before 1912. Although the pentathlon was primarily decided on place points, points were also earned for the marks achieved in the individual events. He won the gold medal. The same day, Thorpe qualified for the high-jump final. He placed fourth and also took seventh place in the long jump.

Thorpe's final event was the decathlon, his first—and as it turned out, only—Olympic decathlon. Strong competition from local favorite Hugo Wieslander was expected. Thorpe, however, easily defeated Wieslander by more than 700 points. He placed in the top four of all ten events. Thorpe's Olympic record of 8,413 points would stand for nearly two decades. Overall, Thorpe won eight of the 15 individual events of the pentathlon and decathlon.

As was the custom of the day, the medals were presented to the athletes during the closing ceremonies of the games. Along with the two gold medals, Thorpe also received two challenge prizes, which were donated by King Gustav V of Sweden for the decathlon and Czar Nicholas II of Russia for the pentathlon. Several sources recount that, when awarding Thorpe his prize, *King Gustav said, "You, sir, are the greatest athlete in the world," to which Thorpe replied, "Thanks, King."*

Thorpe's successes had not gone unnoticed at home, and he was honored with a ticker-tape parade on Broadway. He remembered later, "I heard people yelling my name, and I couldn't realize how one fellow could have so many friends."

Apart from his track and field appearance, Thorpe also played in one of two exhibition baseball games at the 1912 Olympics, which featured two teams composed of U.S. track and field athletes. It was not Thorpe's first try at baseball, as the public would soon learn.

All-Around Champion

After his victories at the Olympic Games in Sweden, on September 2, 1912, Thorpe returned to Celtic Park, the home of the Irish American Athletic Club, in Queens, New York (where he had qualified four months earlier for the Olympic Games), to compete in the Amateur Athletic Union's All-Around Championship. Competing against Bruno Brodd of the Irish

American Athletic Club, and J. Bredemus of Princeton University, he won seven of the ten events contested, and came in second in the remaining three. With a total point score of 7,476 points, Thorpe broke the previous record of 7,385 points set in 1909, (also set at Celtic Park), by Martin Sheridan, the champion athlete of the Irish American Athletic Club. Sheridan, a five-time Olympic gold medalist, was present to watch his record broken and approached Thorpe after the event. He shook his hand saying, "Jim my boy, you're a great man. I never expect to look upon a finer athlete." *Sheridan told a reporter from The New York World, "Thorpe is the greatest athlete that ever lived. He has me beaten fifty ways. Even when I was in my prime, I could not do what he did today."*

Controversy

In 1913, strict rules regarding amateurism were in effect for athletes participating in the Olympics. Athletes who received money prizes for competitions, who were sports teachers, or who had competed previously against professionals, were not considered amateurs and were not allowed to compete.

In late January 1913, U.S. newspapers published stories announcing that Thorpe had played professional baseball. It is not entirely certain which newspaper first published the story; the earliest article found is from the *Providence Times*, but the *Worcester Telegram* is usually mentioned as the first. Thorpe had indeed played professional baseball in the Eastern Carolina League for Rocky Mount, North Carolina, in 1909 and 1910, receiving meager pay; reportedly as little as $2 ($47 in current dollar terms) a game and as much as $35 ($815 in current dollar terms) a week. *College players, in fact, regularly spent summers playing professionally, but most used aliases, unlike Thorpe.*

Although the public did not seem to care much about Thorpe's past, the Amateur Athletic Union (AAU), and especially its secretary James Edward Sullivan, took the case very seriously. Thorpe wrote a letter to Sullivan, in which he admitted playing professional baseball:

> *". . . I hope I will be partly excused by the fact that I was simply an Indian schoolboy and did not know all about such things. In fact, I did not know that I was doing wrong, because I was doing what I knew several other college men had done, except that they did not use their own names . . . ."*

His letter did not help. The AAU decided to withdraw Thorpe's amateur status retroactively and asked the International Olympic Commission (IOC) to do the same. Later that year, the IOC unanimously decided to strip Thorpe of his Olympic titles, medals, and awards, and declared him a professional.

Although Thorpe had played for money, the AAU and IOC did not follow the rules for disqualification. The rulebook for the 1912 Olympics stated that protests had to be made *within* 30 days from the closing ceremonies of the games. The first newspaper reports did not appear until January 1913, about six months after the Stockholm Games had concluded. There also is some evidence that Thorpe's amateur status had been questioned long before the Olympics, but the AAU had ignored the issue until being confronted with it in 1913.

The only positive element of this affair for Thorpe was that, as soon as the news was reported that he had been declared a professional, he received offers from professional sports clubs.

Professional career
A free agent

Declared a rare free agent during the era of the reserve clause, Jim Thorpe had a choice of baseball teams for which to play. He refused a starting position with the Saint Louis Browns to be a reserve with the New York Giants. One of the immediate benefits of joining the team came that October, when the Giants joined the Chicago White Sox for a world tour. Barnstorming across the United States and then around the world, Thorpe was the celebrity of the world tour. Everywhere the teams went; Thorpe increased their publicity and increased the tour's attendance receipts. He met with the Pope and the last khedive of Egypt, and played before 20,000 people in London including King George V. While in Rome, Thorpe was filmed wrestling with another baseball player on the floor of the Coliseum. No copy of that film is known to exist.

Baseball, football, and basketball

Thorpe signed with the New York Giants baseball club in 1913 and played sporadically with them as an outfielder for three seasons. After playing in the minor leagues with the Milwaukee Brewers in 1916, he returned to the Giants in 1917 but was sold to the Cincinnati Reds early in the season. In the "double no-hitter" between Fred Toney of the Reds and Hippo Vaughn of the Chicago Cubs, Thorpe drove in the winning run in the 10th inning. Late in the season, he was sold back to the Giants. Again, he played sporadically for the Giants in 1918 and was traded to the Boston Braves on May 21, 1919, for Pat Ragan. In his career, he amassed 91 runs scored, 82 runs batted in and a.252 batting average over 289 games. He continued to play baseball with teams in the minor leagues until 1922.

But Thorpe had not abandoned football either. He first played professional football in 1913, as a member of the Indiana-based Pine Village Pros, a team that had a several-season winning streak against local teams during the 1910s. By 1915, Thorpe had signed with the Canton Bulldogs They paid him $250 ($5,359 in current dollar terms) a game, a tremendous wage at the time. Before Thorpe's signing, Canton was averaging 1,200 fans a game; 8,000 showed up for his debut against Massillon. The team won titles in 1916, 1917, and 1919. *Thorpe reportedly ended the 1919 championship game by kicking a wind-assisted 95-yard punt from his team's own 5-yard line, effectively putting the game out of reach. In 1920, the Bulldogs were one of 14 teams to form the American Professional Football Association (APFA), which would become the National Football League (NFL) two years later.* Thorpe was nominally the APFA's first president; however, he spent most of the year playing for Canton and a year later was replaced by Joseph Carr. He continued to play for Canton, coaching the team as well. Between 1921 and 1923, Thorpe played for the LaRue, Ohio, and (Marion County, Ohio) Oorang Indians, an all-Native American team. Although the team record was 3-6 in 1922, and 1-10 in 1923, Thorpe played well and was selected for the *Green Bay Press-Gazette's* first All-NFL team in 1923 (the Press-Gazette's team would later be formalized by the NFL as the league's official All-NFL team in 1931).

Thorpe never played for an NFL championship team. He retired from professional football at age 41, having played 52 NFL games for six teams from 1920 to 1928.

Until 2005, most of Thorpe's biographers were unaware of his basketball career. A ticket discovered in an old book that year revealed his career in basketball. By 1926, he was the main feature of the "World Famous Indians" of LaRue, which sponsored traveling football, baseball, and basketball teams. "Jim Thorpe and His World-Famous Indians" barnstormed for at least two years (1927-28) in parts of New York, Pennsylvania, and Marion, Ohio. Although pictures of Thorpe in his WFI basketball uniform were printed on postcards and published in newspapers, this period of his life was not well documented.

In 1926, Thorpe married Freeda V. Kirkpatrick (b.September 19, 1905, d. March 2, 2007). She was working for the manager of the baseball team for which he was playing at the time. They had four sons: Carl, William, Richard and John "Jack". William, Richard and Jack survived their mother, who divorced their father in 1941 after 15 years of marriage.

Lastly, Thorpe married Patricia Askew, who was with him when he died.

Later life

After his athletic career, Thorpe struggled to provide for his family. He found it difficult to work a non-sports job and never held a job for an extended period of time. During the Great Depression in particular, Thorpe had various jobs, among others as an extra for several movies, usually playing an American Indian chief in Westerns. He also worked as a construction worker, a doorman (bouncer), a security guard, and a ditch digger, and he briefly joined the United States Merchant Marine in 1945.Thorpe was a chronic alcoholic during his later life.

By the 1950s, Thorpe had no money left. When he was hospitalized for lip cancer in 1950, he was admitted as a charity case. At a press conference announcing the procedure, Thorpe's wife Patricia wept and pleaded for help, saying, "[W]e're broke . . . . Jim has nothing but his name and his memories. He has spent money on his own people and has given it away. He has often been exploited."

Death

In early 1953, Thorpe suffered his third heart failure, while eating dinner with his wife Patricia Askew in their home in Lomita, California. He was briefly revived by artificial respiration and was able to speak to those around him, but lost consciousness shortly afterward and died on March 28 at the age of 64 years.

Racism

Thorpe, half Caucasian, was raised as an American Indian. His accomplishments occurred during a period of racial inequality in the United States. It has been often suggested that his medals were stripped because of his ethnicity. While it is difficult to prove this, the public comment at the time largely reflected this view. At the time Thorpe won his gold medals, not all Native Americans were recognized as US citizens. (The US government had wanted them to make concessions to adopt European-American ways to receive such recognition.) All American Indians were not granted citizenship until 1924.

Legacy
Olympic awards reinstated

Over the years, supporters of Thorpe attempted to have his Olympic titles reinstated. US Olympic officials, including former teammate and later president of the IOC Avery Brundage, rebuffed several attempts, with Brundage once saying, "Ignorance is no excuse." Most persistent were author Robert Wheeler and his wife, Florence Ridlon. They succeeded in having the AAU and United States Olympic Committee (USOC) overturn their decision and restore Thorpe's amateur status prior to 1913.

In 1982, Wheeler and Ridlon established the Jim Thorpe Foundation and gained support from the US Congress. Armed with this support and evidence from 1912 proving Thorpe's disqualification had occurred after the 30-day time period allowed by Olympics rules, they succeeded in making the case to the IOC. In October 1982, the IOC Executive Committee approved Thorpe's reinstatement. In an unusual ruling, they declared that Thorpe was co-champion with Bie and Wieslander, although both athletes had always said they considered Thorpe to be the only champion. In a ceremony on January 18, 1983, the IOC presented two of Thorpe's children, Gale and Bill, with commemorative medals. Thorpe's original medals were held by museums but were stolen and have not been recovered.

Honors

Thorpe's monument, featuring the quote from Gustav V, still stands there. The grave rests on a mound of soil from Thorpe's native Oklahoma and from the stadium where he won his Olympic medals.

Thorpe's achievements received great acclaim from sports journalists, both during his lifetime and since his death. In 1950, an Associated Press poll of almost 400 sportswriters and broadcasters voted Thorpe the "greatest athlete" of the first half of the 20th century. The same year, the Associated Press named Thorpe the "greatest American football player" of the first half of the century. In 1999, the Associated Press placed him third on its list of top athletes of the century, after Babe Ruth and Michael Jordan. ESPN ranked Thorpe seventh on their list of best North American athletes of the century.

President Richard Nixon, as authorized by Senate Joint Resolution 73, proclaimed Monday, April 16, 1973 as "Jim Thorpe Day" to increase his national recognition. In 1986, the Jim Thorpe Association established an award in his name. The Jim Thorpe Award is awarded annually to the best defensive back in college football. The annual Thorpe Cup athletics meeting is named in his honor.

Jim Thorpe, Pennsylvania

Thorpe's wife Patricia was angry after his death when the government of Oklahoma would not erect a memorial to honor him. When she heard that the small Pennsylvania towns of Mauch Chunk and East Mauch Chunk were desperately seeking to attract business, she made a deal with officials. *The towns bought Thorpe's remains, erected a monument to him, merged and renamed the newly united town in his honor, Jim Thorpe, Pennsylvania. Thorpe had never been there.*

In June 2010, Thorpe's son, Jack, filed a federal lawsuit against the borough of Jim Thorpe, seeking to have his father's remains returned to his homeland and re-interred near other family members in Oklahoma. Citing the Native American Graves Protection and Repatriation Act, Jack Thorpe is arguing to bring his father's remains to the reservation in Oklahoma. There Thorpe's remains would be buried near his father, sisters, and brother, and would be one mile away from the place he was born. Jack Thorpe says the agreement between his stepmother and borough officials was made against the wishes of other family members. They want him buried in Native American land.

Film

Thorpe was memorialized in the film *Jim Thorpe—All-American* (1951) starring Burt Lancaster, with Billy Gray performing as Thorpe as a child. The film was directed by Michael Curtiz. Although Thorpe was listed as a consultant in the credits, he did not earn any money for the movie. In 1931, during the Great Depression, he had sold the film rights to his life story to MGM for $1,500 ($21,400 in current dollar terms). The movie included archival footage of the 1912 and 1932 Olympics, as well as of a banquet in which Thorpe was honored. Thorpe was seen in some long shots in the film; one scene had Thorpe as a coaching assistant. It was also distributed in the United Kingdom, where it was called *Man of Bronze*.

In the 1930s, however, Jim Thorpe appeared in several short films and features. Usually, his roles were little more than cameo appearances.

Identity Theft

Ironically; in the movie about his life, Burt Lancaster, a white actor of Irish descend, was cast in the role of Jim Thorp.

Tony Curtis another white actor of Jewish descend was cast in the role of Ira Hayes the Native American who became a hero for helping to raise the flag on Iwo Jima.

Food for Thought

When all the trees have been cut down, when all the animals have been hunted, when all the waters are polluted, when all the air is unsafe to breathe, only then will you discover you cannot eat money.

Cree Prophecy

Sidney Bechet

(Born May 14, 1897, New Orleans, La., U.S.—died May 14, 1959, Paris, France) U.S. saxophonist. He took up the clarinet at age six, later switching to the more powerful soprano saxophone. His emergence as a soloist from the New Orleans tradition of collective improvisation (see Dixieland) established his reputation in the mid-1920s. He produced a large, warm tone with a wide and rapid vibrato. His mastery of drama and his use of critically timed deviations in pitch ("note bending") had a long-lasting influence, because they were absorbed by his disciple Johnny Hodges. From the late 1940s he was based in Paris.

Musically educated on the streets and cabarets of New Orleans, clarinetist and alto-saxophonist Sidney Bechet (1897-1959) emerged as a major exponent of early jazz. He was to the alto-saxophone what Louis Armstrong had been to the trumpet. Bechet helped set the standard for his instrument, inspiring jazzmen like John Coltrane to study the New Orleans master's tone and immaculate phrasing.

One of seven children, **Sidney Bechet was born on May 14, 1897, in New Orleans, Louisiana. His father, the son of a slave who performed in the city's Congo Square dances, shared a passion for music.** A shoemaker and able dancer, Bechet's father encouraged his children to take up the study of music. As a Creole of color, Bechet grew up within the musical world of New Orleans. Running along parades in "the second line," he watched brass bands play marches and ragtime numbers. Accompanied by his mother Josephine, he attended operas and listened to circus bands. Around age six, Bechet took his older brother Leonard's clarinet and began practicing behind the family home. After she discovered him playing, his mother, instead of punishing him for taking the clarinet, had Bechet play for his older brother. Impressed by his brother's precocious playing, Leonard eventually invited him to join his family-based brass band that featured four of his brothers. Soon after, he sat in with trumpeter Freddie Keppard, marched in Manuel Perez's band, and took lessons from clarinetists George Baquet, Louis de Lisle "Big Eye" Nelson, and Lorenzo Tio.

Introduction to Louis Armstrong

By age twelve Bechet performed with a number of bands including John Robichaux's Orchestra. Around 1908 he performed with trumpeter Bunk Johnson who introduced him to Louis Armstrong. Bechet and Armstrong, along with a drummer, played on the back of a furniture truck, advertising Saturday night boxing. Composer and bandleader, Clarence Williams, in search of a band to promote the sale of his sheet music, hired Bechet to accompany him on a tour. Presuming that the tour was heading north, Bechet and his fellow band members were disappointed when they found themselves in Texas, plugging Williams' numbers in local dime stores. In Galveston, Bechet and the band's pianist Louis Wade quit and made their way back to New Orleans.

Bechet continued to build a reputation as one of the premiere clarinetists in New Orleans. As Martin Williams pointed out in *Jazz Masters of New Orleans*, "It is important to remember . . . that Bechet was then not just a kid in the opinion of New Orleans players. *While still in his teens, he was acknowledged as one of the best clarinetists in the city—to many the best.*"

In the summer of 1917 Bechet embarked on a Southern and Midwestern tour with the Bruce and Bruce Touring Company. The group's last stop was Chicago. Bechet remained in the city and joined Lawrence Duhe's band at the De Luxe Cafe. He then performed with Freddie Keppard's band at the Dreamland and occasionally worked with King Oliver at the De Luxe. In 1919 he briefly rejoined Keppard at the Royal Gardens and took a late-hour job at the Pekin Theatre with the band of ragtime pianist, Tony Jackson.

Joined Southern Syncopated Orchestra

While performing in Chicago Bechet attracted the attention of Will Marion Cook, a classically trained composer. Cook invited him to join his Southern Syncopated Orchestra. As Bechet recounted in his autobiography, *Treat It Gentle*, "Will knew I couldn't read notes . . . and told me, 'Son, I want you to listen to the band and I'll let you know when to rehearse." After informing Cook that he did not need to sit out, Bechet took part in the rehearsal, playing along with the orchestra by ear.

With Cook's orchestra, Bechet toured New York and Europe. In London he bought a straight-model soprano saxophone and began to adapt it into his repertoire. At Buckingham Palace, he entertained the Prince of Wales with his original composition "Characteristic Blues." *Taken with Bechet's fine musicianship, Swiss conductor Ernest Amsermet attended a number of his performances. As quoted in Jelly Roll, Jabbo, and Fats, Amsermet stated: "There is in the Southern Syncopated Orchestra an extraordinary clarinetist who is, so it seems, the first of his race to have composed perfectly formed blues on the clarinet . . . I wish to set down the name of the artist of genius; as for myself I will never forget it—it is Sidney Bechet."*

With the disbanding of Cook's Orchestra, Bechet remained in London with a remnant group led by drummer Benny Peyton. This small ensemble appeared at The Embassy Club and the Hammersmith Palais in London and, for a short time in 1920, played in Paris before returning to the Embassy and Palais. Despite Bechet's musical achievements in England, an arrest for allegedly assaulting a prostitute resulted in his deportation to America.

Returning to New York in the fall of 1921, Bechet performed with society orchestra leader Ford Dabney and played in Donald Heywood's production "How Come?" In Washington D.C. he met singer Bessie Smith. During his brief relationship and musical association with the talented and hard-drinking blues woman, Bechet took Smith to Okeh Records and recorded "Sister Kate," a side that was never released.

Recorded with Clarence Williams' Blue Five

Bechet's earliest and most legendary recordings were with Clarence Williams' Blue Five—sessions that spanned a three year period between 1923 and 1925. Among these ground breaking sides, were "Wild Cat Blues," "Kansas City Man," "Texas Moaner Blues," "Mandy, Make Up Your Mind." Joined by his old-time New Orleans musical associate Louis Armstrong, Bechet performed on Williams' legendary composition "Cake Walkin' Babies From Home." *Proclaimed by many critics as the best of the Williams' series, the song exhibited the brilliant interaction between Bechet and Armstrong. In Jazz Masters of the Twenties, Richard Hadlock wrote that Bechet "was probably the only jazzman in New York at the time who could match Armstrong's brilliance in every way: When the two improvised together, each prodding the other to more daring flights.* As Hadlock added, "Despite Armstrong's authority on most of the Clarence Williams dates, it was the more experienced Bechet who initially set the pace and tone of each performance."

Bechet's next most important association occurred around 1924 when he took a brief job at a white, midtown-cabaret, the Kentucky Club, with the Duke Ellington Orchestra. Though Ellington held Bechet's talent in high regard, he could not tolerate his eccentric habit of bringing a large dog on-stage. As quoted in *American Musicians,* Ellington later related, "When Bechet was blowing, he would say 'I'm going to call Goola this time!' Goola was his dog, a big German shepherd. Goola wasn't always there, but he was calling him anyway with a kind of throaty growl."

Bechet soon left Ellington and opened a restaurant on Lenox Avenue, the Club Basha—a name derived from his nickname Bash. The restaurant proved a short-lived venture. Before long he took to the road once more with Claude Hopkins and Josephine Baker, in the 1925 production "Revue Negre." When the tour broke up in Berlin the next year, Bechet traveled to Russia where he made appearances in Kiev, Kharkov, and Odessa. He was billed as the exemplar of the "Talking Saxophone." Afterward, Bechet returned to Berlin and organized a new production of "Revue Negre" which toured Europe in 1927. Moving to Paris in the summer of 1928, he joined bandleader Noble Sissle at the Les Ambassadors Club. ***Being a product of a tough upbringing, Bechet carried a pistol for protection. Outside a nightclub he got into a dispute with a man which resulted in the accidental wounding of a French woman. Arrested and convicted, he served eleven months in jail and was finally deported.***

Rejoining Noble Sissle in New York, Bechet embarked on a tour of Europe, along with trumpeter Tommy Ladnier. Since his earlier meeting with Ladnier in Europe, Bechet became drawn to his musicianship. In 1931 Bechet and Ladnier formed a six-piece band, the New Orleans Feetwarmers. Eventually establishing themselves at New York's Savoy, they initiated a long and musically creative collaboration. "That was the best band," recalled Bechet in *Profiles in Jazz,* "people liked it and we were all musicianers who understood what jazz really meant." As jazz writer Graham Colombe' observed, in the liner notes for *An Introduction to Sidney Bechet,* "Tommy Ladnier was Bechet's most important sideman of the thirties and they recorded together in 1932 some of the most boisterous and jubilant music of the decade." Among their excellent up-tempo numbers were "Shag," "Sweetie Dear," and "Blackstick." With few musical jobs, Bechet and Ladnier soon opened the Southern Tailor Shop, a combination repair and cleaners operation which doubled as a musicians hangout.

During the 1940s a renewed interest in traditional jazz helped bolster Bechet's career. He worked with a trio at Nick's in Greenwich Village and, through the connections of banjo/guitarist Eddie Condon, appeared at New York Town Hall concerts. Organized by Nesuhi Ertegun, he played at an all-star concert in Washington D.C., with such talents as trombonist Vic

Dickerson and pianist Art Hodes. In 1945 he was briefly reunited with Louis Armstrong at the Jazz Foundation Concert in New Orleans, and soon after he made several sides for the Blue Note label with another famous New Orleans trumpeter, Bunk Johnson.

Moved to France

By 1949 Bechet responded to offers by European promoters, and left for France to appear at the Paris Jazz Festival. After the festival he returned to America and played a short stint at Jimmy Ryan's in New York. In 1951 Bechet took up permanent residence in France and became an international celebrity, earning enough income to buy a small estate outside Paris. *The relaxed racial atmosphere and artistic recognition he received in France was a welcome break from long years of traveling and economic hardship in America.* His musical association with French musician Claude Luter's band provided Bechet with steady work until 1955. Around this time he appeared in a ballet and two films: *Se'rie Noire* with Eric Stroheim and *Blues* featuring Vivane Romance.

Bechet remained busy in the recording studio as well. In 1953 he signed his last contract with the French Vogue label. Despite the varying criticism of the Vogue sides, Bechet's musicianship remained in fine form. Unlike many of the musicians of his era, he was not opposed to perform with be bop-inspired jazzmen. His Vogue sides with modernist drummer Kenny Clarke yielded several notable recordings such as "Klook's Blues."

In 1958 Bechet experienced stomach pains while playing a job in Boston, and was taken to Boston General Hospital. More trustful of the French, he waited to return to his home outside Paris before undergoing surgery. Despite his weakened condition brought on by cancer, Bechet expressed intentions to return to America. Before he was able to complete these arrangements, Bechet died on his birthday, May 14, 1959. Years later, Duke Ellington, in *The Duke Ellington Reader*, paid tribute to his former band member: "Of all the musicians, Bechet was to me the very epitome of jazz. He represented and executed everything that had to do with the beauty of it all, and everything he played in his whole life was original . . . *I honestly think he was the most unique man ever to be in this music—but don't ever try and compare because when you talk about Bechet you just don't talk about anyone else.*"

Quote:

"*Jazz does not belong to one race or culture, but is a gift that America has given the world.*" **Ahmad Alaadeen**

Paul Robeson

Occupation—Singer, Actor, Activist, Lawyer

Introduction

Paul Robeson, a great American singer and actor, spent much of his life actively agitating for equality and fair treatment for all of America's citizens as well as citizens of the world. Robeson brought to his audiences not only a melodious baritone voice and a grand presence, but magnificent performances on stage and screen. Although his outspokenness often caused him difficulties in his career and personal life, he unswervingly pursued and supported issues that only someone in his position could effect on a grand scale. His career flourished in the 1940s as he performed in America and numerous countries around the world. ***He was one of the most celebrated persons of his time.***

Narrative Essay

Paul Leroy Robeson was born in Princeton, New Jersey, on April 9, 1898, the fifth and last child of Maria Louisa Bustill and William Drew Robeson. During these early years the Robeson's experienced both family and financial losses. At the age of six Paul and his siblings, William, Reeve, Ben and Marian suffered the death of their mother in a household fire. This was followed a few years later with their father's loss of his Princeton pastorate. After moving first to Westfield, the family finally settled in Somerville, New Jersey, in 1909, where William Robeson was appointed pastor of St. Thomas AME Zion Church.

Enrolling in Somerville High School, one of only two blacks, Paul Robeson excelled academically while successfully competing in debate, oratorical contests, and showing great promise as a football player. He also got his first taste of acting in the title role of Shakespeare's *Othello*. In his senior year he not only graduated with honors, but placed first in a competitive examination for scholarships to enter Rutgers University. *Although his other male siblings chose all-black colleges, Robeson took the challenge of attending Rutgers, a majority white institution in 1915.*

In college: between 1915 and 1919, Robeson experienced both fame and racism. In trying out for the varsity football team, where blacks were not wanted, he encountered physical brutality. In spite of this resistance, Robeson not only earned a place on the team but was named first on the roster for the All-American college team. He graduated with 15 letters in sports. Academically he was equally successful, elected a member of the prestigious Phi Beta Kappa Society and the Cap and Skull Honor Society of Rutgers. Graduating in 1919 with the highest grade point average in his class, Robeson gave the class oration at the 153d Rutgers Commencement.

With college life behind him, Robeson moved to the Harlem section of New York City to attend law school, first at New York University, later transferring to Columbia University. He sang in the chorus of the musical *Shuffle Along* (1921) by Eubie Blake and Noble Sissle, and made his acting debut in 1920 playing the lead role in *Simon the Cyrenian* by poet Ridgely Torrence. Robeson's performance was so well received that he was congratulated not only by the Harlem YMCA (Young Men's Christian Association) audience but also by members of the Provincetown Players who were in the audience. While working odd jobs and taking part in professional football to earn his college fees, Robeson met Eslanda "Essie" Cardozo Goode. The granddaughter of Francis L. Cardozo, the secretary of state of South Carolina during Reconstruction, she was a graduate of Columbia University and employed as a histological chemist. *She was the first black staff person at Presbyterian Hospital in New York City. The couple married on August 17, 1921, and their son Paul Jr. was born on November 2, 1927.*

To support his family while studying at Columbia Law School, Robeson played professional football for the Akron Pros (1920—1921) and the Milwaukee Badgers (1921—1922), and during the summer of 1922 he went to England to appear in a production of *Taboo*, which was renamed *Voodoo*. Once graduating from Columbia in 1923, Robeson sought work in his new profession, all the while singing at the famed Cotton Club in Harlem. Offered an acting role in 1923 in Eugene O'Neill's *All God's Chillun Got Wings*, Robeson quickly took this opportunity; *he had recently quit a law firm because the secretary refused to take dictation from a black person.*

Although All God's Chillun brought threats by the Ku Klux Klan because of the play's interracial subject matter and the fact that a white woman was to kiss Robeson's hand, it was an immediate success.

It was followed in 1924 by his performances in a revival of *The Emperor Jones,* the play *Rosanne,* and the silent movie *Body and Soul* for Oscar Micheaux, an independent black film maker. In 1925 Robeson debuted in a formal concert at the Provincetown Playhouse. His performance which consisted of Negro spirituals and folk songs was so brilliant that he and his accompanist, Lawrence Brown, were offered a contract with the Victor Talking Machine Company. Encouraged by this success, Robeson and Brown embarked on a tour of their own, but were sorely disappointed. Even though they received good reviews, the crowds were small and they made very little money. What Robeson came to know was that his talents in acting and singing would serve as the combined focus of his career.

Acting and Singing Career

Robeson's acting career started to take off in 1928 when he accepted the role of Joe in a London production of *Show Boat* by Jerome Kern and Oscar Hammerstein. It was his singing of "Ol' Man River" that received the most acclaim regarding the show and earned him a great degree of attention from British socialites. Robeson gave concerts in London at Albert Hall and Sunday afternoon concerts at Drury Lane. In spite of all this attention, Robeson still had to deal with racism. ***In 1929 he was refused admission to a London hotel. Because of the protest raised by Robeson, major hotels in London said they would no longer refuse service to blacks.***

Much attention was given to Robeson's acting and singing and he was embraced by the media. ***The New Yorker magazine in an article by Mildred Gilman referred to Robeson as "the promise of his race," "King of Harlem," and "Idol of his people."*** Robeson returned briefly to America in 1929 to perform at a packed Carnegie Hall. In May of 1930, after establishing a permanent residence in England, Robeson accepted the lead role in Shakespeare's *Othello.* This London production at the Savoy Theatre was the first time since the performance of the great black actor Ira Aldridge in 1860 that a major production company cast a black man in the part of the Moor. Robeson was a tall, strikingly handsome man with a deep, rich, baritone voice and a shy, almost boyish manner. ***The audience was so mesmerized by his performance in Othello that the production had 20 curtain calls.***

> *Accolades for outstanding acting and singing performances were prevalent during the 1930s in Robeson's career, but his personal and home life was surrounded by difficulties. His wife Eslanda "Essie," who had published a book on Robeson, Paul Robeson, Negro (1930), sued for divorce in 1932. Her actions were encouraged*

by the fact that Robeson had fallen in love and planned to marry Yolande Jackson, a white Englishwoman. Jackson, whom Robeson called the love of his life, had originally accepted his proposal but later called the marriage off. It was thought by some who knew the Jackson family well that she was strongly influenced by her father, Tiger Jackson, who was less than tolerant of Robeson and people of color in general. With his marriage plans cancelled, Robeson and his wife came to an understanding regarding their relationship, and the divorce proceedings were cancelled.

Activism

Robeson returned to New York briefly in 1933 to star in the film version of *Emperor Jones* before turning his attention to the study of singing and languages. His stay in the United States was a short one due to his treatment by the racist American film industries and because of criticism by blacks regarding his role as a corrupt emperor. Upon returning to England, Robeson eagerly immersed himself in his studies and mastered several languages. Robeson along with Essie became an honorary member of the West African Students' Union, becoming acquainted with African students Kwame Nkrumah and Jomo Kenyatta, future presidents of Ghana and Kenya, respectively. It is also during this time that Robeson played at a benefit for Jewish refugees which marked the beginning of his political awareness and activism.

Robeson's inclination to aid the less fortunate and the oppressed in their fight for freedom and equality was firmly rooted in his own family history. His father William Drew Robeson was an escaped slave who eventually graduated from Lincoln College in 1878, and his maternal grandfather, Cyrus Bustill, was a slave who was freed by his second owner in 1769 and went on to become an active member of the African Free Society. Recognizing the heritage that brought him so many opportunities, Robeson, between 1934 and 1937 performed in several films that presented blacks in other than stereotypical ways. He acted in such films as *Sanders of the River* (1935), *King Solomon's Mines* (1937) and *Song of Freedom* (1937).

On a trip to the Soviet Union in 1934 to discuss the making of the film *Black Majesty,* Robeson not only had discussions with the Soviet film director Sergei Eisenstein during his trip but was so impressed regarding the education against racism for schoolchildren that he began to study Marxism and Socialist systems in the Soviet Union. He also decided to send his son, nine-year-old Paul Jr., to school in the Soviet Union so that he would not have to contend with the racism and discrimination Robeson confronted in both Europe and America.

Robeson continued acting in films confronting stereotypes of blacks while receiving rave reviews for his success in singing *"Ol' Man River"* in the 1936 film production of *Show Boat*. He also embarked on a more active role in fighting the injustices he found throughout the world. Robeson co-founded the Council on African Affairs to aid in African liberation, sang and spoke at benefit concerts for Basque refugees, supported the Spanish Republican cause, and sang at rallies to support a democratic Spain along with numerous other causes. At a benefit in Albert Hall in London, Robeson is quoted in Philip Foner's *Paul Robeson Speaks* as saying *"The artist must elect to fight for freedom or slavery. I have made my choice. I had no alternative."* This statement echoed a clear and focused direction of Robeson's personal and professional life.

In 1939 Robeson stated his intentions to retire from commercial entertainment and returned to America. He gave his first recital in the United States at Mother AME Zion Church Harlem where his brother Benjamin was pastor. Later on in the same year Robeson premiered the patriotic song "Ballad for Americans" on CBS radio as a preview of a play by the same name. The song was so well received that studio audiences cheered for 20 minutes after the performance while the listening audience exceeded the response even for Orson Welles's famous Martian scare program. Robeson's popularity in the United States soared and he remained the most celebrated person in the country well into the 1940s. He was awarded the esteemed NAACP Spingarn Medal (1945) as well as numerous other awards and recognitions from civic and professional groups. *In the American production of Othello (1943), Robeson's performance placed him among the ranks of great Shakespearean actors. The production ran for 296 performances—over ten months—and toured both the United States and Canada.*

Robeson's political commitments became foremost in his life as he championed causes from South African famine relief to support of an anti-lynching law; in September 1946 he was among the delegation that spoke with President Harry S Truman about anti-lynching legislation. The meeting was a stormy one as Robeson adamantly urged Truman to act, all the while defending the Soviet Union and denouncing United States' allies. In October of the same year when called before the California Legislative Committee on Un-American activities, Robeson declared himself not a member of the Communist Party but praised their fight for equality and democracy. This attempt at branding him as un-American was successful in causing many to distrust his political commitments. Regardless of these events, Robeson decided to retire from concert work and devote himself to gatherings that promoted the causes to which he had dedicated himself.

In 1949 Robeson embarked on a European tour and in doing so spoke out against the discrimination and injustices that blacks in America had to confront. His statements were distorted as they were dispatched back to the United States. *Although Robeson got mixed responses from the black community, the backlash from whites culminated in riot before a scheduled concert in Peekskill, New York, on August 27, 1949; a demonstration by veteran organizations turned into a full-blown riot. Robeson was advised of this and returned to New York. He did agree to do a second concert on September 4 in Peekskill for the people who truly wanted to hear him. The concert did take place but afterwards a riot broke out which lasted into the night leaving over 140 persons seriously injured. With such violence surrounding Robeson's concerts, many groups and sponsors no longer supported him.*

By 1950 Robeson had received so much negative press that he made plans for a European tour. His plans were abruptly halted because the United States government refused to allow him to travel unless he agreed not to make any speeches. With no passport and denied his freedom of speech abroad, Robeson continued to speak out in public forums and through his own monthly newspaper, *Freedom*. Barred from all other forms of media, his own newspaper became his primary platform from 1950 to 1955. His remaining supporters encompassed the National Negro Labor Council, Council on African Affairs, and the Civil Rights Congress. *The NAACP openly attacked Robeson while other black organization shunned him in fear of reprisals. Undaunted by these negative responses, Robeson traveled the United States encouraging groups to fight for their rights and for equal treatment. Even though he suffered from health as well as financial difficulties, Robeson held firm to his convictions and published in 1958 his autobiography—Here I Stand—through a London publishing house.*

On May 10, 1958, Robeson gave his first New York concert in ten years to a packed Carnegie Hall. When the concert was over, he informed the audience that the passport battle had been won. From 1958 to 1963 Robeson traveled to England, the Soviet Union, Austria, and New Zealand. He was showered with awards and played to packed houses throughout his travels. After being hospitalized several times throughout his trip due to a disease of the circulatory system, Robeson returned to the United States. Much had changed since the Civil Rights Act of 1957 and school integration were in full enactment. Robeson was welcomed on his return by *Freedomways*, a quarterly review which saw him as a powerful fighter for freedom. A salute to Robeson was given in 1965 which was chaired by actors Ossie Davis and Ruby Dee along with writer James Baldwin and many other admirers.

Eslanda "Essie" Robeson died of cancer in 1965 at the age of 68 and Robeson went to live with his sister Marian in Philadelphia. He remained in seclusion until he died there on January 23, 1976; on his 75th birthday four days later a "Salute to Paul Robeson" was held in Carnegie Hall. Paul Leroy Robeson's funeral was held at Mother AME Zion Church in Harlem before a crowd of 5,000.

On February 24, 1998, Robeson received a posthumous Grammy lifetime achievement award. His honors are numerous, as Robeson's life is being depicted through exhibits, film festivals, and lectures. Upon the centennial of his birth on April 9, 1998, at least 25 U.S. states and several countries worldwide hosted celebrations of his life and work in every conceivable manner.

Paul Robeson was truly a man who saw a commitment to the oppressed, and particularly black people, as a much more profound calling than the accolades he received for his astonishing talents. His extraordinary voice and engaging acting abilities would have undoubtedly brought him more fame, fortune, and approval than the activist role he pursed instead. ***It is because of this clear vision of justice that he is remembered as a great American and a great citizen of the world.***

Sources

Duberman, Martin B. *Paul Robeson.* New York: Alfred A. Knopf, 1988.

Foner, Philip S. *Paul Robeson Speaks: Writings, Speeches, and Interviews 1918—1974.* New York: Brunner/Mazel Publishers, 1978.

Jackson, Kenneth T., and others, eds. *Dictionary of American Biography.* Supplement Ten, 1976—1980. New York: Charles Scribner's Sons, 1995.

"Robeson Receives Posthumous Grammy." *New York Times,* February 25, 1998.

Southern, Eileen. *Biographical Dictionary of Afro-American and African Musicians.* Westport, CT: Greenwood Press, 1982.

Williams, Michael W., ed. *The African American Encyclopedia.* New York: Marshall Cavendish, 1993.

A Reflection:

If a man doesn't stand for something he will fall for anything.

Joe Louis

Brown Bomber' was a hero to all

The son of an Alabama sharecropper, great grandson of a slave, great, great grandson of a white slave owner became the first African-American to achieve lasting fame and popularity in the 20th century.

In a time when his people were still subject to lynching's, discrimination and oppression, when the military was segregated and African-Americans weren't permitted to play Major League Baseball, Joe Louis was the first African-American to achieve hero worship that was previously reserved for whites only. When he started boxing in the 1930s, there were no African-Americans in positions of public prominence, none who commanded attention from whites.

"What my father did was enable white America to think of him as an American, not as a black," said his son, Joe Louis Jr. "By winning; he became white America's first black hero."

Louis was heavyweight champion of the world in an era when the heavyweight champion was, in the minds of many, the greatest man in the world. Jack Johnson, the first African-American heavyweight champ, wasn't popular with whites. Louis, on the other hand, converted all into his corner. **When "The Brown Bomber" avenged his loss to Germany's Max Schmeling—viewed as a Nazi symbol—the entire country celebrated, not just African-Americans.**

Louis' war-time patriotism in a racially divided country made him a symbol of national unity and purpose. Twice he donated his purse to military relief funds. He endeared himself even more to the American public when he said the U.S. would win World War II "because we're on God's side."

While some accused Louis of being an Uncle Tom, others realized it wasn't in his training or character to be militant. His uncommon sense of dignity, exemplified by his refusal to be pictured with a slice of watermelon, increased his popularity.

When some called Louis "a credit to his race," sportswriter Jimmy Cannon responded, "Yes, Louis is a credit to his race—the human race."

He also was a credit to boxing, which often contributes to the worst in the human race. His championship reign, from 1937 until he retired in 1949, is the longest of any heavyweight. With his powerful left jab, his destructive two-fisted attack that he released with accuracy at short range, and his capacity for finishing a wounded opponent, the 6-foot-1½ fighter defeated all 25 of his challengers, another record.

Louis also was a winner with women. Though married four times, including twice to his first wife, he discreetly enjoyed the company of both African-American and white women, including Lena Horne, Sonja Henie and Lana Turner.

He was born Joseph Louis Barrow on May 13, 1914, in a shack in the cotton-field country near Lafayette, Ala. Besides being African-American, he also was part Indian and part white. His father was committed to a state hospital for the mentally ill before he was 2.

After Louis' mother heard her husband had died (he hadn't, though), she remarried. The children slept three to a bed in Alabama before the family moved to Detroit in the 1920s. Joe was learning cabinet-making in a vocational school and taking violin lessons when he turned to boxing at the request of a schoolmate.

Fighting under the name Joe Louis, so his mother wouldn't find out, he won 50 of 54 amateur bouts and gained the attention of John Roxborough, king of the numbers rackets in Detroit's African-American neighborhoods. Roxborough and Julian Black, a speakeasy owner who also ran numbers, convinced Louis to turn pro in 1934, and they became his managers.

To shape the fighter's image, Roxborough publicized seven commandments, which would be inoffensive to white Americans. They included: Never be photographed with a white woman, never gloat over a fallen (read white) opponent, never engage in fixed fights, and live and fight clean.

Louis won his first 27 fights, 23 by knockout, with his most impressive victories being a sixth-round TKO of Primo Carnera and a fourth-round KO of Max Baer, both former heavyweight champions. His undefeated streak ended on June 19, 1936 when Schmeling detected a chink in Louis' armor: Because Louis carried his left hand low, he was vulnerable to a counter right.

In the fourth round, Schmeling's overhand right dropped Louis, who never recovered; though he lasted until the 12th before two rights by Schmeling ended the fight. In the dressing room, Louis cried.

His road to the title had merely taken a detour. On June 22, 1937, he became the first African-American champ since Johnson when he dethroned James Braddock, knocking out "The Cinderella Man" in the eighth round.

"For one night, in all the dark towns of America, the black man was king," wrote Alistair Cooke.

Louis became a symbol of African-American power in a time when they felt powerless. "Every Negro boy old enough to walk wanted to be the next Brown Bomber," said Malcolm X, then the leader of the militant Black Muslims.

Exactly one year later, Louis exacted his revenge on Schmeling. The fight was for more than the heavyweight championship, more than two individuals competing. It was built into a battle of two ideologies.

In one corner was Schmeling, representing Hitler (though Schmeling wasn't a Nazi) and everything fascism stood for. In the other corner was Louis, representing the U.S. and everything democracy meant. Louis was invited to the White House, where President Franklin Roosevelt felt the champ's biceps. "Joe, we need muscles like yours to beat Germany," he said.

There were reports of messages to Schmeling from Hitler warning him that he had better win for the glory of the Third Reich. Hitler hailed him as a paragon of Teutonic manhood and telephoned him personally before he left the dressing room.

Schmeling wasn't gone from the room long. Before some 70,000 fans at Yankee Stadium, Louis pulverized the reluctant Aryan figurehead, knocking him to the canvas three times. Two years of waiting ended for Louis after 124 seconds, with Schmeling lying broken on the canvas. *Louis had crossed the line from champion to idol as Americans of all color and ancestry celebrated.*

He went through a "Bum of the Month" club until he met former light-heavyweight champ Billy Conn on June 18, 1941. It appeared as if Louis was about to lose his title after 12 rounds, as he trailed by three and two rounds on two officials' scorecards. But Conn ignored his corner's instruction to box with caution, and the result was Louis knocking him out with two seconds left in the 13th round.

Louis enlisted in the Army in 1942 and fought close to 100 exhibitions before some two million servicemen. After the war, he knocked out Conn again *("He can run, but he can't hide")* and won three other fights, including two with Jersey Joe Walcott, before abdicating his title.

However, because he needed money to pay back taxes, he returned. After not fighting for two years, he lost a one-sided decision to his successor as champ, Ezzard Charles, in 1950 and retired for good when Rocky Marciano knocked him out in the eighth round in 1951.

Louis' fights earned him close to $5 million, but the money went like three-minute rounds, mostly due to his extravagances and generosity. The IRS, conveniently forgetting Louis' generosity during the war, demanded a reported $1.2 million in back taxes, interest and penalties, and he suffered the humiliation of competing as a pro wrestler to help pay his debts. Following several stays in hospitals for cocaine addiction and paranoia, he became an "official greeter" at Caesars Palace in Las Vegas.

Louis spent his last four years in a wheelchair before dying of a heart attack at 66 on April 12, 1981 in Las Vegas. He was buried in Arlington National Cemetery at the request of President Ronald Reagan. In death, like in life, he was a hero.

By Larry Schwartz Special to ESPN.com

Something to think about:

"Show me a hero and I will write you a tragedy." **F Scott Fitzgerald**

Josephine Baker
1905—1975

Josephine Baker, immensely popular in Paris as sensuous yet comical dancer in the 1920's, was unfortunately not accepted in racist America until 1973. Famous for her almost non-existent clothing and uninhibited dances, Josephine was known as "Black Venus", "Creole Goddess" and "Black Pearl". Men bestowed on her a myriad of gifts such as diamonds and cars, and she supposedly had 1,500 marriage proposals. She continued her successful stage career for fifty years until her death in 1975.

Coming from humble beginnings, Josephine was born as Freda Josephine Carson in St. Louis, Missouri on June 3, 1906 to Carrie McDonald, a washerwoman, and Eddie Carson, a vaudeville drummer. Eddie soon abandoned them and Carrie married Arthur Martin, who was kind but usually without work.

The young Josephine found work cleaning houses and babysitting for wealthy white families. When she was thirteen she became a waitress, met a man there named Willie Wells whom she married. She left him when the relationship went bad and later married three more times first to Willie Baker in 1921 (she kept his name), Frenchman Jean Lion in 1937 (whom she became a French citizen through), and French orchestra leader Jo Bouillon in 1947 who helped to raise her twelve adopted children.

She began her stage career touring with the Jones Family Band and the Dixie Steppers in 1919, performing in skits. She worked as a dresser for the Dixie Steppers learning the dance routines, so when they needed an extra dancer she got her chance. Her added comical touches made her a box-office draw.

She found stage success at The Plantation Club in New York City, but when she traveled to Paris for "La Revue Negre" they went crazy for her. Her stage success brought money which she spent on clothes, jewelry and pets.

At one time she enjoyed owning a leopard, a chimpanzee, a pig, a snake, a goat, a parrot, parakeets, fish, three cats and seven dogs.

By 1927 Josephine was one of the most photographed women in the world, along with personalities like Gloria Swanson and Mary Pickford. Her earnings set her above any other entertainer in Europe at the time. She was the star in two early movies, Zou-Zou and Princess Tam-Tam. Although her celebrity status was unrivaled in Europe, when she returned to the United States in 1936 to star in the Ziegfeld Follies the public rejected her due to her color.

Returning to France, Josephine participated in World War II as a performer for the soldiers as well as doing undercover work for the French Resistance. She smuggled secret messages written in invisible ink on her music. She also served as a sub-lieutenant in the Women's Auxiliary Air Force. The French government awarded her with the Medal of Resistance and was named a Chevalier of the Legion of Honor.

Visiting the U.S. again in the 1950's, Josephine continued to fight against racism. The Stork Club rejected her as a customer; she began a media battle with pro-segregationist Walter Winchell as her opponent. The NAACP named May 20 as Josephine Baker Day to honor her efforts.

During this time Josephine began adopting children of different races and ethnicities and called them affectionately her *"Rainbow Tribe"*. She lived and promoted her belief that people of various ethnicities can live together harmoniously. She continued to visit the U.S. and met an artist Robert Brady whom she became involved with. Divorced from her fourth husband, Josephine and Robert decided to say wedding vows in an empty church in Acapulco, Mexico to cement their platonic friendship in 1973. Strides had been made in black acceptance, and also in 1973 Josephine performed at New York's Carnegie Hall to a standing ovation even before she had begun.

On April 8, 1975 Josephine performed at the Bobino Theater in Paris before people like Princess Grace of Monaco and Sophia Loren. Even though she was 68 years old, she thrilled the audiences with a medley of her routines from her 50 year career. On April 12, only days later Josephine died from a cerebral hemorrhage. *By Jane Y. Harter*

Wisdom for the Journey

The talent of success is nothing more than doing what you can do well, and doing well whatever you do without thought of fame. If it comes at all it will come because it is deserved, not because it is sought after.

Henry Wadsworth Longfellow

Mahalia Jackson

(Born Oct. 26, 1911, New Orleans, La., U.S.—died Jan. 27, 1972, Evergreen Park, Ill.) U.S. gospel music singer.

As a child, Jackson sang in the choir of the New Orleans church where her father preached. She learned sacred songs but was also exposed to blues recordings by Bessie Smith and Ida Cox. In Chicago she worked at odd jobs while singing with a touring gospel quintet, and she opened several small businesses. Her warm, powerful voice first came to wide public attention in the 1930s, when she participated in a cross-country tour singing songs such as "He's Got the Whole World in His Hands." Closely associated with Thomas A. Dorsey, she sang many of his songs. *"Move on up a Little Higher" (1948) sold more than a million copies, and she became one of the most popular singers of the 1950s and '60s. She first appeared at Carnegie Hall in 1950. Active in the civil rights movement from 1955, she sang at the epochal 1963 civil rights march on Washington.*

Throughout her celebrated career, gospel singer Mahalia Jackson (1911-1972) used her rich, forceful voice and inspiring interpretations of spirituals to move audiences around the world to tears of joy. In the early days, as a soloist and member of church choirs, she recognized the power of song as a means of gloriously reaffirming the faith of her flock. And later, as a world figure, her natural gift brought people of different religious and political convictions together to revel in the beauty of the gospels and to appreciate the warm spirit that underscored the way she lived her life.

The woman who would become known as the "Gospel Queen" was born on October 26, 1911 into a poor family in New Orleans, Louisiana. The Jacksons' Water Street home, a shack between the railroad tracks and the levee of the Mississippi River, was served by a pump that delivered water so dirty that cornmeal had to be used as a filtering agent. Jackson's father, like many blacks in the segregated south, held several jobs; he was a long-shoreman, a barber, and a preacher at a small church. Her mother, a devout Baptist who died when Mahalia was five, took care of the six Jackson children and the house, using washed-up driftwood and planks from old barges to fuel the stove.

Sounds of New Orleans

As a child, Mahalia was taken in by the sounds of New Orleans. She listened to the rhythms of the woodpeckers, the rumblings of the trains, the whistles of the steamboats, the songs of sailors and street peddlers. When the annual festival of Mardi Gras arrived, the city erupted in music. In her bedroom at night, young Mahalia would quietly sing the songs of blues legend Bessie Smith.

But Jackson's close relatives disapproved of the blues, music indigenous to southern black culture, saying it was decadent and claiming that the only acceptable songs for pious Christians were the gospels of the church. In gospel songs, they told her, music was the cherished vehicle of religious faith. As the writer Jesse Jackson (not related to the civil rights leader) said in his biography of Mahalia, *Make a Joyful Noise Unto the Lord!*, **"It was like choosing between the devil and God. You couldn't have it both ways."** Mahalia made up her mind. When Little Haley (the nickname by which she was known as a child) tried out for the Baptist choir, she silenced the crowd by singing "I'm so glad, I'm so glad, I'm so glad I've been in the grave an' rose again . . . ." She became known as "the little girl with the big voice."

At 16, with only an eighth grade education but a strong ambition to become a nurse, Jackson went to Chicago to live with her Aunt Hannah. In the northern city, **to which thousands of southern blacks had migrated after the Civil War to escape segregation, she earned a living by washing white people's clothes for a dollar a day.** After searching for the right church to join, a place whose music spoke to her, she ended up at the Greater Salem Baptist Church, to which her aunt belonged. At her audition for the choir, Jackson's thunderous voice rose above all the others. She was invited to be a soloist and started singing with a quintet that performed at funerals and church services throughout the city. In 1934, she received $25 for her first recording, "God's Gonna Separate the Wheat from the Tares."

Though she sang traditional hymns and spirituals almost exclusively, Jackson continued to be fascinated by the blues. During the Great Depression, she knew she could earn more money singing the songs that her relatives considered profane and blasphemous. But when her beloved grandfather was struck down by a stroke and fell into a coma, Jackson vowed that if he recovered she would never even enter a theater again, much less sing songs of which he would disapprove. He did recover, and Mahalia never broke that vow. She wrote in her autobiography, *Movin' On Up:* "I feel God heard me and wanted me to devote my life to his songs and that is why he suffered my prayers to be answered-so that nothing would distract me from being a gospel singer."

Later in her career, Jackson continued to turn down lucrative requests to sing in nightclubs-she was offered as much as $25,000 a performance in Las Vegas-even when the club owners promised not to serve whisky while she performed. She never dismissed the blues as anti-religious, like her relatives had done: it was simply a matter of the vow she had made, as well as a matter of inspiration. "There's no sense in my singing the blues, because I just don't feel it," she was quoted as saying in *Harper's* magazine in 1956. "In the old, heart-felt songs, whether it's the blues or gospel music, there's the distressed cry of a human being. But in the blues, it's all despair; when you're done singing, you're still lonely and sorrowful. In the gospel songs, there's mourning and sorrow, too, but there's always hope and consolation to lift you above it."

Singing Career Blossomed

In 1939, Jackson started touring with renowned composer Thomas A. Dorsey. Together they visited churches and "gospel tents" around the country, and Jackson's reputation as a singer and interpreter of spirituals blossomed. She returned to Chicago after five years on the road and opened a beauty salon and a flower shop, both of which drew customers from the gospel and church communities. She continued to make records that brought her fairly little monetary reward. In 1946, while she was practicing in a recording studio, a representative from Decca Records overheard her sing an old spiritual she had learned as a child. He advised her to record it, and a few weeks later she did. "Move On Up a Little Higher" became her signature song. The recording sold 100,000 copies overnight and soon passed the two million dollar mark. "It sold like wildfire," Alex Haley wrote in *Reader's Digest.* "Negro disk jockeys played it; Negro ministers praised it from their pulpits. *When sales passed one million, the Negro press hailed Mahalia Jackson as 'the only Negro whom Negroes have made famous.'*"

Jackson began touring again, only this time she did it not as the hand-to-mouth singer who had toured with Dorsey years before. She bought a Cadillac big enough for her to sleep in when she was performing in areas with hotels that failed to provide accommodations for blacks. She also stored food in the car so that when she visited the segregated South she wouldn't have to sit in the backs of restaurants. Soon the emotional and resonant singing of the "Gospel Queen," as she had become known, began reaching the white community as well. She appeared regularly on Studs Terkel's radio show and was ultimately given her own radio and television programs.

On October 4, 1950, Jackson played to a packed house of blacks and whites at New York's Carnegie Hall. She recounted in her autobiography how she reacted to the jubilant audience. "I got carried away, too, and found myself singing on my knees for them. I had to straighten up and say, 'Now we'd best remember we're in Carnegie Hall and if we cut up too much, they might put us out.'" *In her book, she also described a conversation with a reporter who asked her why she thought white people had taken to her traditionally black, church songs. She answered, "Well, honey, maybe they tried drink and they tried psychoanalysis and now they're going to try to rejoice with me a bit."* Jackson ultimately became equally popular overseas and performed for royalty and adoring fans throughout France, England, Denmark, and Germany. *One of her most rewarding concerts took place in Israel, where she sang before an audience of Jews, Muslims, and Christians.*

Participated in Civil Rights Struggles

In the late 1950s and early 1960s, Jackson's attention turned to the growing civil rights movement in the United States. Although she had grown up on Water Street, where black and white families lived together peacefully, she was well aware of the injustice engendered by the Jim Crow laws that enforced racial segregation in the South. At the request of the Reverend Martin Luther King, Jr., Jackson participated in the Montgomery bus boycott. This action had been prompted by Rosa Parks' refusal to move from a bus seat reserved for whites. *During the famous March on Washington in 1963, seconds before Dr. King delivered his celebrated "I Have a Dream" speech, Jackson sang the old inspirational, "I Been 'Buked and I Been Scorned" to over 200,000 people.*

Jackson died in Chicago on January 27, 1972, never having fulfilled her dream of building a nondenominational temple, where people could sing, celebrate life, and nurture the talents of children. *Christian Century* magazine reported that her funeral was attended by over six thousand fans. Singer *Ella Fitzgerald described Jackson as "one of our greatest ambassadors of love . . . this wonderful woman who only comes once in a lifetime."*

Jackson considered herself a simple woman: she enjoyed cooking for friends as much as marveling at landmarks around the world. But it was in her music that she found her spirit most eloquently expressed. She wrote in her autobiography: "Gospel music is nothing but singing of good tidings-spreading the good news. It will last as long as any music because it is sung straight from the human heart. Join with me sometime-whether you're white or colored-and you will feel it for yourself. Its future is brighter than a daisy."

One of Mahalia's most memorable renditions

"If I can help somebody"

If I can help somebody, as I pass along.
If I can cheer somebody, with a word or song,
If I can show somebody, He is travelling wrong
Then my living shall not be in vain

If I can do my duty, as all men ought
If I can bring that duty to a world that's lost
If I can spread a love message that the Master taught
Then my living shall not be in vain

Chorus:

Then my living shall not be in vain—
Then my living shall not be in vain
If I can help somebody, as I pass along
Then my living shall not be in vain.

"Jesse" Owens

James Cleveland "Jesse" Owens (September 12, 1913-March 31, 1980) was an American track and field athlete. He participated in the 1936 Summer Olympics in Berlin, Germany, where he achieved international fame by winning four gold medals: one each in the 100 meters, the 200 meters, the long jump, and as part of the 4x100 meter relay team.

Childhood

James Cleveland Owens was born the seventh of eleven children of Henry and Emma Alexander Owens in Oakville, Alabama on September 12, 1913. "J.C.", as he was called, was nine when the family moved to Cleveland, Ohio for better opportunities, as part of **the Great Migration, when 1.5 million African Americans left the segregated South. His new teacher nicknamed him Jesse. When she asked his name to enter in her roll book, he said J.C., but because of his strong Southern accent, she thought he said "Jesse". The name took and he was known as Jesse Owens for the rest of his life.**
As a boy and youth, Owens took different jobs in his spare time: he delivered groceries, loaded freight cars and worked in a shoe repair shop. During this period, Owens realized that he had a passion for running. Throughout his life, Owens attributed the success of his athletic career to the encouragement of Charles Riley, his junior-high track coach at Fairmount Junior High. Since Owens worked in a shoe repair shop after school, Riley allowed him to practice before school instead.
Owens first came to national attention when he was a student of East Technical High School in Cleveland; he equaled the world record of 9.4 seconds in the 100-yard (91 m) dash and long-jumped 24 feet 9 ½ inches (7.56 m) at the 1933 National High School Championship in Chicago. Owens's record at East Technical High School directly inspired Harrison Dillard to take up track sports.

Ohio State University

Owens attended the Ohio State University after employment was found for his father, ensuring the family could be supported. Affectionately known as the *"Buckeye Bullet,"* Owens won a record eight individual NCAA championships, four each in 1935 and 1936. (The record of four gold medals at the NCAA was equaled only by Xavier Carter in 2006, although his many titles also included relay medals.) *Though Owens enjoyed athletic success, he had to live off campus with other African-American athletes. When he traveled with the team, Owens was restricted to ordering carry-out or eating at "black-only" restaurants. Similarly, he had to stay at "blacks-only" hotels. Owens did not receive a scholarship for his efforts, so he continued to work part-time jobs to pay for school.*

Owens's greatest achievement came in a span of 45 minutes on May 25, 1935 at the Big Ten meet in Ann Arbor, Michigan, where he set three world records and tied a fourth. He equaled the world record for the 100-yard (91 m) sprint (9.4 seconds); and set world records in the long jump (26 feet 8¼ inches (8.13 m), a world record that would last 25 years); 220-yard (201.2 m) sprint (20.3 seconds); and 220-yard (201.2m) low hurdles (22.6 seconds, becoming the first to break 23 seconds). In 2005, NBC sports announcer Bob Costas and University of Central Florida professor of sports history Richard C. Crepeau both chose these wins on one day as the most impressive athletic achievement since 1850.

Owens was a member of Alpha Phi Alpha, the first intercollegiate Greek-letter organization established by and for African Americans.

Berlin Olympics

In 1936, Owens arrived in Berlin to compete for the United States in the Summer Olympics. Adolf Hitler was using the games to show the world a resurgent Nazi Germany. He and other government officials had high hopes that German athletes would dominate the games with victories (the German athletes achieved a "top of the table" medal haul). *Meanwhile, Nazi propaganda promoted concepts of "Aryan racial superiority" and depicted ethnic Africans as inferior.*

Owens surprised many by winning four gold medals: On August 3, 1936 he won the 100m sprint, defeating Ralph Metcalfe; on August 4, the long jump (later crediting friendly and helpful advice from Luz Long, the German competitor he ultimately defeated); on August 5, the 200m sprint; and, after he was added to the 4 x 100 m relay team, he won his fourth on August 9 (a performance not equaled until Carl Lewis won gold medals in the same events at the 1984 Summer Olympics).

Just before the competitions, Owens was visited in the Olympic village by Adi Dassler, the founder of the Adidas athletic shoe company. *He persuaded Owens to use Adidas shoes, the first sponsorship for a male African-American athlete.*

The long-jump victory is documented, along with many other 1936 events, in the 1938 film *Olympia* by Leni Riefenstahl.

On the first day, Hitler shook hands only with the German victors and then left the stadium. Olympic committee officials insisted Hitler greet every medalist or none at all. Hitler opted for the latter and skipped all further medal presentations. On reports that Hitler had deliberately avoided acknowledging his victories, and had refused to shake his hand, Owens recounted:

When I passed the Chancellor he arose, waved his hand at me, and I waved back at him.

Hitler expressed his feelings about Owens and Africans in private. Albert Speer, Hitler's architect and later war armaments minister, recollected:

Each of the German victories, and there were a surprising number of these, made him happy, but he was highly annoyed by the series of triumphs by the marvelous colored American runner, Jesse Owens. People whose antecedents came from the jungle were primitive, Hitler said with a shrug; their physiques were stronger than those of civilized whites and hence should be excluded from future games.

Owens was cheered enthusiastically by 110,000 people in Berlin's Olympic Stadium; on the street, Germans sought his autograph. Owens was allowed to travel with and stay in the same hotels as whites, while at the time blacks in many parts of the United States were denied equal rights. *After a New York City ticker-tape parade of Fifth Avenue in his honor, Owens had to ride the freight elevator at the Waldorf-Astoria to reach the reception honoring him.*

Owens said, "Hitler didn't snub me—it was FDR who snubbed me. The president didn't even send me a telegram." Jesse Owens was never invited to the White House nor bestowed honors by presidents Franklin D. Roosevelt (FDR) or his successor Harry S. Truman during their terms. In 1955, President Dwight D. Eisenhower honored Owens by naming him an "Ambassador of Sports."

Post Olympics

He was quoted saying the secret behind his success was "I let my feet spend as little time on the ground as possible: From the air, fast down, and from the ground, fast up."

After the games had finished, the Olympic team and Owens were all invited to compete in Sweden. He decided to capitalize on his success by returning to the United States to take up some of the more lucrative commercial offers. United States athletic officials were furious and withdrew his amateur status, ending his career immediately. Owens was angry, saying, "A fellow desires something for himself."

Prohibited from amateur sporting appearances to bolster his profile, Owens found the commercial offers all but disappeared. In 1946, he joined Abe Saperstein in the formation of the West Coast Baseball Association (WCBA), a new Negro baseball league; Owens was vice-president and the owner of the Portland (Oregon) Rosebuds franchise. He toured with the Rosebuds, sometimes entertaining the audience in between doubleheader games by competing in races against horses. The WCBA disbanded after only two months. He helped promote the exploitation film *Mom and Dad* in black neighborhoods. He tried to make a living as a sports promoter, essentially an entertainer. He would give local sprinters a ten or twenty-yard start and beat them in the 100-yd (91 m) dash. He also challenged and defeated racehorses; as he revealed later, the trick was to race a high-strung thoroughbred that would be frightened by the starter's shotgun and give him a bad jump. Owens said, "People say that it was degrading for an Olympic champion to run against a horse, but what was I supposed to do? *I had four gold medals, but you can't eat four gold medals.*"

Owens ran a dry-cleaning business and worked as a gas station attendant to earn a living. He eventually filed for bankruptcy. In 1966 he was successfully prosecuted for tax evasion. At rock bottom, he was aided in beginning rehabilitation. The government appointed him a U.S.goodwill ambassador. Owens traveled the world and spoke to companies such as the Ford Motor Company and stakeholders such as the United States Olympic Committee. After he retired, he owned racehorses.

Owens refused to support the black power salute by African-American sprinters Tommie Smith and John Carlos at the 1968 Summer Olympics. He told them:

The black fist is a meaningless symbol. When you open it, you have nothing but fingers-weak, empty fingers. The only time the black fist has significance is when there's money inside. There's where the power lies.

After smoking for 35 years, Owens contracted lung cancer. He died from the disease at age 66 in Tucson, Arizona in 1980. He is buried in Oak Woods Cemetery in Chicago.

A few months before his death, Owens had tried unsuccessfully to convince President Jimmy Carter not to boycott the 1980 Moscow Olympics.

He argued that the Olympic ideal was to be a time-out from war and above politics.

Marriage and family

Owens and Minnie Ruth Solomon met at Fairmount Junior High School in Cleveland when he was 15 years old and she was 13 years old. They dated steadily through high school. Ruth gave birth to their first daughter, Gloria, in 1932. They married in 1935 and had two more daughters together: Marlene, born in 1939, and Beverly, born in 1940. They were married until his death.

Awards, tributes and honors

- In 1970, Owens was inducted to the Alabama Sports Hall of Fame.
- In 1976 he was awarded the Presidential Medal of Freedom by President Gerald Ford.
- In 1980, a new asteroid was discovered by A. Mrkos at Klet which was named as 6758 Jesseowens in honour of Jesse Owens.
- USA Track and Field created the Jesse Owens Award in 1981, which is given annually to the country's top track and field athlete.
- In 1984, an Emmy Award-winning biographical television film of his life, *The Jesse Owens Story*, was released, with Dorian Harewood portraying Owens.
- In 1984 a street near the Olympic Stadium in Berlin was renamed Jesse-Owens-Allee, and the Jesse Owens Realschule/Oberschule (a secondary school) in Berlin-Lichtenberg, was named for him.
- ***On March 28, 1990, Owens was posthumously awarded the Congressional Gold Medal by President George H. W. Bush.***
- ***Two U.S. postage stamps have been issued to honor Owens, one in 1990 and another in 1998.***
- In 1996, Owens's hometown of Oakville, Alabama dedicated Jesse Owens Memorial Park in his honor, at the same time that the Olympic Torch came through the community, 60 years after his Olympic triumph. An article in the *Wall Street Journal* of June 7, 1996, covered the event and included this inscription written by poet Charles Ghigna that appears on a bronze plaque at the Park:
- *May his light shine forever as a symbol for all who run for the freedom of sport, for the spirit of humanity, for the memory of Jesse Owens.*
- In 2001, Ohio State University dedicated Jesse Owens Memorial Stadium for track and field events. The campus also houses three recreational centers for students and staff named in his honor.

- **In 2002, scholar Molefi Kete Asante listed Jesse Owens on his list of 100 Greatest African Americans.**
- In Cleveland, Ohio, a statue of Owens in his Ohio State track suit, was installed at Fort Huntington Park, west of the old Courthouse.
- Phoenix, Arizona named the Jesse Owens Medical Plaza in his honor, as well as Jesse Owens Parkway.
- Jesse Owens Park, located in Tucson, Arizona, is a staple of local youth athletics there.
- At the 2009 World Athletic Championships in Berlin, all members of the United States Track & Field team wore badges with "JO" to commemorate Owens's victories in the same stadium 73 years before.
- In early 2010, the Ohio Historical Society proposed Jesse Owens as a finalist from a statewide vote for inclusion in Statuary Hall at the United States Capitol.

Wisdom for the Journey

"Never underestimate the power of dreams and the influence of the human spirit. We are all the same in this notion: The potential for greatness lives within each of us." **Wilma Rudolph**

"If you don't try to win you might as well hold the Olympics in somebody's back yard" **Jesse Owens**

"Although they only give gold medals in the field of athletics, I encourage everyone to look into themselves and find their own personal dream, whatever that may be—sports, medicine, whatever. The same principles apply."

Jackie Robinson

Jack Roosevelt "Jackie" Robinson (January 31, 1919-October 24, 1972) was the first black Major League Baseball (MLB) player of the modern era. Robinson broke the baseball color line when he debuted with the Brooklyn Dodgers in 1947. As the first black man to play in the major leagues since the 1880s, he was instrumental in bringing an end to racial segregation in professional baseball, which had relegated black players to the Negro leagues for six decades. The example of his character and unquestionable talent challenged the traditional basis of segregation, which then marked many other aspects of American life, and contributed significantly, to the Civil Rights Movement.

Apart from his cultural impact, Robinson had an exceptional baseball career. Over ten seasons, he played in six World Series and contributed to the Dodgers' 1955 World Championship. He was selected for six consecutive All-Star Games from 1949 to 1954, was the recipient of the inaugural MLB Rookie of the Year Award in 1947, and won the National League Most Valuable Player Award in 1949—the first black player so honored. Robinson was inducted into the Baseball Hall of Fame in 1962. *In 1997, Major League Baseball retired his uniform number, 42, across all major league teams.*

Robinson was also known for his pursuits outside the baseball diamond. He was the first black television analyst in Major League Baseball, and the first black vice-president of a major American corporation. In the 1960s, he helped establish the Freedom National Bank, an African-American-owned financial institution based in Harlem, New York. In recognition of his achievements on and off the field, Robinson was posthumously awarded the Presidential Medal of Freedom and the Congressional Gold Medal.

Early life

Robinson was born on January 31, 1919, into a family of sharecroppers in Cairo, Georgia, during a Spanish flu and smallpox epidemic. He was the youngest of five children, after siblings Edgar, Frank, Matthew (nicknamed "Mack"), and Willa Mae. His middle name was in honor of former President Theodore Roosevelt, who died twenty-five days before Robinson was born. After Robinson's father left the family in 1920, they moved to Pasadena, California. The extended Robinson family established itself on a residential plot containing two small houses at 121 Pepper Street in Pasadena. Robinson's mother worked various odd jobs to support the family. Growing up in relative poverty in an otherwise affluent community, Robinson and his minority friends were excluded from many recreational opportunities. As a result, Robinson joined a neighborhood gang, but his friend Carl Anderson persuaded him to abandon it.

John Muir High School

In 1935, Robinson graduated from Washington Junior High School and enrolled at John Muir High School (Muir Tech). Recognizing his athletic talents, Robinson's older brothers Mack (himself an accomplished athlete and silver medalist at the 1936 Summer Olympics) and Frank inspired Jackie to pursue his interest in sports. At Muir Tech, Robinson played several sports at the varsity level and lettered in four of them: football, basketball, track, and baseball. He played shortstop and catcher on the baseball team, quarterback on the football team, and guard on the basketball team. With the track and field squad, he won awards in the broad jump. He was also a member of the tennis team.

In 1936, Robinson won the junior boys singles championship in the annual Pacific Coast Negro Tennis Tournament and earned a place on the Pomona annual baseball tournament all-star team, which included future Hall of Famers Ted Williams and Bob Lemon. In late January 1937, the *Pasadena Star-News* newspaper reported that Robinson "for two years has been the outstanding athlete at Muir, starring in football, basketball, track, baseball and tennis."

Pasadena Junior College

After Muir, Robinson attended Pasadena Junior College (PJC), where he continued his athletic career by participating in basketball, football, baseball, and track. On the football team, he played quarterback and safety. He was a shortstop and leadoff hitter for the baseball team, and he broke school broad jump records held by his brother Mack. As at Muir High School, most of Jackie's teammates were white. While playing football at PJC, Robinson suffered a fractured ankle, complications from which would eventually delay his deployment status while in the military. Also while at PJC, he was elected to the Lancers, a student-run police organization responsible for patrolling various school activities. In 1938, he was elected to the All-Southland Junior College Team for baseball and selected as the region's Most Valuable Player. That year, Robinson was one of ten students named to the school's Order of the Mast and Dagger (*Omicron Mu Delta*), awarded to students performing "outstanding service to the school and whose scholastic and citizenship record is worthy of recognition."

An incident at PJC illustrated Robinson's impatience with authority figures he perceived as racist—a character trait that would resurface repeatedly in his life. On January 25, 1938, he was arrested after vocally disputing the detention of a black friend by police. Robinson received a two-year suspended sentence, but the incident—along with other rumored run-ins between Robinson and police—gave Robinson a reputation for combativeness in the face of racial antagonism. Toward the end of his PJC tenure, Frank Robinson (to whom Robinson felt closest among his three brothers) was killed in a motorcycle accident. The event motivated Jackie to pursue his athletic career at the nearby University of California, Los Angeles (UCLA), where he could remain closer to Frank's family.

UCLA and afterward

After graduating from PJC in spring 1939, Robinson transferred to UCLA, where he became the school's first athlete to win varsity letters in four sports: baseball, basketball, football, and track. He was one of four black players on the 1939 UCLA Bruins football team; the others were Woody Strode, Kenny Washington, and Ray Bartlett. Washington, Strode, and Robinson made up three of the team's four backfield players. At a time when only a handful of black players existed in mainstream college football, this made UCLA college football's most integrated team. In track and field, Robinson won the 1940 NCAA Men's Outdoor Track and Field Championship in the Long Jump, jumping 24'10.5". Belying his future career, baseball was Robinson's "worst sport" at UCLA; he hit.097 in his only season, although in his first game he went 4-for-4 and twice stole home.

While a senior at UCLA, Robinson met his future wife, Rachel Isum, a UCLA freshman who was familiar with Robinson's athletic career at PJC. In the spring semester of 1941, despite his mother's and Isum's reservations, Robinson left college just shy of graduation. He took a job as an assistant

278 | George D. Johnson

athletic director with the government's National Youth Administration (NYA) in Atascadero, California.

After the government ceased NYA operations, Robinson traveled to Honolulu in fall 1941 to play football for the semi-professional, racially integrated Honolulu Bears. After a short season, Robinson returned to California in December 1941 to pursue a career as running back for the Los Angeles Bulldogs of the Pacific Coast Football League. By that time, however, the Japanese attack on Pearl Harbor had taken place, drawing the United States into World War II and ending Robinson's nascent football career.[43]

Military career

In 1942, Robinson was drafted and assigned to a segregated Army cavalry unit in Fort Riley, Kansas. Having the requisite qualifications, Robinson and several other black soldiers applied for admission to an Officer Candidate School (OCS) then located at Fort Riley: *Although the Army's initial July 1941 guidelines for OCS had been drafted as race-neutral, practically speaking few black applicants were admitted into OCS until after subsequent directives by Army leadership. As a result, the applications of Robinson and his colleagues were delayed for several months. After protests by heavyweight boxing champion Joe Louis (then stationed at Fort Riley) and the help of Truman Gibson (then an assistant civilian aide to the Secretary of War), the men were accepted into OCS. This common military experience spawned a personal friendship between Robinson and Louis.* Upon finishing OCS, Robinson was commissioned as a second lieutenant in January 1943. Shortly afterward, Robinson and Isum were formally engaged.

After receiving his commission, Robinson was reassigned to Fort Hood, Texas, where he joined the 761st "Black Panthers" Tank Battalion. While at Fort Hood, 2LT Robinson often used his weekend leave to visit the Rev. Karl Downs, President of Sam Huston College (now Huston-Tillotson University) in nearby Austin, Texas; Downs had been Robinson's pastor at Scott United Methodist Church while Robinson attended PJC.

An event on 6 July 1944 derailed Robinson's military career. While awaiting results of hospital tests on the ankle he had injured in junior college, 2LT Robinson boarded an Army bus with a fellow officer's wife; although the Army had commissioned its own unsegregated bus line, the bus driver ordered Robinson to move to the back of the bus. Robinson refused. The driver backed down, but after reaching the end of the line, summoned the military police, who took Robinson into custody. When Robinson later confronted the investigating duty officer about racist questioning by the officer and his assistant, the officer recommended Robinson be court-martialed. After Robinson's commander in the 761st, Paul L. Bates, refused to authorize the legal action, Robinson was summarily transferred to the 758th Battalion—where the commander quickly consented to charge Robinson with multiple offenses, including, among other charges, public drunkenness—even though Robinson did not drink.

By the time of the court-martial in August 1944, the charges against Robinson had been reduced to two counts of insubordination during questioning. Robinson was acquitted by an all-white panel of nine officers. Although his former unit, the 761st Tank Battalion, became the first black tank unit to see combat in World War II, Robinson's court-martial proceedings prohibited him from being deployed overseas, thus he never saw combat action. After his acquittal, he was transferred to Camp Breckinridge, Kentucky, where he served as a coach for army athletics until receiving an honorable discharge in November 1944. While there, Robinson met an ex-player for the Kansas City Monarchs of the Negro American League, who encouraged Robinson to write the Monarchs and ask for a tryout. Robinson took the ex-player's advice and wrote Monarchs' co-owner Thomas Baird.

Post-military

After his discharge, Robinson briefly returned to his old football club, the Los Angeles Bulldogs. Robinson then accepted an offer from his old friend and pastor Rev. Karl Downs to be the athletic director at Sam Huston College in Austin, then of the Southwestern Athletic Conference. The job included coaching the school's basketball team for the 1944-45 season. As a fledgling program, few students tried out for the basketball team, and Robinson even resorted to inserting himself into the lineup for exhibition games. Although his teams were outmatched by opponents, Robinson was respected as a disciplinarian coach, and drew the admiration of, among others, Langston University basketball player Marques Haynes, a future member of the Harlem Globetrotters.

Baseball career
Negro leagues

In early 1945, while Robinson was at Sam Huston College, the Kansas City Monarchs sent him a written offer to play professional baseball in the Negro leagues. Robinson accepted a contract for $400 ($4,836 in 2010 dollars) per month, a boon for him at the time. Although he played well for the Monarchs, Robinson was frustrated with the experience. He had grown used to a structured playing environment in college, and the Negro leagues' disorganization and embrace of gambling interests appalled him. The hectic travel schedule also placed a burden on his relationship with Isum, with whom he could now only communicate by letter. In all, Robinson played 47 games at shortstop for the Monarchs, hitting.387 with five home runs, and registering 13 stolen bases. He also appeared in the 1945 Negro League All-Star Game, going hitless in five at-bats.

During the season, Robinson pursued potential major league interest. The Boston Red Sox held a tryout at Fenway Park for Robinson and other black players on April 16. The tryout, however, was a farce chiefly designed to assuage the desegregationist sensibilities of powerful Boston City Councilman Isadore Muchnick. Even with the stands limited to management, Robinson was subjected to racial epithets. Robinson left the tryout humiliated, and more than fourteen years later, in July 1959, the Red Sox became the last major league team to integrate its roster.

Other teams, however, had more serious interest in signing a black ballplayer. In the mid-1940s, Branch Rickey, club president and general manager of the Brooklyn Dodgers, began to scout the Negro leagues for a possible addition to the Dodgers' roster. Rickey selected Robinson from a list of promising black players, and interviewed Robinson for possible assignment to Brooklyn's International League farm club, the Montreal Royals. Rickey was especially interested in making sure his eventual signee could withstand the inevitable racial abuse that would be directed at him. *In a famous three-hour exchange on August 28, 1945, Rickey asked Robinson if he could face the racial animus without taking the bait and reacting angrily—a concern given Robinson's prior arguments with law enforcement officials at PJC and in the military. Robinson was aghast: "Are you looking for a Negro who is afraid to fight back?" Rickey replied that he needed a Negro player "with guts enough not to fight back." After obtaining a commitment from Robinson to "turn the other cheek" to racial antagonism, Rickey agreed to sign him to a contract for $600 a month, equal to $7,253 today.*

Although he required Robinson to keep the arrangement a secret for the time being, Rickey committed to formally signing Robinson before November 1, 1945. On October 23, it was publicly announced that Robinson would be assigned to the Royals for the 1946 season. On the same day, with representatives of the Royals and Dodgers present, Robinson formally signed his contract with the Royals. In what was later referred to as "The Noble Experiment", Robinson was the first black baseball player in the International League since the 1880s. *Robinson was not necessarily the best player in the Negro leagues and black talents Satchel Paige and Josh Gibson were upset when Robinson was selected first.*

Rickey's offer allowed Robinson to leave the Monarchs and their grueling bus rides behind, and he went home to Pasadena. That September, he signed with Chet Brewer's Kansas City Royals, a post-season barnstorming team in the California Winter League. Later that off-season, he briefly toured South America with another barnstorming team, while his fiancée Isum pursued nursing opportunities in New York City. On February 10, 1946, Robinson and Isum were married by their old friend, Rev. Karl Downs.

Minor leagues

In 1946, Robinson arrived at Daytona Beach, Florida, for spring training with the Montreal Royals of the Class AAA International League (the designation of "AAA" for the highest level of minor league baseball was first used in the 1946 season). *Robinson's presence was controversial in racially charged Florida. As he was not allowed to stay with his teammates at the team hotel, he lodged instead at the home of a local black politician.* Since the Dodgers organization did not own a spring training facility (the Dodger-controlled spring training compound in Vero Beach known as "Dodgertown" did not open until spring 1948), scheduling was subject to the whim of area localities, several of which turned down any event involving Robinson or Johnny Wright, another black player whom Rickey had signed to the Dodgers' organization in January. *In Sanford, Florida, the police chief threatened to cancel games if Robinson and Wright did not cease training activities there; as a result, Robinson was sent back to Daytona Beach. In Jacksonville, the stadium was padlocked shut without warning on game day, by order of the city's Parks and Public Property director. In DeLand, a scheduled day game was called off, ostensibly because of faulty electrical lighting.*
After much lobbying of local officials by Rickey himself, the Royals were allowed to host a game involving Robinson in Daytona Beach. Robinson made his Royals debut at Daytona Beach's City Island Ballpark on March 17, 1946, in an exhibition game against the team's parent club, the Dodgers. Robinson thus simultaneously became the first black player to openly play for a minor league team and against a major league team since the *de facto* baseball color line had been implemented in the 1880s. Later in spring training, after some less-than-stellar performances, Robinson was shifted from shortstop to second base, allowing him to make shorter throws to first base. Robinson's performance soon rebounded. On April 18, 1946, Roosevelt Stadium hosted the Jersey City Giants' season opener against the Montreal Royals, marking the professional debut of the Royals' Jackie Robinson. In his five trips to the plate, Robinson had four hits, including a three-run home run. He also scored four runs, drove in three, and stole two bases in the Royals' 14-1

victory. Robinson proceeded to lead the International League that season with a.349 batting average and.985 fielding percentage, and he was named the league's Most Valuable Player. *Although he often faced hostility while on road trips (the Royals were forced to cancel a Southern exhibition tour, for example), the Montreal fan base enthusiastically supported Robinson. Whether fans supported or opposed it, Robinson's presence on the field was a boon to attendance; more than one million people went to games involving Robinson in 1946, an amazing figure by International League standards.* In the fall of 1946, following the baseball season, Robinson returned home to California and briefly played professional basketball for the short-lived Los Angeles Red Devils.

Major leagues
Breaking the color barrier (1947)

The following year, six days before the start of the 1947 season, the Dodgers called Robinson up to the major leagues. With Eddie Stanky entrenched at second base for the Dodgers, Robinson played his initial major league season as a first baseman. *On April 15, 1947, Robinson made his major league debut at Ebbets Field before a crowd of 26,623 spectators, including more than 14,000 black patrons.* Although he failed to get a base hit, the Dodgers won 5-3. Robinson became the first player since 1880 to openly break the major league baseball color line. Black fans began flocking to see the Dodgers when they came to town, abandoning their Negro league teams. Robinson's promotion met a generally positive, although mixed, reception among newspapers and white major league players. *However, racial tension existed in the Dodger clubhouse. Some Dodger players insinuated they would sit out rather than play alongside Robinson. The brewing mutiny ended when Dodgers management took a stand for Robinson. Manager Leo Durocher informed the team, "I do not care if the guy is yellow or black, or if he has stripes like a fuckin' zebra. I'm the manager of this team, and I say he plays. What's more, I say he can make us all rich. And if any of you cannot use the money, I will see that you are all traded."*

Robinson was also derided by opposing teams. Some, notably the St. Louis Cardinals, threatened to strike if Robinson played. After the threat, National League President Ford Frick and Baseball Commissioner Happy Chandler let it be known that any striking players would be suspended. Robinson nonetheless became the target of rough physical play by opponents (particularly the Cardinals). At one time, he received a seven-inch gash in his leg. On April 22, 1947, during a game between the Dodgers and the Philadelphia Phillies, Phillies players called Robinson a "nigger" from their dugout and yelled that he should "go back to the cotton fields". Rickey later recalled that Phillies manager Ben Chapman "did more than anybody to unite the Dodgers. When he poured out that string of unconscionable abuse, he solidified and united thirty men."

Robinson received significant encouragement from several major league players. Dodgers' teammate Pee Wee Reese once came to Robinson's defense with the famous line, ***"You can hate a man for many reasons. Color is not one of them."*** In 1948, Reese put his arm around Robinson in response to fans who shouted racial slurs at Robinson before a game in Cincinnati. A statue by sculptor William Behrends, unveiled at KeySpan Park on November 1, 2005, commemorates this event by representing Reese with his arm around Robinson. Jewish baseball star Hank Greenberg, who had to deal with racial epithets during his career, also encouraged Robinson. After colliding with Robinson at first base on one occasion, Greenberg whispered a few words into Robinson's ear, which Robinson later characterized as "words of encouragement." ***Greenberg had advised him that the best way to combat the slurs from the opposing players was to beat them on the field.***

Robinson finished the season with 12 home runs, a league-leading 29 steals, a.297 batting average, a.427 slugging percentage, and 125 runs scored. His cumulative performance earned him the inaugural Major League Baseball Rookie of the Year Award (separate National and American League Rookie of the Year honors were not awarded until 1949).

MVP, Congressional testimony, and film biography (1948-1950)

Following Stanky's trade to the Boston Braves in March 1948, Robinson took over second base, where he logged a.980 fielding percentage that year (second in the National League at the position, fractionally behind Stanky). Robinson had a batting average of.296 and 22 stolen bases for the season. In a 12-7 win against the St. Louis Cardinals on August 29, 1948, he hit for the cycle—a home run, a triple, a double, and a single in the same game. The Dodgers briefly moved into first place in the National League in late August 1948, but they ultimately finished third as the Braves went on to win the league title and lose to the Cleveland Indians in the World Series.

Racial pressure on Robinson eased in 1948 as a number of other black players entered the major leagues. Larry Doby (who broke the color barrier in the American League on July 5, 1947) and Satchel Paige played for the Cleveland Indians, and the Dodgers had three other black players besides Robinson. In February 1948, he signed a $12,500 contract (equal to $112,968 today) with the Dodgers; while a significant amount, this was less than Robinson made in the off-season from a vaudeville tour, where he answered pre-set baseball questions, and a speaking tour of the South. Between the tours, he underwent surgery on his right ankle. Because of his off-season activities, Robinson reported to training camp 30 pounds (14 kg) overweight. He lost the weight during training camp, but dieting left him weak at the plate.

In the spring of 1949, Robinson turned to Hall of Famer George Sisler, working as an advisor to the Dodgers, for batting help. At Sisler's suggestion, Robinson spent hours at a batting tee, learning to hit the ball to right field. Sisler taught Robinson to anticipate a fastball, on the theory that it is easier to subsequently adjust to a slower curveball. Robinson also noted that "Sisler showed me how to stop lunging, how to check my swing until the last fraction of a second". The tutelage helped Robinson raise his batting average from.296 in 1948 to.342 in 1949. In addition to his improved batting average, Robinson stole 37 bases that season, was second place in the league for both doubles and triples, and registered 124 runs batted in with 122 runs scored. For the performance Robinson earned the Most Valuable Player award for the National League. *Baseball fans also voted Robinson as the starting second baseman for the 1949 All-Star Game—the first All-Star Game to include black players.*

That year, a song about Robinson by Buddy Johnson, "Did You See Jackie Robinson Hit That Ball?" reached number 13 on the charts; Count Basie recorded a famous version. Ultimately, the Dodgers won the National League pennant, but lost in five games to the New York Yankees in the 1949 World Series.

Summer 1949 brought an unwanted distraction for Robinson. In July, he was called to testify before the United States House of Representatives' Committee on Un-American Activities (HUAC) concerning statements made that April by black athlete and actor Paul Robeson. Robinson was reluctant to testify, but he eventually agreed to do so, fearing it might negatively affect his career if he declined.

In 1950, Robinson led the National League in double plays made by a second baseman with 133. His salary that year was the highest any Dodger had been paid to that point: $35,000 ($316,311 in 2010 dollars. He finished the year with 99 runs scored, a.328 batting average, and 12 stolen bases. The year saw the release of a film biography of Robinson's life, *The Jackie Robinson Story*, in which Robinson played himself, and actress Ruby Dee played Rachael "Rae" (Isum) Robinson. The project had been previously delayed when the film's producers refused to accede to demands of two Hollywood studios that the movie include scenes of Robinson being tutored in baseball by a white man. **The New York Times wrote that Robinson,**

"doing that rare thing of playing himself in the picture's leading role, displays a calm assurance and composure that might be envied by many a Hollywood star."

Robinson's Hollywood exploits, however, did not sit well with Dodgers co-owner Walter O'Malley, who referred to Robinson as "Rickey's prima donna". In late 1950, Rickey's contract as the Dodgers' team President expired. Weary of constant disagreements with O'Malley, and with no hope of being re-appointed as President of the Dodgers, Rickey cashed out his one-quarter financial interest in the team, leaving O'Malley in full control of the franchise. Rickey shortly thereafter became general manager of the Pittsburgh Pirates. Robinson was disappointed at the turn of events and wrote a sympathetic letter to Rickey, whom he considered a father figure, stating, "Regardless of what happens to me in the future, it all can be placed on what you have done and, believe me, I appreciate it."

Pennant races and outside interests (1951-1953)

Before the 1951 season, O'Malley reportedly offered Robinson the job of manager of the Montreal Royals, effective at the end of Robinson's playing career. O'Malley was quoted in the *Montreal Standard* as saying, "Jackie told me that he would be both delighted and honored to tackle this managerial post"—although reports differed as to whether a position was ever formally offered.

During the 1951 season, Robinson led the National League in double plays made by a second baseman for the second year in a row, with 137. He also kept the Dodgers in contention for the 1951 pennant. During the last game of the season, in the 13th inning, he had a hit to tie the game, and then won the game with a home run in the 14th. This forced a playoff against the New York Giants, which the Dodgers lost.

Despite Robinson's regular-season heroics, the Dodgers lost the pennant on Bobby Thomson's famous home run, known as the Shot Heard 'Round the World, on October 3, 1951. Overcoming his dejection, Robinson dutifully observed Thomson's feet to ensure he touched all the bases. Dodgers' sportscaster Vin Scully later noted that the incident showed "how much of a competitor Robinson was." He finished the season with 106 runs scored, a batting average of.335, and 25 stolen bases.

Robinson had what was an average year for him in 1952. He finished the year with 104 runs, a.308 batting average, and 24 stolen bases. He did, however, record a career-high on-base percentage of.436. The Dodgers improved on their performance from the year before, winning the National League pennant before losing the 1952 World Series to the New York Yankees in seven games. That year, on the television show *Youth Wants to Know,*

Robinson challenged the Yankees' general manager, George Weiss, on the racial record of his team, which had yet to sign a black player. Sportswriter Dick Young, whom Robinson had described as a "bigot", said, "If there was one flaw in Jackie, it was the common one. He believed that everything unpleasant that happened to him happened because of his blackness." The 1952 season was the last year Robinson was an everyday starter at second base. Afterward, Robinson played variously at first, second, and third bases, shortstop, and in the outfield, with Jim Gilliam, another black player, taking over everyday second base duties. Robinson's interests began to shift toward the prospect of managing a major league team. He had hoped to gain experience by managing in the Puerto Rican Winter League, but according to the *New York Post*, Commissioner Happy Chandler denied the request.

In 1953, Robinson had 109 runs, a.329 batting average, and 17 steals, leading the Dodgers to another National League pennant (and another World Series loss to the Yankees, this time in six games). ***Robinson's continued success spawned a string of death threats. He was not dissuaded, however, from addressing racial issues publicly. That year, he served as editor for Our Sports magazine, a periodical focusing on Negro sports issues; contributions to the magazine included an article on golf course segregation by Robinson's old friend Joe Louis. Robinson also openly criticized segregated hotels and restaurants that served the Dodger organization; a number of these establishments integrated as a result, including the five-star Chase Park Hotel in St. Louis.***

World Championship and retirement (1954-1956)

In 1954, Robinson had 62 runs, a.311 batting average, and 7 steals. His best day at the plate was on June 17, when he hit two home runs and two doubles. The following autumn, Robinson won his only championship when the Dodgers beat the New York Yankees in the 1955 World Series. Although the team enjoyed ultimate success, 1955 was the worst year of Robinson's individual career. He hit.256 and stole only 12 bases. The Dodgers tried Robinson in the outfield and as a third baseman, both because of his diminishing abilities and because Gilliam was established at second base. Robinson, then 37 years old, missed 49 games and did not play in Game 7 of the World Series. Robinson missed the game because manager Walter Alston decided to play Gilliam at second and Don Hoak at third base. That season, the Dodgers' Don Newcombe became the first black major league pitcher to win twenty games in a year.

In 1956, Robinson had 61 runs, a.275 batting average, and 12 steals. By then, he had begun to exhibit the effects of diabetes, and to lose interest in the prospect of playing or managing professional baseball. After the season,

Robinson was traded by the Dodgers to the arch-rival New York Giants for Dick Littlefield and $35,000 cash (equal to $280,172 today). The trade, however, was never completed; unbeknownst to the Dodgers, Robinson had already agreed with the president of Chock full o'Nuts to quit baseball and become an executive with the company. Since Robinson had sold exclusive rights to any retirement story to *Look* magazine two years previously, his retirement decision was revealed through the magazine, instead of through the Dodgers organization.

Legacy

Further information: Racial integration in baseball
Robinson's major league debut brought an end to approximately sixty years of segregation in professional baseball, known as the baseball color line. After World War II, several other forces were also leading the country toward increased equality for blacks, including their accelerated migration of to the North, where their political clout grew, and President Harry Truman's desegregation of the military in 1948. Robinson's breaking of the baseball color line and his professional success symbolized these broader changes and demonstrated that the fight for equality was more than simply a political matter. Martin Luther King, Jr. said that he was "a legend and a symbol in his own time", and that he "challenged the dark skies of intolerance and frustration." According to historian Doris Kearns Goodwin, Robinson's "efforts were a monumental step in the civil-rights revolution in America . . . [His] accomplishments allowed black and white Americans to be more respectful and open to one another and more appreciative of everyone's abilities."

Beginning his major league career at the relatively advanced age of twenty-eight, he played only ten seasons, all of them for the Brooklyn Dodgers. During his career, the Dodgers played in six World Series, and Robinson himself played in six All-Star Games. **In 1999, he was posthumously named to the Major League Baseball All-Century Team.**

Robinson's career is generally considered to mark the beginning of the post—" long ball" era in baseball, in which a reliance on raw power-hitting gave way to balanced offensive strategies that used foot speed to create runs through aggressive base running. Robinson exhibited the combination of hitting ability and speed which exemplified the new era. He scored more than 100 runs in six of his ten seasons (averaging more than 110 runs from 1947 to 1953), had a.311 career batting average, a.409 career on-base percentage, a.474 slugging percentage, and substantially more walks than strikeouts (740 to 291). Robinson was one of only two players during the span of 1947-56 to accumulate at least 125 steals while registering a slugging percentage over.425 (Minnie Miñoso was the other). He accumulated 197 stolen bases in total, including 19 steals of home. None of the latter were double steals (in which a player stealing home is assisted by a player stealing another base at the same time). Robinson has been referred to by author David Falkner as "the father of modern base-stealing."

—Robinson, on his legacy

Historical statistical analysis indicates Robinson was an outstanding fielder throughout his ten years in the major leagues and at virtually every position he played. After playing his rookie season at first base, Robinson spent most of his career as a second baseman. He led the league in fielding among second basemen in 1950 and 1951. Toward the end of his career, he played about 2,000 innings at third base and about 1,175 innings in the outfield, excelling at both.

Assessing himself, Robinson said, "I'm not concerned with your liking or disliking me . . . all I ask is that you respect me as a human being." Regarding Robinson's qualities on the field, Leo Durocher said, "Ya want a guy that comes to play. This guy didn't just come to play. He come to beat ya. He come to stuff the goddamn bat right up your ass."

Post-baseball life

Robinson retired from baseball on January 5; 1957.Later that year, after he complained of numerous physical ailments, his doctors diagnosed Robinson with diabetes, a disease that also affected his brothers. Although Robinson adopted an insulin injection regimen, the state of medicine at the time could not prevent continued deterioration of Robinson's physical condition from the disease.

In his first year of eligibility for the Baseball Hall of Fame in 1962, Robinson encouraged voters to consider only his on-field qualifications, rather than his cultural impact on the game. *He was elected on the first ballot, becoming the first black player inducted into the Cooperstown museum.*

In 1965, Robinson served as an analyst for ABC's *Major League Baseball Game of the Week* telecasts, the first black person to do so. On June 4, 1972, the Dodgers retired his uniform number, 42, alongside those of Roy Campanella (39) and Sandy Koufax (32). From 1957 to 1964, Robinson was the vice president for personnel at Chock full o'Nuts; he was the first black person to serve as vice president of a major American corporation. Robinson always considered his business career as advancing the cause of black people in commerce and industry. Robinson also chaired the National Association for the Advancement of Colored People's (NAACP) million-dollar Freedom Fund Drive in 1957, and served on the organization's board until 1967. In 1964, he helped found, with Harlem businessman Dunbar McLaurin, Freedom National Bank—a black-owned and operated commercial bank based in Harlem. He also served as the bank's first Chairman of the Board. In 1970, Robinson established the Jackie Robinson Construction Company to build housing for low-income families.

Robinson was active in politics throughout his post-baseball life. He identified himself as a political independent although he held conservative opinions on several issues, including the Vietnam War (he once wrote Martin Luther King, Jr. to defend the Johnson Administration's military policy). After supporting Richard Nixon in his 1960 presidential race against John F. Kennedy, Robinson later praised Kennedy effusively for his stance on civil rights. He subsequently supported Hubert Humphrey against Nixon in 1968. In 1964, Robinson became one of six national directors for Nelson Rockefeller's Republican presidential campaign and later became special assistant for community affairs when Rockefeller was re-elected governor of New York in 1966.

Protesting the major leagues' ongoing lack of minority managers and central office personnel, Robinson turned down an invitation to appear in an old-timers' game at Yankee Stadium in 1969. He made his final public appearance on October 15, 1972, throwing the ceremonial first pitch before Game 2 of the World Series. He gratefully accepted a plaque honoring the twenty-fifth anniversary of his MLB debut, but also commented, *"I'm going to be tremendously more pleased and more proud when I look at that third base coaching line one day and see a black face managing in baseball." This wish was fulfilled only after Robinson's death: following the 1974 season, the Cleveland Indians gave their managerial post to Frank Robinson (no relation), a Hall of Fame-bound player who would go on to manage three other teams. Despite the success of these two Robinsons and other black players, the number of African-American players in Major League Baseball has declined since the 1970s.*

Family life and death

After Robinson's retirement from baseball, his wife, Rachel Robinson, pursued a career in academic nursing—she became an assistant professor at the Yale School of Nursing and director of nursing at the Connecticut Mental Health Center. She also served on the board of the Freedom National Bank until it closed in 1990. She and Jackie had three children: Jackie Robinson Jr. (born November 18, 1946), Sharon Robinson (born January 13, 1950), and David Robinson (born May 14, 1952).

Robinson's eldest son, Jackie Robinson Jr., had emotional trouble during his childhood and entered special education at an early age. He enrolled in the Army in search of a disciplined environment, served in the Vietnam War, and was wounded in action on November 19, 1965. After his discharge, he struggled with drug problems. Robinson Jr. eventually completed the treatment program at Daytop Village in Seymour, Connecticut, and became a counselor at the institution. On June 17, 1971, at the age of 24, he was killed in an automobile accident. The experience with his son's drug addiction turned Robinson, Sr. into an avid anti-drug crusader toward the end of his life.

Robinson did not long outlive his son. Complications of heart disease and diabetes weakened Robinson and made him almost blind by middle age. On October 24, 1972, he died of a heart attack at home in Stamford, Connecticut, aged fifty-three. Robinson's funeral service on October 27, 1972, at New York City's Riverside Church attracted 2,500 admirers. Many of his former teammates and other famous black baseball players served as pallbearers, and the Rev. Jesse Jackson gave the eulogy. Tens of thousands of people lined the subsequent procession route to Robinson's interment site at Cypress Hills Cemetery in Brooklyn, New York, where he is buried next to his son Jackie and mother-in-law Zellee Isum. Jackie Robinson Parkway also runs through the cemetery.

After Robinson's death, his widow founded the Jackie Robinson Foundation, of which she remains an officer as of 2009. On April 15, 2008, she announced that in 2010 the foundation will be opening a museum devoted to Jackie in Lower Manhattan. Robinson's daughter, Sharon, became a midwife, educator, director of educational programming for MLB, and the author of two books about her father. His youngest son, David, who has ten children, is a coffee grower and social activist in Tanzania.

Awards and recognition

According to a poll conducted in 1947, Robinson was the second most popular man in the country, behind Bing Crosby. In 1999, he was named by Time on its list of the 100 most influential people of the 20th century. Also in 1999, he ranked number 44 on the *Sporting News* list of the 100 Greatest Baseball Players, and was elected to the Major League Baseball All-Century Team as the top vote-getter among second basemen. Baseball writer Bill James, in *The New Bill James Historical Baseball Abstract*, ranked Robinson as the 32nd greatest player of all time strictly on the basis of his performance on the field, noting that he was one of the top players in the league throughout his career. Robinson was among the 25 charter members of UCLA's Athletics Hall of Fame in 1984. In 2002, Molefi Kete Asante included Robinson on his list of 100 Greatest African Americans. Robinson has also been honored by the United States Postal Service on three separate postage stamps, in 1982, 1999, and 2000.

The City of Pasadena has recognized Robinson in several ways. Brookside Park, situated next to the Rose Bowl, features a baseball diamond and stadium named Jackie Robinson Field. The city's Human Services Department operates the Jackie Robinson Center, a community outreach center that provides early diabetes detection and other services. In 1997, a $325,000 bronze sculpture (equal to $440,453 today) by artists Ralph Helmick, Stu Schecter, and John Outterbridge depicting oversized nine-foot busts of Robinson and his brother Mack was erected at Garfield Avenue, across from the main entrance of Pasadena City Hall; a granite footprint lists multiple donors to the commission project, which was organized by the Robinson Memorial Foundation and supported by members of the Robinson family.

MLB has honored Robinson many times since his death. In 1987, both the National and American League Rookie of the Year Awards were renamed the "Jackie Robinson Award" in honor of the first recipient (Robinson's Major League Rookie of the Year Award in 1947 encompassed both leagues). *On April 15, 1997, Robinson's jersey number, 42, was retired by Major League Baseball; no future player on any major league team can wear it.* The number was retired in ceremonies at Shea Stadium to mark the 50th anniversary of Robinson's first game with the Dodgers. A grandfather clause allowed handful of players who wore number 42 as a salute to Robinson, such as the Mets' Butch Huskey and Boston's Mo Vaughn, were allowed to continue wearing the number for as long as they stayed with their current team and did not change their number. The Yankees' Mariano Rivera is the last player in the major leagues to wear jersey number 42 on a regular basis. *This marked the first time that any major American sports league retired a single number throughout the entire league, and has only been done once since then, when the National Hockey League retired Wayne Gretzky's number 99 in 2000.*

As an exception to the retired-number policy, MLB has recently begun honoring Robinson by allowing players to wear number 42 on April 15, Jackie Robinson Day. For the 60th anniversary of Robinson's major league debut, MLB invited players to wear the number 42 on Jackie Robinson Day in 2007. The gesture was originally the idea of outfielder Ken Griffey, Jr., who sought Rachel Robinson's permission to wear the number. After receiving her permission, Commissioner Bud Selig not only allowed Griffey to wear the number, but also extended an invitation to all major league teams to do the same. Ultimately, more than 200 players wore number 42, including the entire rosters of the Los Angeles Dodgers, New York Mets, Houston Astros, Philadelphia Phillies, St. Louis Cardinals, Milwaukee Brewers, and Pittsburgh Pirates. The tribute was continued in 2008, when, during games on April 15, all members of the Mets, Cardinals, Washington Nationals, and Tampa Bay Rays wore Robinson's number 42. On June 25, 2008, MLB installed a new plaque for Robinson at the Baseball Hall of Fame commemorating his off-the-field impact on the game as well as his playing statistics. *In 2009, all uniformed personnel (players, managers, coaches, and umpires) wore number 42 on April 15.*

At the November 2006 groundbreaking for a new ballpark for the New York Mets, Citi Field, it was announced that the main entrance, modeled on the one in Brooklyn's old Ebbets Field, would be called the Jackie Robinson Rotunda. The rotunda was dedicated at the opening of Citi Field on April 16, 2009. It honors Robinson with large quotations spanning the inner curve of the facade and features a large freestanding statue of his number, 42, which has become an attraction in itself. Mets owner Fred Wilpon announced that, in conjunction with Citigroup and the Jackie Robinson Foundation, the Mets will create a Jackie Robinson Museum and Learning Center, located at the headquarters of the Jackie Robinson Foundation at One Hudson Square in lower Manhattan. The main purpose of the museum will be to fund scholarships for "young people who live by and embody Jackie's ideals."

Robinson has also been recognized outside of baseball. In December 1956, the NAACP recognized him with the Spingarn Medal, which it awards annually for the highest achievement by an African-American. President Ronald Reagan posthumously awarded Robinson the Presidential Medal of Freedom on March 26, 1984, and on March 2, 2005, President George W. Bush gave Robinson's widow the Congressional Gold Medal, the highest civilian award bestowed by Congress; Robinson was only the second baseball player to receive the award, after Roberto Clemente. On August 20, 2007, California Governor Arnold Schwarzenegger and his wife, Maria Shriver, announced that Robinson was inducted into the California Hall of Fame, located at The California Museum for History, Women and the Arts in Sacramento.

A number of buildings have been named in Robinson's honor. The UCLA Bruins baseball team plays in Jackie Robinson Stadium, which, because of the efforts of Jackie's brother Mack, features a memorial statue of Robinson by sculptor Richard H. Ellis. City Island Ballpark in Daytona Beach, Florida—the baseball field that became the Dodgers' de facto spring training site in 1947—was renamed Jackie Robinson Ballpark in 1989. The New York Public School system has named a middle school after Robinson, and Dorsey High School plays at a Los Angeles football stadium named after him. In

1976, his home in Brooklyn, the Jackie Robinson House, was declared a National Historic Landmark. Robinson also has an asteroid named after him, 4319 Jackierobinson. ***In 1997, the United States Mint issued a Jackie Robinson commemorative silver dollar, and five dollar gold coin.***

Quote:

Do not go where the path may lead, go instead where there is no path and leave a trail.—Ralph Waldo Emerson

Charlie Sifford

Charles Sifford (born June 2, 1922) was an African American professional golfer who helped to desegregate the PGA of America.

Sifford was born in Charlotte, North Carolina. He began work as a caddy at the age of thirteen. Later he competed in the golf tournaments that black golfers organized for themselves as they were excluded from the PGA of America, and worked as a personal golf coach for band leader Billy Eckstine. *He first attempted to qualify for a PGA Tour event at the 1952 Phoenix Open, using an invitation obtained by former World heavyweight boxing champion Joe Louis and was subjected to threats and racial abuse there and at other tournaments.* In 1957 he won the Long Beach Open, which was not an official PGA Tour event, but was co-sponsored by the PGA and had some well known white players in the field. He became a member of the Tour in 1961 and went on to win two official money events. He also won the 1975 PGA Seniors' Championship, then the leading tournament for golfers over fifty.

In 2004, Sifford became the first African American inducted into the World Golf Hall of Fame. He chose the fellow Hall of Fame member South African Gary Player to present him for induction. On June 22, 2006, he received an honorary degree from the University of St Andrews as a Doctor of Laws. He also received the 2007 Old Tom Morris Award from the Golf Course Superintendents Association of America, GCSAA's highest honor.

In 2009, the Northern Trust Open created an exemption for a player who represents the advancement of diversity in golf; it is named in honor of Sifford and is referred to as the Charlie Sifford Exemption

There will be those who will argue that Charlie Sifford got into the World Golf Hall of Fame not on merit but as a symbol, that his two PGA Tour victories and one PGA Seniors Championship did not warrant the honor. And they would be right, but not for the reasons they think.

Yes, Mr. Sifford is a symbol. He is a symbol of courage and determination as well as a symbolic reminder of a time in America's

all-too-recent past we should remember with sadness and shame. Mr. Sifford is a reminder that many of the things we tend to take for granted—such as the right to be served in a restaurant or attend a state university—were not inalienable rights bestowed from above, as our Founding Fathers said, but rather hard-fought victories earned by those held somewhere down below.

Mr. Sifford did much more than win two PGA Tour events. He was part of a movement that changed America. While it would perhaps be too much of a stretch to say that without Mr. Sifford we would not have Tiger Woods today, it would not be an exaggeration to say that without Mr. Sifford—and the others who fought against the PGA's "Caucasian Only" clause—the arrival of an enormously talented player of color in professional golf would have been further delayed. Certainly, there were many in 1961, when Mr. Sifford became the first black to play fulltime on the PGA Tour, who were as determined to block the integration of the tour as Mr. Sifford was to overturn that injustice.

Was Charlie Sifford a revolutionary? Perhaps not: But he was part of a revolutionary movement. Think about this: Blacks were not allowed on the PGA Tour until 1961. Arnold Palmer had already won two Masters by then. And the first black did not play in the Masters—Lee Elder—until 1975, the year Tiger Woods was born. Our past is not as distant as we sometimes try to pretend it is. That Mr. Sifford, at the age of 81, has been granted access to the Hall of Fame under the Lifetime Achievement category is—in the words President Lincoln used at Gettysburg—"fitting and proper." *Mr. Sifford's achievement did more than benefit golf. It benefited America.*

Mr. Sifford was a very good though not great golfer. And he was a significant though not singular pioneer. Mr. Sifford was part of the post World War II civil rights movement that had Rosa Parks refusing to sit in the back of the bus and James Meredith risking his life to get into the University of Mississippi. But Mr. Sifford was also part of a movement in which countless unnamed heroes were beaten and many killed because they dared stand up for rights we tend today to think were always there for all Americans. His induction into the Hall of Fame in November is an honor not just for Mr. Sifford but for all those of forgotten name who fought for equality.

In the world of sports there was the track star Jesse Owens, the boxer Joe Louis—whose son Joe Louis Barrow heads the First Tee program—and Jackie Robinson, who broke the color barrier in major league baseball. In golf there were early pioneers such as Bill Spiller. But while the inclusion of Mr. Sifford into the Hall of Fame is a fitting symbolic recognition not just of his ordeal as a pioneer but also a recognition of those who fought the good fight with him, it is also a sad reminder of a current condition that is just as shameful as the Caucasian Only clause of more than 40 years ago.

296 | George D. Johnson

Grab a PGA Tour media guide from the mid 1970s—around the time Tiger Woods was born—and search the pages for black faces. You will find Rafe Botts, Pete Brown, Jim Dent, Calvin Peete, Curtis Sifford, Nathaniel Starks, Bobby Stroble, Jim Thorpe and Charlie Sifford. Now pick up this year's tour media guide and search for a native-born American of African descent. There is one—Tiger Woods. And that is one more black face than you will find on the LPGA

Certainly, this is not the fault of the tours. In fact, it was at the initiative of the PGA Tour that the First Tee—which tries to bring children from non-golf backgrounds into the game—was created. And the LPGA is one of the most integrated leagues in any sport, largely on the strength of foreign players. But the lack of American-born minorities in professional golf does say something about the way the game has evolved in this country.

Caddie programs—the traditional way in which kids of modest means were exposed to the game—have been replaced at many golf clubs by revenue-generating carts. And public golf is so overcrowded at the courses that are affordable—and let's not kid ourselves into thinking that a $200 green fee course is public golf—that players are being driven away from the game by six-hour rounds. ***More and more, the PGA Tour has become the workplace of players who have gone through the finishing school of country club golf.***

The country club was not where Mr. Sifford learned the game. And it was also not where Sam Snead, Ben Hogan, Byron Nelson and Gene Sarazen learned the game—except in this regard: They all were exposed to the game by being caddies. If the talent pool for golf has shrunk—and that appears to be the case—it is not just for people of color but for people of modest means.

When Charlie Sifford is inducted into the World Golf Hall of Fame on Nov. 15 in St. Augustine, Fla., it will be a significant day in the history of golf. The game will have its first black member of the Hall of Fame. And it will be a time to remember all those pioneers who walked with him. But it will also be a time to remember how much more there is to do. It will be a time to celebrate the one and only black member of the Hall of Fame, and a time to remember that there is still one and only one black member of the PGA Tour.

Attributed to Ron Sirak is the Executive Editor of Golf World magazine

Reflection:

It's interesting to note that a Tiger now roams freely throughout the world, on terrain where a lion was once shunned as a predator.

Bobo Brazil

*Houston Harris (July 10, 1923—January 20, 1998) was an American professional wrestler, better known by his ring name, **Bobo Brazil**. Harris was credited with breaking down barriers of racial segregation in professional wrestling. Harris is considered one of the first successful African-American professional wrestlers, and is often referred to as "the Jackie Robinson of professional wrestling.*

Professional wrestling career

Harris was trained by Joe Savoldi after meeting him at matches at the Naval Armory. Originally, Harris was to be known as "Boo-Boo Brazil", but a promoter misprinted his first name as "Bobo" in an advertisement and it stuck.

Early in his career, some wrestling promoters would match Brazil against fellow African-American wrestlers, including Ernie Ladd and Abdullah the Butcher. Fans clamored to see Brazil face opponents of any type and Brazil would have many matches with competitors such as Killer Kowalski, Dick the Bruiser, Johnny Valentine, and The Sheik, who feuded with Bobo over the course of several decades. These and other rivals would all fall victim to Brazil's finishing maneuver, the Coco Butt. Brazil also once wrestled Gene Simmons to a draw, and challenged Bruno Sammartino for the WWWF Championship in a battle of two top babyface competitors. *On October 18, 1962 Bobo Brazil made history by becoming the first Black American to win the NWA World Heavyweight Title by defeating "Nature Boy" Buddy Rogers.* (This distinction is usually given to Ron Simmons, the first recognized African-American world champion after winning the WCW World Heavyweight Championship). Although Bobo Brazil initially refused the title (because of an "injury" that Rogers had claimed to have), Brazil was awarded the title the next day after doctors had found nothing wrong with Rogers. However, this title change is not recognized by the NWA.

*On October 9, 1970, El Mongol and Bobo Brazil defeated Mr.
Ito and The Great Ota in the first racially mixed match in Atlanta
history.*

Brazil served as a mentor to wrestler "Soulman" Rocky Johnson. Brazil's
manager was James Dudley, the first African-American to be in charge of
a major arena in the United States. Dudley would run to the ring waving a
towel, as Brazil followed behind.

Brazil retired in the 1990s after a four decade career and was inducted
into the WWF Hall of Fame in 1994 by Ernie Ladd. The following year,
Brazil inducted Ladd into the WWE Hall of Fame.

Personal life

Harris was born in Little Rock, Arkansas but later moved to Benton
Harbor, Michigan. He played baseball and worked in a steel mill. After
retiring from wrestling, Harris ran a restaurant.

Harris had six children. Harris died on January 20, 1998 at the Lakeland
Medical Center in St. Joseph, Michigan. He had been admitted to the hospital
on January 14, after suffering a series of strokes. [1]

Points to Ponder

*Television is an invention that permits you to be entertained in your living
room by people you wouldn't have in your home.* **David Frost**

*When it comes to wresting I am like the old lady who kissed to cow, everyone
to his own liking.*

The Cotton Club:

Since its inception in 1923, The Cotton Club has gained worldwide notoriety for booking the finest musical entertainment in the country. The Cotton Club has been home to numerous legendary greats, including Duke Ellington, Cab Calloway, Ethel Waters and Lena Horne. After some renovation and a grand re-opening in December 1977, The Cotton Club continues to live up to its star-studded legacy. With a warm, intimate interior, The Cotton Club allows its patrons to enjoy the simple things in life—delectable food, raw talent and good company.

Since its inception in 1923, The Cotton Club has gained worldwide notoriety for booking the finest musical entertainment in the country. The Cotton Club has been home to numerous legendary greats, including Duke Ellington, Cab Calloway, Ethel Waters and Lena Horne.

It all began when Heavyweight Boxer Jack Johnson opened an establishment at 142nd street and Lenox Avenue, New York City: Club DeLux.

The failure of this club in 1923 forced Jack Johnson to sell it to gangster Owney Madden. Madden had been seeking a Harlem location from which he could sell his Madden's #1 beer. Thus, The Cotton Club was born.

Madden and his gangster cohorts devised The Cotton Club motif. The name (synonymous with its location in Harlem) was chosen to conjure up thoughts of a stylish plantation environment. To further this connotation, while enhancing the décor of the Club, all musicians and performers were black, and, with rare exceptions, the owners and all the guests were white.

The Club's "white only" policy heightened its appeal for patronage: not only for "downtown" New Yorkers but also for world-wide visitors. Featuring the most talented black entertainers it could get its hands on, The Cotton Club attracted a host of celebrity clientele, including Bing Crosby, Jimmy Durante, Fanny Brice, Irving Berlin, Cole Porter, Dorothy Kilgallen, Doris Duke, as well as the famous Dutch

Shultz. Many of the early black entertainers got their start at The Cotton Club, such as Duke Ellington, Ethel Waters, Cab Calloway, Bill "Bojangles" Robinson, Dorothy Dandridge, Avon Long, Lena Horne and the Nicholas Brothers.

The Cotton Club was definitely the hot-spot to be for both guests and performers. It was not only the aristocratic sphere of Harlem, but of the whole nightclub scene. Only the wealthiest, most influential, famous or notorious went there or could get in. Not only did The Club give its clientele the opportunity to rub shoulders with celebrities and gangsters, but it also exposed them to The Club's unmatched décor, cuisine and entertainment.

The Cotton Club, in its grand return to Harlem, reopened its doors in 1978 with Cab Calloway and other noted entertainers as the featured attraction. Mr. John Beatty, the current owner of The Cotton Club, has instituted a policy of operation whereby formerly excluded clientele can now patronize The Club.

Quote:

" I can't sing in no nightclub. People can't put their minds on the Lord in a place like that." **Mahalia Jackson**

Savoy Ballroom

About the Savoy Ballroom.
Owned by Moe Gale, a Jewish man, and managed by Charles Buchanan, a black man, the Savoy Ballroom opened its doors on March 12, 1926 right in the middle of Harlem, between 140th and 141st Streets on Lenox Avenue. The vision of the two young men created one of the first racially integrated public places in the country, which proved to be a wise business decision as well, attracting a wide range of clientele. The ballroom was on the second floor of a two-story building stretching the entire block. The ground floor of the building housed the entrance to the ballroom at the center of the block signified by the marquee extending out over the sidewalk and various stores. The spacious basement checkrooms could serve up to 5,000 patrons with swift and efficient ease. Billed as the "World's finest ballroom," the Savoy was complete with large luxurious carpeted lounges and mirrored walls. The block long ballroom had two bandstands, colored spotlights and a spring-loaded wooden dance floor. Approximately 700,000 patrons visited the ballroom annually; and, consequently, the floor had to be completely replaced every three years. The Savoy was appropriately nicknamed, ***"The home of happy feet,"*** and it was also known among the regular patrons as "the Track" for the elongated shape of the dance floor.

The staff of 90 permanent employees at the Savoy included musicians, waiters, cashiers, floor attendants, porters and administrative assistants. There were also hostesses with whom a visitor, mostly from downtown, could dance for a dime or be tutored on the latest steps, as well as a team of bouncers clad in black tuxedos and bow ties. The bouncers were ex-boxers, basketball players etc., who would rush in on a moment's notice and put out any person.

Over 250 name and semi-name bands were featured at the Savoy. The house bands included those of Fess Williams, Chick Webb, Erskine Hawkins and Al Cooper's Savoy Sultans, just to name a few. The two bandstands allowed continuous live music all night, and provided the stage for the famous battles of bands. The most famous, and one of the most highly publicized, was the battle of Chick Webb vs. Benny Goodman, when both bands were at the crest of their popularity. Future Be-bop stars like Dizzy Gillespie, Charlie Parker, Art Blakey and Thelonious Monk played there too. As a matter of fact, Teddy Hill, who later became a manager at Minton's Playhouse, also led a house band at the Savoy at one point.

A long succession of dance fads were launched from the Savoy that swept the nation and overseas in response to ever changing music trends from Dixieland, ragtime, jazz, blues, swing, stomp, boogie-woogie, bop to countless Peabody, waltz, one-step, two-step and rumba variations. *Among the countless dance styles originated and developed at the Savoy were: The Flying Charleston, The Lindy Hop, The Stomp, The Big Apple, Jitterbug Jive, Peckin', Snakehips, Rhumboogie and intricate variations of the Peabody, the Shimmy, Mambo, etc . . .*

Herbert White, a.k.a. Whitey, an ex-boxer and bouncer at the Savoy, organized and cultivated a group of young Lindy Hoppers and had them appear in theaters around the world as well as in films. *The Lindy Hop, purportedly named after Charles Lindbergh's solo trans-Atlantic flight in 1927, signifies the entire historical period known as the Swing Era, and was the staple dance at the Savoy until it closed its doors in 1958.* Although the building eventually gave way to a much needed housing complex, the Lindy Hoppers from the Savoy and their heirs dominated the annual Harvest Moon Ball in Madison Square Garden until the 1980's. The Savoy tradition of the Lindy Hop continues to thrive to this date thanks to films and other documented accounts as well as living legends such as Norma Miller and Frankie Manning.

Wisdom for the Journey

"I would believe only in a God that knows how to dance." ~*Friedrich Nietzsche*

"Then David danced before the LORD with all his might; and David was wearing a linen ephod." 2ⁿᵈ Samuel 6:14 (NKJV)

Part Seven:

Significant Events

We hold these truths to be self-evident, that all men are created equal, that they are endowed by their Creator with certain unalienable Rights that among these are Life, Liberty and the pursuit of Happiness.

Declaration of Independence

The Indian Wars

Background:

The Cheyenne are a Native American nation of the Great Plains, closely allied with the Arapaho and loosely allied with the Lakota (Sioux). They are one of the most famous and prominent Plains tribes.

The Cheyenne nation is composed of two united tribes, the Sotaae'o and the Tsitsistas, which translates to "Like Hearted People".

The Cheyenne nation comprised 10 bands, spread all over the Great Plains, from southern Colorado to the Black Hills in South Dakota.

In the early 1800s the tribe split into two factions: the southern band staying near the Platte Rivers and the northern band living near the Black Hills near the Lakota tribes.

The Cheyenne of Montana and Oklahoma both speak the Cheyenne language, with only a handful of vocabulary items different between the two locations. The Cheyenne language is a tonal language and is part of the larger Algonquian language group.

In 1851, the first Cheyenne 'territory' was established in northern Colorado. The Fort Laramie Treaty of 1851 granted this territory.

Today this former territory includes the cities of Fort Collins, Denver and Colorado Springs. *Not long after 1851, the Cheyenne had lost this land due to the influx of settlers due to the gold rush.*

In the Indian Wars, the Cheyenne were the victims of the Sand Creek Massacre in which the Colorado Militia killed 600 Cheyenne. In the early morning on November 27, 1868 the Battle of Washita River started when United States Army Lieutenant Colonel George Armstrong Custer led the 7th U.S. Cavalry in an attack on a band of peaceful Cheyenne legally living on reservation land with Chief Black Kettle. 103 Cheyenne were killed, mostly women and children.

The Indian Wars

The Indian Wars were a series of conflicts between the United States and Native American peoples ("Indians") of North America. The wars, which ranged from colonial times to the Wounded Knee massacre and "closing" of the American frontier in 1890, collectively resulted in the conquest of American Indian peoples and their decimation, assimilation, or forced relocation to Indian reservations.

The term Indian Wars is misleading because it groups American Indians under a single heading. American Indians were (and remain) a diverse category of peoples with discrete histories; throughout the wars, they were not a single people any more than Europeans were. Living in societies organized in a variety of ways (the terms tribe or nation are not always accurate), American Indians usually made decisions about war and peace at the local level, though they sometimes fought as part of complex formal alliances such as the Iroquois Confederation, or in temporary confederacies inspired by charismatic leaders such as Tecumseh.

There are other problems with the term Indian Wars. It creates a category which has traditionally been used to relegate the long story of American Indian warfare to a minor footnote in U.S. history. The term also tends to obscure American Indian involvement in other wars. *For example, American Indians fought extensively in the American Revolutionary War and the War of 1812, two wars which had massive consequences for Native Americans, yet these conflicts have not traditionally been labeled as Indian Wars.*

To see the Indian wars as a racial war between Indians and European-Americans ("whites") overlooks the complex historical reality of the struggle. Indians and whites often fought alongside each other; Indians often fought against Indians. For example, although the Battle of Horseshoe Bend is often described as an "American victory" over the Creek Indians, the victors were a combined force of Cherokees, Creeks, and Tennessee militia led by Andrew Jackson. *From a broad perspective, the Indian wars were about the conquest of Native American peoples by the United States; up close it was rarely quite as simple as that.*

Citing figures from an 1894 estimate by the United States Census Bureau, one scholar has noted that the more than 40 Indian wars from 1775 to 1890 reportedly claimed the lives of some 45,000 Indians and 19,000 whites. This rough estimate includes women and children, since noncombatants were often killed in frontier warfare.

Sand Creek Massacre

The Sand Creek Massacre refers to an infamous incident in the Indian Wars of the United States that occurred on November 29, 1864 when Colorado Militia troops in the Colorado Territory massacred an undefended village of Cheyenne and Arapaho encamped on the territory's eastern plains. The attack was initially reported in the press as a victory against a bravely-fought defense by the Cheyenne. Within weeks, however, eyewitnesses came forward offering conflicting testimony, leading to a military investigation and two Congressional investigations into the events.

Starting the 1850s, the gold rush in the Rocky Mountains (then part of the western Kansas Territory) had brought a flood of white settlers into the mountains and the surrounding foothills. The sudden immigration came into conflict with the Cheyenne and the Arapaho who inhabited the area, eventually leading to the Colorado War in 1864. The violence between the Native Americans and the miners spread, prompting territorial governor John Evans to send Colonel John Chivington to quiet the Indians.

After a few skirmishes and a decisive warpath on the part of the Indians, the Cheyennes and Arapahos were ready for peace and camped near Fort Lyon on the eastern plains.

Both of the tribes had signed a treaty with the United States just three years before in which they ceded their lands to the United States and agreed to move to the Indian reservation to the south of Sand Creek, demarcated by a line to be run due north from a point on the northern boundary of New Mexico, fifteen miles west of Purgatory River, and extending to the Sandy Fork of the Arkansas River.

Chief Black Kettle, a chief of a group of mostly Southern Cheyennes—and some Arapahoe's, some 550 in number, reported to Fort Lyon in an effort to declare peace. After having done so, he and his band camped out at nearby Sand Creek, less than 40 miles north. Having heard the Indians had surrendered, Chivington and his 700 troops of the First Colorado Cavalry, Third Colorado Cavalry and a company of First New Mexico Volunteers marched to their campsite in order to obtain an easy victory.

On the morning of November 29, 1864, the army shot down people as if they were buffalo, killing as many as 150, or about one-quarter of the entire group. The dead were mainly old men, women and children and the cavalry lost only 9 or 10 killed and three dozen wounded.

One man, Silas Soule, a Massachusetts abolitionist, refused to follow Colonel Chivington's orders. He did not allow his cavalry company to fire into the crowd. After the massacre, some tribal members decided to join the Dog Soldiers, a group of Cheyenne who decided there could be no successful negotiations with the white men and were waging war against them.

The nation was shocked by the brutality of the massacre and the army decided to investigate Chivington's role. Silas Soule was extremely willing to testify against him. *After he testified, Soule was murdered by Charles W. Squires. It is believed that Chivington had a hand in this murder.*

The Northern Cheyenne also participated in the Battle of the Little Bighorn, which took place on June 25, 1876. The Cheyenne, along with the Lakota and a small band of Arapaho, annihilated George Armstrong Custer and his contingent.

It is estimated that population of the encampment of the Cheyenne, Lakota and Arapaho along the Little Bighorn River was around 10,000; which would make it one of the largest gathering of Native Americans in North America in pre-reservation times.

Battle of the Little Bighorn

The Battle of the Little Bighorn, also called Custer's **Last Stand,** was an engagement between a Lakota-Northern Cheyenne combined force and the 7th Cavalry of the United States Army, June 25—June 26, 1876 near the Little Bighorn River in the eastern Montana Territory. The battle was the most famous incident in the Indian Wars and was a remarkable victory for the Lakota and Northern Cheyenne. The U.S. cavalry detachment commanded by Lt. Col. George Armstrong Custer was killed to the last man, but overall, the majority of U.S. soldiers survived the fight.

The U.S. forces were sent to attack the Indians based on Indian Inspector's E.C. Watkins report (issued on November 9, 1875) that stated that hundreds of Lakota and Northern Cheyenne associated with Sitting Bull and Crazy Horse were hostile to the United States. U.S. interest in Indian lands (including the gold-rich Black Hills) also played an important role.

As the larger wing of the troops under Gen. Alfred Terry, Custer's force arrived at an overlook 14 miles east of the Little Bighorn River in what is now the state of Montana, on the night of June 24. The rest of the column was marching toward the mouth of the Little Bighorn, to provide a blocking action by the 26th.

The presence of what was judged a very large encampment of Indians was reported to the general by his Crow Indian scouts. Despite this warning, on June 25, Custer divided his regiment into four commands and moved forward to attack the encamped Indians, who were expected to flee at the first sign of attack. The first battalion to attack was commanded by Major Marcus Reno and preceded by about a dozen Arikara and friendly Sioux scouts.

His orders, given by Custer without accurate knowledge of the village's size, location, or propensity to stand and fight, were to pursue the Indians and "bring them to battle." However, Custer did promise to "support . . . [Reno] with the whole outfit." Reno's force crossed the Little Bighorn at the mouth of what is today called Reno Creek, and immediately realized that the Lakota and Northern Cheyenne were present "in force and . . . not running away."

Sending a message to Custer, but hearing nothing in return, Reno launched its offensive northward. He stopped a few hundred yards short of the village, however, and dismounted, unwilling to attack the enormous village with his roughly 125 men. In about 20 minutes of long distance firing, he had taken only one casualty, but the odds against him had become more obvious, and Custer had not reinforced him.

Reno ordered a retreat to nearby woods, and then made a disorderly retreat to the river and up to the top of the bluffs on the other side, suffering heavy casualties along the way. Reno was at the head of this movement and called it a charge; no bugle calls were heard, and a number of men were left in the woods. The river crossing was unguarded, and a number of men died there.

At the top of the bluffs, Reno's force was met by a battalion commanded by Captain Frederick Benteen This force had been on a lateral scouting mission, and had been summoned by Custer to "Come on . . . big village, be quick . . . bring pacs . . ." Benteen's coincidental arrival on the bluffs was just in time to save Reno's men from annihilation. This combined force was then reinforced by a smaller command escorting the expedition's pack train. Benteen did not continue on towards Custer for at least an hour, in spite of the fact that heavy gunfire was heard from the north. Benteen's inactivity prompted later criticism that he had failed to follow orders to "march to the sound of the guns."

The gunfire heard on the bluffs (by everyone except Reno and Benteen) was from Custer's fight. His 210 men engaged the Lakota and Northern Cheyenne (or had been engaged by them) some 3.5 miles to the north. Having driven Reno's force if not into oblivion, at least into chaos, the warriors were free to pursue Custer. The route taken by Custer to his "Last Stand" has been a subject of debate. It does seem clear that after ordering Reno to charge, Custer continued down Reno Creek to within about a half mile of the Little Bighorn, but then turned north, and climbed up the bluffs, reaching the same spot to which Reno would soon retreat. From this point, he could see Reno, on the other side of the river, charging the village.

Custer then rode north along the bluffs, and descended into a drainage called Medicine Tail Coulee, which led to the river. Some historians believe that part of Custer's force descended the coulee, going west to the river and attempting unsuccessfully to cross into the village. Other authorities believe that Custer never approached the river, but rather continued north across the coulee and up the other side, where he gradually came under attack. By the time Custer realized he was badly outnumbered by the Indians who came from the Reno fight, according to this theory, it was too late to break through back to the south, where Reno and Benteen could have provided reinforcement.

Within about 2 hours, Custer's battalion was annihilated to the last man. Only two men from the U.S. side later claimed to have seen Custer engage the Indians: a young Crow whose name translated as Curley, and a trooper named Peter Thompson, who had fallen behind Custer's column.

Accounts of the last moments of Custer's forces vary, but all agree that Crazy Horse personally led one of the large groups of Lakota who overwhelmed the cavalrymen. While exact numbers are difficult to determine, it is clear that the Northern Cheyenne and Lakota outnumbered the U.S. force by approximately 3:1, a ratio which was extended to 5:1 during the piecemeal parts of the battle. In addition, some of the Indians were armed with repeating Sharps and Winchester rifles, while the U.S. forces carried single-shot carbines, which had a slow rate of fire, tended to jam, and were difficult to operate from horseback.

After their fight with Custer was finished, the Lakota and Northern Cheyenne came back to attack the remaining US forces under Benteen and Reno, who had finally ventured toward the audible firing of the Custer fight. For 24 hours the outcome of this struggle was in doubt, but Benteen's leadership secured the US lines. At this point, the US forces under Terry approached from the North, and the Indians drew off to the south. The Indian dead had mostly been removed from the field.

The U. S. dead were given hasty burials, and the wounded were given what treatment was available at that time; six would later die of their wounds. Custer was found to have been shot in the temple and in the left chest; either wound would have been fatal. He may also have been shot in the arm. He was found near the top of the hill where the large obelisk now stands, inscribed with the names of the U.S. dead. *Most of the dead had been stripped of their clothing, mutilated, and were in an advanced state of deterioration, such that identification of many of the bodies was impossible.*

From the evidence, it was impossible to determine what exactly had transpired, but there was not much evidence of prolonged organized resistance. Several days after the battle, the young Crow scout Curly gave an account of the battle which indicated that Custer had attacked the village after crossing the river at the mouth of Medicine Tail Coulee, and had been driven back across the river, retreating up the slope to the hill where his body was later found. This scenario seemed compatible with Custer's aggressive style of warfare, and with some of the evidence found on the ground, and formed the basis for many of the popular accounts of the battle.

Of the U.S. forces killed at Little Bighorn, 210 died with Custer while another 52 died serving under Reno. Six men died later as a result of wounds. Casualty figures on the Indian side included perhaps 40 killed.

The battle was the subject of an army Court of Inquiry in 1879 in which Reno's conduct was scrutinized. Some testimony was presented suggesting that he was drunk, and a coward, but since none of this came from army officers, Reno was not officially condemned. Other factors have been identified which may have contributed to the outcome of the fight: it is apparent that a number of the U.S. troopers were inexperienced and poorly trained. Benteen has been criticized for "dawdling" on the first day of the fight, and disobeying Custer's order. Both Reno and Benteen were heavy drinkers whose subsequent careers were truncated. Terry has been criticized for his tardy arrival on the scene.

Custer's contributions to the U.S. defeat were, at least, faulty intelligence and poor communication, which resulted in an uncoordinated attack against a larger force. For years a debate raged as to whether Custer himself had disobeyed Terry's order not to attack the village until reinforcements arrived. Finally, almost a hundred years after the fight, a document surfaced which indicated that Terry actually had given Custer considerable freedom to do as he saw fit. Custer's widow actively affected the historiography of the battle by suppressing criticism of her husband.

A number of participants decided to wait for her death before disclosing what they knew . . . however, she outlived almost all of them. As a result, the event was recreated along tragic Victorian lines in numerous books, films and other media. The story of Custer's purported heroic attack across the river, however, was undermined by the account of participant Gall, who told Lieutenant Edward S. Godfrey that Custer never came near the river. Godfrey incorporated this into his important publication in 1892 in The Century Magazine.

In spite of this, however, Custer's legend was embedded in the American imagination as a heroic American officer fighting valiantly against savage forces. By the end of the 20th century, the general recognition of the mistreatment of the various Native American nations in the conquest of the American west, and the perception of Custer's role in it, have changed the image of the battle and of Custer.

The Little Bighorn is now popularly viewed as the confrontation between a reckless and ambitious agent of U.S. expansion against courageous warriors defending their land and way of life. *It should be noted that most of the occupants of the large village attacked by Custer were non-combatants.*

The memorials to U.S. troops have now been supplemented by markers celebrating the Indians who fought there. Many of the Native Americans in the fight including Crazy Horse played a leading role in this battle and the Battle of Rosebud one week before. On Memorial Day 1999 the first of five red granite markers denoting where warriors fell during the battle were placed on the battlefield for Cheyenne warriors, Lame White Man and Noisy Walking The warrior markers dot the ravines and hillsides like the white marble markers representing where soldiers fell. Since then, markers have been added for the Sans Arc Lakota warrior, Long Road and the Minneconjou Lakota, Dog's Back Bone.

On June 25, 2003 an unknown Lakota warrior marker was placed on Wooden Leg Hill, east of Last Stand Hill to honor a warrior who was killed during the battle as witnessed by the Northern Cheyenne warrior, Wooden Leg. The first Indian Memorial was dedicated on June 25, 2003.

The bill that changed the name of the battlefield from Custer Battlefield National Monument to Little Bighorn Battlefield National Monument also called for an Indian Memorial to be built near Last Stand Hill. President George H. W. Bush signed the bill into law on December 10, 1991. The Little Bighorn Battlefield National Monument is located in southeastern Montana near Crow Agency, Montana and administered by the National Park Service.

Following the Battle of the Little Bighorn, attempts by the U.S. Army to capture and escort the Cheyenne intensified.

A group of 972 Cheyenne were escorted to Indian Territory in Oklahoma in 1877.

There the conditions were dire, the Northern Cheyenne were not used to the climate and soon many became ill with malaria. In 1878, the two principal Chiefs, Little Wolf and Morning Star (Dull Knife) pressed for the release of the Cheyenne so they could travel back north. That same year a group of an estimated 350 Cheyenne left Indian Territory to travel back north.

This group was led by Chiefs Little Wolf and Morning Star. The Army and other civilian volunteers were in hot pursuit of the Cheyenne as they traveled north. It is estimated that a total of 13,000 Army soldiers and volunteers were sent to pursue the Cheyenne. The band soon split.

One group was led by Little Wolf, and the other by Morning Star. Little Wolf and his band made it back to Montana. Morning Star and his band were captured and escorted to Ft. Robinson, Nebraska. There Morning Star and his band were sequestered.

They were ordered to return to Oklahoma but they refused.

Conditions at the fort grew tense through the end of 1878 and soon the Cheyenne were confined to barracks with no food, water or heat.

In January of 1879, Morning Star and his group broke out of Ft. Robinson. Most of the group was gunned down as they ran away from the fort.

It is estimated that only approximately 50 survived the breakout to reunite with the other Northern Cheyenne in Montana.

Through determination and sacrifice, the Northern Cheyenne had earned their right to remain in the north near the Black Hills.

In 1884, by Executive Order, a reservation, the Northern Cheyenne Indian Reservation was established in southeast Montana. This reservation was expanded in 1890, the current western border is the Crow Indian Reservation and the eastern border is the Tongue River.

For 400 years, the Cheyenne have gone through 4 stages of culture. First they lived in the Eastern Woodlands and were a sedentary/agricultural people, planting corn, and beans.

Next they lived in present day Minnesota/South Dakota and continued their farming tradition and also started hunting the bison of the Great Plains.

During the third stage the Cheyenne abandoned their sedentary/farming lifestyle and became a full-fledged Plains horse culture tribe.

The fourth stage is the reservation phase.

Spiritual Practices

Cheyenne religion recognized two principal deities, the Wise One Above and a God who lived beneath the ground. In addition, four spirits lived at the points of the compass.

The Cheyenne were among the Plains tribes who performed the sun dance in its most elaborate form. They placed heavy emphasis on visions in which an animal spirit adopted the individual and bestowed special powers upon him so long as he observed some prescribed law or practice.

Their most venerated objects, contained in a sacred bundle, were a hat made from the skin and hair of a buffalo cow and four arrows—two painted for hunting and two for battle. These objects were carried in war to insure success over the enemy.

The Cheyenne practiced shamanism—dance, medicine.

Quote:

"In My Father's house are many mansions; if it were not so, I would have told you. I go to prepare a place for you. And if I go and prepare a place for you, I will come again and receive you to Myself; that where I am, there you may be also." **Jesus (John 14:2-4) NKJV**

Crazy Horse

Crazy Horse (Lakota: *Tȟašúnke Witkó* (in Standard Lakota Orthography), literally "His-Horse-Is-Crazy" or "His-Horse-Is-Spirited"; ca. 1840-September 5, 1877) was a Native American war leader of the Oglala Lakota. He took up arms against the U.S. Federal government to fight against encroachments on the territories and way of life of the Lakota people, including leading a war party at the Battle of the Little Bighorn in June 1876. After surrendering to U.S. troops under General Crook in 1877, Crazy Horse was fatally wounded by a military guard while allegedly resisting imprisonment at Camp Robinson in present-day Nebraska. *He ranks among the most notable and iconic of Native American tribal members and has been honored by the U.S. Postal Service with a 13 ¢ Great Americans series postage stamp.*

Early life

Sources differ on the precise year of Crazy Horse's birth, but they agree he was born between 1840 and 1845. According to a close friend, he and Crazy Horse "were both born in the same year at the same season of the year", which census records and other interviews place at about 1845. Encouraging Bear, an Oglala medicine man and spiritual adviser to the Oglala war leader, reported that Crazy Horse was born "in the year in which the band to which he belonged, the Oglala, stole One Hundred Horses, and in the fall of the year", a reference to the annual Lakota calendar or winter count. Among the Oglala winter counts, the stealing of 100 horses is noted by Cloud Shield, and possibly by American Horse and Red Horse owner, equivalent to the year 1840-41. Oral history accounts from relatives on the Cheyenne River Reservation place his birth in the spring of 1840. Probably the most credible source, however, is Crazy Horse's own father. On the evening of his son's death, the elderly man told Lieutenant H. R. Lemly that his son "would soon have been thirty-seven, having been born on the South Cheyenne River in the fall of 1840."

314

Crazy Horse was named at birth *Cha-O-Ha* (In the Wilderness or Among the Trees, meaning he was one with nature.) His mother's nickname for him was "Curly" or "Light Hair"; his light curly hair resembled that of his mother.

Family

Crazy Horse was born to Oglala Lakota parents. His father, born in 1810, was also named Crazy Horse. One account said that after the son had reached maturity and shown his strength, his father gave him his name and took a new one, *Waglula* (Worm). (Another version of how the son Crazy Horse acquired his name was that he took it after having a vision.) His mother was Rattling Blanket Woman (born 1814). Rattling Blanket Woman was the daughter of Black Buffalo and White Cow (also known as Iron Cane). Black Buffalo is famous for stopping Lewis and Clark on the Bad River.

Rattling Blanket Woman was the younger sister of Lone Horn (born between 1790 and 1795, and died in 1875) and also of Good Looking Woman (born 1810). Her younger sister was named Looks at It (born 1815); later given the name They Are Afraid of Her. Crazy Horse's cousin (son of Lone Horn) was Touch the Clouds. He saved his life at least once and was with Crazy Horse when he died. It has been claimed Crazy Horse's mother was Minneconjou and the sister of Spotted Tail, who was a Brule head chief.

In the summer of 1844, Waglula (Worm) went on a buffalo hunt. He came across a Minneconjou Lakota village under attack by Crow warriors. He led his small party of warriors to the village and rescued it. Corn, the head man of the village, had lost his wife in the raid. In gratitude he gave *Waglula* his two eldest daughters as wives: Iron Between Horns (age 18) and Kills Enemy (age 17). Corn's youngest daughter, Red Leggins, who was 15 at the time, requested to go with her sisters; all became Waglula's wives. (Painter, George Catlin made a portrait of Corn while visiting the tribe in 1832.)

Visions

Crazy Horse lived in the Lakota camp with his younger brother, High Horse (son of Iron Between Horns and *Waglula* and a cousin Little Hawk. (Little Hawk was the nephew of his maternal step-grandfather, Corn). The camp was attacked by Lt. Grattan and 28 other US troopers during the Grattan massacre.

After witnessing the death of Lakota leader Conquering Bear, Crazy Horse began to get trance visions. His father *Waglula* took him to what today is Sylvan Lake, South Dakota, where they both sat to do a *hemblecha* (vision quest). A red-tailed hawk led them to their respective spots in the hills; as the trees are tall in the Black Hills, they could not always see where they were going. Crazy Horse sat between two humps at the top of a hill north and to the east of the lake. Waglula sat south of Harney Peak but north of his son.

Crazy Horse's vision first took him to the South, where in Lakota spirituality one goes upon death. He was brought back and was taken to the West in the direction of the *wakiyans* (thunder beings*). **He was given a medicine bundle to protect him for life.** One of his animal protectors would be the white owl which, according to Lakota spirituality, would give extended life. He was also shown his "face paint" for battle, to consist of a yellow lightning bolt down the left side of his face, and white powder. He would wet this and put marks over his vulnerable areas; when dried, the marks looked like hailstones. His face paint was similar to that of his father, who used a red lightning strike down the right side of his face and three red hailstones on his forehead. Crazy Horse put no makeup on his forehead and did not wear a war bonnet. He was given a sacred song that is still sung by the Oglala people today. Lastly, he was told he would be a protector of his people.

A contemporary tribesman and cousin of Crazy Horse, in his classic text, *Black Elk Speaks: being the life story of a holy man of the Oglala Sioux* was said to provide an account of Crazy Horse's vision from which he derived his name.

> "When I was a man, my father told me something about that vision. Of course he did not know all of it; but he said that Crazy Horse dreamed and went into the world where there is nothing but the spirits of all things. That is the real world that is behind this one, and everything we see here is something like a shadow from that world. He was on his horse in that world, and the horse and himself on it and the trees and the grass and the stones and everything were made of spirit, and nothing was hard, and everything seemed to float. His horse was standing still there, and yet it danced around like a horse made only of shadow, and that is how he got his name, which does not mean that his horse was crazy or wild, but that in his vision it danced around in that queer way.
>
> It was this vision that gave him his great power, for when he went into a fight, he had only to think of that world to be in it again, so that he could go through anything and not be hurt. Until he was killed at the Soldiers' Town on White River, he was wounded only twice, once by accident and both times by some one of his own people when he was not expecting trouble and was not thinking; never by an enemy."

This story appears to be an addition by John G. Neihardt, as his original interview transcripts with Black Elk make no mention of the origination of Crazy Horse's name.

Crazy Horse received a black stone from a medicine man named Horn Chips to protect his horse, a black-and-white "paint" which he named *Inyan* (rock or stone). He placed the stone behind the horse's ear, so that the medicine from his vision quest and Horn Chips would combine; he and his horse would be one in battle.

Title of "Shirt Wearer"

Through the late 1850s and early 1860s, Crazy Horse's reputation as a warrior grew, as did his fame among the Lakota. The Lakota conveyed accounts of him in their oral histories; they had no written language. His first kill was a Shoshone raider who had killed a Lakota woman washing buffalo meat along the Powder River. Crazy Horse fought in numerous battles between the Lakota and their traditional enemies, the Crow, Shoshone, Pawnee, Blackfeet, and Arikara, among Plains tribes.

In 1864, after the Third Colorado Cavalry decimated Northern Cheyenne in the Sand Creek Massacre, Lakota Oglala and Minneconjou bands allied with them against the US military. Crazy Horse was present at the Battle of Red Buttes and the subsequent Platte River Bridge Station Battle in July 1865. Because of his fighting ability, in 1865 Crazy Horse was named an *Ogle Tanka Un* (Shirt Wearer, or war leader) by the tribe.

Fetterman Massacre

On December 21, 1866, Crazy Horse and six other warriors, both Lakota and Cheyenne, decoyed Capt. William Fetterman's 53 infantrymen and 27 cavalry troopers under Lt. Grummond into an ambush. They had been sent out from Fort Phil Kearny to follow up on an earlier attack on a wood train. Crazy Horse lured Fetterman's infantry up what Wyoming locals now call Massacre Hill. Grummond's cavalry followed the other six decoys along Peno Head Ridge and down toward Peno Creek, where several Cheyenne women taunted the soldiers. Meanwhile, Cheyenne leader Little Wolf and his warriors, who had been hiding on the opposite side of Peno Head Ridge, blocked the return route to the fort. The Lakota warriors swept over Massacre Hill to attack the infantry. Additional Cheyenne and Lakota hiding in the buck brush along Peno Creek effectively surrounded the soldiers. Seeing that they were surrounded, Grummond headed his cavalry back to Fetterman.

The combined warrior forces of nearly 1,000 killed all the US soldiers, in what became known as the Fetterman Massacre. It was the Army's worst defeat on the Great Plains up to that time.

Wagon Box Fight

On August 2, 1867, Crazy Horse participated in the Wagon Box Fight, also near Fort Phil Kearny. Lakota forces numbering between 1000 and 2000 attacked a wood-cutting crew near the fort. Most of the soldiers fled to a circle of wagon boxes without wheels, using them for cover as they fired at the Lakota. The Lakota took substantial losses, as the soldiers were firing new breech-loading rifles. These could fire ten times a minute compared to the old muzzle-loading rate of three times a minute. The Lakota charged after the soldiers fired, expecting the delay of their older muskets before being able to fire again. The soldiers suffered only five killed and two wounded, while the Lakota suffered between 50 and 120 casualties. Many Lakota were buried in the hills surrounding Fort Phil Kearny in Wyoming.

Controversy over his first wife

In the fall of 1867, Crazy Horse invited Black Buffalo Woman to accompany him on a buffalo hunt in the Slim Buttes area of present-day northwestern South Dakota. She was the wife of No Water, who had a reputation as drinking too much. It was Lakota custom to allow a woman to divorce her husband at any time. She did so by moving in with relatives or with another man, or by placing the husband's belongings outside their lodge. Although some compensation might be required to smooth over hurt feelings, the rejected husband was expected to accept his wife's decision. No Water was away from camp when Crazy Horse and Black Buffalo Woman left for the buffalo hunt.

No Water tracked down Crazy Horse and Black Buffalo Woman in the Slim Buttes area. When he found them in a tipi, he called Crazy Horse's name from outside. When Crazy Horse answered, No Water stuck a pistol into the tipi and aimed for Crazy Horse. Touch the Clouds, Crazy Horse's first cousin and son of Lone Horn, was sitting in the tipi nearest the entry. He knocked the pistol upward as No Water fired, deflecting the bullet to Crazy Horse's upper jaw. No Water left, with Crazy Horse's relatives in hot pursuit. No Water ran his horse until it died and continued on foot until he reached the safety of his own village.

Several elders convinced Crazy Horse and No Water that no more blood should be shed. As compensation for the shooting, No Water gave Crazy Horse three horses. Because Crazy Horse was with a married man's wife, he was stripped of his title as Shirt Wearer (leader). At about the same time, the warrior Little Hawk was killed by a group of miners in the Black Hills while escorting some women to the new agency created by the Treaty of 1868.

Second and third wives

In addition to his first wife Black Buffalo Woman, Crazy Horse married Black Shawl Woman, a member of the Oglala Lakota and relative of Spotted Tail. The elders sent her to heal Crazy Horse after his altercation with No Water. Crazy Horse and Black Shawl Woman were married in 1871. Black Shawl gave birth to Crazy Horse's only child, a daughter named They Are Afraid of Her, who died in 1873. Black Shawl outlived Crazy Horse. She died in 1927 during the influenza outbreaks of the 1920s.

While married to Black Shawl Woman, Crazy Horse took Helena "Nellie" Laravie as his third wife. Nellie, also referred to as *Chi-Chi* and Brown Eyes Woman, was the daughter of a French trader and a woman of the Cheyenne tribe. William Garnett's first-hand account of Crazy Horse's surrender alludes to Nellie as the "half blood woman" who caused Crazy Horse to fall into a "domestic trap which insensibly led him by gradual steps to his destruction."

Great Sioux War of 1876-77

On June 17, 1876, Crazy Horse led a combined group of approximately 1,500 Lakota and Cheyenne in a surprise attack against brevetted Brigadier General George Crook's force of 1,000 cavalry and infantry, and allied 300 Crow and Shoshone warriors in the Battle of the Rosebud. The battle, although not substantial in terms of human losses, delayed Crook's joining with the 7th Cavalry under George A. Custer. It contributed to Custer's subsequent defeat at the Battle of the Little Bighorn.

A week later at 3:00 p.m. on June 25, 1876, Custer's 7th Cavalry attacked a large encampment of Cheyenne and Lakota bands along the Little Bighorn River, marking the beginning of his last battle. Crazy Horse's actions during the battle are unknown. Possibly Crazy Horse entered the battle by repelling the first attack led by Major Marcus Reno, but it is also possible that he was still in his lodge waiting for the larger battle with Custer.

Hunkpapa Warriors led by Chief Gall led the main body of the attack. Crazy Horse's tactical and leadership role in the battle remains ambiguous. While some historians think that Crazy Horse led a flanking assault, ensuring the death of Custer and his men, the only proven fact is that Crazy Horse was a major participant in the battle. His personal courage was attested to by several eye witness Indian accounts. Waterman, one of only five Arapaho warriors who fought, said that Crazy Horse "was the bravest man I ever saw.

He rode closest to the soldiers, yelling to his warriors. All the soldiers were shooting at him, but he was never hit." Sioux battle participant, Little Soldier, said, *"The greatest fighter in the whole battle was Crazy Horse."*

On September 10, 1876, Captain Anson Mills and two battalions of the Third Cavalry captured a Miniconjou village of 36 lodges in the Battle of Slim Buttes, South Dakota. Crazy Horse and his followers attempted to rescue the camp and its headman, (Old Man) American Horse. They were unsuccessful. The soldiers killed American Horse and much of his family after they holed up in a cave for several hours.

On January 8, 1877, Crazy Horse's warriors fought their last major battle at Wolf Mountain, against the US Cavalry in the Montana Territory. His people struggled through the winter, weakened by hunger and the long cold. Crazy Horse decided to surrender with his band to protect them, and went to Camp Robinson in Nebraska.

Surrender and death

Crazy Horse and other northern Oglala leaders arrived at the Red Cloud Agency, located near Camp Robinson, Nebraska, on May 5, 1877. Together with He Dog, Little Big Man, Iron Crow and others, they met in a solemn ceremony with First Lieutenant William P. Clark as the first step in their formal surrender.

For the next four months, Crazy Horse resided in his village near the Red Cloud Agency. The attention that Crazy Horse received from the Army drew the jealousy of Red Cloud and Spotted Tail, two Lakota who had long before come to the agencies and adopted the white ways. Rumors of Crazy Horse's desire to slip away and return to the old ways of life started to spread at the Red Cloud and Spotted Tail agencies. In August 1877, officers at Camp Robinson received word that the Nez Perce of Chief Joseph had broken out of their reservations in Idaho and were fleeing north through Montana toward Canada. When asked by Lieutenant Clark to join the Army against the Nez Perce, Crazy Horse and the Miniconjou leader Touch the Clouds objected, saying that they had promised to remain at peace when they surrendered. According to one version of events, Crazy Horse finally agreed, saying that he would fight "till all the Nez Perce were killed". But his words were apparently misinterpreted by half-Tahitian scout, Frank Grouard (not be confused with Fred Gerard, another U.S. Cavalry scout during the summer of 1876), who reported that Crazy Horse had said that he would "go north and fight until not a white man is left". When he was challenged over his interpretation, Grouard left the council. Another interpreter, William Garnett, was brought in but quickly noted the growing tension.

With the growing trouble at the Red Cloud Agency, General George Crook was ordered to stop at Camp Robinson. A council of the Oglala leadership was called, then canceled, when Crook was incorrectly informed that Crazy Horse had said the previous evening that he intended to kill the general during the proceedings. Crook ordered Crazy Horse's arrest and then departed, leaving the military action to the post commander at Camp Robinson, Lieutenant Colonel Luther P. Bradley. Additional troops were brought in from Fort Laramie and on the morning of September 4, 1877, two columns moved against Crazy Horse's village, only to find that it had scattered during the night. Crazy Horse fled to the nearby Spotted Tail Agency with his sick wife (who had become ill with tuberculosis). After meeting with military officials at the adjacent military post of Camp Sheridan, Crazy Horse agreed to return to Camp Robinson with Lieutenant Jesse M. Lee, the Indian agent at Spotted Tail.

On the morning of September 5, 1877, Crazy Horse and Lieutenant Lee, accompanied by Touch the Clouds as well as a number of Indian scouts, departed for Camp Robinson. Arriving that evening outside the adjutant's office, Lieutenant Lee was informed that he was to turn Crazy Horse over to the Officer of the Day. Lee protested and hurried to Bradley's quarters to debate the issue, but without success. Bradley had received orders that Crazy Horse was to be arrested and forwarded under the cover of darkness to Division Headquarters. Lee turned the Oglala war chief over to Captain James Kennington, in charge of the post guard, who accompanied Crazy Horse to the post guardhouse. *Once inside, no doubt realizing the fate that was about to befall him, Crazy Horse struggled with the guard and Little Big Man and attempted to escape. Just outside the door of the guardhouse, Crazy Horse was stabbed with a bayonet of one of the members of the guard. He was taken to the adjutant's office where he was tended by the assistant post surgeon at the post, Dr. Valentine McGillycuddy, and died late that night.*

The following morning, Crazy Horse's body was turned over to his elderly parents who took it to Camp Sheridan, placing it on a scaffold there. The following month when the Spotted Tail Agency was moved to the Missouri River, Crazy Horse's parents moved the body to an undisclosed location. There are at least four possible locations as noted on a state highway memorial near Wounded Knee, South Dakota. His final resting place remains unknown.

Controversy over his death

Dr. McGillycuddy, who treated Crazy Horse after he was stabbed, wrote that Crazy Horse "died about midnight." According to military records he died before midnight, making it September 5, 1877.

John Gregory Bourke's memoirs of his service in the Indian wars, *On the Border with Crook*, details an entirely different account of Crazy Horse's death. Bourke's account was from an interview with Crazy Horse's relative and rival, Little Big Man, who was present at Crazy Horse's arrest and wounding. The interview took place over a year after Crazy Horse's death. Little Big Man's account is that, as Crazy Horse was being escorted to the guardhouse he suddenly pulled from under his blanket two knives, one in each hand. One knife was reportedly fashioned from the end of an army bayonet. Little Big Man, standing immediately behind Crazy Horse and not wanting the soldiers to have any excuse to kill him, seized Crazy Horse by both elbows, pulling his arms up and behind him. As Crazy Horse struggled to get free, Little Big Man abruptly lost his grip on one elbow, and Crazy Horse's released arm drove his own knife deep into his own lower back. Blood splattered all over them as the attempt to escape was still possible. The guard stabbed him with his bayonet in his back, already punctured. He fell and surrendered to the guards and his commentators.

When Bourke asked about the popular account of the Guard bayoneting Crazy Horse, Little Big Man explained that the guard had thrust with his bayonet, but that Crazy Horse's struggles resulted in the guard's thrust missing entirely and his bayonet being lodged into the frame of the guardhouse door.

Little Big Man related that, in the hours immediately following Crazy Horse's wounding, the camp Commander had suggested the story of the guard being responsible as a means of hiding Little Big Man's involvement in Crazy Horse's death, and thereby avoiding any inter-clan reprisals.

Little Big Man's account, as related by Bourke, is questionable, as it is the only one of as many as 17 eyewitness sources (aside from one other account that states the eyewitness was "not sure" of the identity of the perpetrator) from Lakota, US Army, and "mixed-blood" individuals which fails to attribute Crazy Horse's death to a soldier at the guardhouse.

The "last words" often attributed to Crazy Horse contains a terse implication of the guard. This widely published account directly contradicts the prior, witnessed statement made to the Post Commander:

> *"My friend, I do not blame you for this. Had I listened to you this trouble would not have happened to me. I was not hostile to the white men. Sometimes my young men would attack the Indians who were their enemies and took their ponies. They did it in return. We had buffalo for food, and their hides for clothing and for our tepees. We preferred hunting to a life of idleness on the reservation, where we were driven against our will. At times we did not get enough to eat and we were not allowed to leave the reservation to hunt. We preferred our own way of living. We were no expense to the*

government. All we wanted was peace and to be left alone. Soldiers were sent out in the winter, they destroyed our villages. The "Long Hair" [Custer] came in the same way. They say we massacred him, but he would have done the same thing to us had we not defended ourselves and fought to the last. Our first impulse was to escape with our squaws and papooses, but we were so hemmed in that we had to fight. After that I went up on the Tongue River with a few of my people and lived in peace. But the government would not let me alone. Finally, I came back to the Red Cloud Agency. Yet, I was not allowed to remain quiet. I was tired of fighting. I went to the Spotted Tail Agency and asked that chief and his agent to let me live there in peace. I came here with the agent [Lee] to talk with the Big White Chief but was not given a chance. They tried to confine me. I tried to escape, and a soldier ran his bayonet into me. I have spoken."

The identity of the soldier accused of being responsible for the bayoneting of Crazy Horse is also debatable. Only one eyewitness account actually identifies the soldier as Private William Gentles. Historian Walter M. Camp circulated copies of this account to individuals who had been present who questioned the identity of the soldier and provided two additional names. To this day, the identification remains questionable.

There is also a theory that Crazy Horse's guard Little Big Man was bought off by the white men and he was the one who stabbed Crazy Horse in the back.

Photograph controversy

Most sources question whether Crazy Horse was ever photographed. Dr. McGillycuddy doubted any photograph of the war leader had been taken. In 1908, Walter Camp wrote to the agent for the Pine Ridge Reservation inquiring about a portrait. "I have never seen a photo of Crazy Horse," Agent Brennan replied, "nor am I able to find any one among our Sioux here who remembers having seen a picture of him. Crazy Horse had left the hostiles but a short time before he was killed and it's more than likely he never had a picture taken of himself."

In 1956, a small tintype portrait purportedly of Crazy Horse was published by J. W. Vaughn in his book *With Crook at the Rosebud*. The photograph had belonged to the family of the scout, Baptiste "Little Bat" Garnier. Two decades later, the portrait was again published with further details about how the photograph was produced at Camp Robinson, though the editor of the book "remained unconvinced of the authenticity of the photograph."

Recently, the original tintype was on exhibit at the Custer Battlefield Museum in Garryowen, Montana, who have promoted the image as the only authentic portrait of Crazy Horse. Historians however continue to refute the identification.

Experts argue that the tintype was taken a decade or two after 1877. The evidence includes the individual's attire (such as the length of the hair pipe breastplate and the ascot tie). In addition, no other photograph with the same painted backdrop has been found. Several photographers passed through Camp Robinson and the Red Cloud Agency in 1877—including James H. Hamilton, Charles Howard, David Rodocker and possibly Daniel S. Mitchell—but none of them used the backdrop that appears in the tintype. After the death of Crazy Horse, Private Charles Howard produced at least two images of the famed war leader's alleged scaffold grave, located near Camp Sheridan, Nebraska.[

Crazy Horse Memorial

Crazy Horse is commemorated by the incomplete Crazy Horse Memorial in the Black Hills of South Dakota—a monument carved into a mountain, in the tradition of the Mount Rushmore National Memorial (on which Korczak Ziółkowski had worked with Gutzon Borglum). The sculpture was begun by Ziółkowski in 1948. When completed, it will be 641 ft (195 m) wide and 563 ft (172 m) high. It is still incomplete because of funding constraints. Although the sculpture was originally requested by Henry Standing Bear and other Sioux elders, it has been criticized by some American Indian activists (most notably Russell Means) as exploitative of Sioux culture and Crazy Horse's memory as well as desecrating sacred ground. Crazy Horse's memorial statue depicts him pointing out toward his land in the Black Hills. His famous quote is *"my lands are where my dead lie buried."*

Quote:

"I will both lie down in peace, and sleep; For You alone, O Lord, make me dwell in safety." (Psalm 4:8)

Chief Joseph
Nez Pierce (1840-1904)

Chief Joseph, known by his people as In-mut-too-yah-lat-lat (Thunder coming up over the land from the water), was best known for his resistance to the U.S. Government's attempts to force his tribe onto reservations. The Nez Perce were a peaceful nation spread from Idaho to Northern Washington. The tribe had maintained good relations with the whites after the Lewis and Clark expedition. Joseph spent much of his early childhood at a mission maintained by Christian missionaries.

In 1855 Chief Joseph's father, Old Joseph, signed a treaty with the U.S. that allowed his people to retain much of their traditional lands. In 1863 another treaty was created that severely reduced the amount of land, but Old Joseph maintained that this second treaty was never agreed to by his people.

A showdown over the second "non-treaty" came after Chief Joseph assumed his role as Chief in 1877. *After months of fighting and forced marches, many of the Nez Perce were sent to a reservation in what is now Oklahoma, where many died from malaria and starvation.*

Chief Joseph tried every possible appeal to the federal authorities to return the Nez Perce to the land of their ancestors. In 1885, he was sent along with many of his band to a reservation in Washington where, *according to the reservation doctor, he later died of a broken heart.*

Quotes from Chief Joseph:

I have carried a heavy load on my back ever since I was a boy. I realized then that we could not hold our own with the white men. We were like deer. They were like grizzly bears. We had small country. Their country was large. We were contented to let things remain as the Great Spirit Chief made them. They were not, and would change the rivers and mountains if they did not suit them.

I am tired of fighting . . . . from where the sun now stands, I will fight no more.

Our fathers gave us many laws, which they had learned from their fathers. These laws were good. They told us to treat all people as they treated us; that we should never be the first to break a bargain; that is was a disgrace to tell a lie; that we should speak only the truth; that it was a shame for one man to take another's wife or his property without paying for it.

Suppose a white man should come to me and say, "Joseph, I like your horses. I want to buy them."

I say to him, "No, my horses suit me; I will not sell them."

Then he goes to my neighbor and says, "Pay me money, and I will sell you Joseph's horses."

The white man returns to me and says, "Joseph, I have bought your horses and you must let me have them."

If we sold our lands to the government, this is the way they bought them.

I am not a child, I think for myself. No man can think for me.

If the white man wants to live in peace with the Indian, he can live in peace. Treat all men alike. Give them a chance to live and grow.

All men were made brothers. The earth is the mother of all people, and all people should have equal rights upon it. You might as well expect the rivers to run backward as that any man who was born free should be contented when penned up and denied liberty to go where he pleases.

If you tie a horse to a stake, do you expect him to grow fat? If you pen an Indian up on a small spot of earth, and compel him to stay there, he will not be contented, nor will he grow and prosper.

The earth and myself are of one mind.

We were taught to believe that the Great Spirit sees and hears everything, and that he never forgets, that hereafter he will give every man a spirit home according to his deserts; if he has been a good man, he will have a good home; if he has been a bad man, he will have a bad home.

This I believe and all my people believe the same.

Good words do not last long unless they amount to something. Words do not pay for my dead people. They do not pay for my country, now overrun by white men. They do not protect my father's grave. They do not pay for all my horses and cattle.

Good words cannot give me back my children. Good words will not give my people good health and stop them from dying. Good words will not get my people a home where they can live in peace and take care of themselves.

I am tired of talk that comes to nothing. It makes my heart sick when I remember all the good words and all the broken promises. There has been too much talking by men who had no right to talk.

It does not require many words to speak the truth.

We do not want churches because they will teach us to quarrel about God, as the Catholics and Protestants do. We do not want that.

We may quarrel with men about things on earth, but we never quarrel about the Great Spirit.

I believe much trouble and blood would be saved if we opened our hearts more. I will tell you in my way how the Indian sees things. The white man has more words to tell you how they look to him, but is does not require many words to seek the truth.

Too many misinterpretations have been made . . . too many misunderstandings . . .

The Great Spirit Chief who rules above all will smile upon this land . . . and this time the Indian race is waiting and praying.

I am tired of talk that comes to nothing.

Indian Proverbs

Until you walk a mile in another man's moccasins you can't imagine the smell.
Only he who wears the shoe feels the pinch.

The Chinese Railroad Men

Chinese peasants from the Canton Province began arriving on California's shores in 1850, pushed by poverty and overpopulation from their homeland—and pulled forward by rumors of the *Gum Sham*, the Mountain of Gold, that awaited them across the ocean. Initially, they took five-year stints in the mines, after which they prospected or accepted jobs as laborers, domestic workers, and fishermen. *As their presence increased, the Chinese immigrants faced growing prejudice and an increasingly restrictive laws limiting opportunity.* When Leland Stanford was elected governor of California in 1862, he promised in his inaugural address to protect the state from "the dregs of Asia." Stanford, at least, would change his tune.

Labor Shortage

In early 1865 the Central Pacific had work enough for 4,000 men. Yet contractor Charles Crocker barely managed to hold onto 800 laborers at any given time. Most of the early workers were Irish immigrants. Railroad work was hard, and management was chaotic, leading to a high attrition rate. The Central Pacific management puzzled over how it could attract and retain a work force up to the enormous task. *In keeping with prejudices of the day, some Central Pacific officials believed that Irishmen were inclined to spend their wages on liquor, and that the Chinese were also unreliable. Yet, due to the critical shortage, Crocker suggested that reconsideration be given to hiring Chinese. He encountered strong prejudice from foreman James Harvey Strobridge.*

Impressive Workers

Strobridge's attitude changed when a group of Irish laborers agitated over wages. Crocker told Strobridge to recruit some Chinese in their place. Instantly, the Irishmen abandoned their dispute. Sensing at least that fear of competition might motivate his men, Strobridge grudgingly agreed to hire 50 Chinese men as wagon-fillers. Their work ethic impressed him, and he hired more Chinese workers for more difficult tasks. Soon, labor recruiters were scouring California, and Crocker hired companies to advertise the work in China. The number of Chinese workers on CP payrolls began increasing by the shipload. Several thousand Chinese men had signed on by the end of that year; the number rose to a high of 12,000 in 1868, comprising at least 80% of the Central Pacific workforce. "Wherever we put them, we found them good," Crocker recalled, "and they worked themselves into our favor to such an extent that if we found we were in a hurry for a job of work, it was better to put Chinese on at once."

"Celestials"

The Chinese workers were punctual, willing, and well-behaved—sometimes referred to as "Celestials" in reflection of their spiritual beliefs. They were quite unlike their Caucasian counterparts, who quickly resented the growing competition and harassed the foreigners. Crocker and Strobridge made clear to the Irishmen that they could work alongside the Chinese crews or be replaced by them. The ultimatum may not have cured the anger of the white crews, but it sufficed to quell rebellion.

Less Pay

The Chinese teams were organized into groups of 20 under one white foreman; as the difficulty of construction increased, so often did the size of the gangs. Initially, *Chinese employees received wages of $27 and then $30 a month, minus the cost of food and board. In contrast, Irishmen were paid $35 per month, with board provided.*

Healthier Habits

Workers lived in canvas camps alongside the grade. In the mountains, wooden bunkhouses protected them from the drifting snow, although these were often compromised by the elements. Each gang had a cook who purchased dried food from the Chinese districts of Sacramento and San Francisco to prepare on site. While Irish crews stuck to an unvarying menu of boiled food—beef & potatoes—the Chinese ate vegetables and seafood, and kept live pigs and chickens for weekend meals. To the dull palates of the Irishmen, the Chinese menu was a full-blown sensory assault. The newcomers seemed alien in other ways: they bathed themselves, washed their clothes, stayed away from whiskey. Instead of water they drank lukewarm tea, boiled in the mornings and dispensed to them throughout the day. In such a manner they avoided the dysentery that ravaged white crews.

A Famous Retort

As work crews approached the summit, Strobridge continued to doubt the suitability of Chinese to certain tasks. When a group of Irish masons struck for higher wages, Crocker suggested using Chinese men in their place. The foreman objected. Famously, Crocker replied, *"Did they not build the Chinese Wall, the biggest piece of masonry in the world?"* Strobridge acquiesced, and Chinese crews were soon laying stone.

The Ten-Mile Day

Toward the end of the line, Crocker was so convinced of the skill of his Irish and Chinese workers that he decided to try for a record by laying 10 miles of track in one day. April 28, 1868 was the appointed day, and Crocker had prepared well. "One by one, platform cars dumped their iron, two miles of material in each trainload, and teams of Irishmen fairly ran the five-hundred-pound rails and hardware forward," writes author David Bain. "Straighteners led the Chinese gangs shoving the rails in place and keeping them to gauge while spikers walked down the ties, each man driving one particular spike and not stopping for another, moving on to the next rail; levelers and fillers followed, raising ties where needed, shoveling dirt beneath, tamping and moving on . . . ." Watching the scene was a team of soldiers. Its commander praised Crocker and his workers for their effort to lay so much rail in so little time. "Mr. Crocker, I never saw such organization as that; it was like an army marching over the ground and leaving a track built behind them."

Wisdom for the Journey

No problem is insurmountable. With a little courage, teamwork and determination a person can overcome anything. **B. Dodge**

It is a fact that in the right formation, the lifting power of many wings can achieve twice the distance of any bird flying alone. **~Author Unknown**

No man is an island, entire of itself; every man is a piece of the continent.
~John Donne

Who Was Jim Crow?

The name Jim Crow is often used to describe the segregation laws, rules, and customs which arose after Reconstruction ended in 1877 and continued until the mid-1960s. How did the name become associated with these "Black Codes" which took away many of the rights which had been granted to Blacks through the 13th, 14th, and 15th Amendments?

> *"Come listen all you galls and boys,*
> *I'm going to sing a little song,*
> *My name is Jim Crow.*
> *Weel about and turn about and do jis so,*
> *Eb'ry time I weel about I jump Jim Crow."*

These words are from the song, "Jim Crow," as it appeared in sheet music written by Thomas Dartmouth "Daddy" Rice. Rice, a struggling "actor" (he did short solo skits between play scenes) at the Park Theater in New York, happened upon a Black person singing the above song—some accounts say it was an old Black slave who walked with difficulty, others say it was a ragged Black stable boy. Whether modeled on an old man or a young boy we will never know, however, it is clear that in 1828 Rice appeared on stage as "Jim Crow"—an exaggerated, highly stereotypical Black character.

Rice, a White man, was one of the first performers to wear blackface makeup—his skin was darkened with burnt cork. His Jim Crow song-and-dance routine was an astounding success that took him from Louisville to Cincinnati to Pittsburg to Philadelphia and finally to New York in 1832. He then performed to great acclaim in London and Dublin. By then "Jim Crow" was a stock character in minstrel shows, along with counterparts Jim Dandy and Zip Coon. **Rice's subsequent blackface characters were Sambos, Coons, and Dandies: White audiences were receptive to the portrayals of Blacks as singing, dancing, grinning fools.**

By 1838, the term "Jim Crow" was being used as a collective racial epithet for Blacks, not as offensive as nigger, but as offensive as coon or darkie. Obviously, the popularity of minstrel shows aided the spread of Jim Crow as a racial slur. This use of the term did not last past a half century. By the end of the 19th Century, the words Jim Crow were less likely to be used to derisively describe Blacks; instead, the phrase Jim Crow was being used to describe laws and customs which oppressed Blacks.

The minstrel show was one of the first native forms of American entertainment, and Rice was rightly regarded as the "Father of American minstrelsy." He had many imitators. In 1843, four White men from Virginia, billed as the "Virginia Minstrels," darkened their faces and imitated the singing and dancing of Blacks. They used violins, castanets, banjos, bones and tambourines. Their routine was successful and they were invited to tour the country. In 1845, the Christy Minstrels (for whom Stephen Foster wrote some of his most popular songs) originated many features of the minstrel show, including the seating of the blackface performers in a semicircle on stage, with the tambourine player (Mr. Tambo) at one end, and the bones player (Mr. Bones) at the other; the singing of songs, called Ethiopian melodies, with harmonized choruses; and the humorous banter of jokes between the endmen and the performer in the middle seat (Mr. Interlocutor). These performers were sometimes called "Ethiopian Delineators" and the shows were popularly referred to **as "Coon shows."**

Rice, and his imitators, by their stereotypical depictions of Blacks, helped to popularize the belief that Blacks were lazy, stupid, inherently less human, and unworthy of integration. During the years that Blacks were being victimized by lynch mobs, they were also victimized by the racist caricatures propagated through novels, sheet music, theatrical plays, and minstrel shows. Ironically, years later when Blacks replaced White minstrels, the Blacks also "blackened" their faces, thereby pretending to be Whites pretending to be Blacks. They, too, performed the Coon Shows which dehumanized Blacks and helped establish the desirability of racial segregation.

Daddy Rice, the original Jim Crow, became rich and famous because of his skills as a minstrel. However, he lived an extravagant lifestyle, and when he died in New York on September 19, 1860, he was in poverty.

The minstrel shows were popular between 1850 and 1870, but they lost much of their national popularity with the coming of motion pictures and radios. Unfortunately for Blacks, the minstrel shows continued in small towns, and worse, caricatured portrayals of Blacks found greater expression in motion pictures and radios.

Minstrel Man BY Langston Hughes

Because my mouth
Is wide with laughter
And my throat
Is deep with song,
You do not think
I suffer after
I have held my pain
So long?

Because my mouth
Is wide with laughter,
You do not hear
My inner cry?
Because my feet
Are gay with dancing,
You do not know
I die?

About the Ku Klux Klan

The Ku Klux Klan is a racist, anti-Semitic movement with a commitment to extreme violence to achieve its goals of racial segregation and white supremacy. *Of all the types of right-wing hate groups that exist in the United States, the Klan remains the one with the greatest number of national and local organizations around the country.*

More than 40 different Klan groups exist, many having multiple chapters, or "klaverns," including a few that boast a presence in a large number of states. There are over a hundred different Klan chapters around the country, with a combined strength of members and associates that may total around 5,000.

After a period of relative quiet, Ku Klux Klan activity has spiked noticeably upwards in 2006, as Klan groups have attempted to exploit fears in America over gay marriage, perceived "assaults" on Christianity, crime and especially immigration.

Founder: Confederate Civil War veterans Captain John C. Lester, Major James R. Crowe, John D. Kennedy, Calvin Jones, Richard R. Reed, And Frank O. McCord

Founded: 1866

Headquarters: Each different Klan group has its own headquarters.

Background: The Klan has fragmented into more than 40 separate factions of varying sizes. There is no "one" Ku Klux Klan.

Estimated size: There are over a hundred different chapters in the various Klan organizations, with varying memberships. *Overall, there may be as many as 5,000 members and associates of the Ku Klux Klan. The Klan is strongest in the South and in the Midwest.*

Criminal Activity: *The Klan has a relatively high association with criminal activity, ranging from hate crimes to acts of domestic terrorism.*

Media: Mass mailings, leafleting and the Internet.

Strategy: Public rallies and protests, "adopt a highway" programs and other attention getting stunts, Internet.

Ideology: *White supremacist ideology not far from that of neo-Nazis, although it tends to be more Christian-oriented and to stress nativism.*

Affiliations: National Socialist Movement, Aryan Nations, Christian Identity groups.

Financial support: Little. Most funding comes from membership dues and sales of Klan paraphernalia.

The Ku Klux Klan first emerged following the Civil War as America's first true terrorist group. Since its inception, the Ku Klux Klan has seen several cycles of growth and collapse, and in some of these cycles the Klan has been more extreme than in others. In all of its incarnations, however, the Klan has maintained its dual heritage of hate and violence.

At first, the Ku Klux Klan focused its anger and violence on African-Americans, on white Americans who stood up for them, and against the federal government which supported their rights. Subsequent incarnations of the Klan, which typically emerged in times of rapid social change, added more categories to its enemies list, including Jews, Catholics (less so after the 1970s), homosexuals, and different groups of immigrants.

In most of these cases, these perceived enemies were minority groups that came into direct economic competition with the lower—and working-class whites that formed the core constituency of the Klan in most of its incarnations.

The Ku Klux Klan was overshadowed in the late 1990s and early 2000s by growing neo-Nazi activity; however, by 2005 neo-Nazi groups had fallen on hard times, with many groups collapsing or fragmenting. This collapse has helped create a rise of racist skinhead activity, but has also provided new opportunities for Klan groups.

In addition, in the early 2000s, many communities in the United States began to experiences a significant influx of immigrants, especially Hispanics, for the first time in their histories. A single-issue movement opposing immigration has helped create fear and anxiety about immigration in the minds of many Americans.

Many Ku Klux Klan groups have attempted to take advantage of that fear and uncertainty, using anti-immigration sentiments for recruitment and propaganda purposes, and to attract publicity.

Reflections:

A Rattlesnake, if cornered will become so angry it will bite itself. That is exactly what the harboring of hate and resentment against others is—a biting of oneself. We think we are harming others in holding these spites and hates, but the deeper harm is to ourselves. ~E. Stanley Jones

Hating people is like burning down your own house to get rid of a rat.

~Henry Emerson Fosdick

Wounded Knee Massacre

The **Wounded Knee Massacre** occurred on December 29, 1890 near Wounded Knee Creek (Lakota: *Cankpe Opi Wakpala*) on the Lakota Pine Ridge Indian Reservation. On the day before, a detachment of the U.S. 7th Cavalry Regiment commanded by Major Samuel M. Whitside intercepted Spotted Elk's (Big Foot) band of Miniconjou Lakota and 38 Hunkpapa Lakota near Porcupine Butte and escorted them 5 miles westward (8 km) to Wounded Knee Creek where they made camp.

The rest of the 7th Cavalry Regiment arrived led by Colonel James Forsyth and surrounded the encampment supported by four Hotchkiss guns.

On the morning of December 29, the troops went into the camp to disarm the Lakota. One version of events claims that during the process of disarming the Lakota, a deaf tribesman named Black Coyote was reluctant to give up his rifle claiming he had paid a lot for it. A scuffle over Black Coyote's rifle escalated and a shot was fired which resulted in the 7th Cavalry opening firing indiscriminately from all sides, killing men, women, and children, as well as some of their own fellow troopers. Those few Lakota warriors who still had weapons began shooting back at the attacking troopers, who quickly suppressed the Lakota fire. The surviving Lakota fled, but U.S. cavalrymen pursued and killed many who were unarmed.

By the time it was over, at least 150 men, women, and children of the Lakota Sioux had been killed and 51 wounded (4 men, 47 women and children, some of whom died later); some estimates placed the number of dead at 300. Twenty-five troopers also died, and thirty-nine were wounded (6 of the wounded would also die). It is believed that many were the victims of friendly fire, as the shooting took place at close range in chaotic conditions.

Prelude

In the years prior to the Massacre, the U.S. Government continued to coerce the Lakota into signing away more of their lands. The large bison herds, as well as other staple species of the Sioux diet, had been driven nearly to extinction. Congress failed to keep its treaty promises (as still does today) to feed, house, clothe and protect reservation lands from encroachment by settlers and gold miners; as well as failing to properly oversee the Indian Agents. As a result there was unrest on the reservations.

General Miles' Telegraph

General Miles sent this telegraph from Rapid City to General John Schofield in Washington, D.C. on December 19, 1890:

> *"The difficult Indian problem cannot be solved permanently at this end of the line. It requires the fulfillment of Congress of the treaty obligations that the Indians were entreated and coerced into signing. They signed away a valuable portion of their reservation, and it is now occupied by white people, for which they have received nothing.*
>
> *They understood that ample provision would be made for their support; instead, their supplies have been reduced, and much of the time they have been living on half and two-thirds rations. Their crops, as well as the crops of the white people, for two years have been almost total failures.*
>
> *The dissatisfaction is wide spread, especially among the Sioux, while the Cheyenne's have been on the verge of starvation, and were forced to commit depredations to sustain life. These facts are beyond question, and the evidence is positive and sustained by thousands of witnesses."*

It was during this time of suffering and degradation that news spread among the reservations of a Paiute prophet named Wovoka, founder of the Ghost Dance religion. *He had a vision that the Christian Messiah, Jesus Christ, had returned to earth in the form of a Native American.*

The Messiah would raise all the Native American believers above the earth. During this time the white man would disappear from Native lands, the buffalo herds and all the other animals would return in abundance and the ghosts of their ancestors would return to earth—hence the word "Ghost" in

"Ghost Dance". They would then return to earth to live in peace. This would all be brought about by performance of the "Ghost Dance". While performing the Ghost Dance they would wear special Ghost Dance shirts, which they believed to be bulletproof.

The sight of the many Great Basin and Plains tribes performing the Ghost Dance alarmed some whites. Among them was the Indian Agent at the Standing Rock Agency where Chief Sitting Bull lived. ***US officials decided to take some of the chiefs into custody in order to quell the so-called "Messiah Craze."*** The military's original plan was to have Sitting Bull's friend Buffalo Bill aid in the plan to reduce the chance of violence. Standing Rock agent Royer, who was ill experienced in native affairs, overrode the military and sent the Indian police to arrest Sitting Bull.

On December 15, 1890, 40 Indian policemen arrived at Chief Sitting Bull's house to arrest him. Crowds gathered to protest the arrest, and the first shot was fired when Sitting Bull tried to pull away from his captors, killing the officer who had been holding him. Additional shots were fired, resulting in the death of eight of Sitting Bull's supporters and six policemen. After Sitting Bull's death, 200 members of his Hunkpapa band, fearful of reprisals, fled Standing Rock to join Chief Spotted Elk (later to be known as "Big Foot") and his Miniconjou band at the Cheyenne River Indian Reservation.

Spotted Elk and his band, along with 38 Hunkpapa, left the Cheyenne River Reservation on December 23 to journey to the Pine Ridge Indian Reservation to seek shelter with Red Cloud.

A portion of a letter from former Indian Agent Valentine T. Mcgillycuddy:

> *"As for the "Ghost Dance" too much attention has been paid to it. It was only the symptom [sic] or surface indication of a deep rooted, long existing difficulty; as well treat the eruption of small pox as the disease and ignore the constitutional disease."*
>
> *"As regards disarming the Sioux, however desirable it may appear, I consider it neither advisable, nor practicable. I fear it will result as the theoretical enforcement of prohibition in Kansas, Iowa and Dakota; you will succeed in disarming and keeping disarmed the friendly Indians because you can, and you will not succeed with the mob element because you cannot."*
>
> *"If I were again to be an Indian Agent, and had my choice, I would take charge of 10,000 armed Sioux in preference to a like number of disarmed ones; and furthermore agree to handle that number, or the whole Sioux nation, without a white soldier. Respectfully, etc., V.T. McGillycuddy.*

> *P.S. I neglected to state that up to date there has been either a*
> *Sioux outbreak or war. No citizen in Nebraska or Dakota has been*
> *killed, molested or can show the scratch of a pin, and no property*
> *has been destroyed off the reservation."*

The Massacre

On December 28, 1890, Chief Spotted Elk of the Miniconjou Lakota nation and 350 of his followers were intercepted by a 7th Cavalry detachment under Major Samuel M. Whitside southwest of the badlands near Porcupine Butte. John Shangreau, a scout and interpreter who was half Sioux, advised that they not be disarmed immediately, as it would lead to violence. The troopers escorted the Lakota about five miles westward (8 km) to Wounded Knee Creek where they made camp. Later that evening, Col. James W. Forsyth and the rest of the 7th Cavalry arrived, bringing the number of troopers at Wounded Knee to 500. In contrast, there were 350 Native Americans, of whom all but 120 were women and children.

The troopers surrounded Spotted Elk's encampment and set up four rapid fire Hotchkiss guns. At daybreak on December 29, 1890, Col. Forsyth ordered the surrender of weapons and the immediate removal and transportation of the Indians from the "zone of military operations" to awaiting trains. **Specific details of what triggered the fight are debated.** According to some accounts, a medicine man named Yellow Bird began to perform the Ghost Dance, reiterating his assertion to the Lakota that the ghost shirts were bulletproof. As tension mounted, Black Coyote refused to give up his rifle; he was deaf and had not understood the order. Another Indian said: "Black Coyote is deaf." (He did not speak English). When the soldier refused to heed his warning, he said "Stop! He cannot hear your orders!" At that moment, two soldiers seized Black Coyote from behind, and in the struggle (allegedly), his rifle discharged. At the same moment Yellow Bird threw some dust into the air, and approximately five young Lakota men with concealed weapons threw aside their blankets and fired their rifles at Troop K of the 7th. After this initial exchange, the firing became indiscriminate.

According to commanding Gen. Nelson A. Miles, a "scuffle occurred between one warrior who had [a] rifle in his hand and two soldiers. ***The rifle was discharged and a massacre occurred, not only the warriors but the sick Chief Spotted Elk, and a large number of women and children who tried to escape by running and scattering over the prairie were hunted down and killed."***

At first the struggle was fought at close range; fully half the Indian men were killed or wounded before they had a chance to get off any shots. Some of the Indians grabbed rifles they had been hiding and opened fire on the soldiers. With no cover, and with many of the Sioux unarmed, this phase of the fighting lasted a few minutes at most. While the Indian warriors and soldiers were shooting at close range, other soldiers used the Hotchkiss guns against the tipi camp full of women and children. It is believed that many of the troops on the battlefield were victims of friendly fire from their own Hotchkiss guns. The Indian women and children fled the camp, seeking shelter in a nearby ravine from the crossfire. The officers had lost all control of their men. Some of the soldiers fanned out to run across the battlefield and finish off wounded Indians. Others leaped onto their horses and pursued the Lakota (men, women and children), in some cases for miles across the prairies. By the end of the fighting, which lasted less than an hour, at least 150 Lakota had been killed and 50 wounded. Army casualties numbered 25 dead and 39 wounded.

Eyewitness accounts

- Dewey Beard (Iron Tail, 1862-1955), Minneconjou Lakota survivor: as told to Eli S. Ricker :

"*. . . then many Indians broke into the ravine; some ran up the ravine and to favorable positions for defense.*"

- Black Elk (1863-1950); medicine man, Oglala Lakota:

"*I did not know then how much was ended. When I look back now from this high hill of my old age, I can still see the butchered women and children lying heaped and scattered all along the crooked gulch as plain as when I saw them with eyes young. And I can see that something else died there in the bloody mud, and was buried in the blizzard. A people's dream died there. It was a beautiful dream . . . . the nation's hoop is broken and scattered. There is no center any longer, and the sacred tree is dead.*" (Source: Black Elk Speaks, c. 1932)

- American Horse (1840-1908); Chief, Oglala Lakota:

"*There was a woman with an infant in her arms who was killed as she almost touched the flag of truce . . . A mother was shot down with her infant; the child not knowing that its mother was dead was still nursing . . . The women as they were fleeing with their babies were killed together, shot right through . . . and after most all of them had been killed a cry was made that all those who were not killed or wounded should come forth and they would be safe. Little boys . . . came out of their places of refuge, and as soon as they came in sight a number of soldiers surrounded them and butchered them there.*"

- Edward S. Godfrey; Captain; commanded Co. D of the Seventh Cavalry:

"I know the men did not aim deliberately and they were greatly excited. I don't believe they saw their sights. They fired rapidly but it seemed to me only a few seconds till there was not a living thing before us; warriors, squaws, children, ponies, and dogs . . . went down before that unaimed fire."(Godfrey was a Lieutenant in Captain Benteen's force during the Battle of the Little Bighorn)

- Hugh McGinnis; First Battalion, Co. K, Seventh Cavalry: *General Nelson A. Miles, who visited the scene of carnage, following a three day blizzard, estimated that around 300 snow shrouded forms were strewn over the countryside. He also discovered to his horror that helpless children and women with babes in their arms had been chased as far as two miles from the original scene of encounter and cut down without mercy by the troopers. . . . Judging by the slaughter on the battlefield it was suggested that the soldiers simply went berserk. For who could explain such a merciless disregard for life? . . . As I see it the battle was more or less a matter of spontaneous combustion, sparked by mutual distrust . . . .*

Aftermath

Following a three-day blizzard, the military hired civilians to bury the dead Lakota. The burial party found the deceased frozen in contorted positions; they were gathered up and placed in a common grave on a hill overlooking the encampment from which some of the fire from the Hotchkiss guns originated. It was reported that four infants were found alive, wrapped in their deceased mothers' shawls. In all, 84 men, 44 women, and 18 children reportedly died on the field, while at least seven Lakota were mortally wounded they later hired civilians to remove the bodies and bury them in a mass grave. General Nelson Miles denounced Colonel Forsyth and relieved him of command. ***An exhaustive Army Court of Inquiry convened by Miles criticized Forsyth for his tactical dispositions but otherwise exonerated him of responsibility. The Court of Inquiry, however, was not conducted as a formal court-martial.***

The Secretary of War concurred with the decision and reinstated Forsyth to command of the 7th Cavalry. Testimony indicated that for the most part troops attempted to avoid non-combatant casualties. Nevertheless, Miles ignored the results of the Court of Inquiry and continued to criticize Forsyth, who he believed had deliberately disobeyed his commands in order to destroy the Indians. *Miles promoted the conclusion that Wounded Knee was a deliberate massacre rather than a tragedy caused by poor decisions, in an effort to destroy the career of Forsyth. This was later understood and Forsyth was promoted to Major General.*

The American public's reaction to the battle at the time was generally favorable. Many non-Lakota living near the reservations interpreted the battle as the defeat of a murderous cult; others confused Ghost Dancers with Native Americans in general. In an editorial response to the event, the young newspaper editor L. Frank Baum, later the author of *The Wonderful Wizard of Oz*, wrote in the *Aberdeen Saturday Pioneer* on January 3, 1891:

The Pioneer has before declared that our only safety depends upon the total extermination of the Indians. Having wronged them for centuries, we had better, in order to protect our civilization, follow it up by one more wrong and wipe these untamed and untamable creatures from the face of the earth. In this lies future safety for our settlers and the soldiers who are under incompetent commands. Otherwise, we may expect future years to be as full of trouble with the redskins as those have been in the past.

More than 80 years after the massacre, beginning on February 27, 1973, Wounded Knee was the site of the Wounded Knee incident, a 71-day standoff between federal authorities and militants of the American Indian Movement.

Skirmish at Drexel Mission

Historically, Wounded Knee is generally considered to be the end of the collective multi-century series of conflicts between colonial and U.S. forces and American Indians, known collectively as the Indian Wars. It led to a dramatic decline in the Ghost Dance movement; however, it was not the last armed conflict between Native Americans and the United States.

A related skirmish took place at Drexel Mission the day after the Battle of Wounded Knee. One soldier died and six were wounded from K Troop, 7th Cavalry. Lakota casualties were not recorded. After news of Wounded Knee reached them, Lakota Ghost Dancers from bands that had surrendered fled, burning several buildings at the mission as they left. They ambushed a squadron of the 7th Cavalry that responded to the incident and pinned it down until a relief force from the 9th Cavalry arrived. The 9th had been trailing the Lakota from the White River. Lieutenant James D. Mann, who had been a key participant in the outbreak of firing at Wounded Knee, died of his wounds 17 days later at Fort Riley, Kansas, on January 15, 1891. The Drexel Mission skirmish is often overlooked.

Medal of Honor Controversy

The Army awarded twenty Medals of Honor, its highest award, for the action. Native American activists have urged the medals be withdrawn, as they say they were "Medals of Dishonor". According to Lakota tribesman William Thunder Hawk, "The Medal of Honor is meant to reward soldiers who act heroically. But at Wounded Knee, they didn't show heroism; they showed cruelty." In 2001, the National Congress of American Indians passed two resolutions that condemned the Medals of Honor awards and called on the U.S. government to rescind them.

> *Historian Will G. Robinson noted that in contrast, only three Medals of Honor were awarded among the 64,000 South Dakotans who fought for four years of World War II.*

Some of the citations on the medals awarded to the troopers at Wounded Knee state that they went in pursuit of Lakota who were trying to escape or hide.

Remembrance

A church was built on the hill behind the mass grave in which the victims had been buried. In 1903, descendants of those who died in the massacre erected a monument at the gravesite. The memorial lists many of those who died at Wounded Knee along with an inscription that reads:

> *"This monument is erected by surviving relatives and other Ogalala [sic] and Cheyenne River Sioux Indians in memory of the Chief Big Foot massacre December 29, 1890. Col. Forsyth in command of US troops. Big Foot was a great chief of the Sioux Indians. He often said, "I will stand in peace till my last day comes." He did many good and brave deeds for the white man and the red man. Many innocent women and children who knew no wrong died here*

Beginning in 1986, a group began the Big Foot Memorial Riders to continue to honor the victims of the Wounded Knee Massacre; this ceremony has grown increasingly larger every year since then, and riders subject themselves to the cold weather as well as the lack of food and water as they retrace the path that their family members took to Wounded Knee. They carry with them a white flag to symbolize their hope for world peace, and to continue to honor and remember the victims so that they will not be forgotten.

Some family members are still seeking compensation from the U.S. Government as heirs of the victims, but they have been unsuccessful in receiving any monetary settlement.

Popular culture

The phrase, *"Bury my heart at Wounded Knee" comes from the 1931 poem* "American Names" by Stephen Vincent Benet. The poem is about Benet's love of American place names and makes no reference to the battle. However, when the line was used as the title of a 1970 book—*Bury My Heart at Wounded Knee* by historian Dee Brown—it became popularly attached to the incident. Brown's book raised awareness of the massacre and became a best seller, and Benet's phrase has since been used many times in songs and other references to the battle. Perhaps the best known is "Bury My Heart at Wounded Knee", written by Buffy Sainte-Marie and featured on her 1992 album *Coincidence and Likely Stories.*

Other artists who have written or recorded songs referring to the massacre at Wounded Knee include Johnny Cash (1972's "Big Foot", which like many of Cash's songs about Native Americans is strongly sympathetic).

Over heard in passing:

"Tell me if you can; in countries like Afghanistan, Iraq, and Somalia, to name just a few, who have little money or munitions factories, where do the terrorist get all their guns and ammunition?"

"The same place the Indians got theirs."

National Association for the Advancement of Colored People

The **National Association for the Advancement of Colored People,** usually abbreviated as **NAACP** (pronounced en double-ay cee pee), is one of the oldest and most influential civil rights organizations in the United States. Its mission is "to ensure the political, educational, social, and economic equality of rights of all persons and to eliminate racial hatred and racial discrimination". *Its name, retained in accordance with tradition, is one of the last surviving uses of the term colored people.*

The NAACP bestows the annual Image Awards for achievement in the arts and entertainment, and the annual Spingarn Medals for outstanding positive achievement of any kind, on deserving African Americans. It has its headquarters in Baltimore, Maryland.

Organization

The NAACP's headquarters are in Baltimore, Maryland, with additional regional offices in California, New York, Michigan, Missouri, Georgia and Texas. Each regional office is responsible for coordinating the efforts of state conferences in the states included in that region. Local, youth, and college chapters organize activities for individual members.

The NAACP is run nationally by a 64-member board led by a chair. The board elects one person as the President and chief executive officer for the organization; Benjamin Jealous is its most recent (and youngest) President, selected to replace Bruce S. Gordon, who resigned in March 2007. Civil Rights Movement activist and former Georgia State Senator Julian Bond was chairman until replaced in February 2010 by health-care administrator Roslyn M. Brock.

Departments within the NAACP govern areas of action. Local chapters are supported by the Branch and Field Services department and the Youth and

College department. The Legal Department focuses on court cases of broad application to minorities, such as systematic discrimination in employment, government, or education. The Washington, D.C., bureau is responsible for lobbying the U.S. government, and the Education Department works to improve public education at the local, state and federal levels. The goal of the Health Division is to advance health care for minorities through public policy initiatives and education.

As of 2007, the NAACP had approximately 425,000 paying and non-paying members.

Pre-History: The Niagara Movement

In 1905, a group of 32 prominent, outspoken African Americans met to discuss the challenges facing "people of color" (a term used to describe people who were not white) and possible strategies and solutions. Among the issues they were concerned about was the disfranchisement of blacks in the South starting in 1890 to 1908, when Southern legislatures ratified new constitutions creating barriers to voter registration and more complex election rules. Voter registration and turnout dropped markedly in the South as a result. *Men who had been voting for 30 years were told they did not "qualify" to register.*

Because hotels in the U.S. were segregated, the men convened under the leadership of Harvard scholar W. E. B. Du Bois at a hotel (Fort Erie Hotel) on the Canadian side of Niagara Falls in Fort Erie, Ontario. As a result, the group came to be known as the Niagara Movement. A year later, three whites joined the group: journalist William E. Walling, social worker Mary White Ovington, and social worker Henry Moskowitz, then Associate Leader of the New York Society for Ethical Culture.

The fledgling group struggled for a time with limited resources and internal conflict and disbanded in 1910. Many members of the Niagara Movement then went on to join the NAACP. Although both organizations shared membership and overlapped in their existence, the Niagara Movement was a separate organization and is historically thought of as having a more radical platform than the NAACP. *The Niagara Movement was formed exclusively by African Americans, while the initial meeting which birthed the idea of the NAACP was with three white people.*

History
The Birth of the NAACP

The Race Riot of 1908 in Lincoln's hometown of Springfield, Illinois had highlighted the urgent need for an effective civil rights organization in the U.S. This event is often cited as the catalyst for the formation of the NAACP. Mary White Ovington, journalist William English Walling and Henry Moscowitz met in New York City in January 1909 and the NAACP was born. Solicitations for support went out to more than 60 prominent Americans, and a meeting date was set for February 12, 1909. This was intended to coincide with the 100th anniversary of the birth of President Abraham Lincoln, who emancipated enslaved African Americans. While the meeting did not take place until three months later, this date is often cited as the founding date of the organization.

The NAACP was founded on February 12, 1909 by a diverse group composed of Du Bois, Ida B. Wells, Archibald Grimké, Henry Moscowitz, Mary White Ovington, Oswald Garrison Villard, William English Walling (the last son of a former slave-holding family), and Florence Kelley, a social reformer and friend of Du Bois.

On May 30, 1909, the Niagara Movement conference took place at New York City's *Henry Street Settlement House*, from which an organization of more than 40 individuals emerged, calling itself the National Negro Committee. Du Bois played a key role in organizing the event and presided over the proceedings. Also in attendance was African-American journalist and anti-lynching crusader Ida B. Wells-Barnett. At its second conference on May 30, 1910, members chose as the organization's name the *National Association for the Advancement of Colored People* and elected its first officers, who were:

- National President, Moorfield Storey, Boston
- Chairman of the Executive Committee, William English Walling
- Treasurer, John E. Milholland (a Lincoln Republican and Presbyterian from New York City and Lewis, NY)
- Disbursing Treasurer, Oswald Garrison Villard
- Executive Secretary, Frances Blascoer
- Director of Publicity and Research, Dr. W.E.B. Du Bois.

The NAACP was incorporated a year later in 1911. The association's charter delineated its mission:

To promote equality of rights and to eradicate caste or race prejudice among the citizens of the United States; to advance the interest of colored citizens; to secure for them impartial suffrage; and to increase their opportunities for securing justice in the courts, education for the children, employment according to their ability and complete equality before law.

The conference resulted in a more influential and diverse organization, where the leadership was predominantly white and heavily Jewish American. In fact, at its founding, the NAACP had only

one African American on its executive board, Du Bois himself. It did not elect a black president until 1975, although executive directors had been African American. The Jewish community contributed greatly to the NAACP's founding and continued financing. Jewish historian Howard Sachar writes in his book *A History of Jews in America* of how, "In 1914, Professor Emeritus Joel Spingarn of Columbia University became chairman of the NAACP and recruited for its board such Jewish leaders as Jacob Schiff, Jacob Billikopf, and Rabbi Stephen Wise." Early Jewish-American co-founders included Julius Rosenwald, Lillian Wald, Rabbi Emil G. Hirsch and Wise.

According to Pbs.org "Over the years Jews have also expressed empathy (capability to share and understand another's emotion and feelings) with the plight of Blacks. In the early 1900s, Jewish newspapers drew parallels between the Black movement out of the South and the Jews' escape from Egypt, pointing out that both Blacks and Jews lived in ghettos, and calling anti-Black riots in the South "pogroms". Stressing the similarities rather than the differences between the Jewish and Black experience in America, Jewish leaders emphasized the idea that both groups would benefit the more America moved toward a society of merit, free of religious, ethnic and racial restrictions." Pbs.org further states, "The American Jewish Committee, the American Jewish Congress, and the Anti-Defamation League were central to the campaign against racial prejudice. Jews made substantial financial contributions to many civil rights organizations, including the NAACP, the Urban League, the Congress of Racial Equality, and the Student Non-Violent Coordinating Committee. *About 50 percent of the civil rights attorneys in the South during the 1960s were Jews, as were over 50 percent of the Whites who went to Mississippi in 1964 to challenge Jim Crow Laws.*"

As a member of the Princeton chapter of the NAACP, Albert Einstein corresponded with Du Bois, and in 1946 Einstein called racism "America's worst disease". Du Bois continued to play a pivotal role in the organization and served as editor of the association's magazine, *The Crisis*, which had a circulation of over 30,000.

Moorfield Storey, who was white, was the president of the NAACP from its founding to 1915. Storey was a long-time classical liberal and Grover Cleveland Democrat who advocated *laissez-faire* free markets, the gold standard, and anti-imperialism. Storey consistently and aggressively championed civil rights; not only for blacks but also for Native Americans and immigrants (he opposed immigration restrictions).

Fighting Jim Crow and disfranchisement

In its early years, the NAACP concentrated on using the courts to overturn the Jim Crow statutes that legalized racial segregation. In 1913, the NAACP organized opposition to President Woodrow Wilson's introduction of racial segregation into federal government policy, offices, and hiring.

By 1914, the group had 6,000 members and 50 branches. It was influential in winning the right of African Americans to serve as officers in World War I. Six hundred African-American officers were commissioned and 700,000 men registered for the draft. *The following year, the NAACP organized a nationwide protest, with marches in numerous cities, against D.W. Griffith's silent movie Birth of a Nation, a film that glamorized the Ku Klux Klan. As a result, several cities refused to allow the film to open.*

The NAACP began to lead lawsuits targeting disfranchisement and racial segregation early in its history. It played a significant part in the challenge of *Guinn v. United States* (1915) to Oklahoma's discriminatory grandfather clause that disfranchised most black citizens while exempting many whites from certain voter registration requirements. It persuaded the Supreme Court of the United States to rule in *Buchanan v. Warley* in 1917 that state and local governments cannot officially segregate African Americans into separate residential districts. The Court's opinion reflected the jurisprudence of property rights and freedom of contract as embodied in the earlier precedent it established in *Lochner v. New York*.

In 1916, when the NAACP was just seven years old, Chairman Joel Spingarn invited James Weldon Johnson to serve as field secretary. Johnson was a former U.S. consul to Venezuela and a noted scholar and columnist. Within four years, Johnson was instrumental in increasing the NAACP's membership from 9,000 to almost 90,000. In 1920, Johnson was elected head of the organization. Over the next ten years, the NAACP escalated its lobbying and litigation efforts, becoming internationally known for its advocacy of equal rights and equal protection for the "American Negro".

The NAACP devoted much of its energy during the interwar years to fighting the lynching of blacks throughout the United States by working for legislation, lobbying and educating the public. *The organization sent its field secretary Walter F. White to Phillips County, Arkansas, in October 1919, to investigate the Elaine Race Riot. More than 200 black tenant farmers were killed by roving white vigilantes and federal troops after a deputy sheriff's attack on a union meeting of sharecroppers left one white man dead. White published his report on the riot in the Chicago Daily News. The NAACP organized the appeals for twelve black men sentenced to death a month later based on the fact that testimony used in their convictions was obtained by beatings and electric shocks.* It gained a groundbreaking Supreme Court decision in *Moore v. Dempsey* 261 U.S. 86 (1923) that significantly expanded the Federal courts' oversight of the states' criminal justice systems in the years to come. White investigated eight race riots and 41 lynching's for the NAACP and directed its study *Thirty Years of Lynching in the United States*.

The NAACP also spent more than a decade seeking federal legislation against lynching, but Southern white Democrats voted as a block against it or used the filibuster in the Senate to block passage. Because of disfranchisement, there were no black representatives from the South in Congress and the region had essentially a one-party system of Democrats. The NAACP regularly displayed a black flag stating "A Man Was Lynched Yesterday" from the window of its offices in New York to mark each lynching.

In alliance with the American Federation of Labor, the NAACP led the successful fight to prevent the nomination of John Johnston Parker to the Supreme Court, based on his support for denying the vote to blacks and his anti-labor rulings. It organized support for the Scottsboro Boys. The NAACP lost most of the internecine battles with the Communist Party and International Labor Defense over the control of those cases and the strategy to be pursued in that case.

The organization also brought litigation to challenge the "white primary" system in the South. Southern states had created white-only primaries as another way of barring blacks from the political process. Since southern states were one-party states, the primaries were the only competitive contests. In 1944 in Smith v. Allwright, the Supreme Court ruled against the white primary. Although states had to retract legislation related to the white primaries, the legislatures soon came up with new methods to limit the franchise for blacks.

The board of directors of the NAACP created the Legal Defense Fund in 1939 specifically for tax purposes. It functioned as the NAACP legal department. Intimidated by the Department of the Treasury and the Internal Revenue Service, the Legal and Educational Defense Fund, Inc., became a separate legal entity in 1957, although it was clear that it was to operate in accordance with NAACP policy: After 1961 serious disputes emerged between the two organizations, creating considerable confusion in the eyes and minds of the public.

Desegregation

With the rise of private corporate litigators like the NAACP to bear the expense, civil suits became the pattern in modern civil rights litigation. The NAACP's Legal department, headed by Charles Hamilton Houston and Thurgood Marshall, undertook a campaign spanning several decades to bring about the reversal of the "separate but equal" doctrine announced by the Supreme Court's decision in *Plessy v. Ferguson*.

The NAACP's Baltimore chapter, under president Lillie Mae Carroll Jackson, challenged segregation in Maryland state professional schools by supporting the 1935 *Murray v. Pearson* case argued by Marshall. Houston's victory in *Missouri ex rel. Gaines v. Canada* (1938) led to the formation of the NAACP Legal Defense fund in 1940.

The campaign for desegregation culminated in a unanimous 1954 Supreme Court decision in *Brown v. Board of Education* that held state-sponsored segregation of elementary schools was unconstitutional. Bolstered by that victory, the NAACP pushed for full desegregation throughout the South. Starting on December 5, 1955, NAACP activists, including E.D. Nixon, its local president, and Rosa Parks, who had served as the chapter's Secretary, helped organize a bus boycott in Montgomery, Alabama. This was designed to protest segregation on the city's buses, two-thirds of whose riders were black. The boycott lasted 381 days.

The State of Alabama responded by effectively barring the NAACP from operating within its borders because of its refusal to divulge a list of its members. The NAACP feared members could be fired or face violent retaliation for their activities. Although the Supreme Court eventually overturned the state's action in *NAACP v. Alabama*, 357 U.S. 449 (1958), the NAACP lost its leadership role in the Civil Rights Movement while it was barred from Alabama.

New organizations such as the Southern Christian Leadership Conference (SCLC) and the Student Nonviolent Coordinating Committee (SNCC) rose up with different approaches to activism. These newer groups relied on direct action and mass mobilization to advance the rights of African Americans, rather than litigation and legislation. Roy Wilkins, NAACP's executive director, clashed repeatedly with Dr. Martin Luther King, Jr. and other civil rights leaders over questions of strategy and leadership within the movement.

The NAACP continued to use the Supreme Court's decision in Brown to press for desegregation of schools and public facilities throughout the country. Daisy Bates, president of its Arkansas state chapter, spearheaded the campaign by the Little Rock Nine to integrate the public schools in Little Rock, Arkansas.

By the mid-1960s, the NAACP had regained some of its preeminence in the Civil Rights Movement by pressing for civil rights legislation. ***The March on Washington for Jobs and Freedom took place on August 28, 1963. That fall President John F. Kennedy sent a civil rights bill to Congress before he was assassinated.***

President Lyndon B. Johnson worked hard to persuade Congress to pass a civil rights bill aimed at ending racial discrimination in employment, education and public accommodations, and succeeded in gaining passage in July 1964. He followed that with passage of the Voting Rights Act of 1965, which provided for protection of the franchise, with a role for federal oversight and administrators in places where voter turnout was historically low.

After Kivie Kaplan died in 1975, scientist W. Montague Cobb became President of the NAACP and served until 1982. Benjamin Hooks, a lawyer and clergyman, was elected as the NAACP's executive director in 1977, after the retirement of Roy Wilkins.

The 1990s: crisis and restored strength

In the 1990s, the NAACP ran into debt. The dismissal of two leading officials further added to the picture of an organization in deep crisis.

In 1993 the NAACP's Board of Directors narrowly selected Reverend Benjamin Chavis over Reverend Jesse Jackson to fill the position of Executive Director. A controversial figure, Chavis was ousted eighteen months later by the same board that had hired him. They accused him of using NAACP funds for an out-of-court settlement in a sexual harassment lawsuit. Following the dismissal of Chavis, Myrlie Evers-Williams narrowly defeated NAACP chairperson William Gibson for president in 1995, after Gibson was accused of overspending and mismanagement of the organization's funds.

In 1996 Congressman Kweisi Mfume, a Democratic Congressman from Maryland and former head of the Congressional Black Caucus, was named the organization's president. Three years later strained finances forced the organization to drastically cut its staff, from 250 in 1992 to just fifty.

In the second half of the 1990s, the organization restored its finances, permitting the NAACP National Voter Fund to launch a major get-out-the-vote offensive in the 2000 U.S. presidential elections. 10.5 million African Americans cast their ballots in the election. This was one million more than four years before, and the NAACP's effort was credited by observers as playing a significant role in Democrat Al Gore's winning several states where the election was close, such as Pennsylvania and Michigan.

Lee Alcorn controversy

During the 2000 Presidential election, Lee Alcorn, president of the Dallas NAACP branch, criticized Al Gore's selection of Senator Joe Lieberman for his Vice-Presidential candidate because Lieberman was Jewish. On a gospel talk radio show on station KHVN, Alcorn stated, "If we get a Jew person, then what I'm wondering is, I mean, what is this movement for, you know? Does it have anything to do with the failed peace talks?" . . ." So I think we need to be very suspicious of any kind of partnerships between the Jews at that kind of level because we know that their interest primarily has to do with money and these kinds of things."

NAACP President Kweisi Mfume immediately suspended Alcorn and condemned his remarks. Mfume stated, "I strongly condemn those remarks. I find them to be repulsive, anti-Semitic, anti-NAACP and anti-American. Mr. Alcorn does not speak for the NAACP, its board, its staff or its membership. We are proud of our long-standing relationship with the Jewish community and I personally will not tolerate statements that run counter to the history and beliefs of the NAACP in that regard."

Alcorn, who had been suspended three times in the previous five years for misconduct, subsequently resigned from the NAACP and started his own organization called the Coalition for the Advancement of Civil Rights. Alcorn criticized the NAACP, saying, "I can't support the leadership of the NAACP. Large amounts of money are being given to them by large corporations that I have a problem with." Alcorn also said, "I cannot be bought. For this reason I gladly offer my resignation and my membership to the NAACP because I cannot work under these constraints."

Alcorn's remarks were also condemned by the Reverend Jesse Jackson, Jewish groups and George W. Bush's rival Republican presidential campaign. Jackson said he strongly supported Lieberman's addition to the Democratic ticket, saying, "When we live our faith, we live under the law. He [Lieberman] is a firewall of exemplary behavior." Al Sharpton, another prominent African-American leader, said, "The appointment of Mr. Lieberman was to be welcomed as a positive step." The leaders of the American Jewish Congress praised the NAACP for its quick response, stating that: "It will take more than one bigot like Alcorn to shake the sense of fellowship of American Jews with the NAACP and black America . . . Our common concerns are too urgent, our history too long, and our connection too sturdy, to let anything like this disturb our relationship."[24]

NAACP and George W. Bush

In 2004, President George W. Bush (2001-2009) became the first sitting U.S. president since Herbert Hoover (1929-1933) to fail to address the NAACP when he declined an invitation to speak to its national convention. The White House originally said the president had a schedule conflict with the NAACP convention, slated for July 10-15, 2004. On July 10, 2004, however, Bush's spokesperson said that Bush had declined the invitation to speak to the NAACP because of harsh statements about him by its leaders. In an interview, Bush said, "I would describe my relationship with the current leadership as basically nonexistent. You've heard the rhetoric and the names they've called me." Bush also mentioned his admiration for some members of the NAACP and said he would seek to work with them "in other ways."

NAACP and tax exempt status

The Internal Revenue Service informed the NAACP in October 2004 that it was investigating its tax-exempt status based on Julian Bond's speech at its 2004 Convention in which he criticized President George W. Bush as well as other political figures. In general, the US Internal Revenue Code prohibits organizations granted tax-exempt status from "directly or indirectly participating in, or intervening in, any political campaign on behalf of (or in opposition to) any candidate for elective public office." The NAACP denounced the investigation as retaliation for its success in increasing the number of African Americans who vote. In August 2006, the IRS investigation concluded with the agency's finding "that the remarks did not violate the group's tax-exempt status."

NAACP and youth

This aspect of the NAACP came into existence in 1936 and now is made of over 600 groups and totaling over 30,000 individuals. The NAACP Youth & College Division is a branch of the NAACP in which youth are actively involved. The Youth Council is composed of hundreds of state, county, high school and college operations where youth (and college students) volunteer to share their voices or opinions with their peers and address issues that are local and national. Sometimes volunteer work expands to a more international scale. Committing to the Youth Council may reward young people with travel opportunities or scholarships.

In 2003, NAACP President and CEO, Kweisi Mfume, appointed Brandon Neal, the National Youth and College Division Director Currently, Stefanie L. Brown serves as the NAACP's National Youth & College Division Director. A graduate and former Student Government President at Howard University, Stefanie previously served as the National Youth Council Coordinator of the NAACP.

Mission of the Youth & College Division

"The mission of the NAACP Youth & College Division shall be to inform youth of the problems affecting African Americans and other racial and ethnic minorities; to advance the economic, education, social and political status of African Americans and other racial and ethnic minorities and their harmonious cooperation with other peoples; to stimulate an appreciation of the African Diaspora and other people of color's contribution to civilization; and to develop an intelligent, militant effective youth leadership."

ACT-SO program

Since 1978 the NAACP has sponsored the Afro-Academic, Cultural, Technological and Scientific Olympics (ACT-SO) program for high school youth around the United States. The program is designed to recognize and award African American youth who demonstrate accomplishment in academics, technology, and the arts. Local chapters sponsor competitions in various categories of achievement for young people in grades 9-12. Winners of the local competitions are eligible to proceed to the national event at a convention held each summer at locations around the United States. Winners at the national competition receive national recognition along with cash awards and various prizes.

National Urban League

*The **National Urban League** (NUL), formerly known as the **National League on Urban Conditions Among Negroes**, is a nonpartisan civil rights organization based in New York City that advocates on behalf of African Americans and against racial discrimination in the United States. **It is the oldest and largest community-based organization of its kind in the nation.***

History

The Committee on Urban Conditions Among Negroes was founded in New York City on September 29, 1910 by Ruth Standish Baldwin and Dr. George Edmund Haynes, among others. It merged with the Committee for the Improvement of Industrial Conditions Among Negroes in New York (founded in New York in 1906) and the National League for the Protection of Colored Women (founded in 1905), and was renamed the National League on Urban Conditions Among Negroes.

In 1918, Eugene K. Jones took the leadership of the organization and under his direction, the League significantly expanded its multifaceted campaign to crack the barriers to black employment, spurred first by the boom years of the 1920s, and then, by the desperate years of the Great Depression.

In 1920 the organization took the present name, the National Urban League. ***The mission of the Urban League movement is "to enable African Americans to secure economic self-reliance, parity, power and civil rights."***

In 1941, Lester Granger was appointed Executive Secretary and led the NUL's effort to support the March on Washington proposed by A. Phillip Randolph, Bayard Rustin and A. J. Muste to protest racial discrimination in defense work and the Armed Forces. During the African-American Civil Rights Movement (1955-1968), his insistence that the NUL continue its strategy of "education and persuasion" prevailed.

357

In 1961, Whitney Young became executive director amidst the explosion of the civil rights movement which provoked a change for the League. Young substantially expanded the League's fund-raising ability—and made the League a full partner in the civil rights movement. *In 1963, the NUL hosted the planning meetings of A. Philip Randolph, Martin Luther King, Jr., and other civil rights leaders for the March on Washington.* During Young's ten-year tenure at the League, he initiated programs like "Street Academy," an alternative education system to prepare high school dropouts for college, and "New Thrust," an effort to help local black leaders identify and solve community problems. Young also pushed for federal aid to cities.

In 1994, Hugh Price was appointed to the League's top office at a critical moment for the League, for Black America, and for the nation as a whole.

In 2003, Marc Morial was appointed the league's eighth President and Chief Executive Officer. Since his appointment to the National Urban League, Morial has worked to reenergize the movement's diverse constituencies by building on the strengths of the NUL's 95 year old legacy and increasing the organization's profile both locally and nationally.

Current status

Today, there are over 100 local affiliates of the National Urban League located in 35 states and the District of Columbia.

The National Urban League is an organizational member of the Coalition to Stop Gun Violence, which advocates gun control, and in 1989, was the beneficiary of all proceeds from the Stop the Violence Movement and their hip hop single, "Self Destruction".

In February 2010 the Urban League of Essex County announced their partnership with The National Association of Professional Women to form a national "Open Doorways" project, designed to offer young inner-city middle school girls an opportunity to benefit from professional female role models.

Light from the BOOK

"And we know that all things work together for good to those who love God, to those who are the called according to His purpose."—"What then shall we say to these things? If God is for us, who can be against us?" (Romans 8:28 ... 31)

Japanese-American Internment Camps

A historical fact that is not really "common knowledge" is the fact that, during World War II, over 100,000 Japanese-American individuals, the vast majority of which were actually American citizens, were rounded up and shipped eventually to internment camps. These consisted of poorly-constructed barracks surrounded by barbed wire, sentry posts and armed guards.

They were put in these camps, not because they had been tried and found guilty of something, but because either they or their parents or ancestors were from Japan and, as such, they were deemed a "threat" to national security. They were also easily identifiable due to their race. There was not a similar large-scale roundup of German or Italian-Americans, even though we were also fighting them during World War II.

These people were forced to abandon their businesses, their homes and, in many cases, their families as some individuals were taken elsewhere and held, again without trial, for years. *The Japanese-Americans suffered severe economic losses, personal humiliation and, in a some cases, death, due to this relocation.*

The relocation itself was ordered by the then President of the United States, Franklin D. Roosevelt, and by an act of Congress.

The Japanese-American (Nisei) and the Japanese aliens (Issei) on the West Coast were rounded up and moved to assembly centers and then to internment camps. Few Japanese living in the East or Midwestern portions of the U.S., though, were treated the same way.

What is extremely interesting is that the Nisei and Issei living in Hawaii were not subject to a mass evacuation even though they formed a third of the population in Hawaii and were a lot closer to Japan than the Japanese-Americans on the West Coast of the U.S.

The reasons they weren't rounded up were both cultural and economic.

360 George D. Johnson

"There was no mass relocation and internment in Hawaii, where the population was one-third Japanese American. It would have been impossible to transport that many people to the mainland, and the Hawaiian economy would have collapsed without Japanese American workers. "*-from the book Japanese American Internment Camps by Gail Sakurai, 2002*

"Ironically, the territory with the largest Japanese population saw the least discrimination. More than one third of all residents of Hawaii had some Japanese ancestry. Japanese labor was considered vital to the civilian and military economics of the Hawaiian Islands. Besides, the views of Delos Emmons, military commander of Hawaii, were the opposite of those of General DeWitt."*-from the book Japanese-American internment in American History, 1996.*

As noted in some of the other reviews, there were a very small number of people arrested and detained in Hawaii and a small number that voluntarily went to the mainland camps, but primarily so they could find relatives. ***There was not a single act of sabotage in Hawaii by the Japanese Americans during the entire war.***

In addition, since there were so many people of Japanese ancestry already living in Hawaii, about a third of the population, racism was not at all the kind of problem it was on the west coast.

Although prejudice and discrimination played major roles in the internment, economics and jealousy did also, as many Californians were jealous of the economic success that the Japanese-American farmers and store owners enjoyed. Thus arose a lot of the anti-Japanese-American feeling in the same way that some people despise Jewish people, largely due to their economic successes. ***The hard work, self-sacrifice, and strong efforts by the Japanese-Americans and Jewish people are overlooked and ignored when people of prejudice proclaim their judgments against Japanese-Americans and Jewish people.***

The fact that the internment did happen here in the U.S. is something to never forget since what has happened once could very well happen again, especially in these days of growing anti-immigrant, anti-foreigner feelings in the U.S.

Points to Ponder

Whoever refuses to remember the inhumanity is prone to new risks of infection.

Richard von Weizsaecker

Man's inhumanity to man makes countless thousands mourn!

Robert Burns

The Case Of The "Scottsboro Boys"

The International Labor Defense's (ILD) involvement in the Scottsboro case, more than any other event, crystallized black support for the radical political movements, especially the Communist Party, in the 1930s. Accused of raping two white women (Ruby Bates and Victoria Price) on a freight train near Paint Rock, Alabama, nine young black men (Charlie Weems, Ozie Powell, Clarence Norris, Olen Montgomery, Willie Roberson, Haywood Patterson, Andy and Roy Wright, Eugene Williams), ages thirteen to twenty-one, were arrested on March 25, 1931, tried without adequate counsel, and hastily convicted on the basis of shallow evidence. All but Roy Wright were sentenced to death. Already in the midst of a mass anti-lynching campaign begun a year earlier, the ILD gained the confidence of the defendants and their parents, initiated a legal and political campaign for their freedom, and in the process waged a vicious battle for control over the case with the NAACP, who accused the Communists of using the young men for propaganda purposes.

The Scottsboro case was not simply an isolated instance of injustice, the Communists argued, but represented a common manifestation of national oppression and class rule in the South. Maintaining that a fair and impartial trial was impossible, the Party and its auxiliaries publicized the case widely in order to apply mass pressure on the Alabama justice system. Protests erupted throughout the country and as far away as Paris, Moscow, and South Africa, and the governor of Alabama was bombarded with telegrams, postcards and letters demanding the immediate release of the "Scottsboro Boys." *Through Scottsboro and other related cases, black and white Communists gained entrance into churches lodges, and clubs in the African-American community, and eventually the ILD was regarded by some as a welcome addition to the panoply of "racial defense"* organizations. Moreover, although the "Scottsboro Boys" the defendants were denied the right of counsel. For the new Scottsboro trials, which opened on March 27, 1933, the ILD had retained renowned criminal lawyer Samuel Leibowitz. More significant, a month before the trial date Ruby Bates repudiated the rape charge. Yet, despite new evidence and a brilliant defense, the all-white jury still found the Scottsboro defendants guilty—a verdict that seemed to buttress the Communists' interpretation of justice under capitalism and augmented the ILD's popularity in the black community. In fact, pressure from black militants and some sympathetic clergy and middle-class spokesmen compelled the virulently anticommunist NAACP secretary, Walter White, to develop a working relationship with the ILD in the spring of 1933. Several months later, however, in an unprecedented decision, Alabama circuit Judge James E. Horton overturned the March 1933 verdict and ordered a new trial.

Following a number of incredibly foolish legal and ethical mistakes (including an attempt to bribe Victoria Price), star lawyer Samuel Leibowitz bolted the ILD, which began to lose its prestige in the mid-1930s. With support of conservative black leaders, white liberals, and clergymen, Leibowitz founded the American Scottsboro Committee (ASC) in 1934. However, hostilities between the two bodies were slightly mitigated a year later when the ILD turned to the coalition-building politics of the Popular Front. In a tenuous alliance the ILD, ASC, NAACP, and ACLU, formed the Scottsboro Defense Committee, which opted for a more reformist, legally oriented campaign in lieu of mass tactics. After failing to win the defendants' release in a 1936 trial, the SDC agreed to a strange plea bargain in 1937 whereby four defendants were released and the remaining five endured lengthy prison sentences—the last defendant was not freed until 1950.

Although the ILD did not win the defendants' unconditional release, its campaign to "Free the Scottsboro Boys" had tremendous legal and political implications during the early 1930s. For example, in one of the ILD's many appeals, a 1935 U.S. Supreme Court ruled that the defendant's constitutional rights were violated because blacks were systematically excluded from the jury rolls—a landmark opinion that spurred a battle to include African Americans on the jury rolls. Moreover, the realization that limited mass interracial action was possible challenged traditional liberalism and the politics of racial accommodation; the often scorned tactics of "mass pressure" would eventually be a precedent for civil rights activity two decades later.
Attributed to—Robin D. G. Kelley

Wisdom for the Journey

If you are neutral in situations of injustice, you have chosen the side of the oppressor. If an elephant has its foot on the tail of a mouse and you say that you are neutral, the mouse will not appreciate your neutrality. **Desmond Tutu**

Little Rock Nine

The **Little Rock Nine** *was a group of African-American students who were enrolled in Little Rock Central High School in 1957. The ensuing Little Rock Crisis, in which the students were initially prevented from entering the racially segregated school by Arkansas Governor Orval Faubus, and then attended after the intervention of President Eisenhower, is considered to be one of the most important events in the African-American Civil Rights Movement.* On their first day of school, troops from the Arkansas National Guard would not let them enter the school and they were followed by mobs making threats to lynch.

The U.S. Supreme Court issued its historic *Brown v. Board of Education* of Topeka, Kansas, 347 U.S. 483, on May 17, 1954. The decision declared all laws establishing segregated schools to be unconstitutional, and it called for the desegregation of all schools throughout the nation.

After the decision the National Association for the Advancement of Colored People (NAACP) attempted to register black students in previously all-white schools in cities throughout the South. In Little Rock, the capital city of Arkansas, the Little Rock School Board agreed to comply with the high court's ruling. Virgil Blossom, the Superintendent of Schools, submitted a plan of gradual integration to the school board on May 24, 1955, which the board unanimously approved. The plan would be implemented during the fall of the 1957 school year, which would begin in September 1957. By 1957, the NAACP had registered nine black students to attend the previously all-white Little Rock Central High, selected on the criteria of excellent grades and attendance. The nicknamed "Little Rock Nine" consisted of Ernest Green (b. 1941), Elizabeth Eckford (b. 1941), Jefferson Thomas (1942-2010), Terrence Roberts (b. 1941), Carlotta Walls LaNier (b. 1942), Minnijean Brown (b. 1941), Gloria Ray Karlmark (b. 1942), Thelma Mothershed (b. 1940), and Melba Beals (b. 1941). Ernest Green was the first African American to graduate from Central High School.

National Guard blockade

Several segregationist councils threatened to hold protests at Central High and physically block the black students from entering the school. Governor Orval Faubus deployed the Arkansas National Guard to support the segregationists on September 4, 1957. The sight of a line of soldiers blocking nine black students from attending high school made national headlines and polarized the city. Regarding the accompanying crowd, one of the nine black students, Elizabeth Eckford, recalled "they moved closer and closer . . . Somebody started yelling . . . I tried to see a friendly face somewhere in the crowd—someone who maybe could help. I looked into the face of an old woman and it seemed a kind face, but when I looked at her again, she spat on me." On September 9, "The Council of Church Women" issued a statement condemning the governor's deployment of soldiers to the high school and called for a citywide prayer service on September 12. Even President Dwight Eisenhower attempted to de-escalate the situation and summoned Governor Faubus to meet him. The President warned the governor not to interfere with the Supreme Court's ruling.

Armed escort

The next day, Woodrow Mann, the Mayor of Little Rock, asked President Eisenhower to send federal troops to enforce integration and protect the nine students. On September 24, the President ordered the 101st Airborne Division of the United States Army to Little Rock and federalized the entire 10,000 member Arkansas National Guard, taking it out of the hands of Governor Faubus. The 101st took positions immediately, and the nine students successfully entered the school on the next day, Wednesday, September 25, 1957.

A tense year

By the end of September 1957, the nine were admitted to Little Rock Central High under the protection of the U.S. Army (and later the Arkansas National Guard), but they were still subjected to a year of physical and verbal abuse (being spat on and called names) by many of the white students. Melba Pattillo had acid thrown into her eyes. Another one of the students, Minnijean Brown, was verbally confronted and abused. She said "I was one of the kids 'approved' by the school officials. We were told we would have to take a lot and were warned not to fight back if anything happened. One girl ran up to me and said, 'I'm so glad you're here.

Won't you go to lunch with me today?' I never saw her again." Minnijean Brown was also taunted by members of a group of white, male students in December 1957 in the school cafeteria during lunch. She dropped her lunch—a bowl of chili—onto the boys and was suspended for six days. Two months later, after more confrontation, Brown was suspended for the rest of the school year. She transferred to New Lincoln High School in New York City. As depicted in the 1982 made-for-TV docudrama *Crisis at Central High*, white students were only punished when their offense was "both egregious and witnessed by an adult".

The following year

In August 1958, Faubus called a special session of the state legislature to pass a law allowing him to close public schools to avoid integration and to lease the closed schools to private school corporations—and the following year the public school system closed for the year. This is known as "The Lost Year." In June 1959, a federal court declared the state's school-closing law unconstitutional. School re-opened in September, 1959, with just two of the original nine students re-enrolling—Jefferson Thomas and Carlotta Walls.

Analysis
Governor Faubus

Governor Faubus' opposition to desegregation may have been politically and racially motivated. Faubus had indicated that he would consider bringing Arkansas into compliance with the high court's decision in 1956. However, desegregation was opposed by his own southern conservative Democratic Party, which dominated all Southern politics at the time. Faubus risked losing political support in the upcoming 1958 Democratic gubernatorial primary if he showed support for integration.

Most histories of the crisis conclude that Faubus, facing pressure as he campaigned for a third term, decided to appease racist elements in the state by calling out the National Guard to prevent the black students from entering Central High.

Harry Ashmore, the editor of the *Arkansas Gazette*, won a 1958 Pulitzer Prize for his editorials on the crisis. Ashmore portrayed the fight over Central High as a crisis manufactured by Faubus; in his interpretation, Faubus used the Arkansas National Guard to keep black children out of Central High School because he was frustrated by the success his political opponents were having in using segregationist rhetoric to stir white voters.

Congressman Brooks Hays, who tried to mediate between the federal government and Faubus, was later defeated by a last minute write-in candidate,

Dale Alford, a member of the Little Rock School Board who had the backing of Faubus's allies. A few years later, despite the incident with the "Little Rock Nine", Faubus ran as a moderate segregationist against Dale Alford, who was challenging Faubus for the Democratic nomination for governor in 1962.

Legacy

Little Rock Central High School still functions as part of the Little Rock School District, and is now a National Historic Site that houses a Civil Rights Museum, administered in partnership with the National Park Service, to commemorate the events of 1957.

Two made-for-television movies have dramatized the events of the crisis: the 1981 CBS movie *Crisis at Central High*, and the 1993 Disney Channel movie *The Ernest Green Story*.

In 1996, seven of the Little Rock Nine appeared on *The Oprah Winfrey Show*. They came face to face with a few of the white students who had tormented them as well as one student who had befriended them.

In 2007, the United States Mint made available a commemorative silver dollar to "recognize and pay tribute to the strength, the determination and the courage displayed by African-American high school students in the fall of 1957." The face depicts students accompanied by a soldier, with nine stars symbolizing the Little Rock Nine. The reverse depicts an image of Little Rock Central High School, circa 1957. Proceeds from the coin sales are to be used to improve the National Historic Site. **On December 9, 2008, the Little Rock Nine were invited to attend the inauguration of President-elect Barack Obama, the first African-American to be elected President.**

On February 9, 2010, Marquette University honored the group by presenting them with the Père Marquette Discovery Award, the university's highest honor, one that had previously been given to Mother Teresa, Archbishop Desmond Tutu, Karl Rahner, and the Apollo 11 astronauts, among other notables.

Wisdom for the Journey

The courage of life is often a less dramatic spectacle than the courage of a final moment; but it is no less a magnificent mixture of triumph and tragedy. A man does what he must—in spite of personal consequences, in spite of obstacles and dangers and pressures—and that is the basis of all morality.—John F. Kennedy

If we have the courage and tenacity of our forebears, who stood firmly like a rock against the lash of slavery, we shall find a way to do for our day what they did for theirs.—Mary Mcleod Bethune

Murder of Emmett Till

Emmett Louis "Bobo" Till (July 25, 1941-August 28, 1955) *was an African-American boy who at fourteen years old was murdered in Money, Mississippi after reportedly flirting with a white woman. Till was from Chicago, Illinois visiting his relatives in the Mississippi Delta region when he was dared to speak to 21-year-old Carolyn Bryant, the married proprietor of a small grocery store. Several nights later, Carolyn Bryant's husband Roy and his half-brother J. W. Milam, arrived at Till's great-uncle's house where they took Till, transported him to a barn, beat him and gouged out one of his eyes, before shooting him through the head and disposing of his body in the Tallahatchie River, weighting it with a 70-pound (32 kg) cotton gin fan tied around his neck with barbed wire. His body was discovered and retrieved from the river three days later.*

Till was returned to Chicago and his mother, who had raised him mostly by herself, insisted on a public funeral service with an open casket to show the world the brutality of the killing. Tens of thousands attended his funeral or viewed his casket and images of his mutilated body were published in two black magazines, rallying popular black support and white sympathy across the country. Intense scrutiny was brought to bear on the condition of black civil rights in Mississippi, with newspapers around the country critical of the state. Although initially local newspapers and law enforcement officials decried the violence against Till and called for justice, they soon began responding to national criticism by defending Mississippians, which eventually transformed into support for the killers. The trial attracted a vast amount of press attention. Bryant and Milam were acquitted of Till's kidnapping and murder, but a year later, protected by double jeopardy, they admitted to killing him in a magazine interview. *Till's murder is noted as one of the leading events that motivated the African-American Civil Rights Movement.*

Problems identifying Till affected the trial, partially leading to Bryant's and Milam's acquittals, and the case was officially reopened by the United States Department of Justice in 2004. As part of the investigation, the body was exhumed and autopsied resulting in a positive identification. He was reburied in a new casket, which is standard practice in cases of body exhumation. ***His original casket was donated to the Smithsonian Institution.*** Events surrounding Emmett Till's life and death, according to historians, continue to resonate with people, and almost every story about Mississippi returns to Till, *or* the region in which he died, in "some spiritual, homing way".

Provoking incident

Till arrived on August 21, 1955. On August 24, he and cousin Curtis Jones skipped church where Wright was preaching, joining some local boys as they went to Bryant's Grocery and Meat Market to buy candy. The teenagers were children of sharecroppers and had been picking cotton all day. The market was owned by a white couple, 24-year-old Roy Bryant and his wife Carolyn, and mostly catered to the local sharecropper population. Carolyn was alone in the store that day; her sister-in-law was in the rear of the store watching children. Jones left Till with the other boys while Jones played checkers across the street. According to Jones, the other boys reported that Till had a photograph of an integrated class at the school he attended in Chicago, and Till bragged to the boys that the white children in the picture were his friends. He pointed to a white girl in the picture, or referred to a picture of a white girl that had come with his new wallet, and stated that she was his girlfriend. One or more of the local boys dared Till to speak to 21-year-old Carolyn Bryant.

The facts of what transpired in the store are still disputed, but according to several versions, Till may have wolf-whistled at Bryant. A newspaper account following his disappearance stated that Till sometimes whistled to alleviate his stuttering. His speech was sometimes unclear; his mother claimed he had particular difficulty with pronouncing "b" sounds, and may have whistled to overcome problems asking for bubble gum. Other stories claim Till may have grabbed Carolyn Bryant's hand and asked her for a date, or said "Bye, baby" as he left the store, or "You needn't be afraid of me, baby, I've been with white women before". Carolyn Bryant later asserted that Till had grabbed her at the waist and asked her for a date. She said the young man also used "unprintable" words.

In any event, Carolyn Bryant was so alarmed she ran outside to a car to retrieve a pistol from under the seat. Upon seeing her do this, the teenagers left immediately. One of the other boys ran across the street to tell Curtis Jones what happened. When the older man Jones was playing checkers with heard the story, he urged the boys to leave quickly, fearing violence. Carolyn Bryant told others of the events at the store, and the story spread quickly. Jones and Till declined to tell Mose Wright, fearing they would get in trouble. Till expressed a desire to return home to Chicago. Roy Bryant was on an extended trip hauling shrimp to Texas and did not return home until August 27.

Murder

When Roy Bryant returned home and was told of what had transpired, he aggressively questioned several young black men who entered the store. That evening, Bryant, with a black man named J. W. Washington, approached a young black man walking along a road. Bryant ordered Washington to seize the young man, put him in the back of his pickup truck, and took him to be identified by an as-yet unnamed companion of Carolyn's who had witnessed the episode with Till. Friends or parents vouched for the young men in Bryant's store, and Carolyn's companion denied that the young man Bryant and Washington seized was the one who had accosted her. Somehow, however, Bryant learned that the young man who had done it was from Chicago and was staying with Mose Wright. Several witnesses overheard Bryant and his 36-year-old half-brother J. W. Milam deciding to take Till from his house.

In the early morning hours—between 2.00 and 3.30—on Sunday, August 28, 1955, Roy Bryant, Milam, and another man (who may have been black) drove to Mose Wright's house. Milam was armed with a pistol and a flashlight. He asked Wright if he had three boys in the house from Chicago. Till shared a bed with another cousin; there were eight people in the small two-bedroom cabin. Milam asked Wright to take them to **"the nigger who did the talking"**. When they asked Till if it was he, he replied, "Yeah", for which they threatened to shoot him and told him to get dressed. The men threatened to kill Wright if he reported what he had seen. Till's great-aunt offered the men money, but they did not respond. They put Till in the back of a pickup truck and drove to a barn at the Clint Shurden Plantation in Drew. **Till was pistol-whipped and placed in the bed of the pickup truck** again and covered with a tarpaulin. Throughout the course of the night, Bryant, Milam, and witnesses recall them being in several locations with Till. According to some witnesses, they took Till to a shed behind Milam's home in the nearby town of Glendora where they beat him again and tried to decide what to do. Witnesses recall between two and four white men and two and four black men who were either in or surrounding the pickup truck where Till was seated. Others passed by Milam's shed to the sounds of someone being beaten. Accounts differ as to when Till was shot; either in Milam's shed or by the Tallahatchie River. He was driven to Bryant's store where several people noticed blood pooling in the truck bed. Bryant explained he killed a deer, and in one instance showed the body to a black man who questioned him, saying ***"that's what happens to smart niggers"***.

> *"Well, what else could we do? He was hopeless. I'm no bully; I never hurt a nigger in my life. I like niggers—in their place—I know how to work 'em. But I just decided it was time a few people got put on notice. As long as I live and can do anything about it, niggers are gonna stay in their place. Niggers ain't gonna vote where I live. If they did, they'd control the government. They ain't gonna go to school with my kids. And when a nigger gets close to mentioning sex with a white woman, he's tired o' livin'. I'm likely to kill him. Me and my folks fought for this country, and we got some rights. I stood there in that shed and listened to that nigger throw that poison at me, and I just made up my mind. 'Chicago boy,' I said, 'I'm tired of 'em sending your kind down here to stir up trouble. Goddam you, I'm going to make an example of you—just so everybody can know how me and my folks stand." J. W. Milam, Look magazine, 1956*

In an interview with William Bradford Huie in *Look* magazine in 1956, Bryant and Milam stated that their intention was to beat Till and throw him off an embankment into the river to frighten him. They told Huie that while they were beating Till, however, he called them bastards, declared he was as good as they, and had in the past had sexual encounters with white women. They then put Till in the back of their truck, drove to a cotton gin to take a 70-pound (32 kg) fan—the only time they admitted to being worried, thinking that by this time in early daylight they would be spotted and accused of stealing—and drove for several miles along the river looking for a place to dispose of Till. They shot him by the river and weighted his body with the fan.

Mose Wright stayed on his front porch for twenty minutes waiting for Till to return. He did not go back to bed. He and another man went into Money, got gasoline, and drove around trying to find Till. Unsuccessful, they returned home by 8.00 am. After hearing from Wright he would not call the police because he feared for his life, Curtis Jones placed a call to the Leflore County Sheriff and another to his mother in Chicago, who, hysterical, called Mamie Till Bradley. Wright and his wife also drove to Sumner, where Elizabeth's Wright's brother contacted the sheriff.

Bryant and Milam were questioned by Leflore County Sheriff George Smith. They admitted they had taken the boy from his great-uncle's yard but claimed they turned him loose the same night in front of Bryant's store. Bryant and Milam were arrested for kidnapping. Word got out that Till was missing, and soon Mississippi state field secretary for the National Association for the Advancement of Colored People (NAACP) Medgar Evers, and Amzie Moore, head of the Bolivar County chapter, became involved, disguising themselves as cotton pickers and going into the cotton fields in search of any information that might help find Till.

Three days after his abduction, Till's swollen and disfigured body was found by two boys fishing in the Tallahatchie River. His head was very badly damaged, had been shot above the right ear, an eye was dislodged from the socket, there was evidence that he had been beaten on the back and the hips, and his body weighted to the fan blade, fastened around his neck with barbed wire. He was nude, but wearing a silver ring with the initials "L. T." and "May 25, 1943" carved in it.

Confusion about Till's whereabouts and a positive identification of the body retrieved from the river compounded issues in the case that eventually influenced the trial. Hodding Carter in the *Delta Democrat-Times*, a local Mississippi newspaper, reported that Till may have been hidden by his relatives or perhaps returned to Chicago for his safety. The body's face was unrecognizable due to trauma and the result of being submerged in water. Mose Wright was called to the river and identified Till. The silver ring Till wore was removed and returned to Wright, and further passed to the district attorney. Stories from witnesses, both black and white, conflict about whether the ring was on Till's body and who knew he had worn it previously.

A thought worth remembering:

It is often easier to become outraged by injustice half a world away than by oppression and discrimination half a block from home.

Carl T. Rowan

James Earl "J.E." Chaney
(May 30, 1943-June 21, 1964)

James Earl "J.E." Chaney was one of three American civil rights workers who were murdered during Freedom Summer by members of the Ku Klux Klan near Philadelphia, Mississippi. The others were Andrew Goodman and Michael Schwerner.

Chaney was a native of Meridian and the eldest son in a family of five children. His mother, a domestic servant, was protective; his father, a plasterer, left his mother when James was in his mid-teens. He was slightly built, but athletic. He was described as shy in public, but a cutup in his home.

In October, 1963, Chaney began volunteer work at the Meridian office of the Congress on Racial Equality (CORE). He impressed Michael Schwerner, the head of the office, and was recommended for a full-time post with the organization.

Chaney was involved with the Core's Freedom Summer campaign. On 21st June, 1964, Chaney, along with Andrew Goodman and Michael Schwerner, went to Longdale to visit Mt. Zion Methodist Church, a building that had been fire-bombed by the Ku Klux Klan because it was going to be used as a Freedom School.

On the way back to the CORE office in Meridian, the three men were arrested by Deputy Sheriff Cecil Price. Later that evening they were released from the Neshoba jail only to be stopped again on a rural road where a white mob shot them dead and buried them in a earthen dam.

When Attorney General Robert Kennedy heard that the men were missing, he arranged for Joseph Sullivan of the Federal Bureau of Investigations (FBI) to go to Mississippi to discover what has happened. On 4th August, 1964, FBI agents found the bodies in an earthen dam at Old Jolly Farm.

On 13th October, Ku Klux Klan member, James Jordon, confessed to FBI agents that he witnessed the murders and agreed to co-operate with the investigation. Eventually nineteen men were arrested and charged with violating the civil rights of Chaney, Michael Schwerner and Andrew Goodman. This included Sheriff Lawrence Rainey and Deputy Sheriff Cecil Price.

On 24th February, 1967, Judge William Cox dismissed seventeen of the nineteen indictments. However, the Supreme Court overruled him and the Mississippi Burning Trial started on 11th October, 1967. The main evidence against the defendants came from James Jordon, who had taken part in the killings. Another man, Horace Barnette had also confessed to the crime but refused to give evidence at the trial.

Jordan claimed that Price had released Chaney, Andrew Goodman and Michael Schwerner at 10.25, but re-arrested them before they were able to cross the border into Lauderdale County. Price then took them to the deserted Rock Cut Road where he handed them over to the Ku Klux Klan.

On 21st October, 1967, seven of the men were found guilty of conspiring to deprive Goodman, Schwerner and Chaney of their civil rights and sentenced to prison terms ranging from three to ten years. This included James Jordon (4 years) and Cecil Price (6 years) but Sheriff Lawrence Rainey was acquitted.

Civil Rights activists led by Ruth Schwerner-Berner, the former wife of Michael Schwerner and Ben Chaney, the brother of James Chaney, continued to campaign for the men to be charged with murder. Eventually, it was decided to charge Edgar Ray Killen, a Ku Klux Klan member and part-time preacher, with more serious offences related to this case. ***On June 21, 2005, the forty-first anniversary of the crime, Killen was found guilty of the manslaughter of the three men.***

Quote;

Nothing in all the world is more dangerous than sincere ignorance and conscientious stupidity. Martin Luther King Jr.

Civil Rights March on Washington

The March on Washington for Jobs and Freedom took place in Washington, D.C., on August 28, 1963. Attended by some 250,000 people, it was the largest demonstration ever seen in the nation's capital, and one of the first to have extensive television coverage.

Background

1963 was noted for racial unrest and civil rights demonstrations. Nationwide outrage was sparked by media coverage of police actions in Birmingham, Alabama, where attack dogs and fire hoses were turned against protestors, many of whom were in their early teens or younger. Martin Luther King, Jr., was arrested and jailed during these protests, writing his famous "Letter From Birmingham City Jail," which advocates civil disobedience against unjust laws. Dozens of additional demonstrations took place across the country, from California to New York, culminating in the March on Washington. President Kennedy backed a Civil Rights Act, which was stalled in Congress by the summer.

Coalition

The March on Washington represented a coalition of several civil rights organizations, all of which generally had different approaches and different agendas. The "Big Six" organizers were James Farmer, of the Congress of Racial Equality (CORE); Martin Luther King, Jr., of the Southern Christian Leadership Conference (SCLC); John Lewis, of the Student Nonviolent Coordinating Committee (SNCC); A. Philip Randolph, of the Brotherhood of Sleeping Car Porters; Roy Wilkins, of the National Association for the Advancement of Colored People (NAACP); and Whitney Young, Jr., of the National Urban League.

The stated demands of the march were the passage of meaningful civil rights legislation; the elimination of racial segregation in public schools; protection for demonstrators against police brutality; a major public-works program to provide jobs; the passage of a law prohibiting racial discrimination in public and private hiring; a $2 an hour minimum wage; and self-government for the District of Columbia, which had a black majority.

Opposition

President Kennedy originally discouraged the march; for fear that it might make the legislature vote against civil rights laws in reaction to a perceived threat. Once it became clear that the march would go on, however, he supported it.

While various labor unions supported the march, the AFL-CIO remained neutral.

Outright opposition came from two sides. White supremacist groups, including the Ku Klux Klan, were obviously not in favor of any event supporting racial equality. On the other hand, the march was also condemned by some civil rights activists who felt it presented an inaccurate, sanitized pageant of racial harmony; *Malcolm X called it the "Farce on Washington," and members of the Nation of Islam who attended the march faced a temporary suspension.*

The March on Washington

Nobody was sure how many people would turn up for the demonstration in Washington, D.C. Some travelling from the South were harassed and threatened. *But on August 28, 1963, an estimated quarter of a million people—about a quarter of whom were white—marched from the Washington Monument to the Lincoln Memorial, in what turned out to be both a protest and a communal celebration.* The heavy police presence turned out to be unnecessary, as the march was noted for its civility and peacefulness. The march was extensively covered by the media, with live international television coverage.

The event included musical performances by Marian Anderson; Joan Baez; Bob Dylan; Mahalia Jackson; Peter, Paul, and Mary; and Josh White: Charlton Heston—representing a contingent of artists, including Harry Belafonte, Marlon Brando, Diahann Carroll, Ossie Davis, Sammy Davis Jr., Lena Horne, Paul Newman, and Sidney Poitier—read a speech by James Baldwin.

The speakers included all of the "Big Six" civil-rights leaders (James Farmer, who was imprisoned in Louisiana at the time, had his speech read by Floyd McKissick); Catholic, Protestant, and Jewish religious leaders; and labor leader Walter Reuther. The one female speaker was Josephine Baker, who introduced several "Negro Women Fighters for Freedom," including Rosa Parks.

Noteworthy Speeches

The two most noteworthy speeches came from John Lewis and Martin Luther King, Jr.

Lewis represented the Student Nonviolent Coordinating Committee, a younger, more radical group than King's. The speech he planned to give, circulated beforehand, was objected to by other participants; it called Kennedy's civil rights bill "too little, too late," asked "which side is the federal government on?" and declared that they would march "through the Heart of Dixie, the way Sherman did" and "burn Jim Crow to the ground—nonviolently." In the end, he agreed to tone down the more inflammatory portions of his speech, but even the revised version was the most controversial of the day, stating:

The revolution is at hand, and we must free ourselves of the chains of political and economic slavery. The nonviolent revolution is saying, "We will not wait for the courts to act, for we have been waiting hundreds of years. We will not wait for the President, nor the Justice Department, nor Congress, but we will take matters into our own hands, and create a great source of power, outside of any national structure that could and would assure us victory." For those who have said, "Be patient and wait!" we must say, "Patience is a dirty and nasty word." We cannot be patient, we do not want to be free gradually, we want our freedom, and we want it now. We cannot depend on any political party, for the Democrats and the Republicans have betrayed the basic principles of the Declaration of Independence.

King's speech remains one of the most famous speeches in American history. He started with prepared remarks, saying he was there to "cash a check" for "Life, Liberty and the pursuit of Happiness," while warning fellow protesters not to "allow our creative protest to degenerate into physical violence. Again and again, we must rise to the majestic heights of meeting physical force with soul force." But then he departed from his script, shifting into the "I have a dream" theme he'd used on prior occasions, drawing on both "the American dream" and religious themes, *speaking of an America where his children "will not be judged by the color of their skin but by the content of their character." He followed this with an exhortation to "let freedom ring" across the nation, and concluded with:*

"And when this happens, when we allow freedom to ring, when we let it ring from every village and every hamlet, from every state and every city, we will be able to speed up that day when all of God's children, black men and white men, Jews and Gentiles, Protestants and Catholics, will be able to join hands and sing in the words of the old Negro spiritual, "Free at last, free at last. Thank God Almighty, we are free at last."

Wisdom for the Journey

"No man can put a chain about the ankle of his fellow man without at last finding the other end fastened about his own neck."
~**Frederick Douglass, speech, Civil Rights Mass Meeting, Washington, D.C., 1883**

James Earl Ray

James Earl Ray (March 10, 1928-April 23, 1998) was an American murderer convicted of the assassination of American civil rights activist Dr. Martin Luther King, Jr. He was convicted on March 10, 1969 after entering a guilty plea to forgo a jury trial. If Ray had been found guilty by jury trial he would have been electrocuted. He was sentenced to ninety-nine years in prison. He later recanted his confession and tried unsuccessfully to gain a trial. He died in prison of hepatitis C.

Early life

James Earl Ray came from a poor family in Alton, Illinois, and left school at age fifteen. He joined the US Army at the close of World War II and served in Germany. He was convicted of his first crime, a burglary in California, in 1949.

In 1952 he served two years for armed robbery of a taxi driver in Illinois. In 1955, he was convicted of mail fraud. After an armed robbery in Missouri in 1959, Ray was sentenced to twenty years in prison for repeated offenses. He escaped from prison in 1967 by hiding in a truck transporting bread from the prison bakery.

Assassination of Martin Luther King, Jr.

Martin Luther King was shot and killed by a sniper on April 4, 1968, while standing on the second-floor balcony of the Lorraine Motel in Memphis, Tennessee.

Capture and trial

On June 8, 1968, a little more than two months after King's death, Ray was captured at London's Heathrow Airport while trying to leave the United Kingdom on a false Canadian passport. At check-in the ticket agent noticed the name on his passport was on a Royal Canadian Mounted Police watch list. He was using the name of Ramon George Sneyd. At the airport, officials noticed that Ray carried another passport under a second name. The UK quickly extradited Ray to Tennessee, where he was charged with King's murder. He confessed to the crime on March 10, 1969, although he recanted this confession three days later. After pleading guilty he was sentenced to ninety-nine years in prison. Ray entered a guilty plea on the advice of his attorney, Percy Foreman, in order to avoid a potential trial conviction, which could have led to a sentence of death. The method of execution in Tennessee at the time would have been electrocution.

Ray fired Foreman as his attorney and derisively called him "Percy Four-flusher," thereafter. Ray began claiming that a man he had met in Montreal, who used the alias "Raul", had been deeply involved. Instead he asserted that he did not "personally shoot Dr. King," but may have been, "partially responsible without knowing it," hinting at a conspiracy. This version of King's assassination and his fleeing Ray sold to William Bradford Huie. Huie investigated this story and discovered Ray sometimes lied. Ray told Huie he purposely left the rifle with his fingerprints on it behind in plain sight because he wanted to become a famous criminal. Ray was convinced he was so smart that he would not be caught. He believed Governor of Alabama, George Wallace, would soon be elected President and Ray would only be confined for a short time. He spent the remainder of his life attempting unsuccessfully to withdraw his guilty plea and secure a trial.

1977 escape

On June 11, 1977, Ray made his second appearance on the FBI Most Wanted Fugitives list, this time as the 351st entry. He and six other convicts had escaped from Brushy Mountain State Penitentiary in Petros, Tennessee on June 10, 1977. They were recaptured on June 13, three days later, and returned to prison. A year was added to Ray's previous sentence, to total 100 years.

Ray had hired Jack Kershaw as his attorney, who promoted Ray's claim that he was not responsible for the shooting, which was said to have been the result of a conspiracy of the otherwise unidentified man named "Raul". Kershaw and his client met with representatives of the United States House Select Committee on Assassinations and convinced the committee to run ballistics tests—which ultimately proved inconclusive—that would show that Ray had not fired the fatal shot. Kershaw claimed that the escape was additional proof that Ray had been involved in a conspiracy that had provided him with the outside assistance he would have needed to break out of jail. Kershaw convinced Ray to take a polygraph test as part of an interview with

Playboy. **The magazine said that the test results showed "that Ray did, in fact, kill Martin Luther King Jr. and that he did so alone".** Ray fired Kershaw after discovering that the attorney had been paid $11,000 by the magazine in exchange for the interview and hired conspiracy theorist Mark Lane to provide him with legal representation.

Later developments

In 1997, King's son Dexter met with Ray, and publicly supported his efforts to obtain a retrial. Loyd Jowers, a restaurant owner in Memphis, was brought to civil court and sued as being part of a conspiracy to murder Martin Luther King. Jowers was found legally liable, and the King family accepted $100 in restitution, an amount chosen to show that they were not pursuing the case for financial gain.

Dr. William Pepper, a friend of King in the last year of his life, represented Ray in a televised mock trial in an attempt to get him the trial he never had. Pepper later represented the King family in a wrongful death civil trial against Loyd Jowers. The King family has since concluded that Ray did not have anything to do with the murder of Martin Luther King.

Death

Ray died in prison on April 23, 1998, at seventy years of age, from complications related to kidney disease and liver failure caused by Hepatitis C. He probably contracted the disease through a blood transfusion given after he sustained a stabbing while at Brushy Mountain State Penitentiary. Ray was survived by seven siblings. His brother Jerry Ray told CNN that his brother did not want to be buried or have his final resting place in the United States because of "the way the government has treated him." Ray was cremated and his ashes were flown to Ireland, the home of his family's ancestors.

Legacy

On January 19, 2002, a plaque in Lauderhill, Florida was unveiled in tribute to Martin Luther King's life. The text was supposed to read "Thank you James Earl Jones for keeping the dream alive." The name was instead that of James Earl Ray. The plaque was soon fixed.

Quote:

Assassination has never changed the history of the world. *Benjamin Disraeli*

Epilogue:

There is so much history to be discovered that I could not possibly tell it all in *Profiles in Hue*. What I have tried to do is whet the appetite of those who would like to digest a little more food for thought and education.

The Internet is rich with *free* information on just about every subject and personality imaginable. And all we have to do is adhere to the WORD that says, *"Seek and you shall find"* (Luke 11:19).

From my perspective on history, in the final roundup of human affairs, there will come a time when this civilization, as we now know it, will amount to nothing more than a fly speck on the sands of time. So, *"what is your life? It is even a vapor that appears for a little time and then vanishes away"* (James 4:14). We come and we go like the ripples on a stream. King Solomon, the wisest and riches man who ever lived, reminds us that, *"All is vanity and striving after the wind"* (Eccl. 1:14).

Looking back through the telescope of time, history has taught me that there are only two kinds of riches that one can accumulate: those we take with us into eternity and those that we leave behind for someone else.

Even though I never made history, it was history that made me. The greatest lesson I have learned from history *is what not to do.*

HIS
George D. Johnson

BIOGRAPHICAL SKETCH

George D. Johnson resides in Harrisburg. PA

He was born on January 23, 1928 and was married to Maybelle Adams Johnson for 36 years until her death in July 2002 He was educated in the Philadelphia public school system and attended St. Joseph's College, Institute of Industrial Relations.

Mr. Johnson worked for the United States Department of Labor for twenty-two years as a Labor Relations Specialist until his retirement on June 1, 1987. Moreover, he belonged to the United Steelworkers of America (AFL-CIO) and worked as a Labor Columnist for the *Philadelphia Tribune*. He was also president of the Local Union 2948 American Federation of Government Employees for sixteen years. Beyond this, he was an instructor of Labor Studies at the Pennsylvania State University @, the Delaware County Campus.

Mr. Johnson is an ordained Christian minister and was interim pastor for one year at 1st Zion Baptist Church.

Mr. Johnson is also founder and president of *Light of the Savior Ministries. (Founded in 1979) Light of the Savior Ministries* is a non-denominational Christian organization that shares the teachings of Christ with individuals of all walks of life, Light *of the Savior Ministries* also provides counseling in the principles of Christian living and aids the poor through financial assistance and guidance.

Mr. Johnson enjoys music appreciation and computer sciences. His favorite hobbies are football and baseball He is also the author of *"Except For The Grace"* which is his personal autobiography, "'Light From the Book", "More Light From the Book", "What's Wrong With Society And Can it be Fixed?", "Wisdom", "Wisdom II" "The Lamp Lighter," and "The Lamp Lighter II."

Except For The Grace and Light From The Book" are available through Trafford Publishing

Suite 6E-2333 Government Street, Victoria, BC Canada V8T 4P4 Toll Free 1-866-638-6884

More Light From the Book and What's Wrong with Society, Wisdom, Wisdom II and The Lamp Lighter's are available through Xlibris Corporation—I-888-795-4274